Abstractions

Leou

Abstractions 4

ISBN : 9781086839074

nicolaslehoux.com

Abstractions
tome4

art
Leou

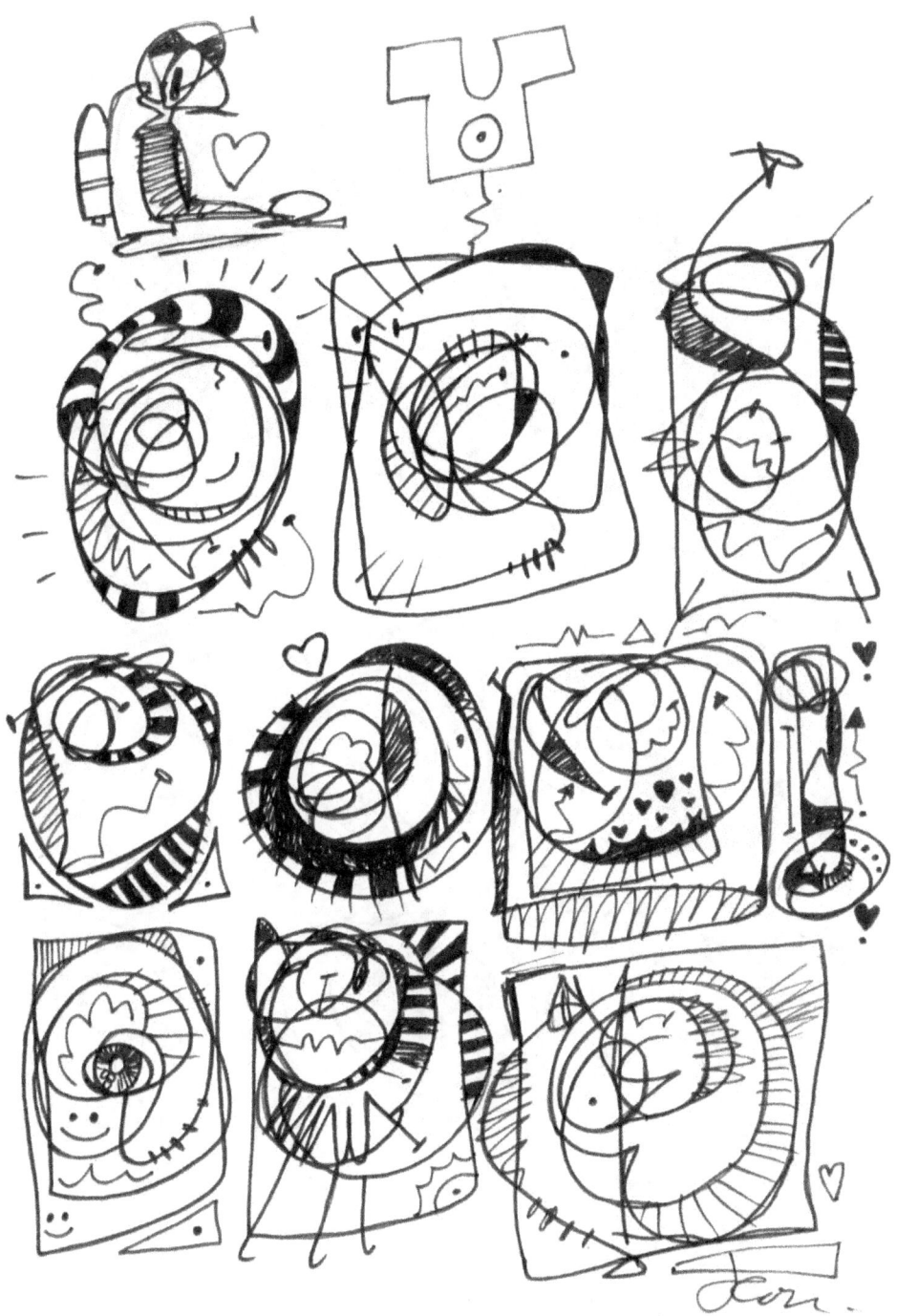

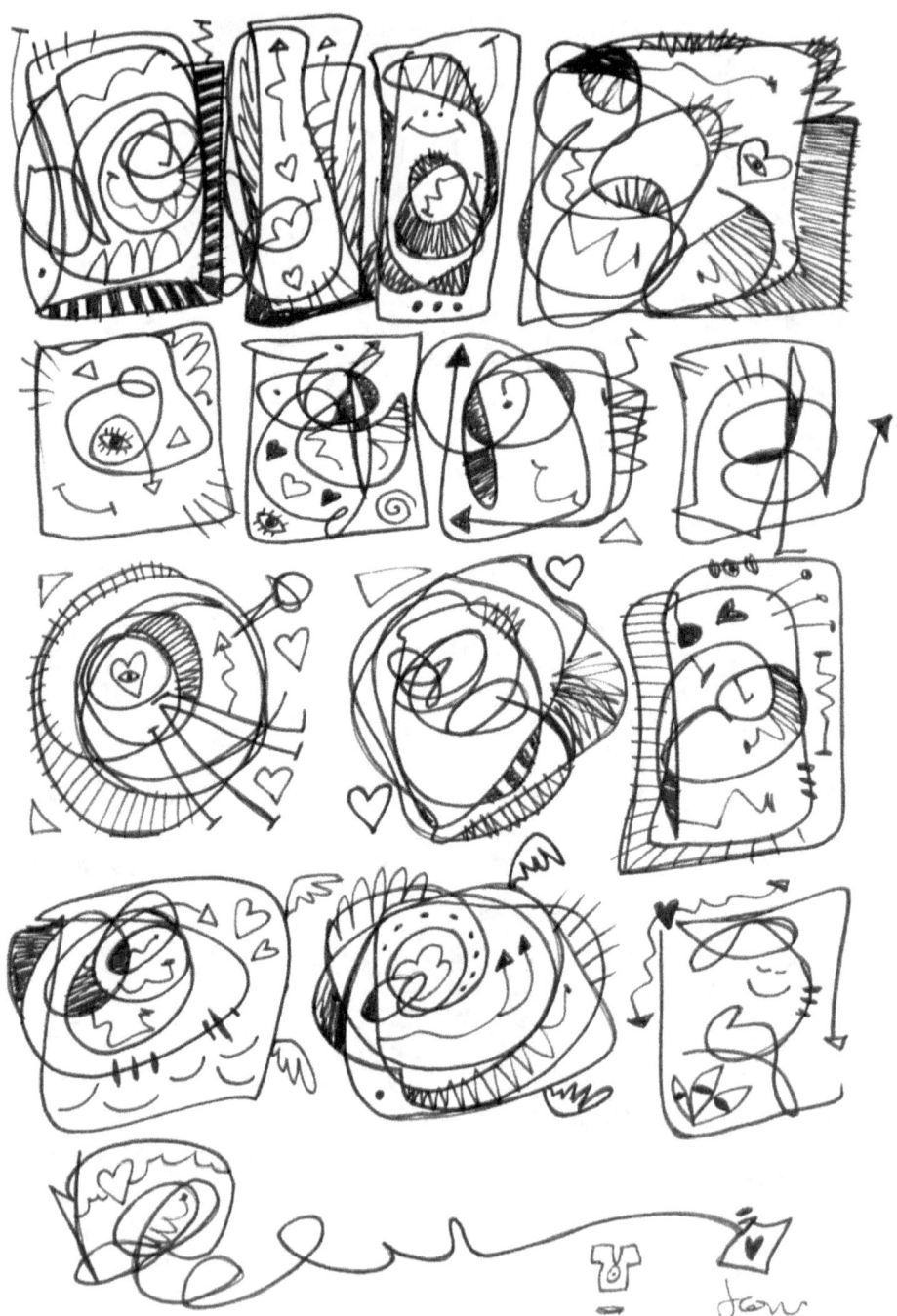

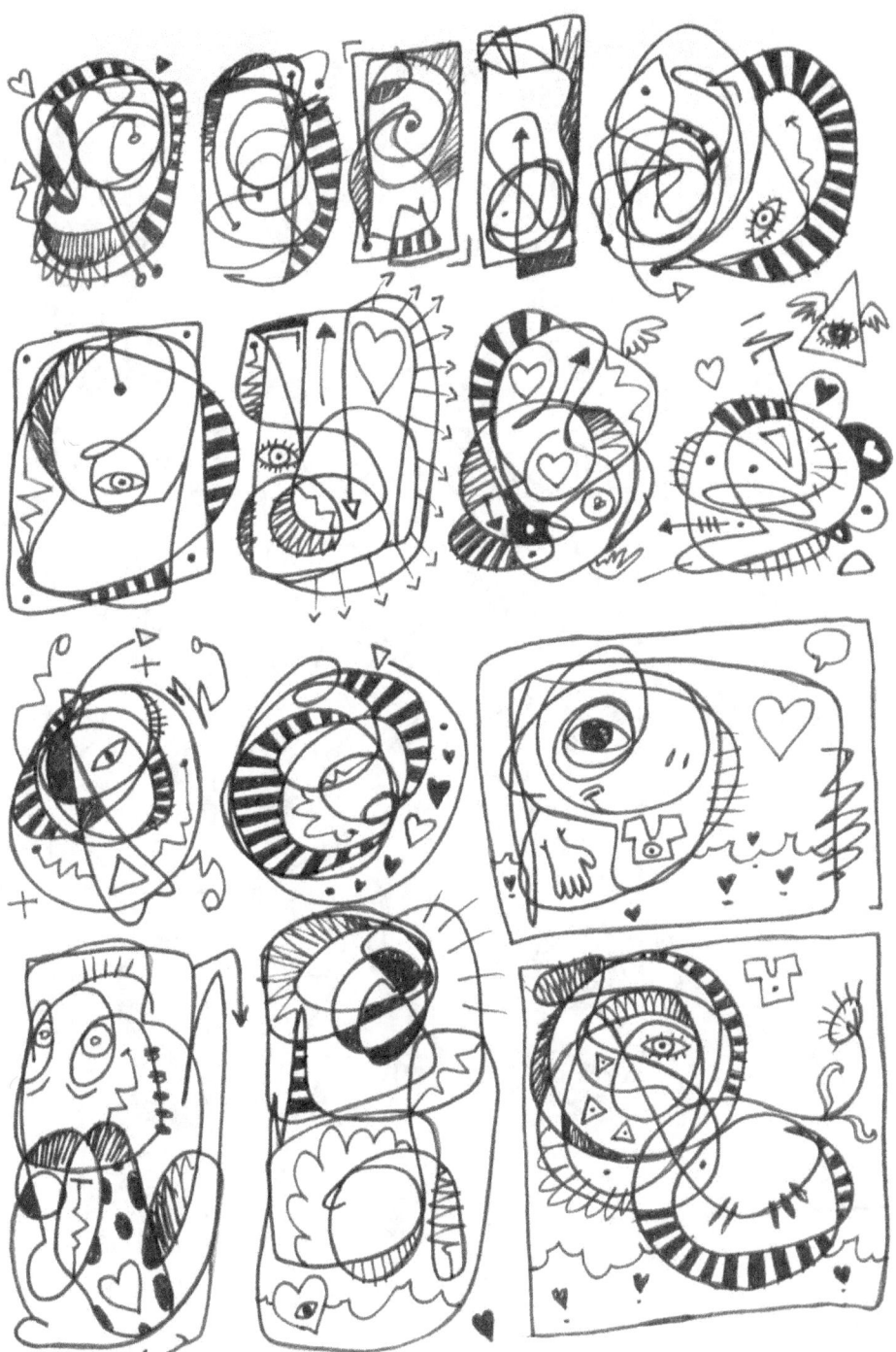

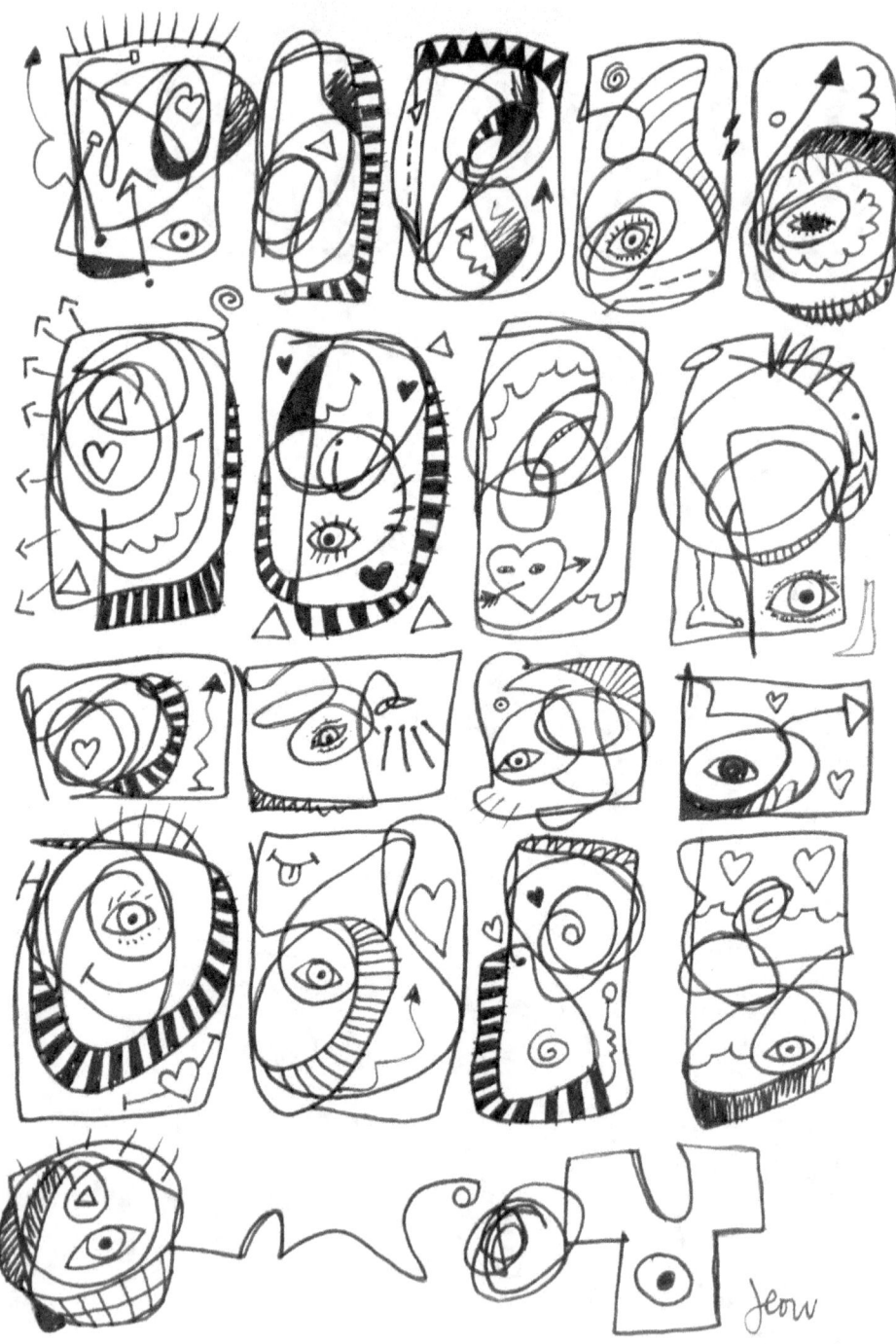

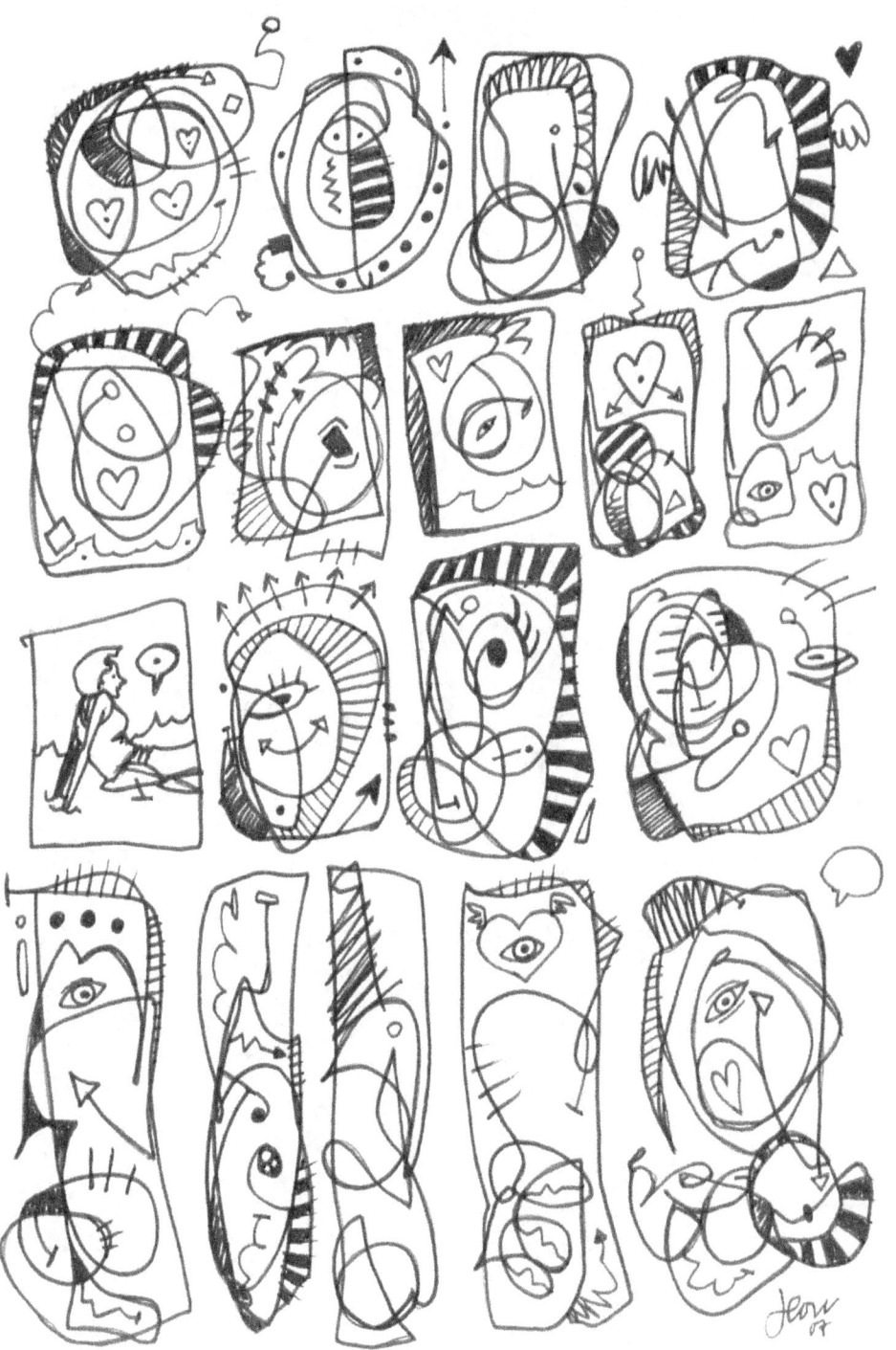

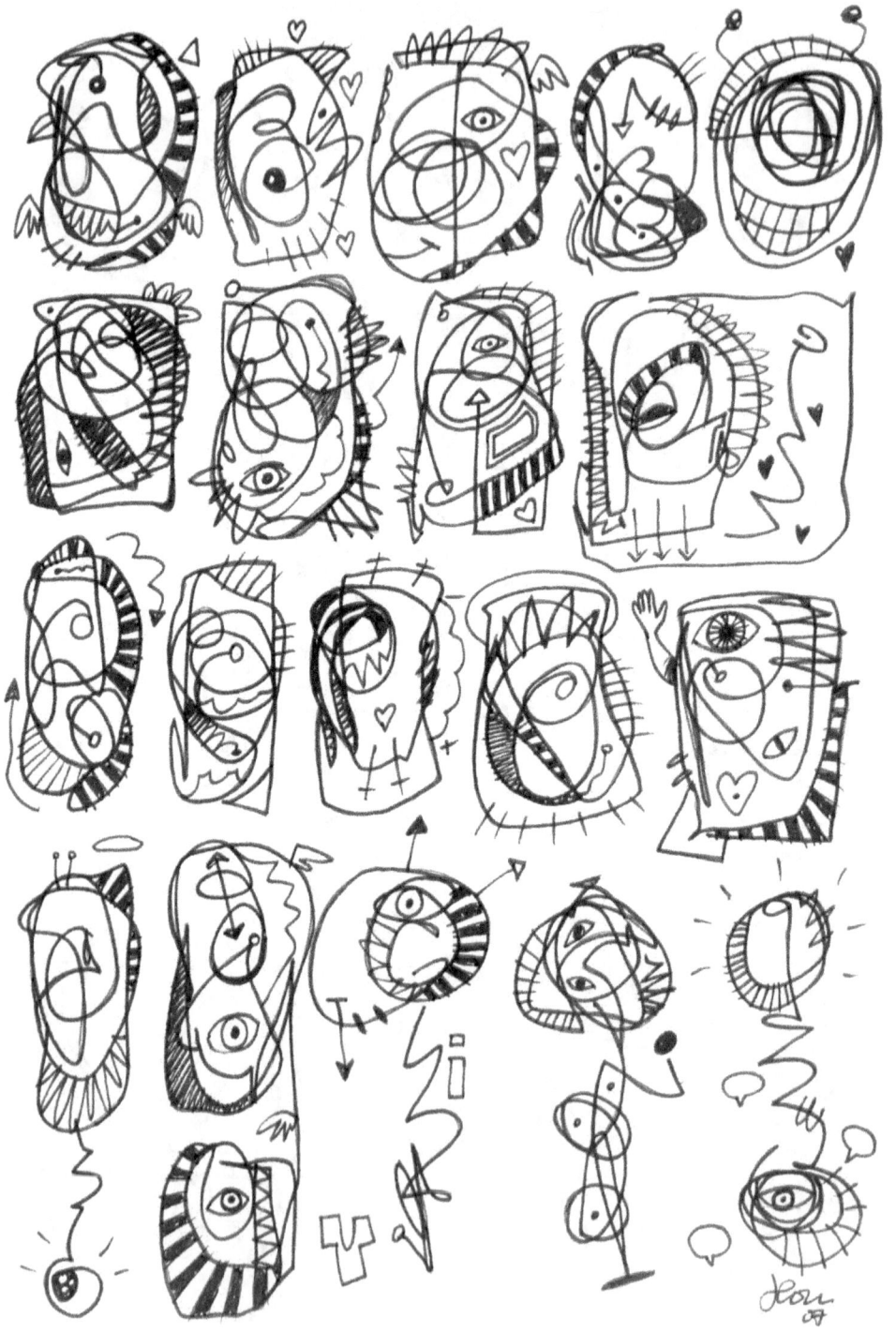

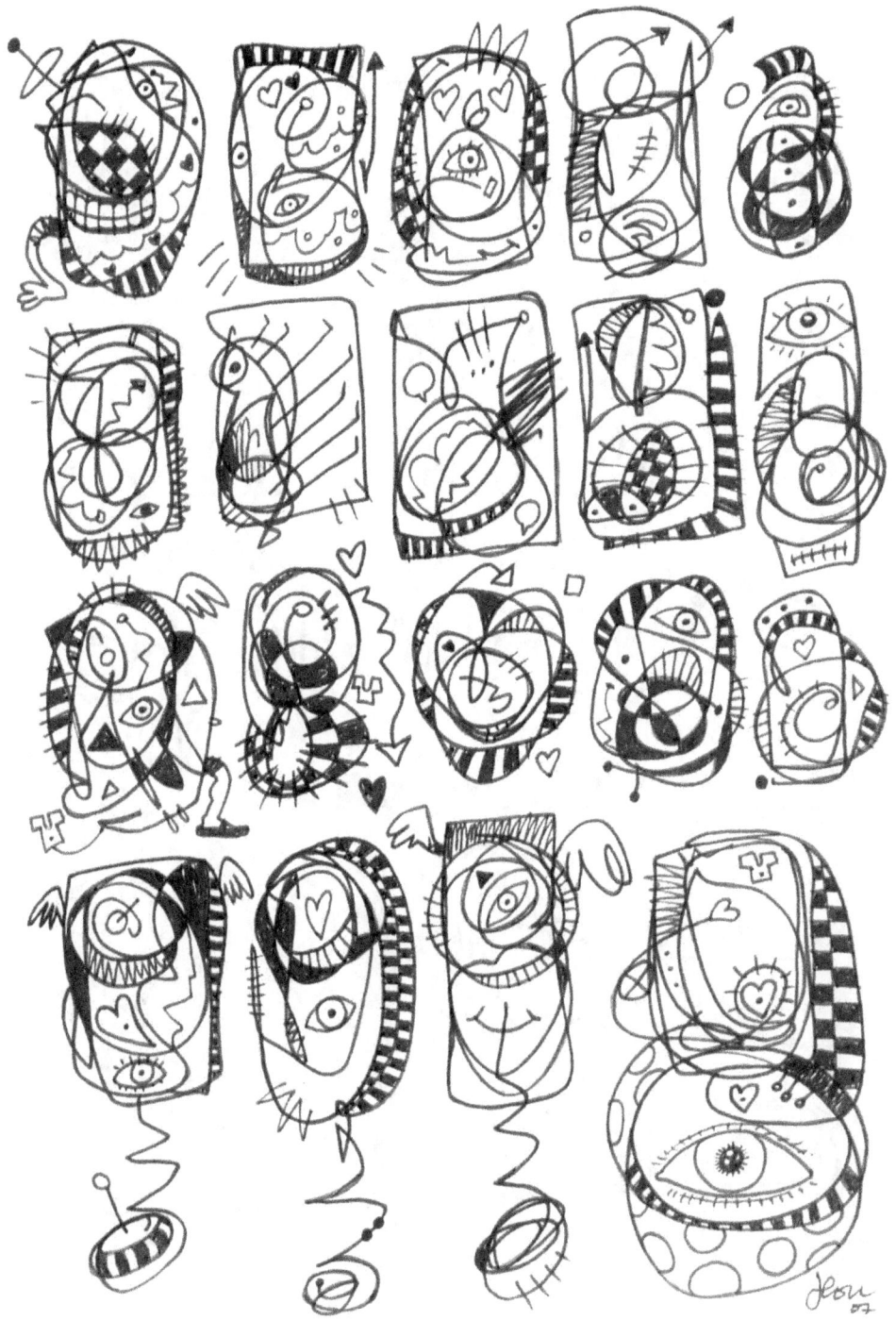

13

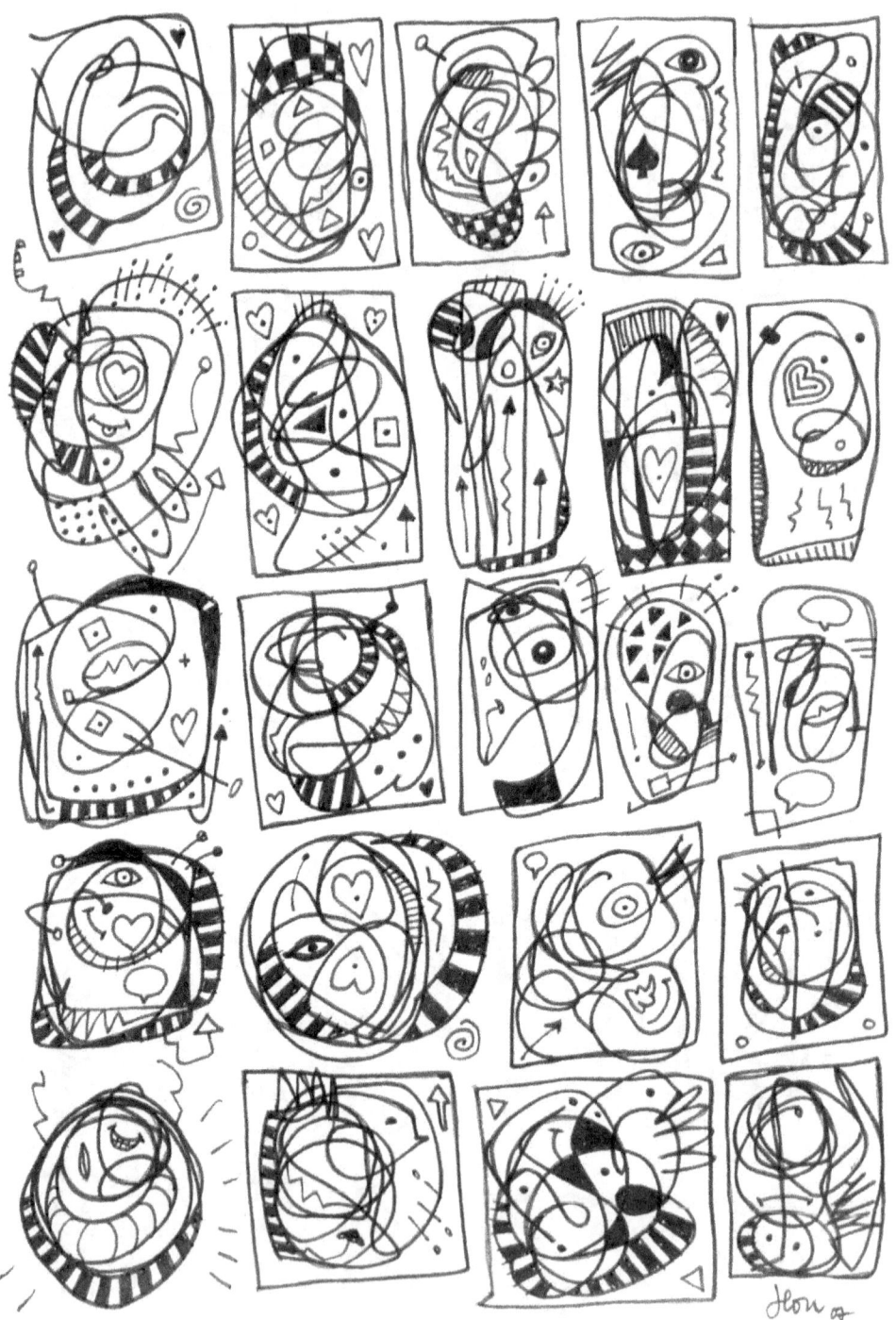

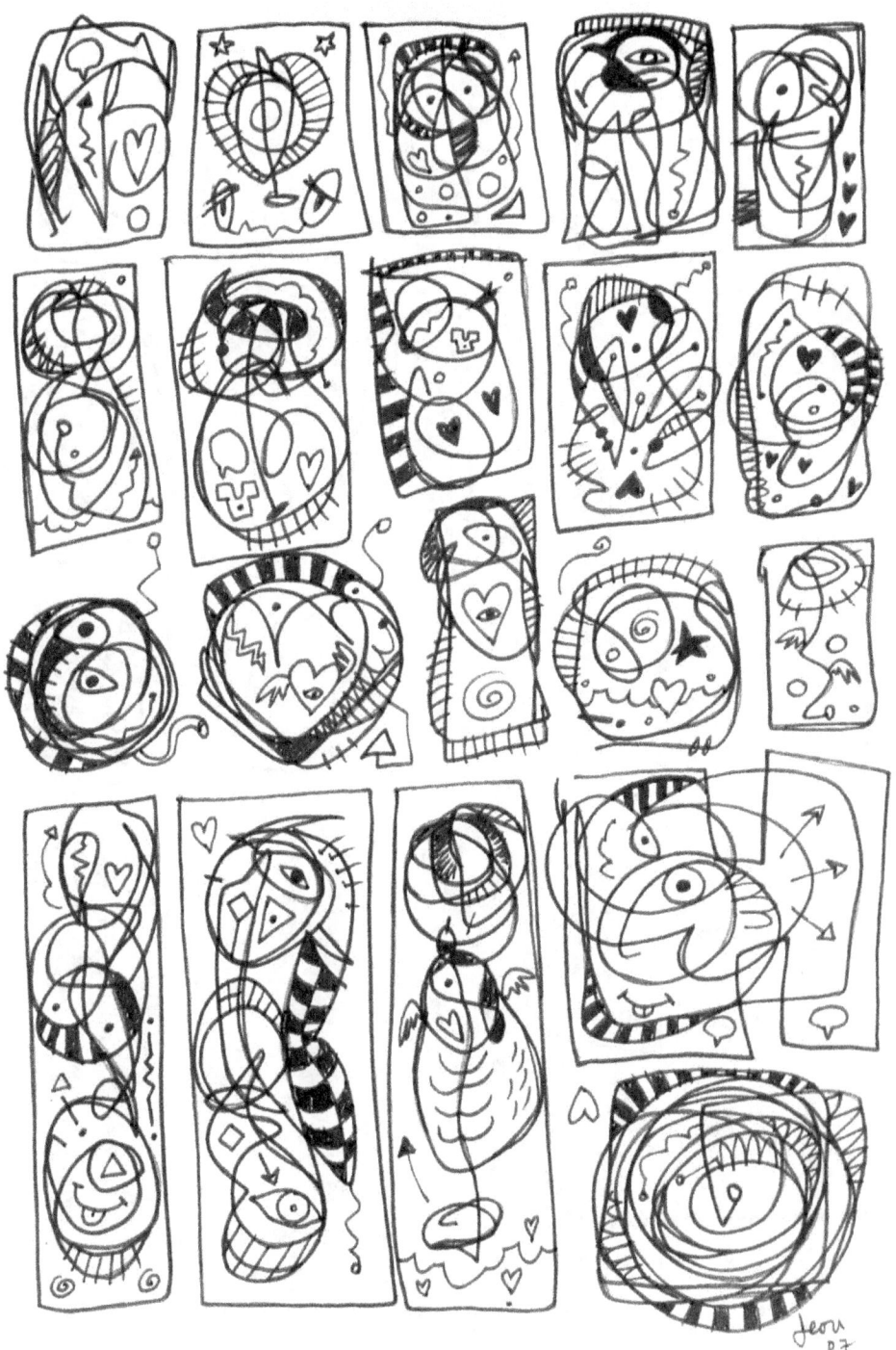

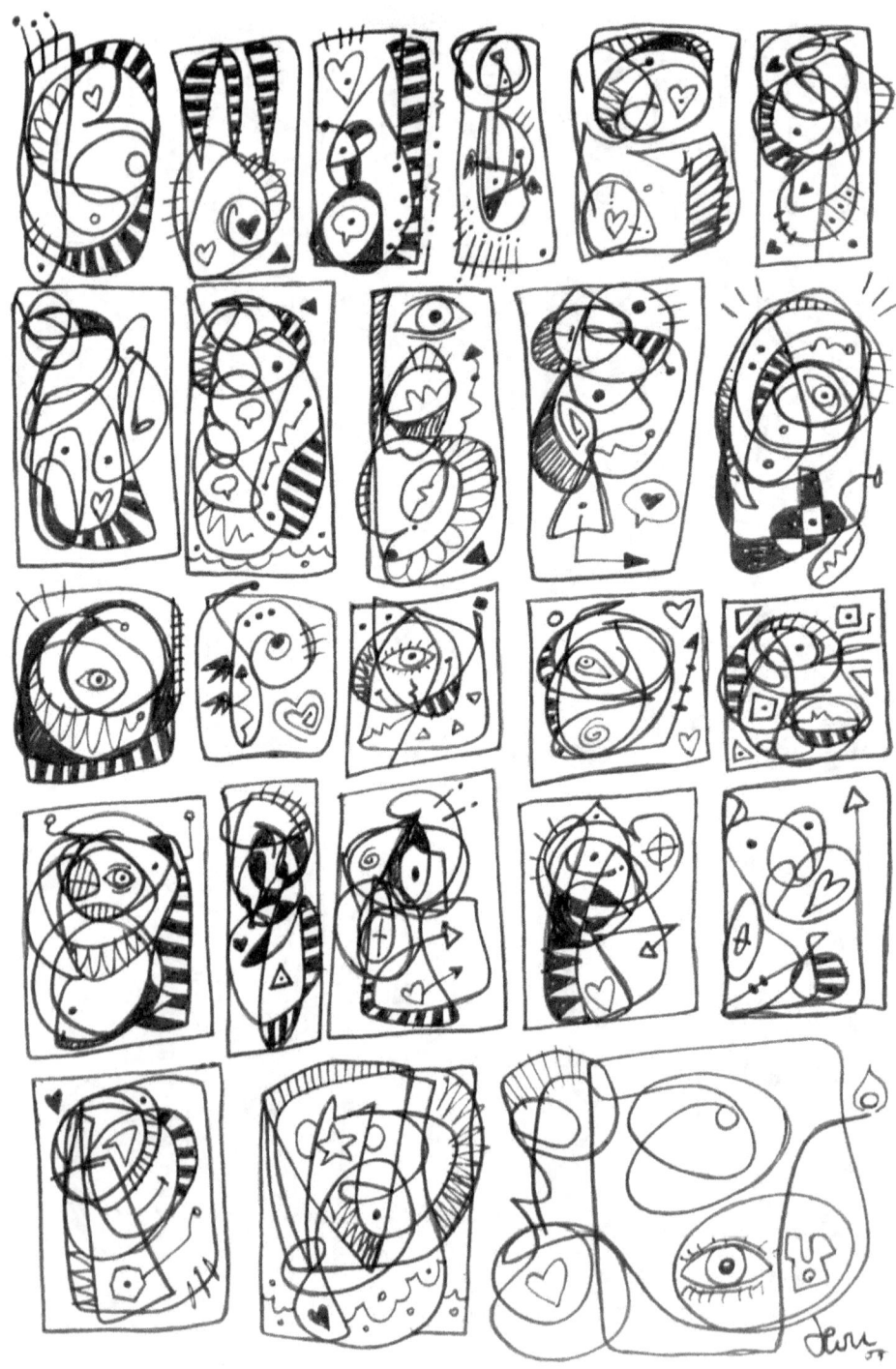

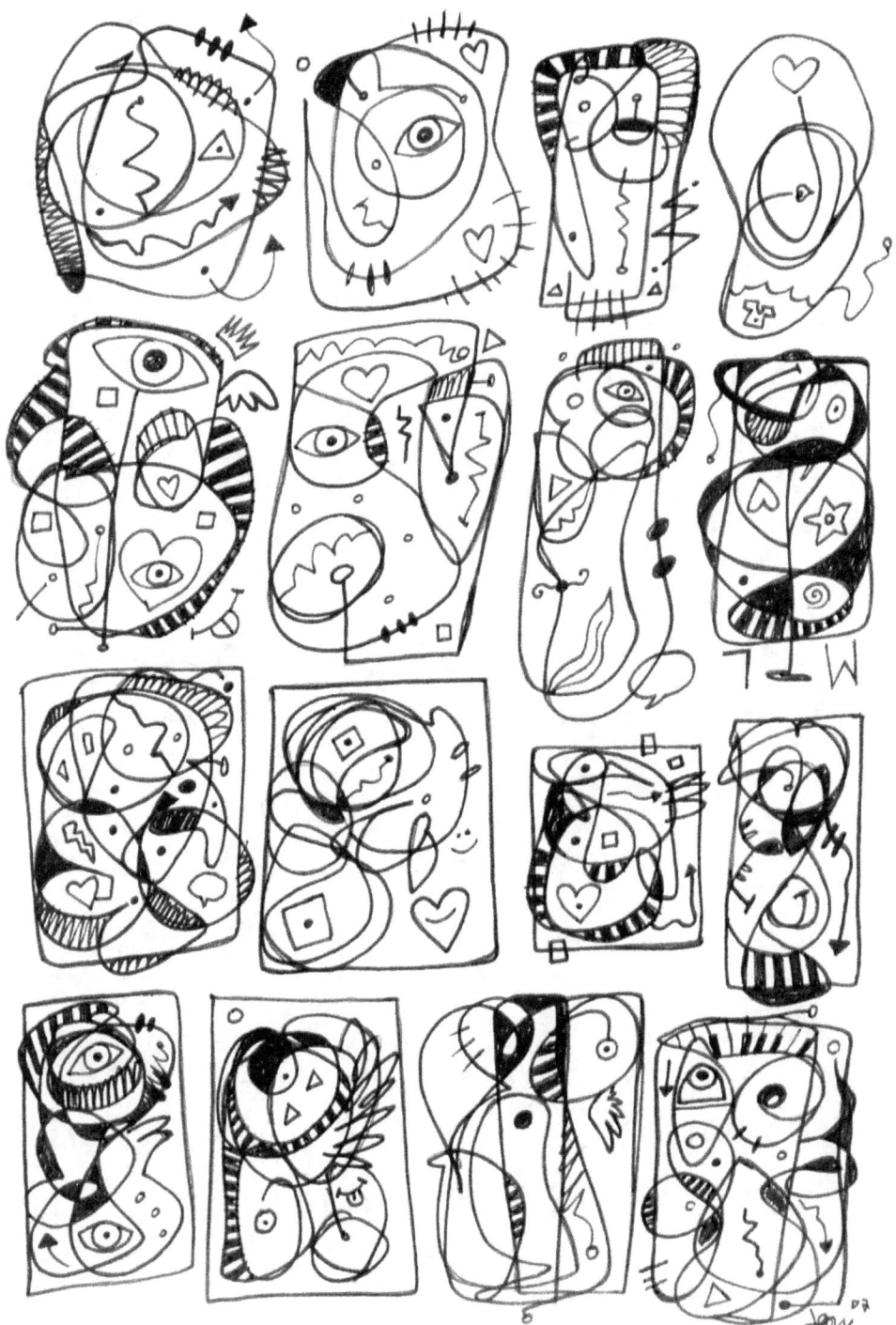

17

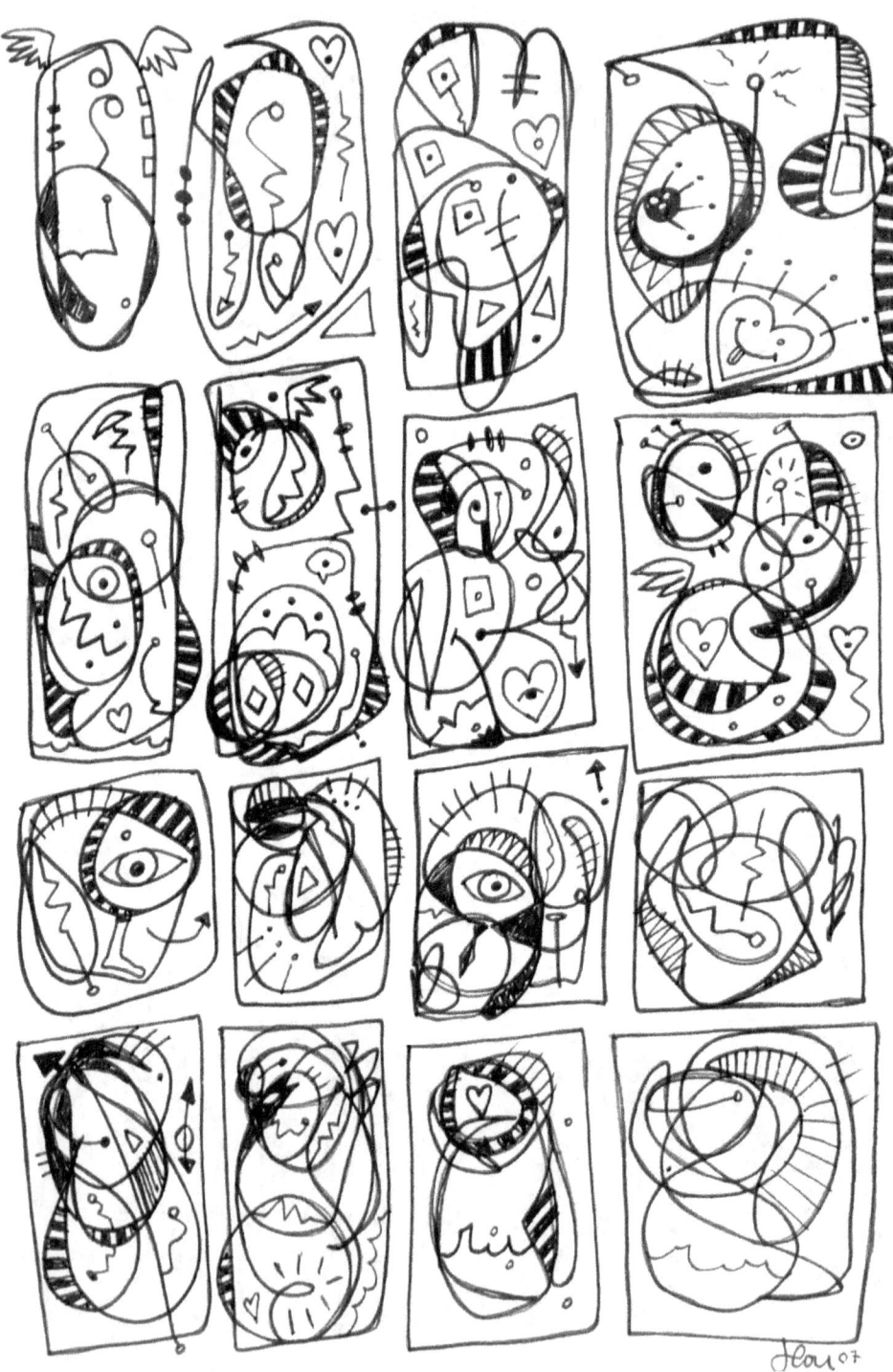

18

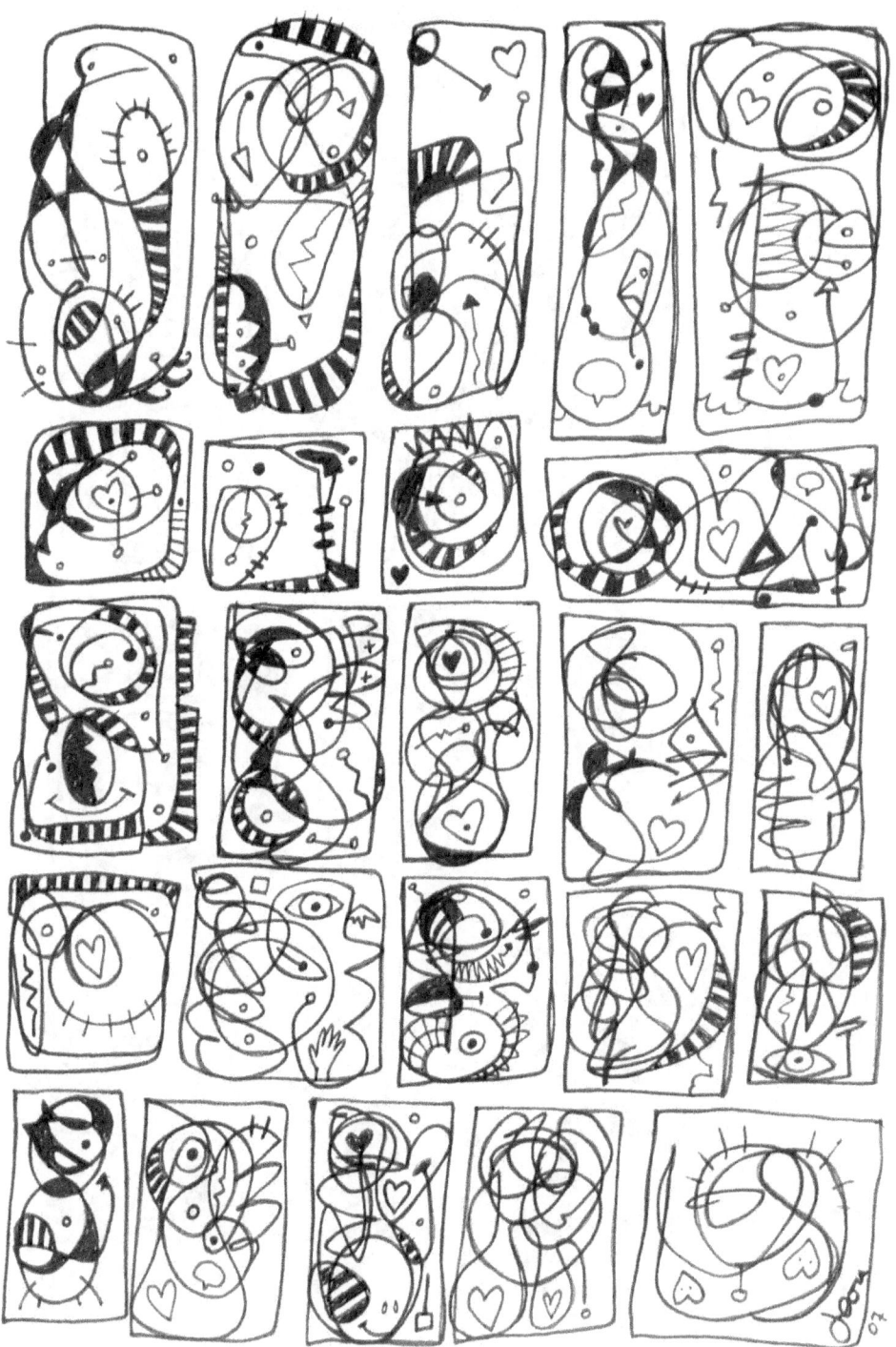

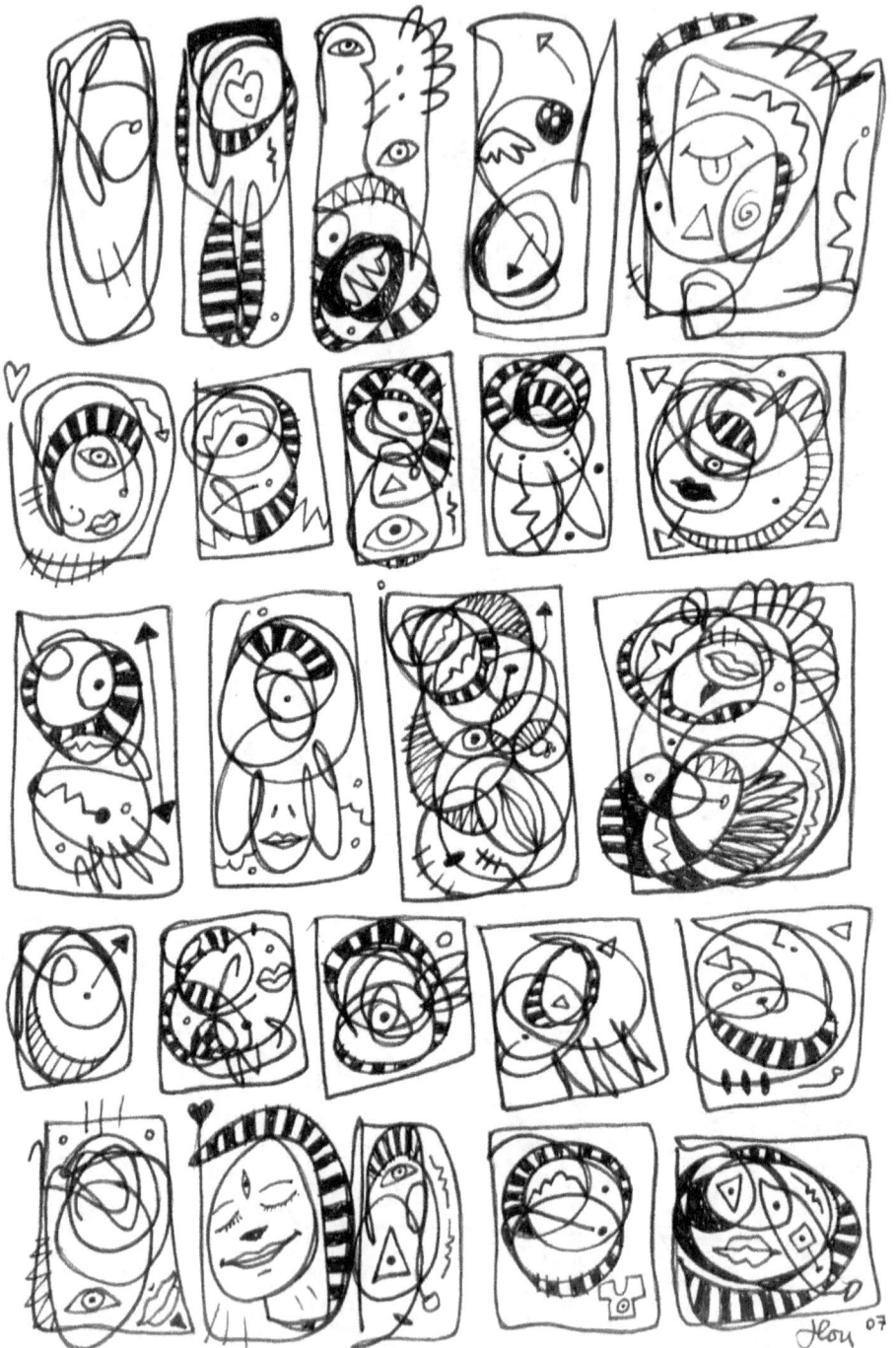

20

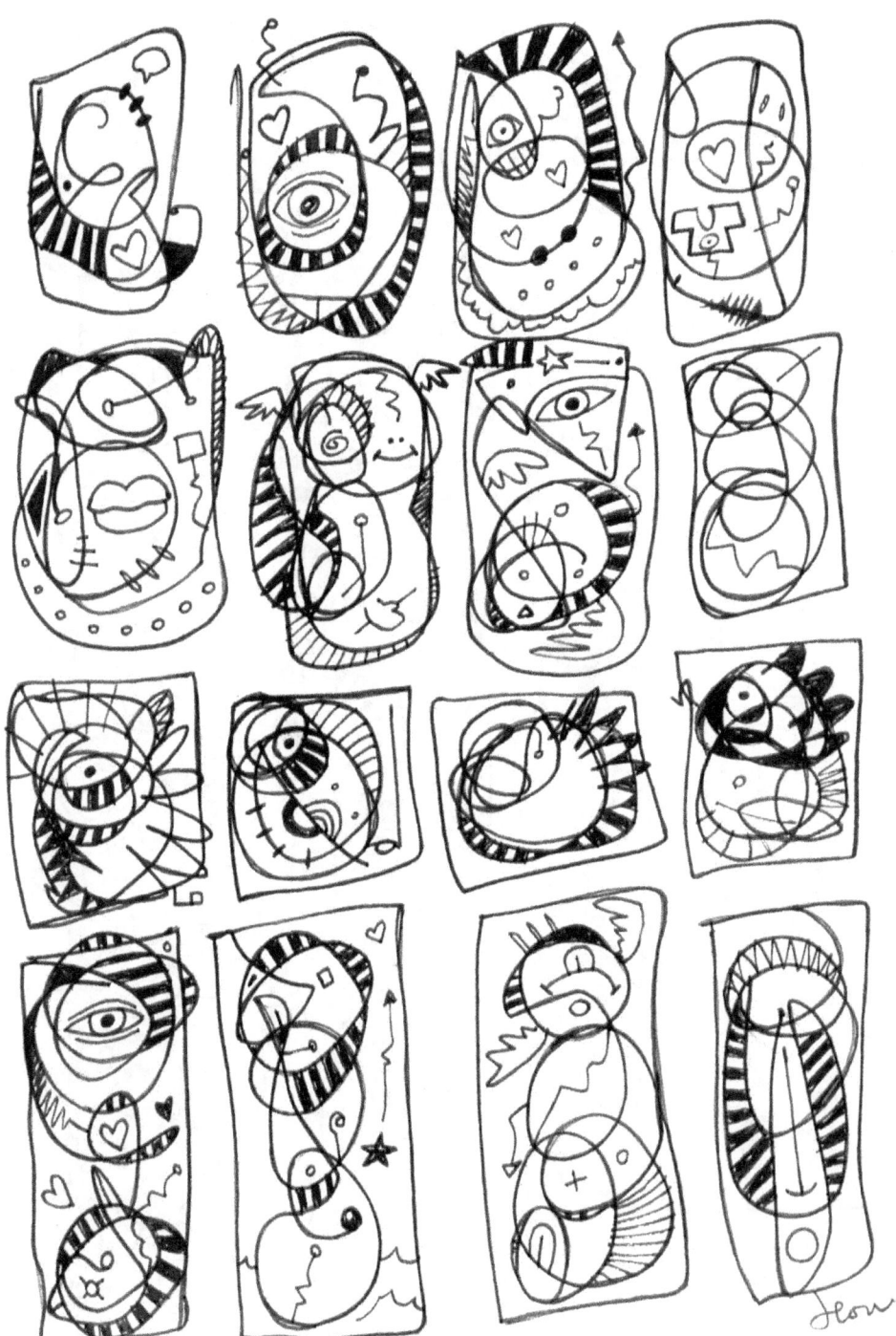

21

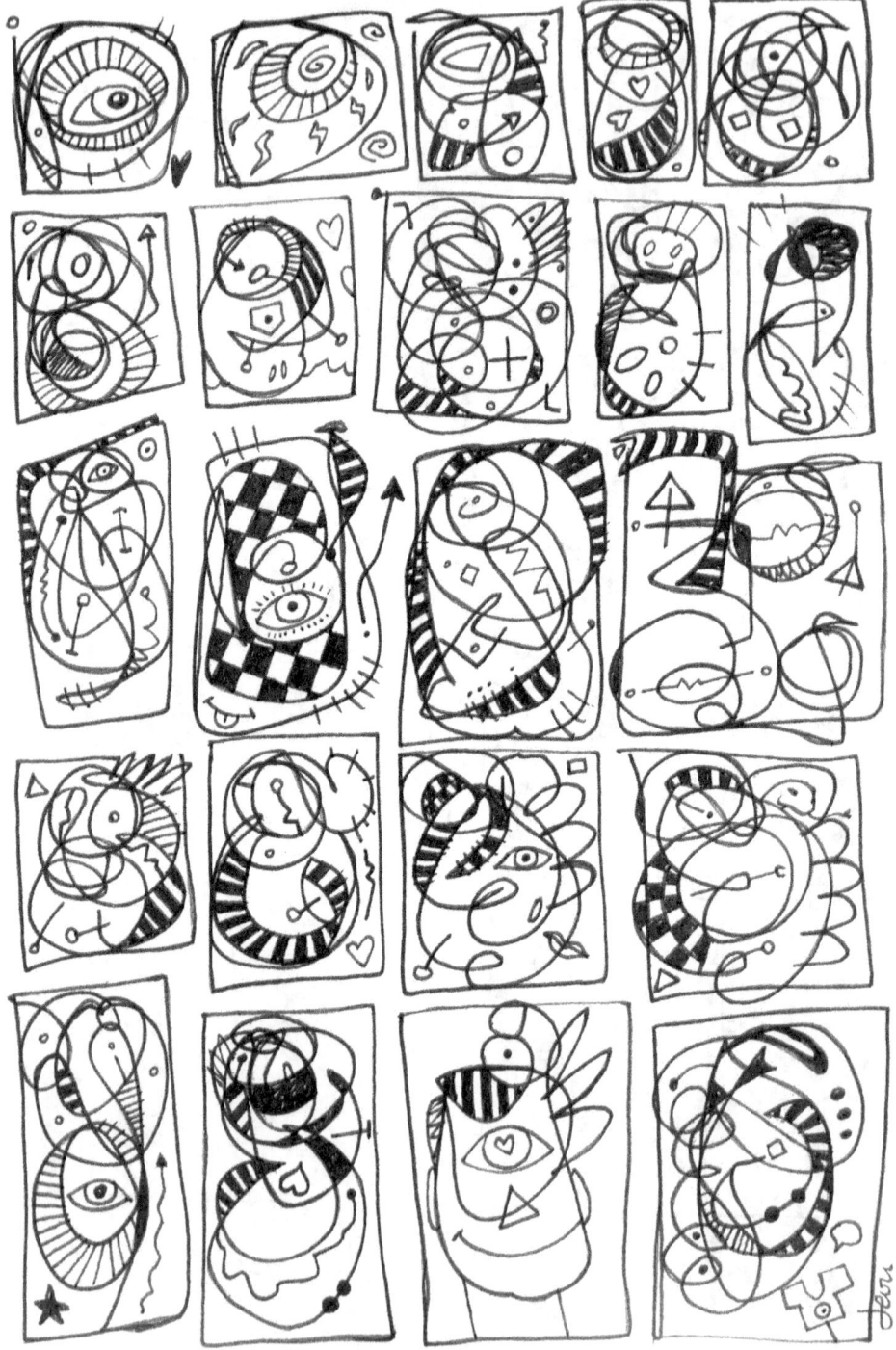

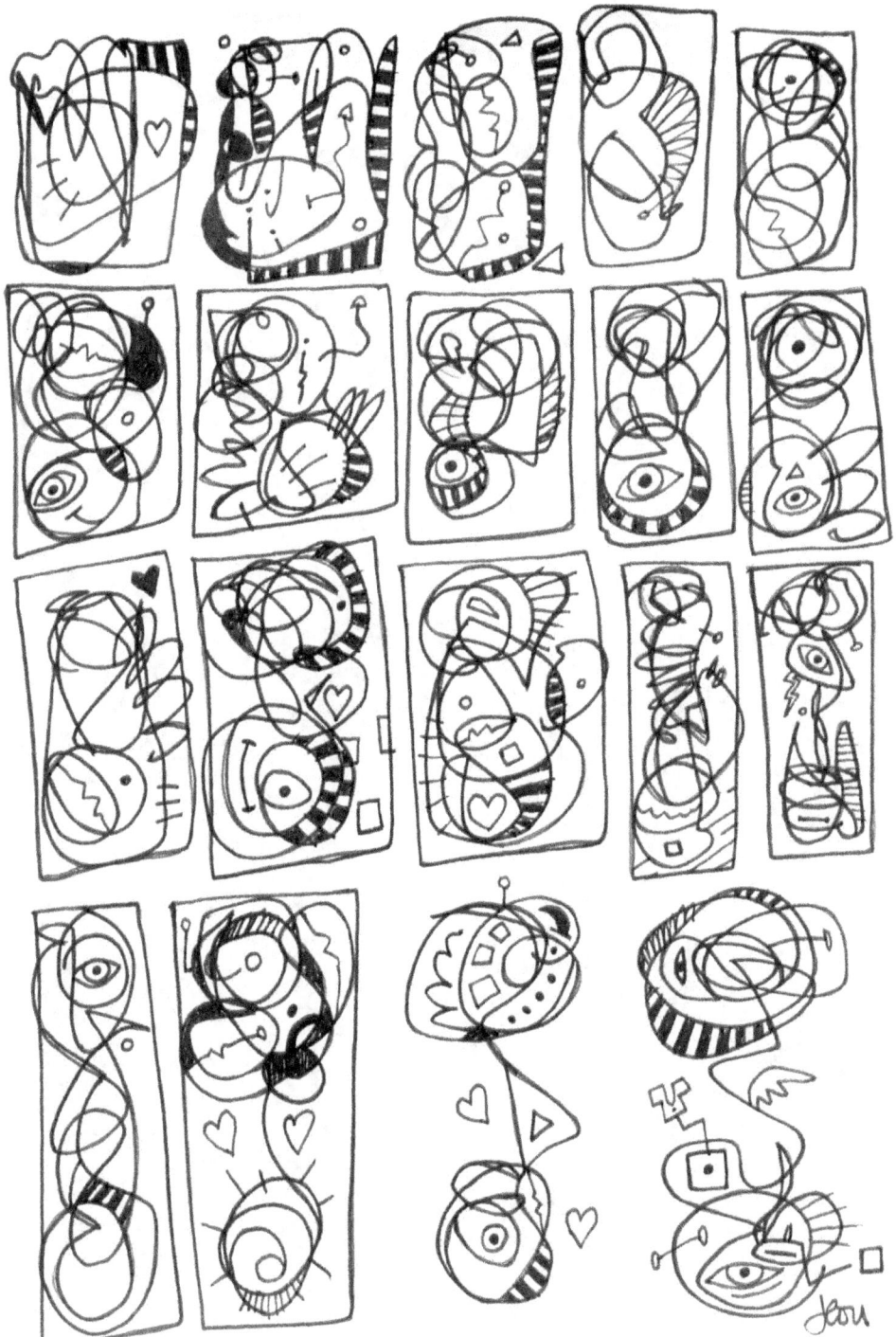

23

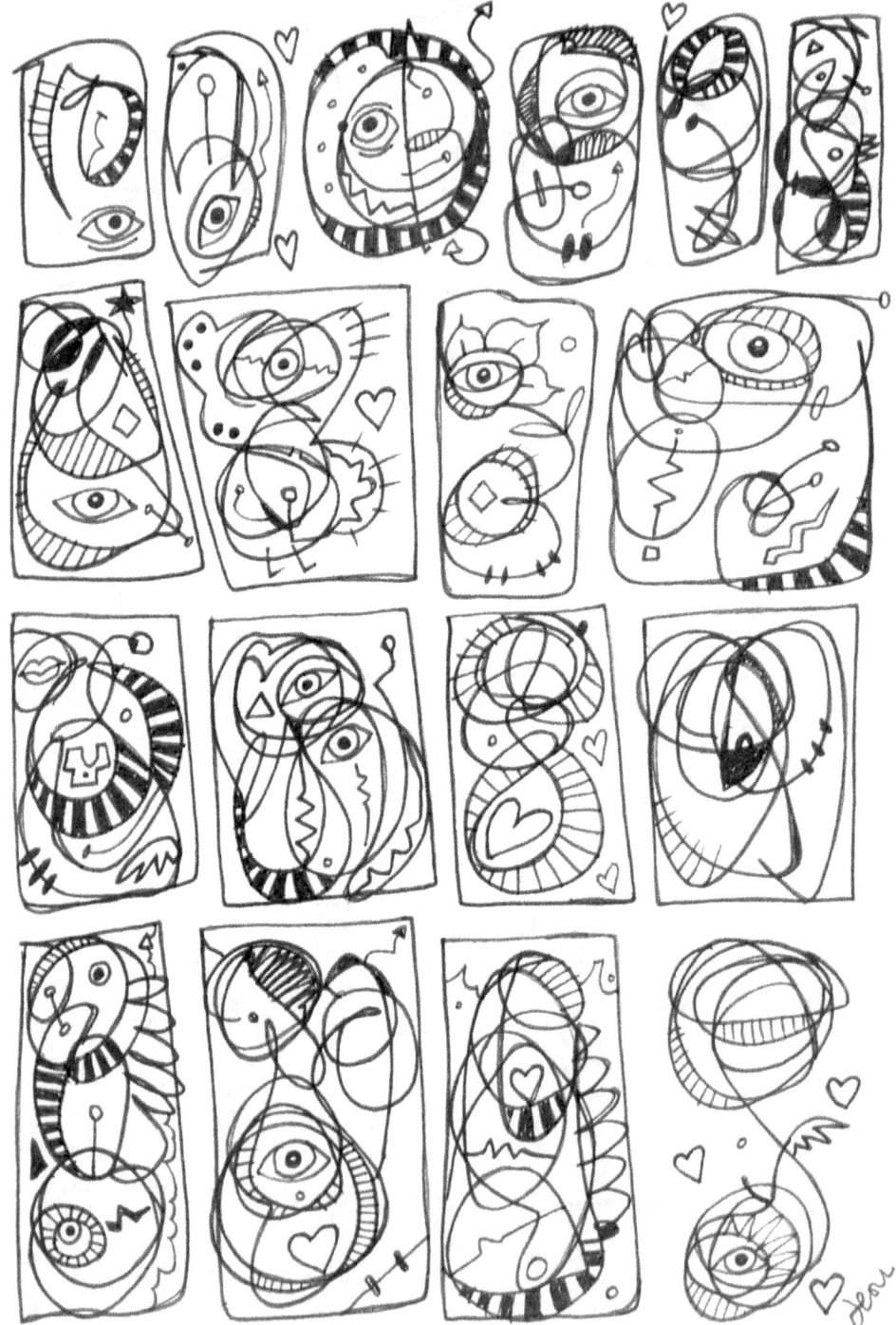

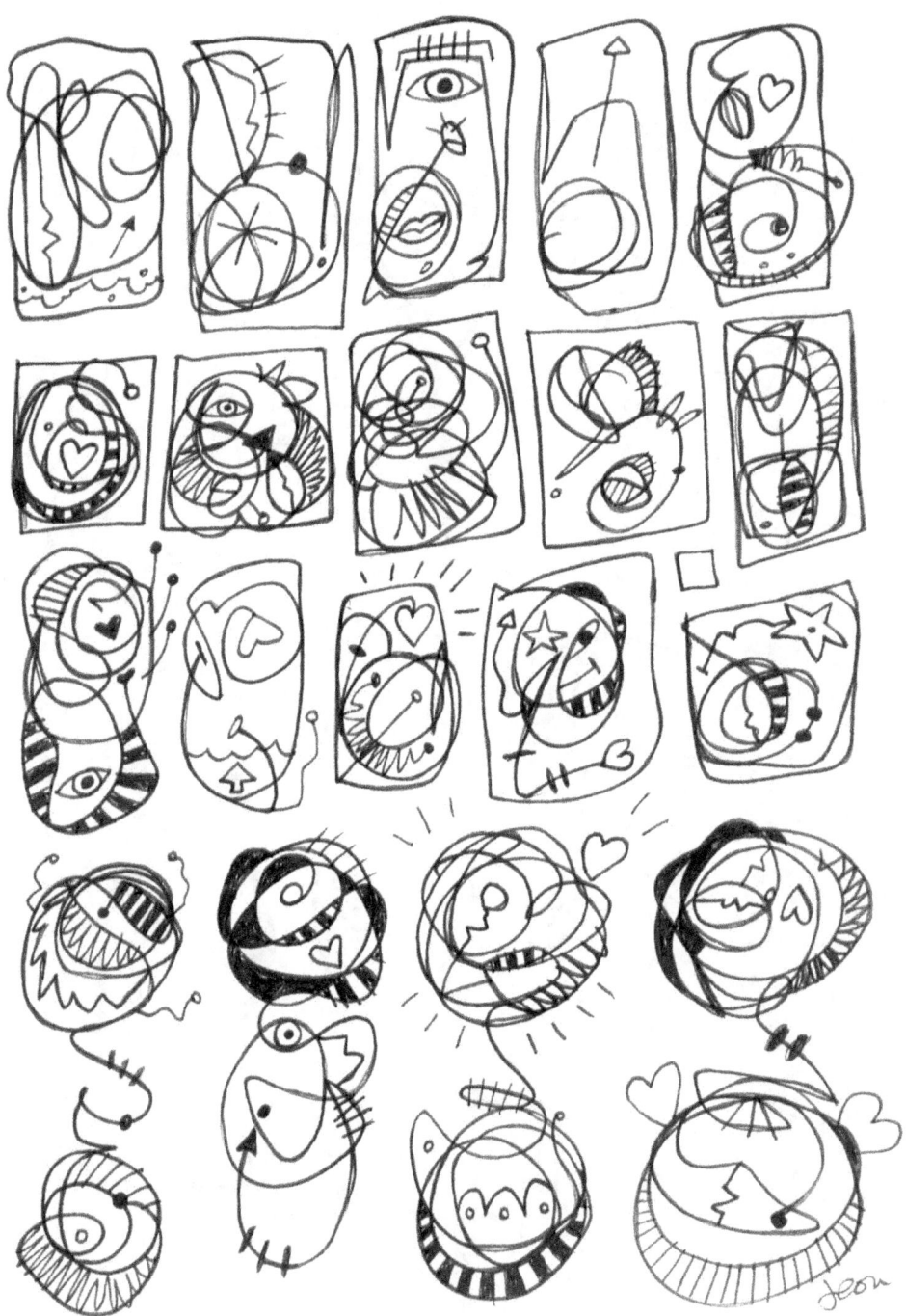

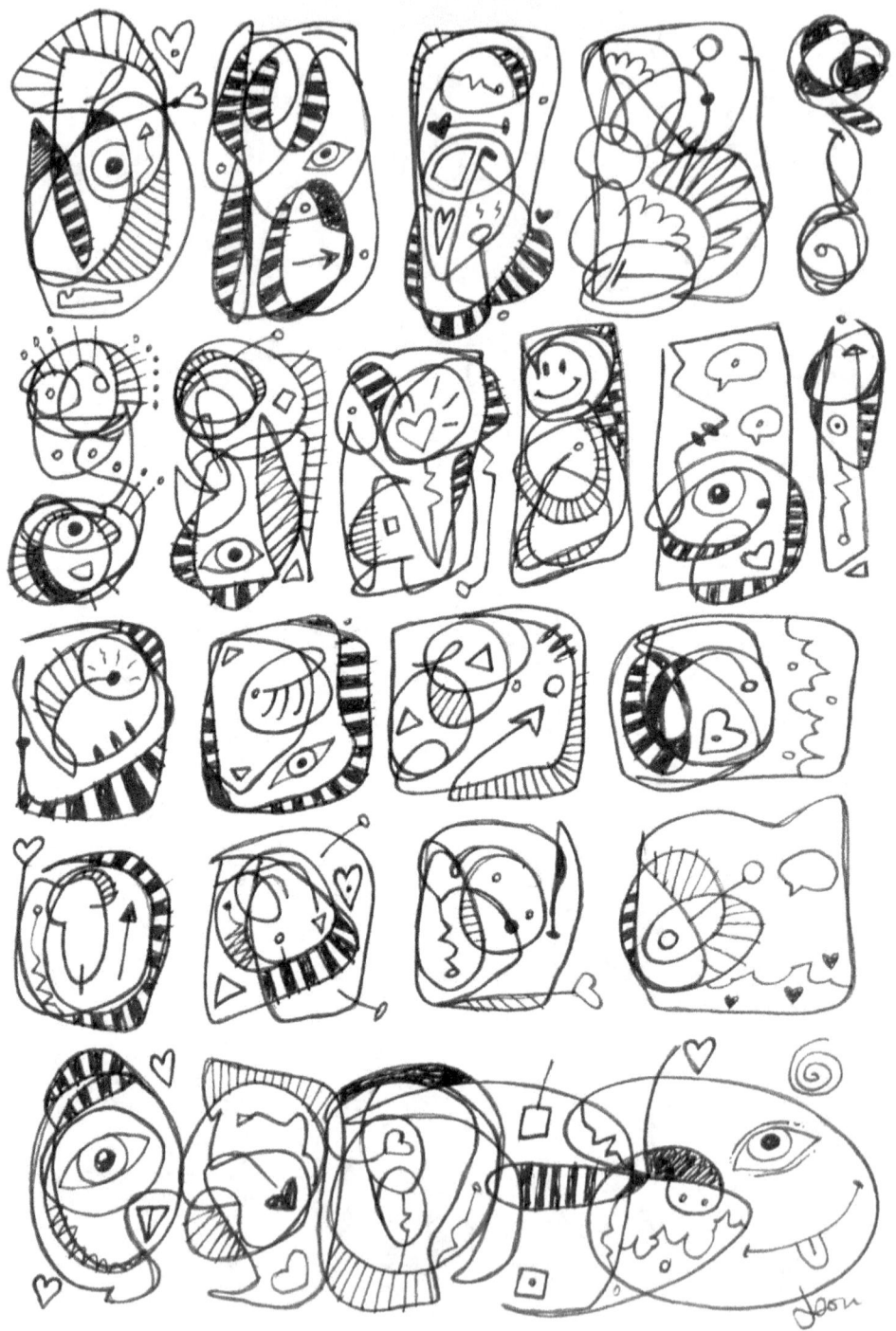

26

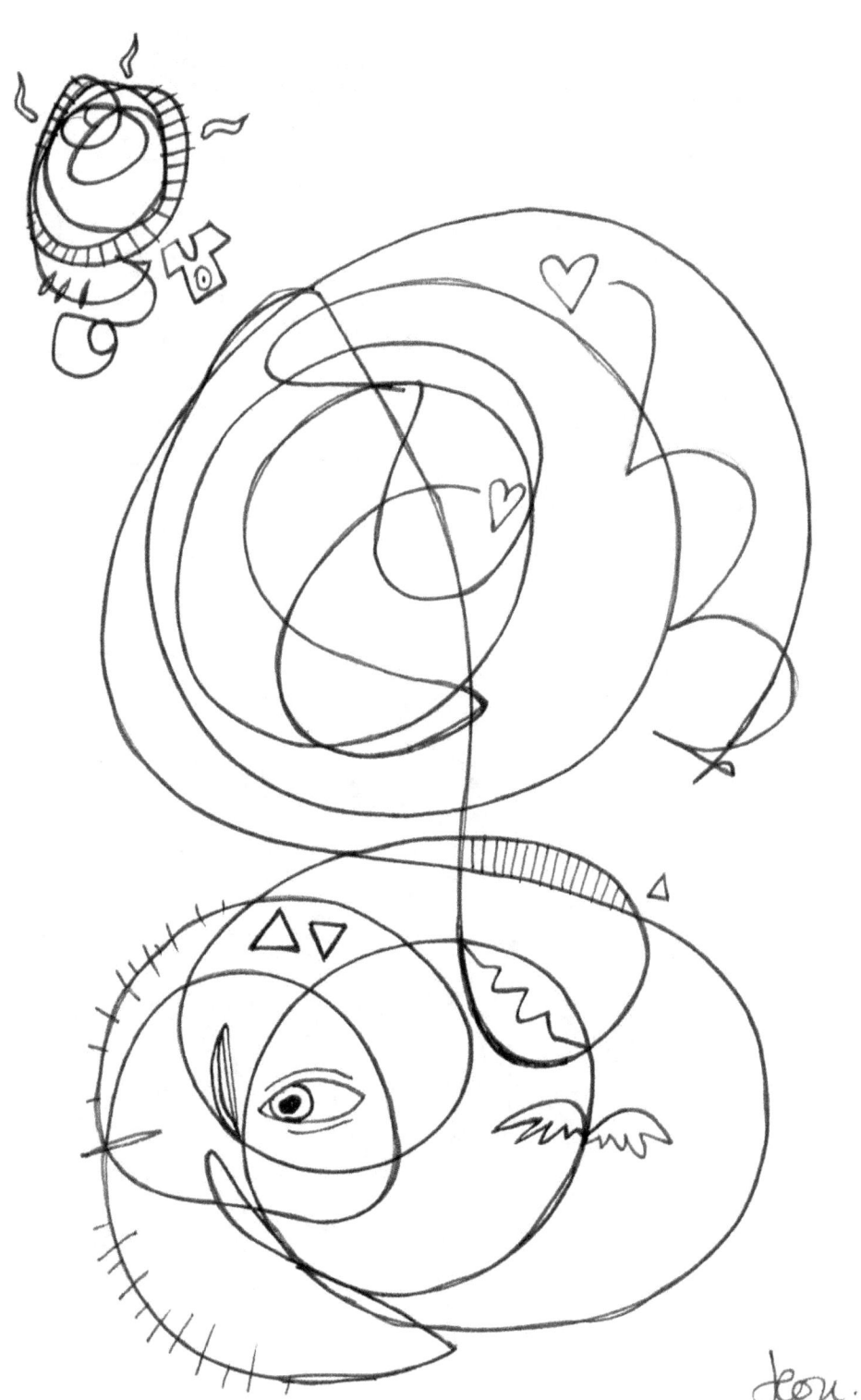

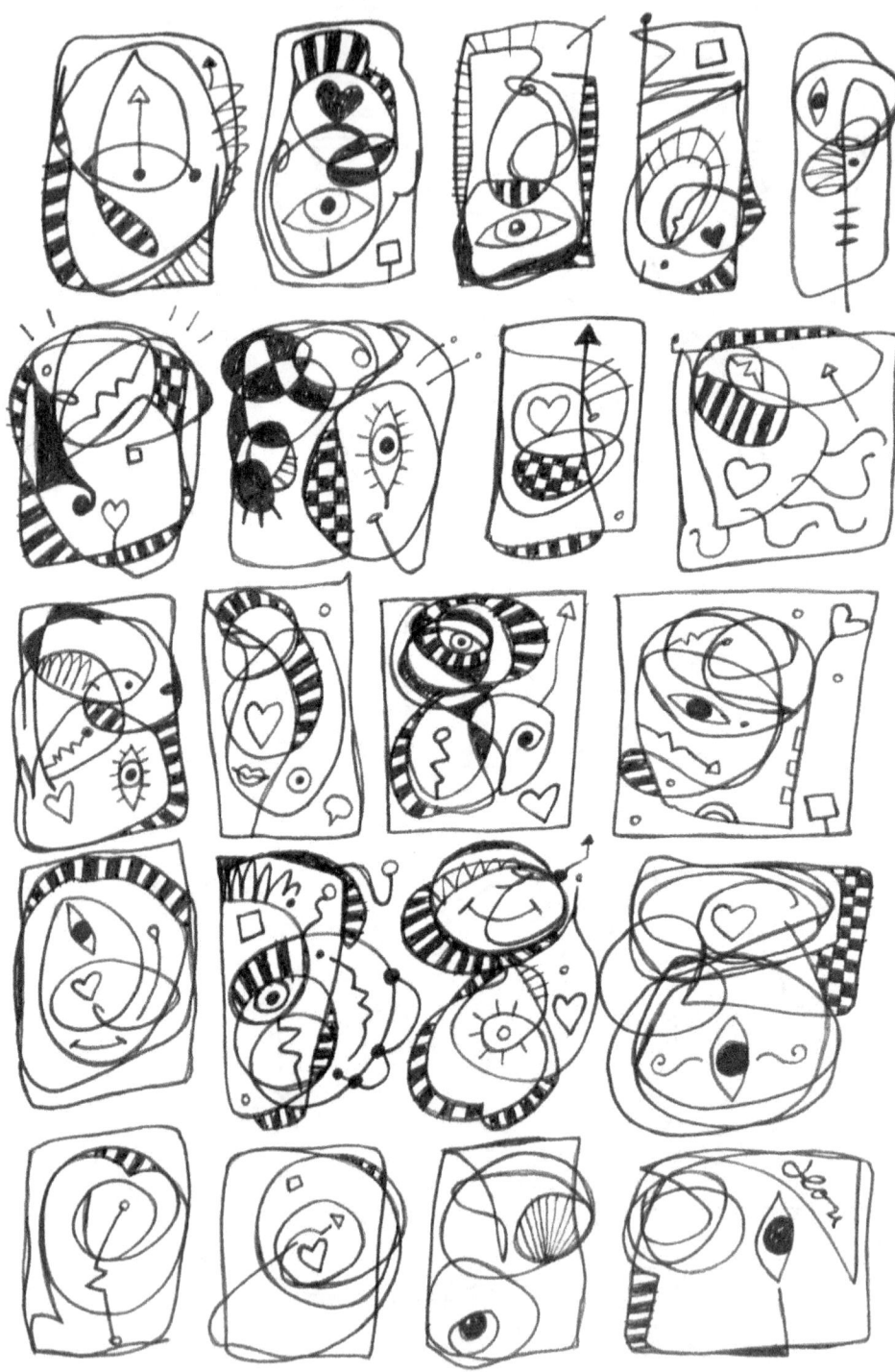

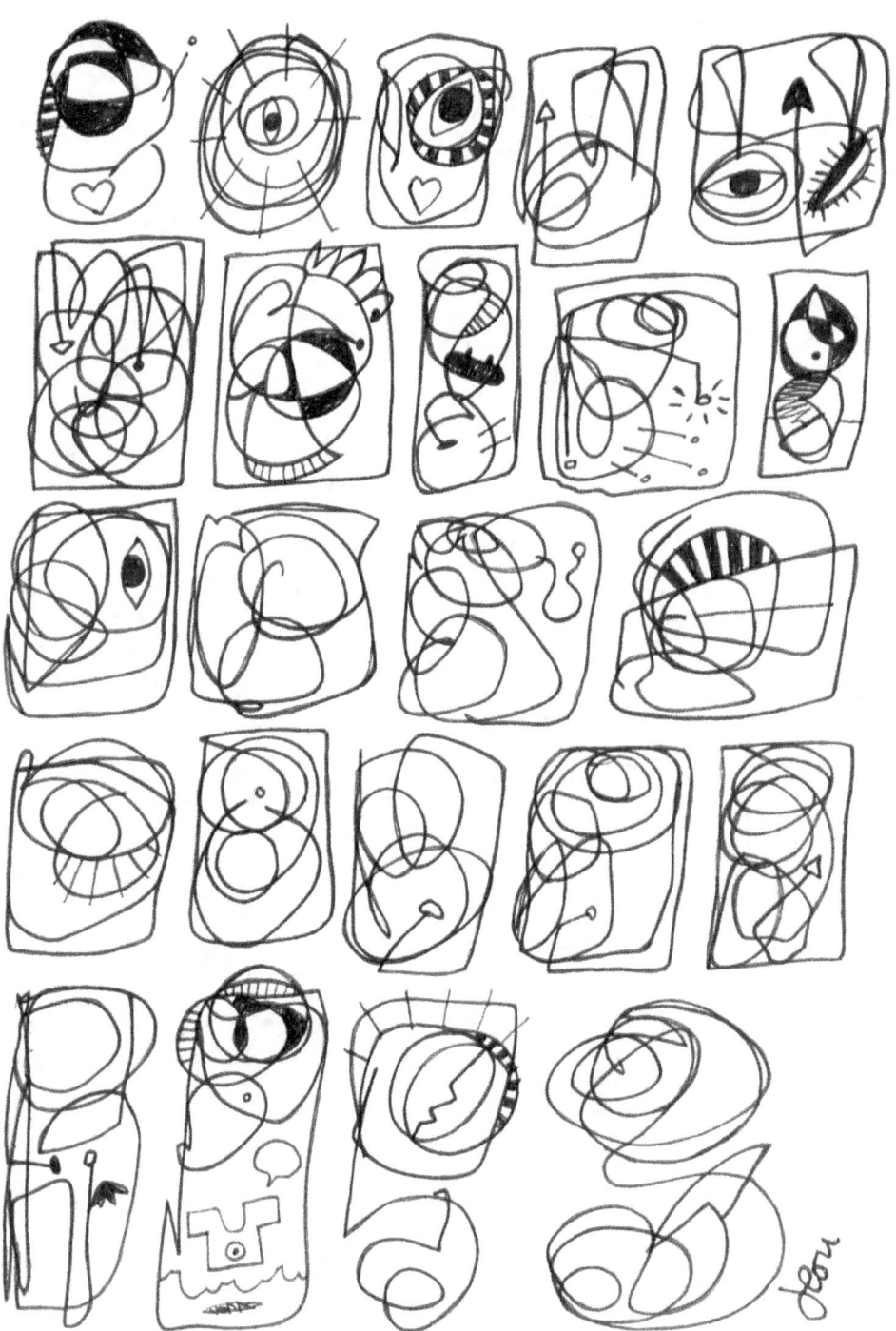

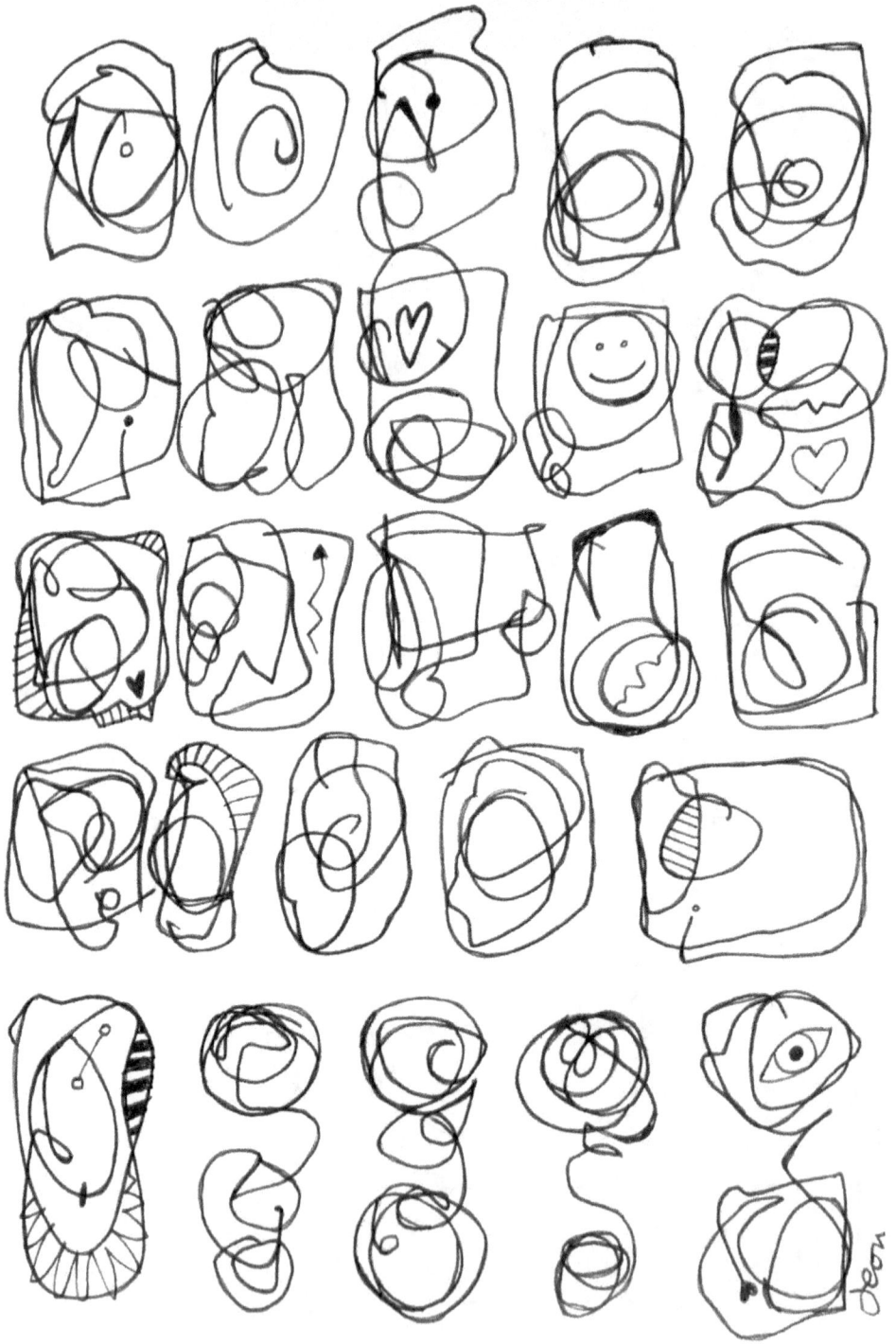

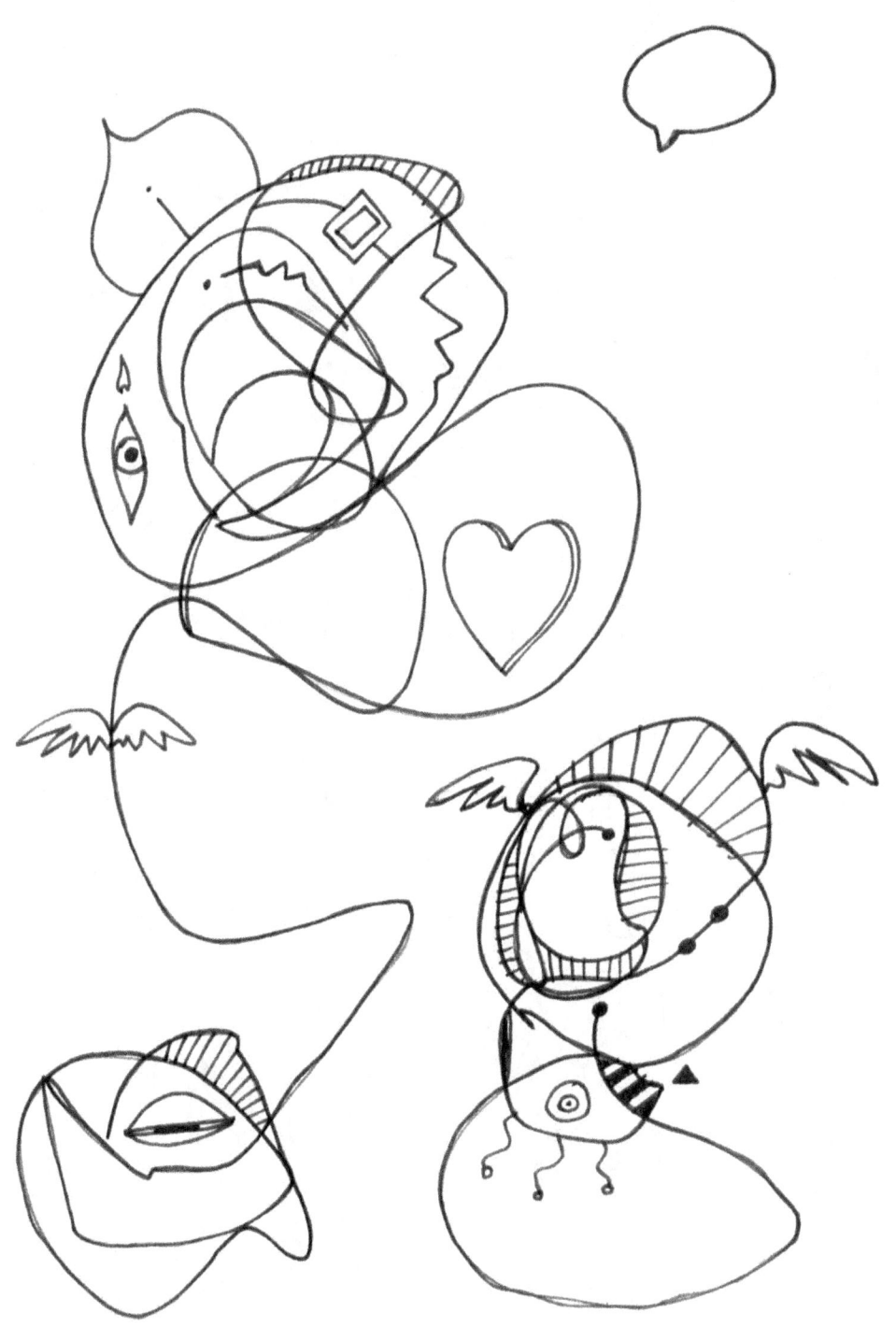

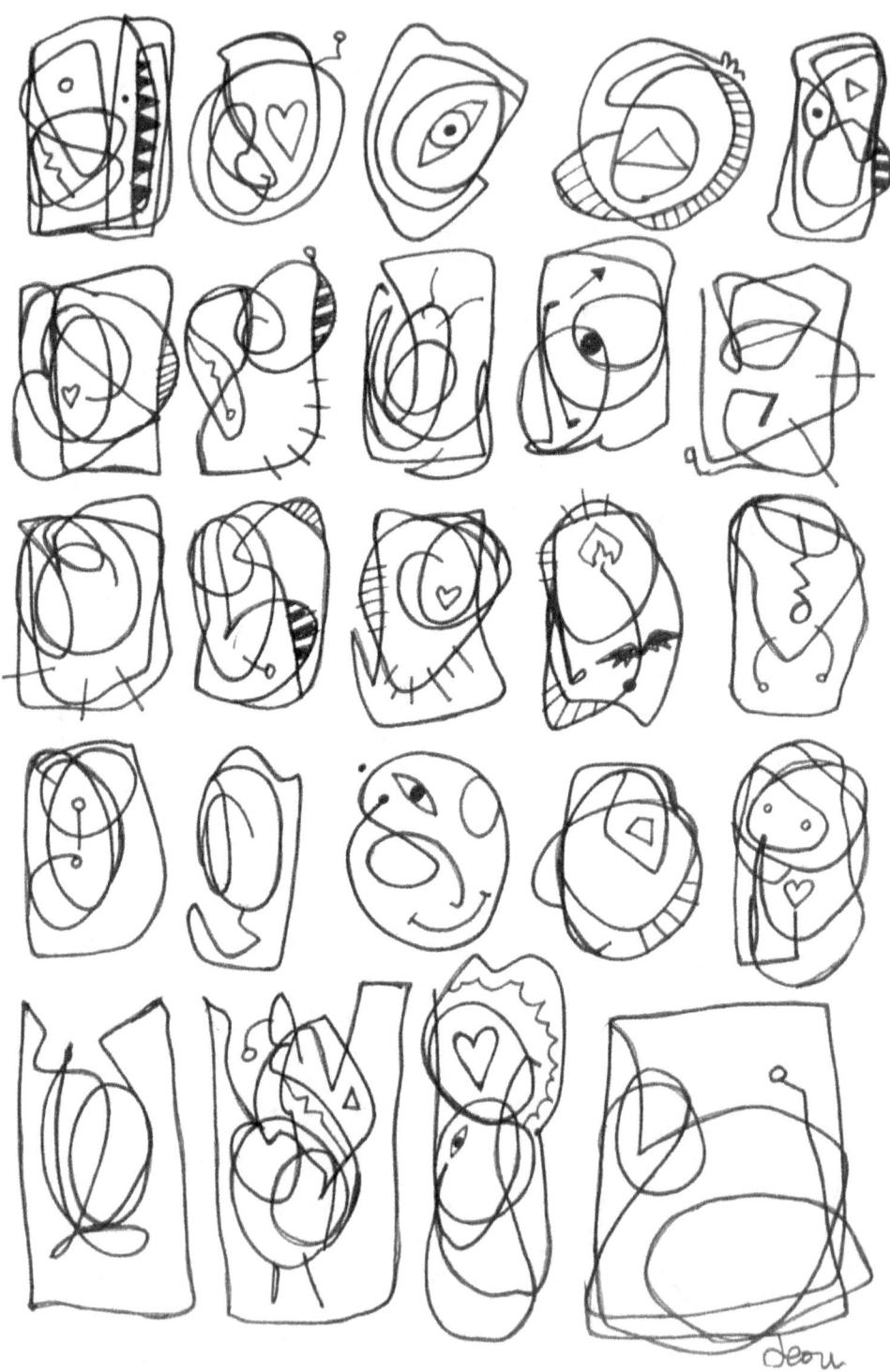

32

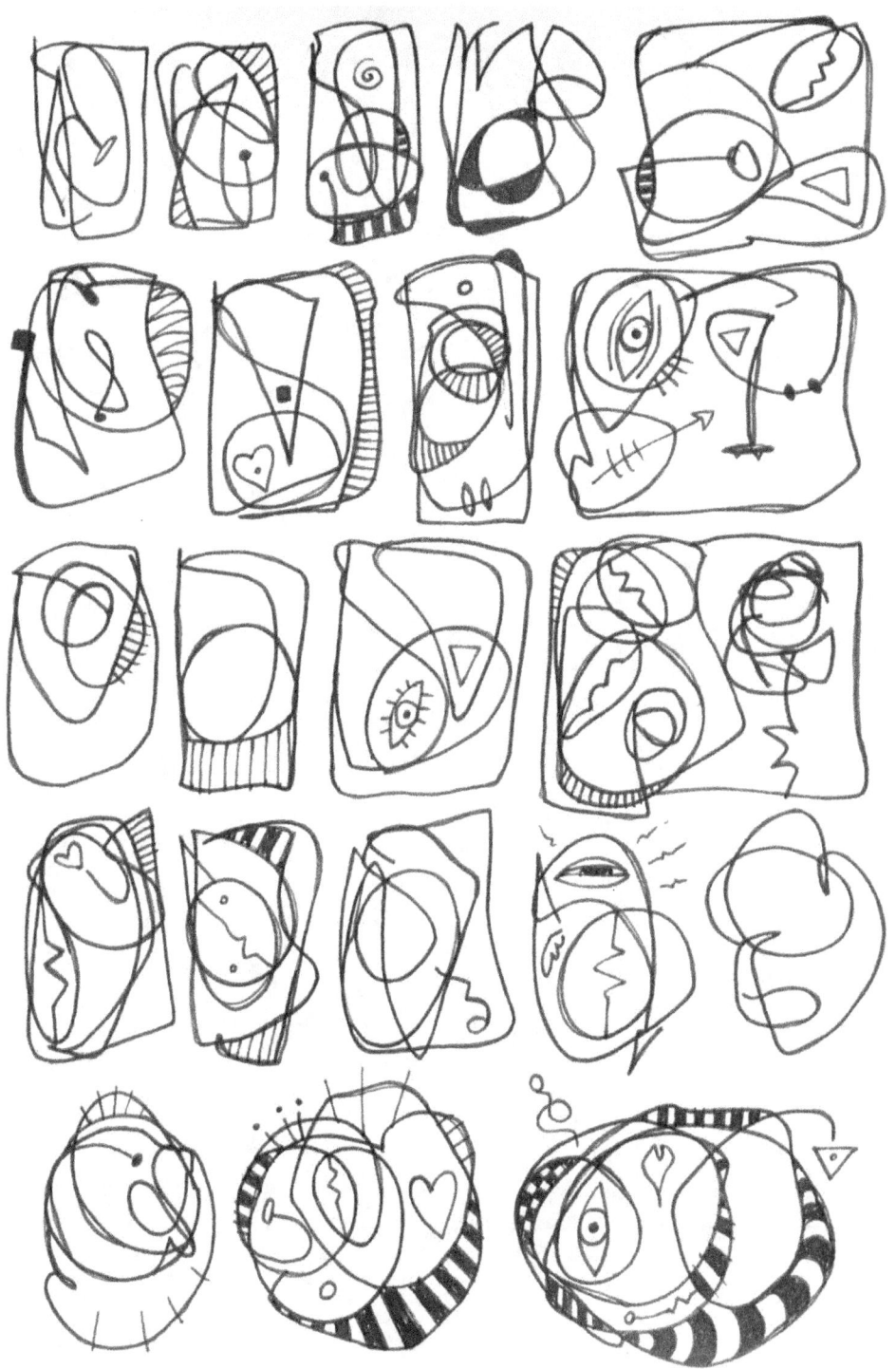

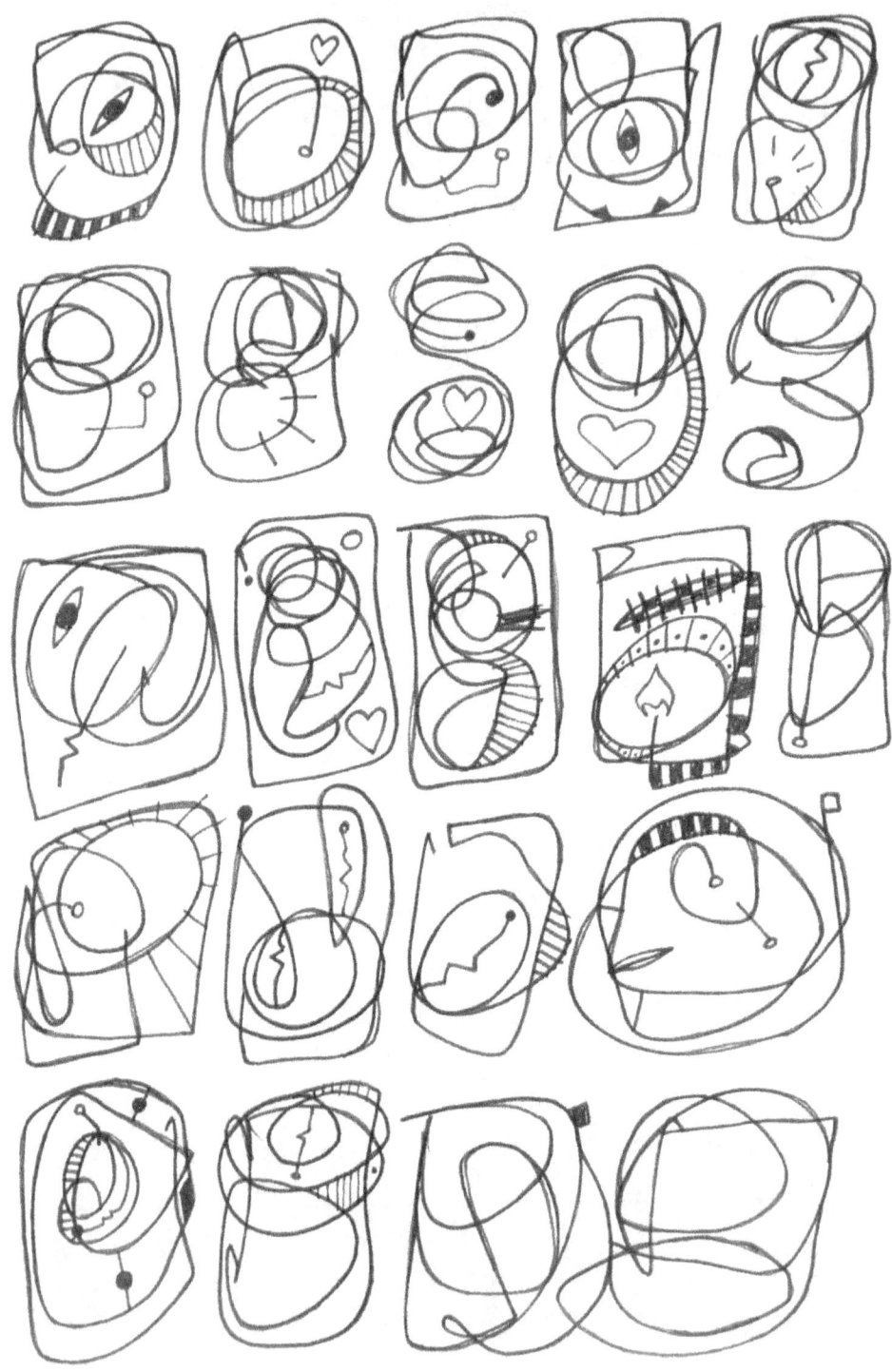

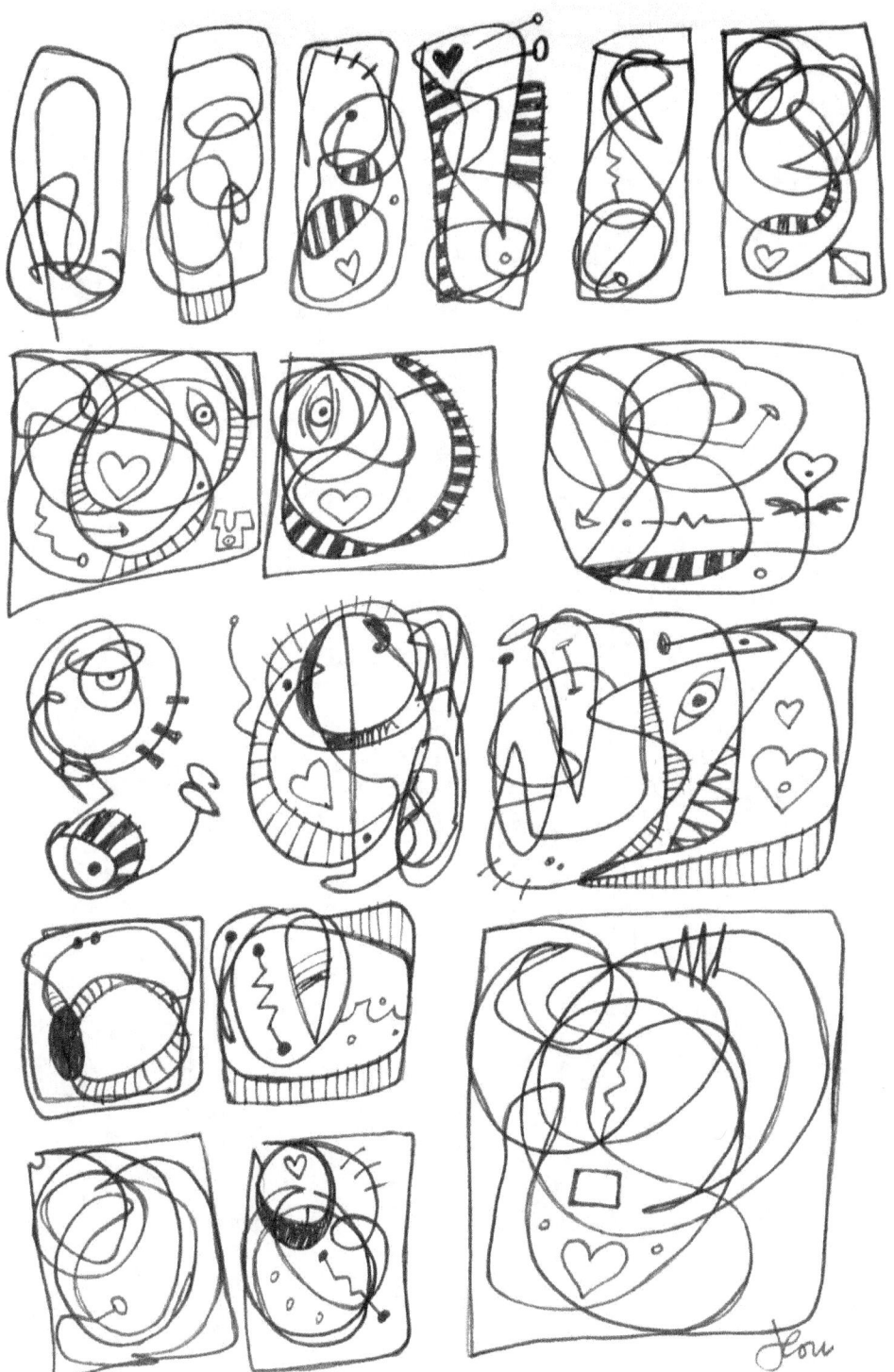

35

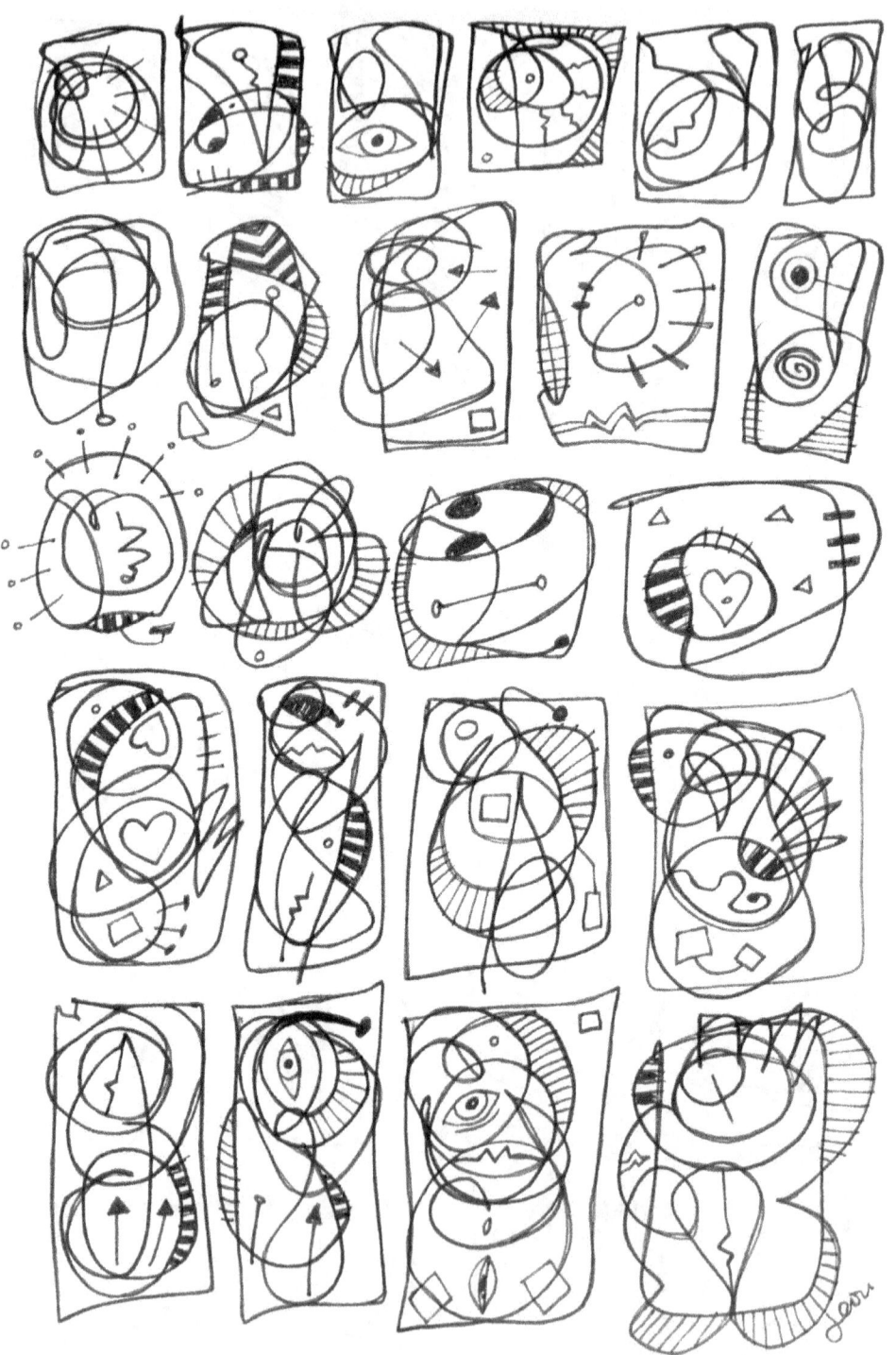

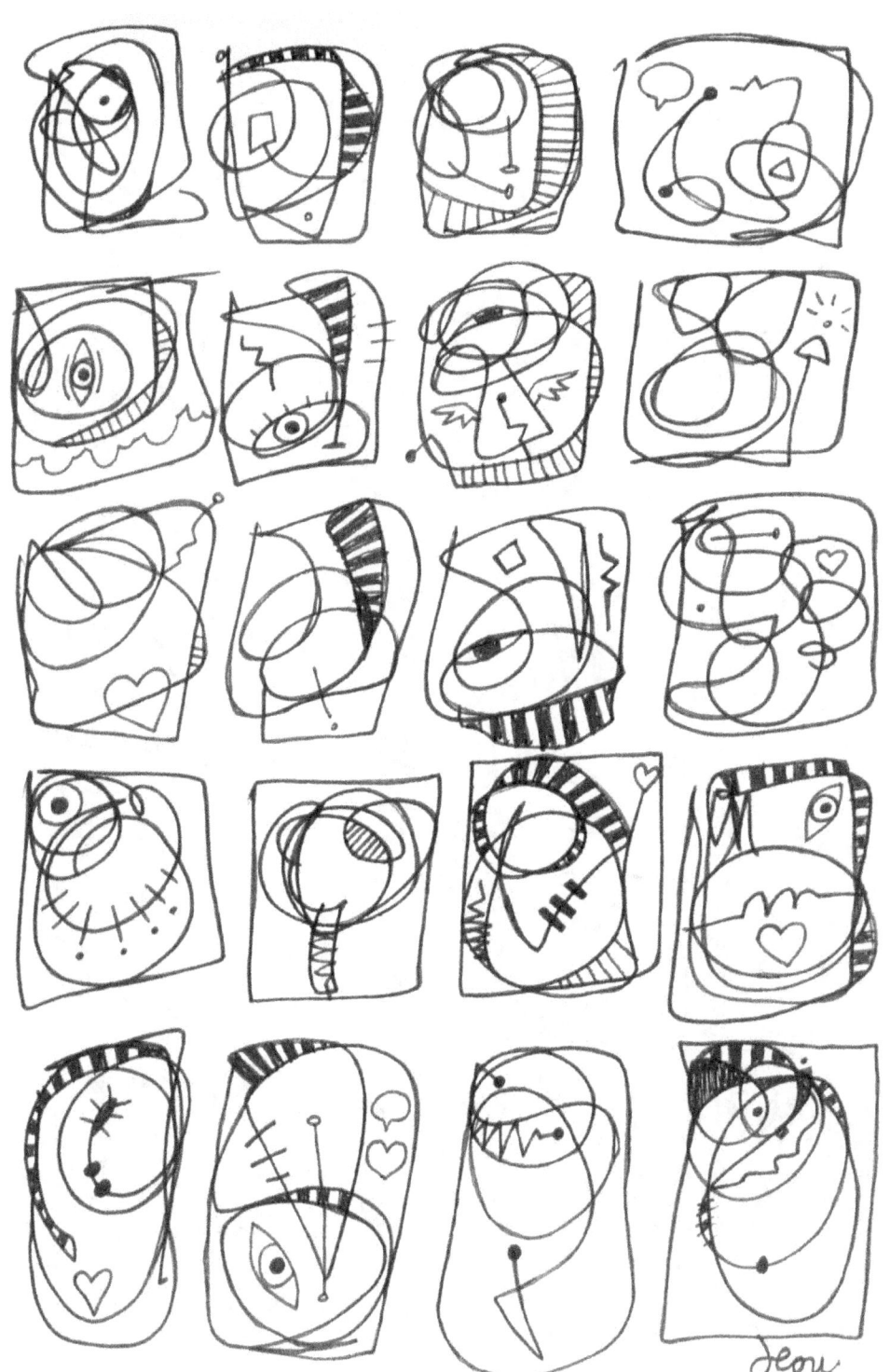

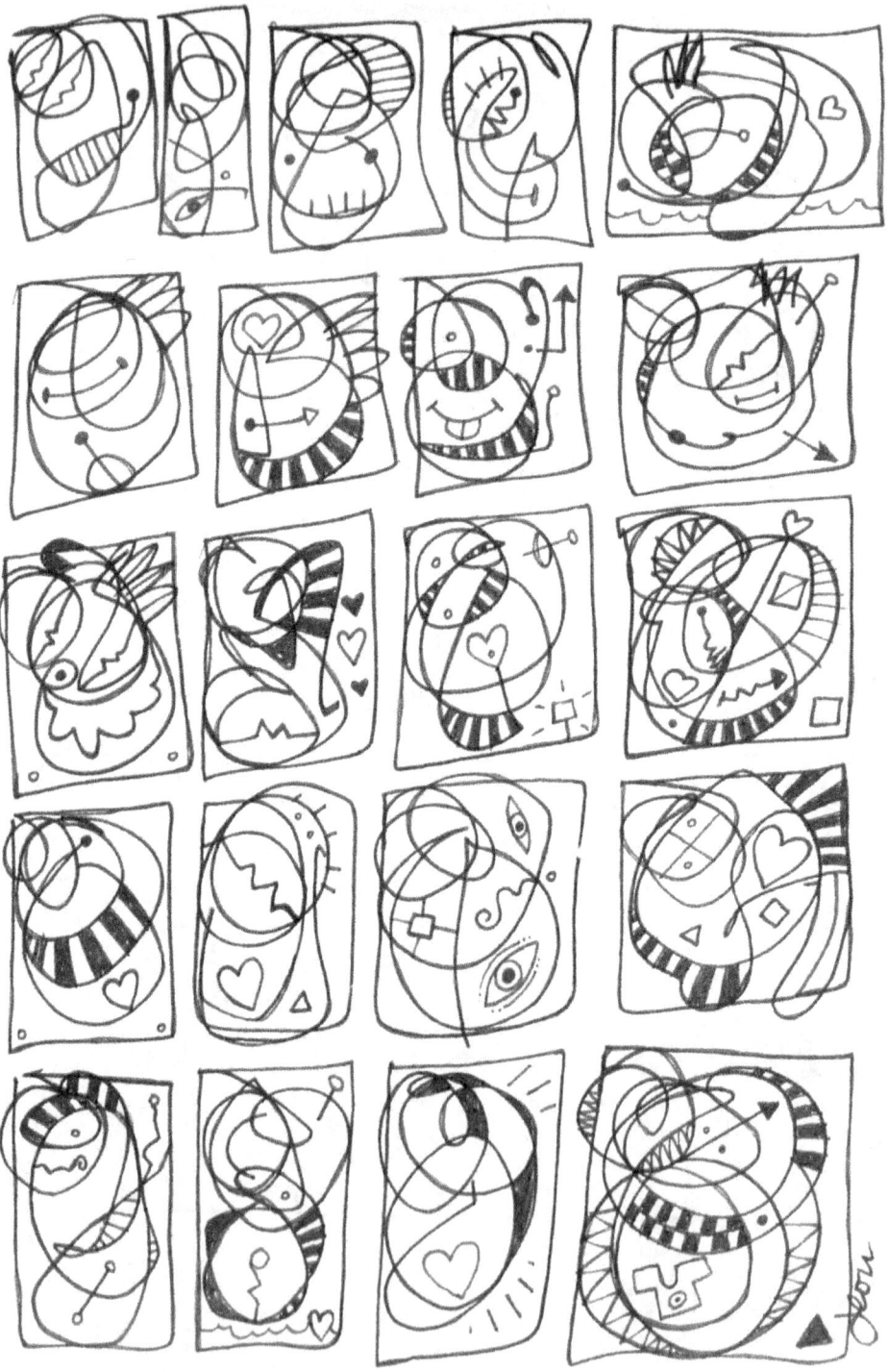

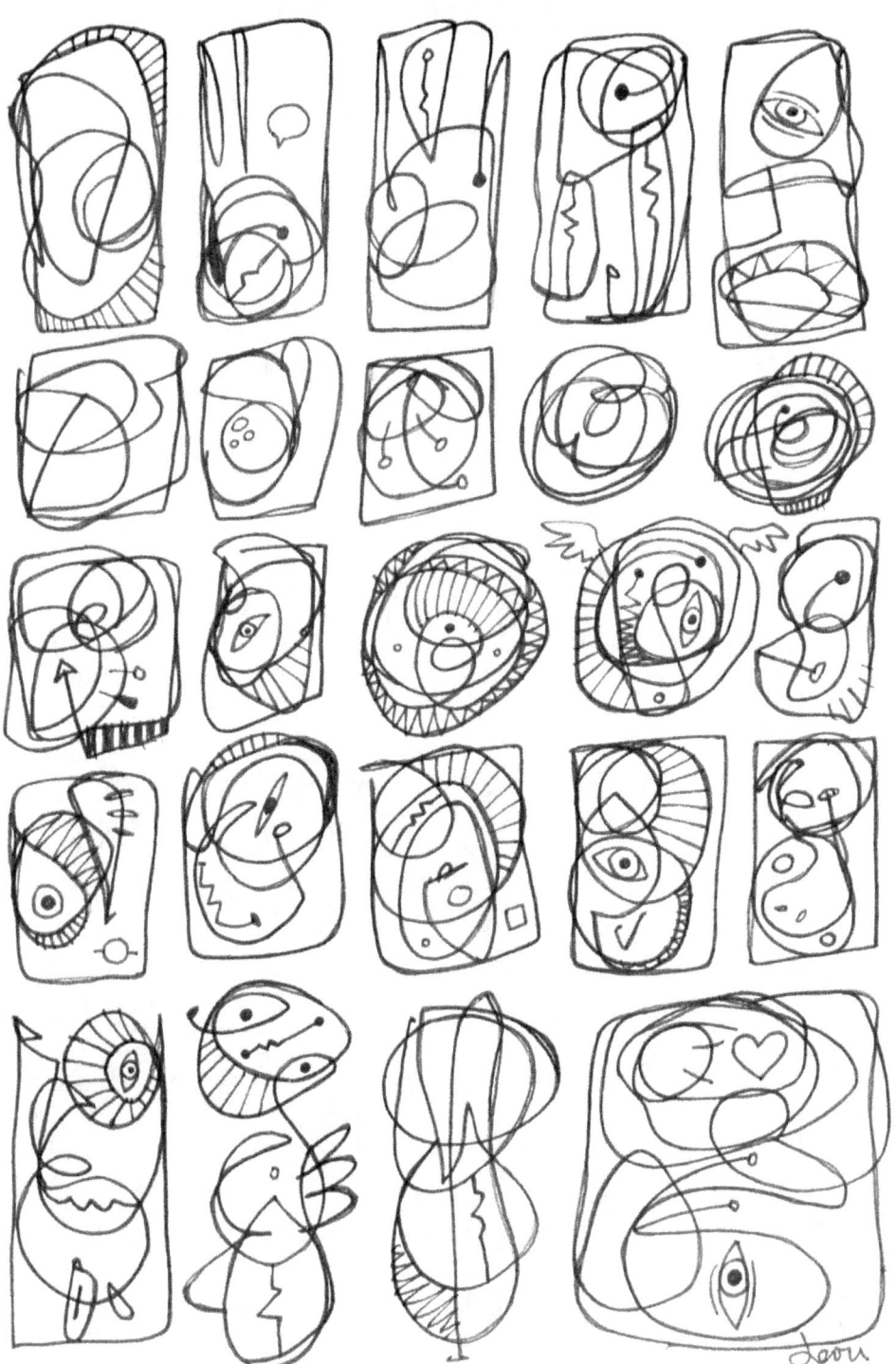

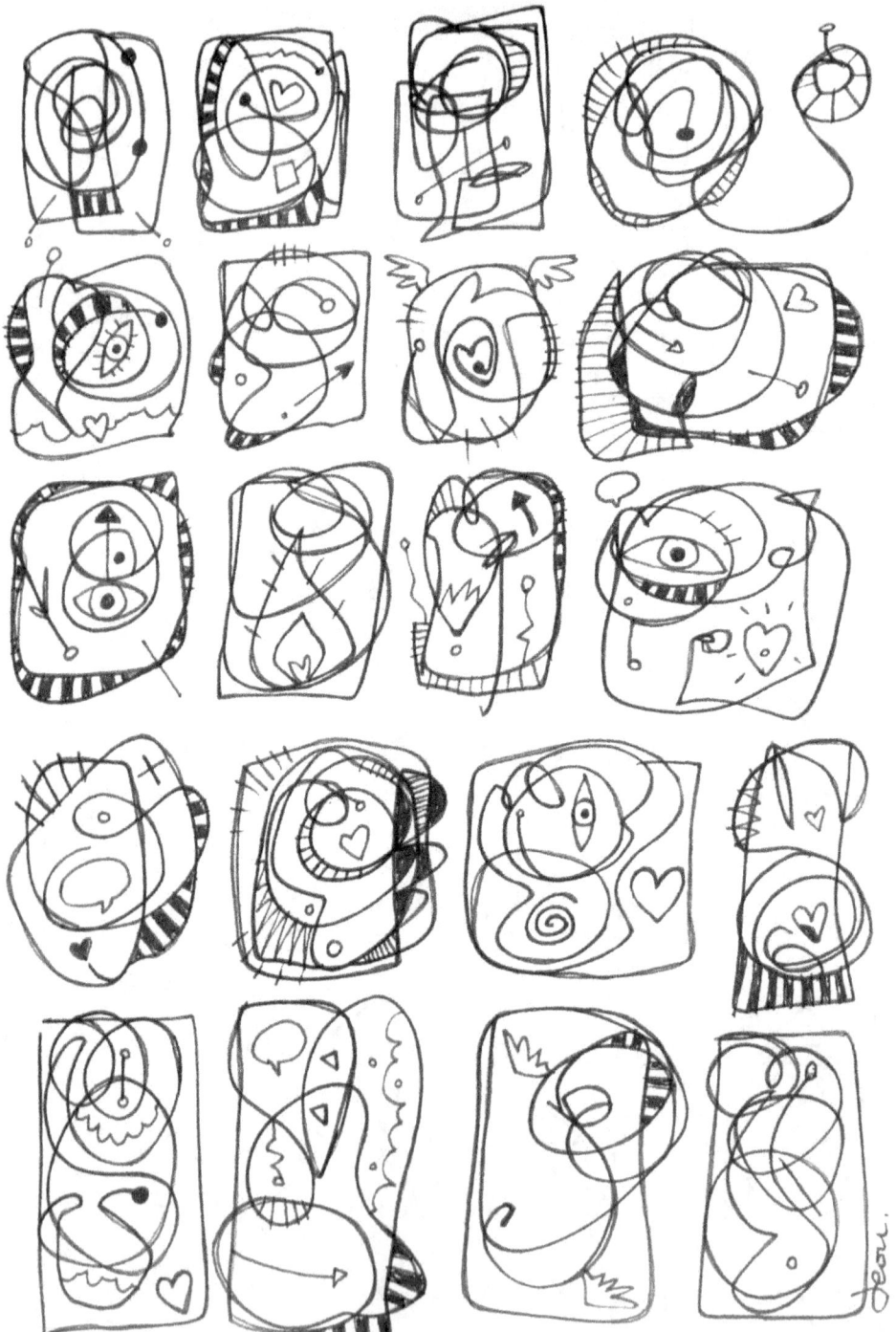

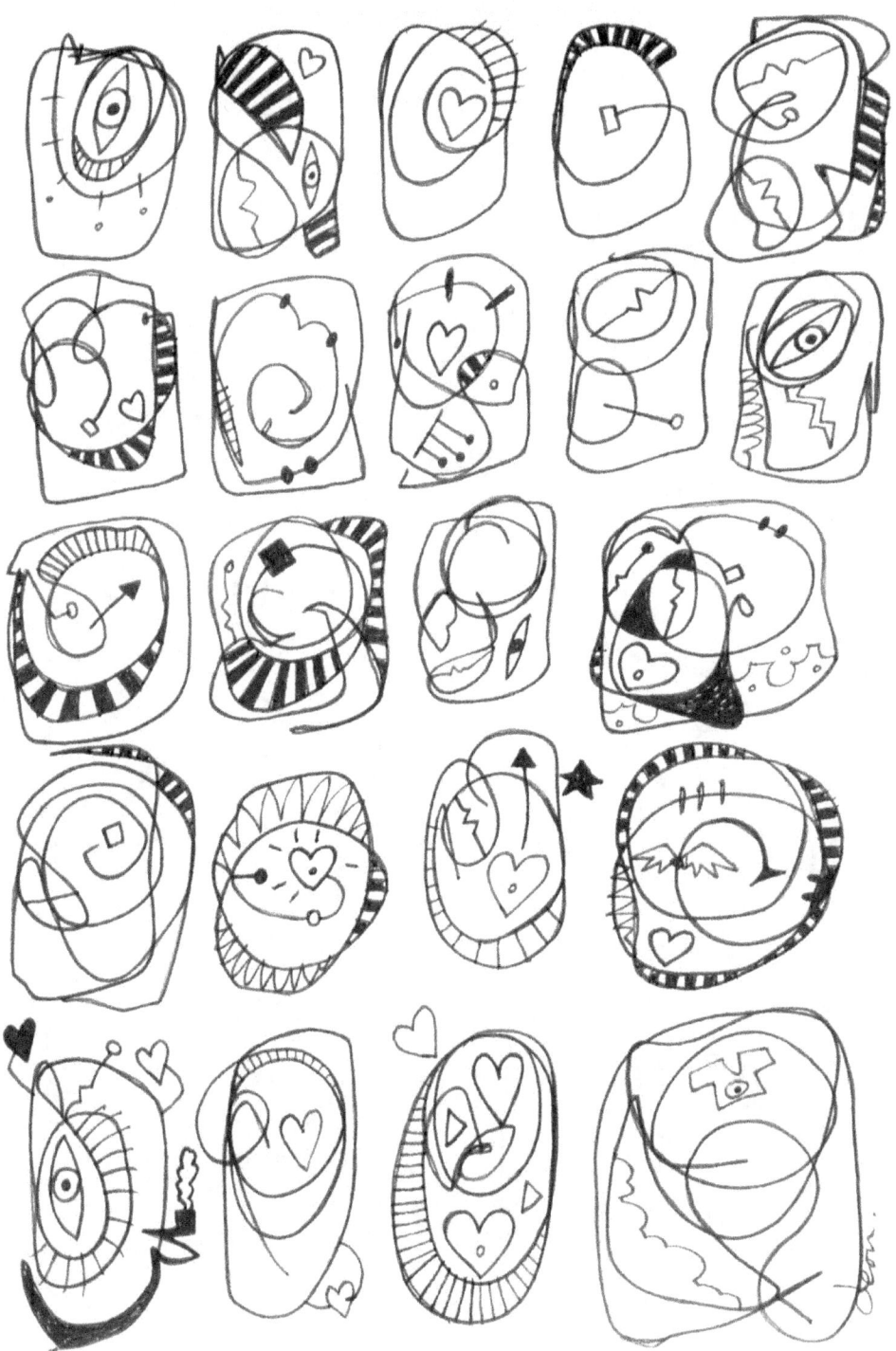

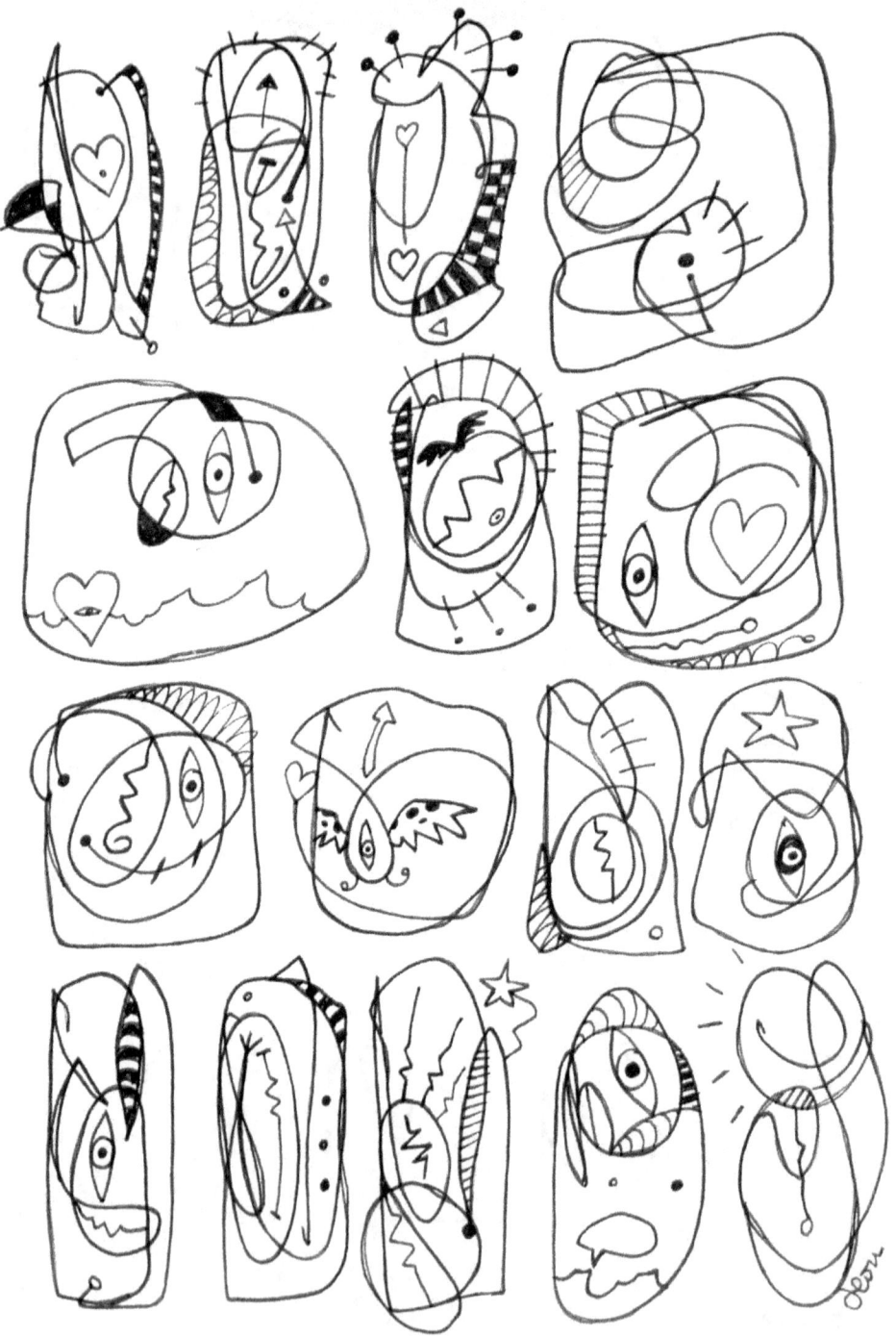

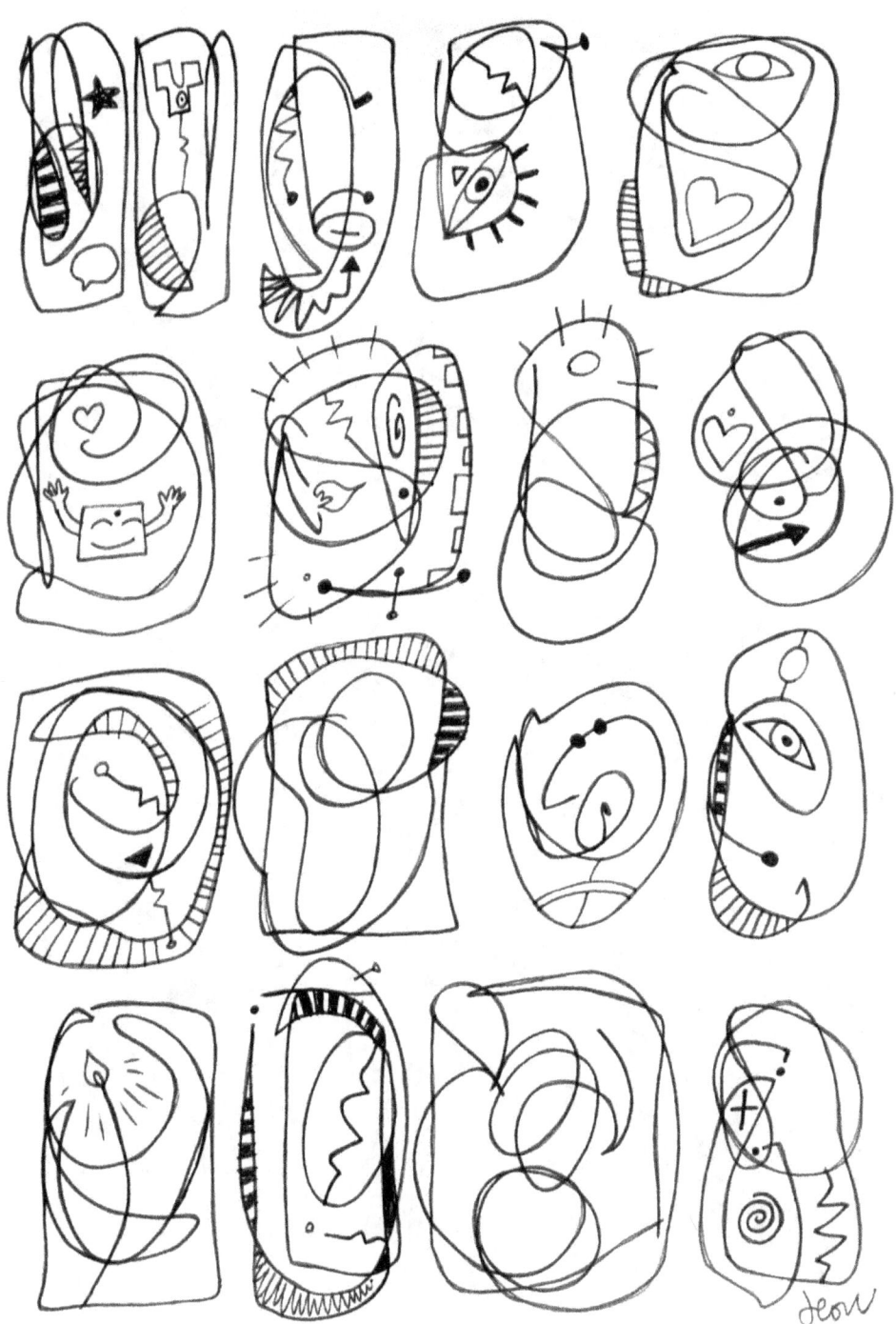

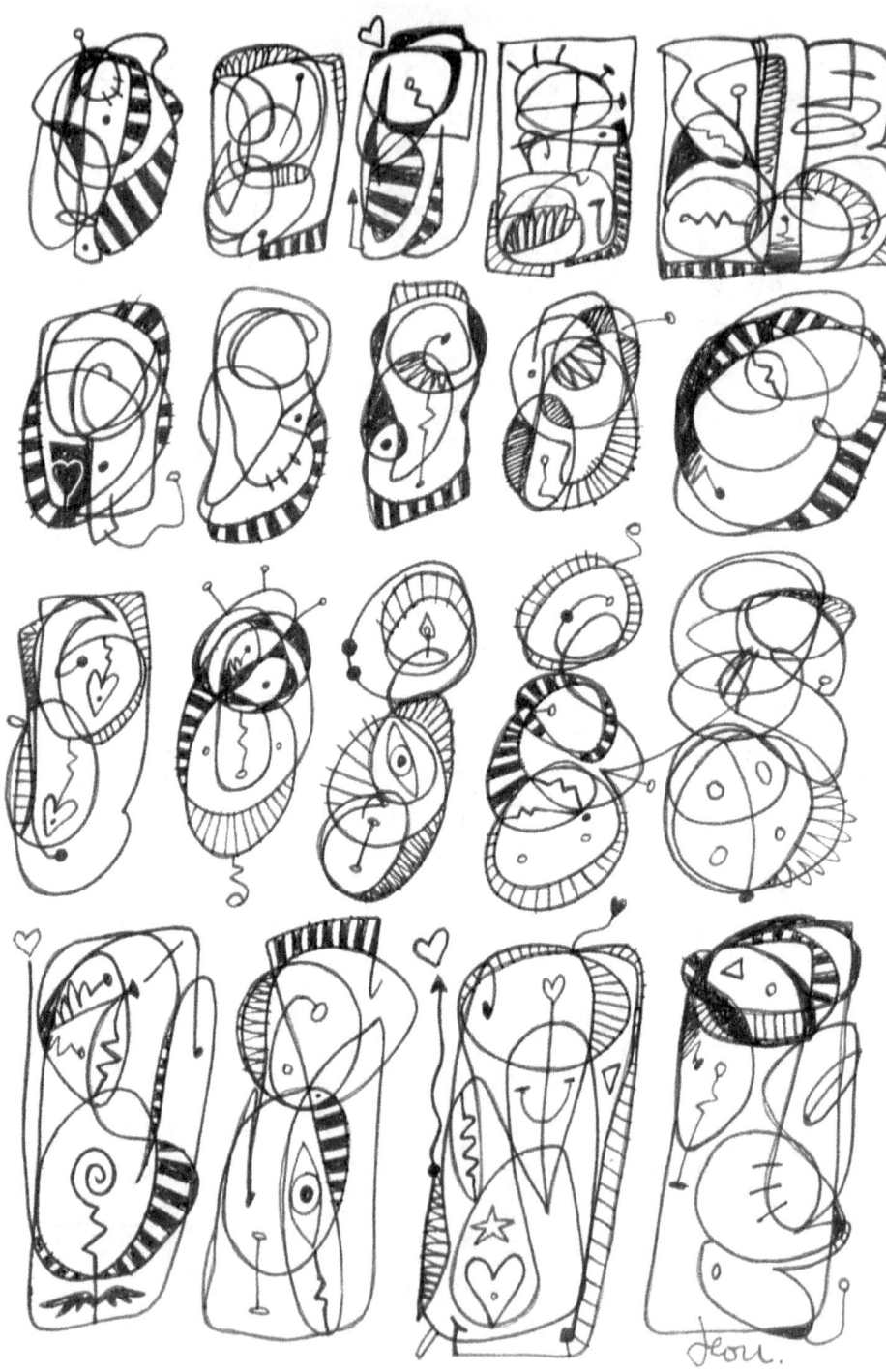

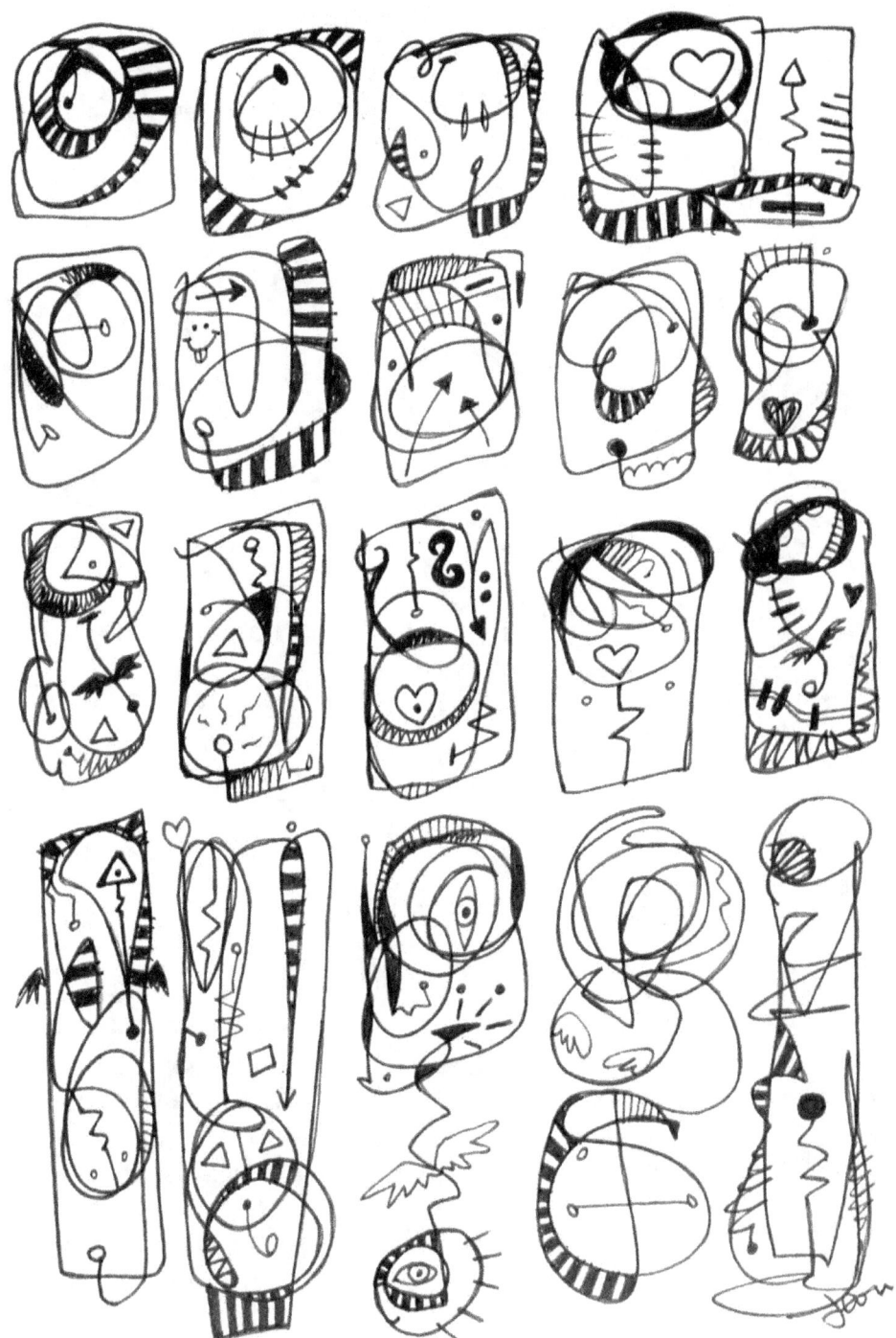

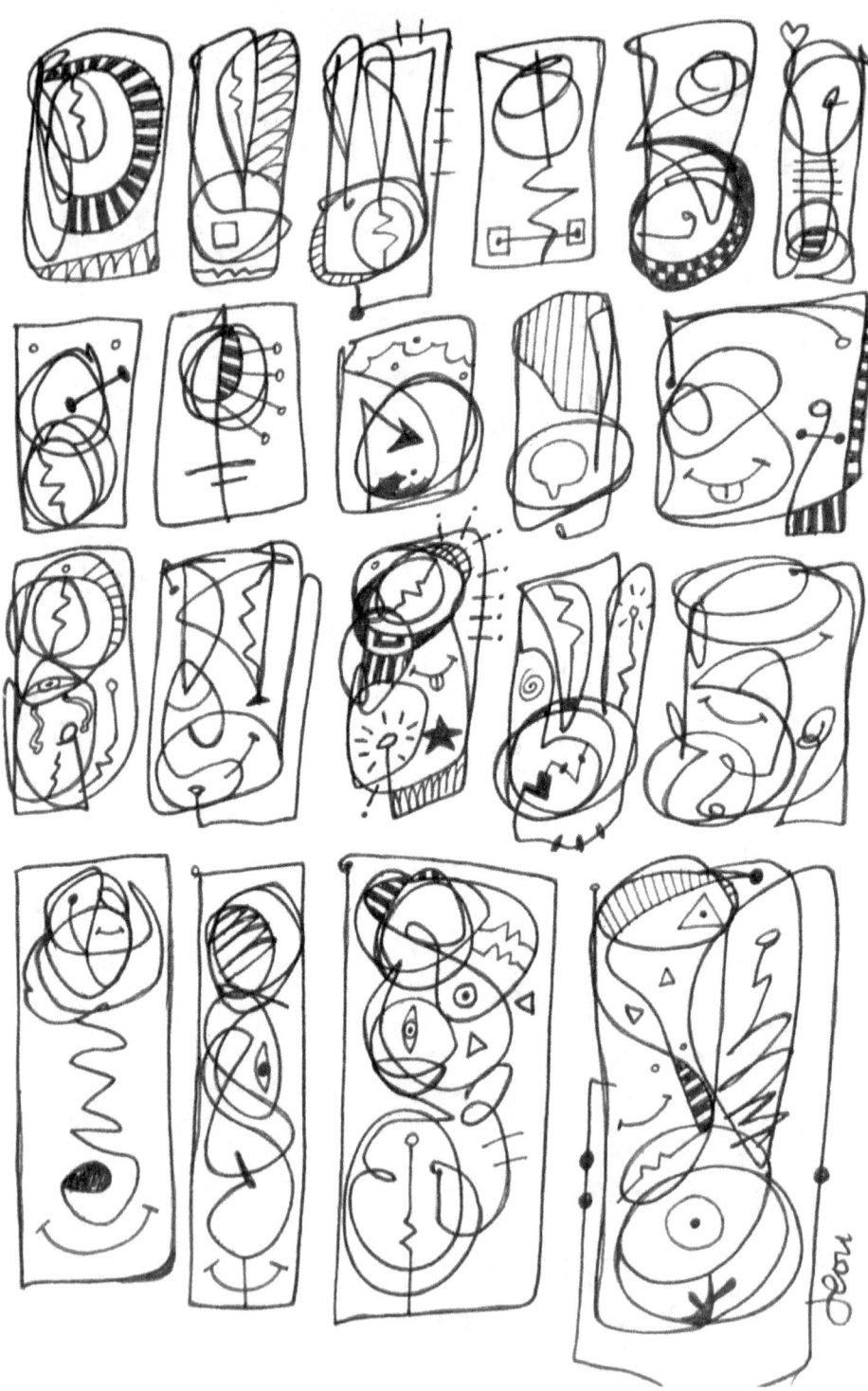

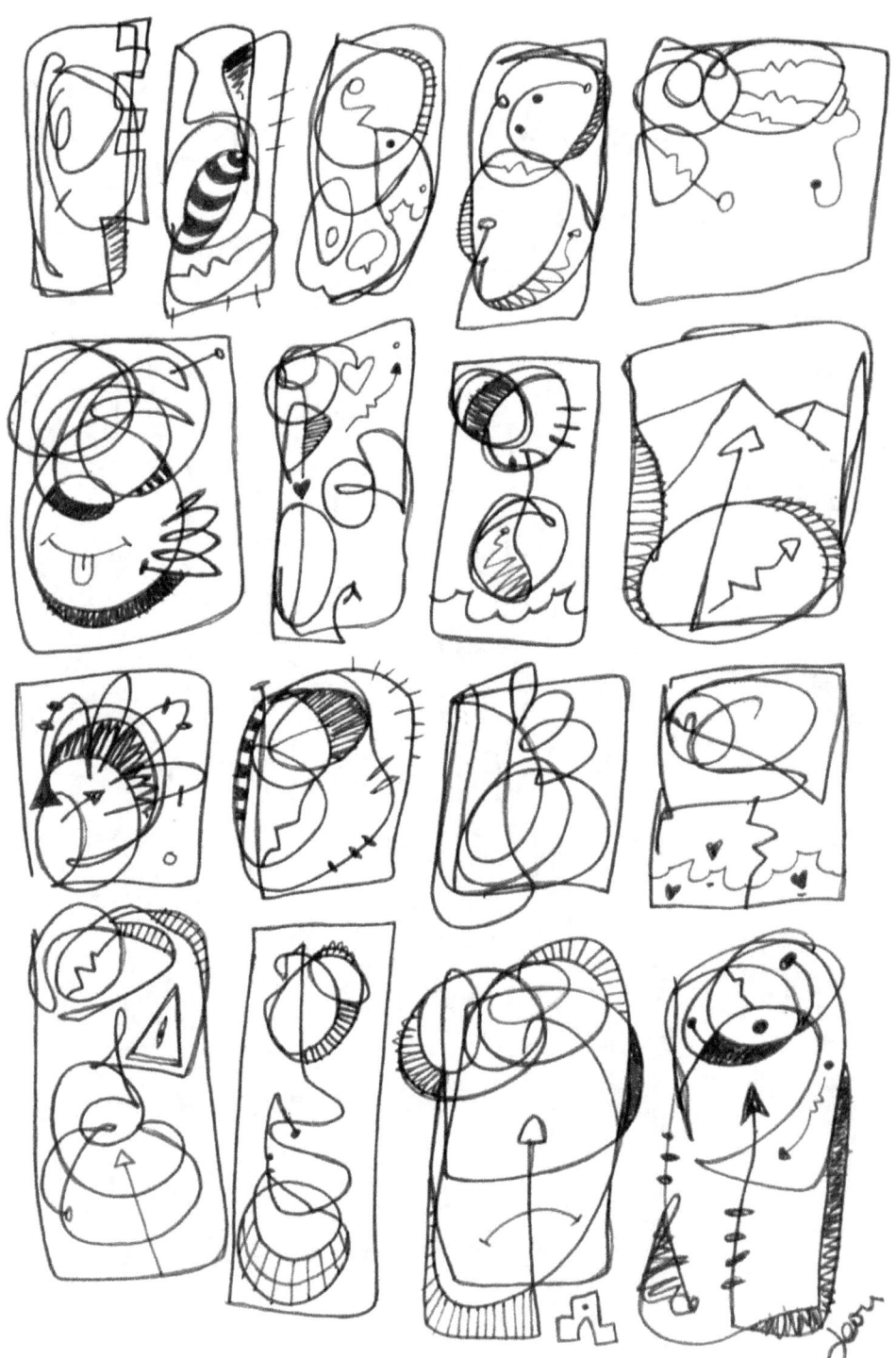

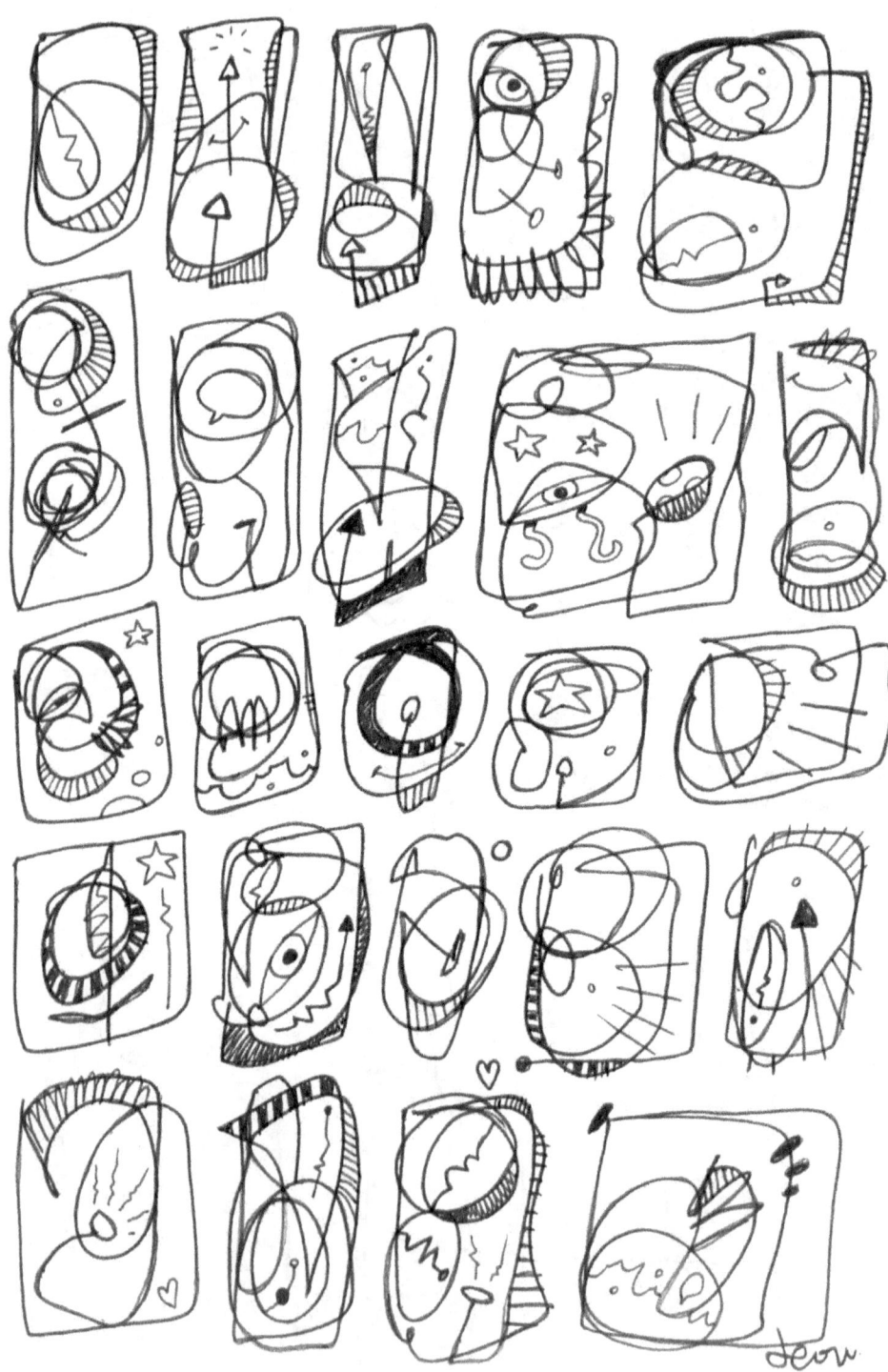

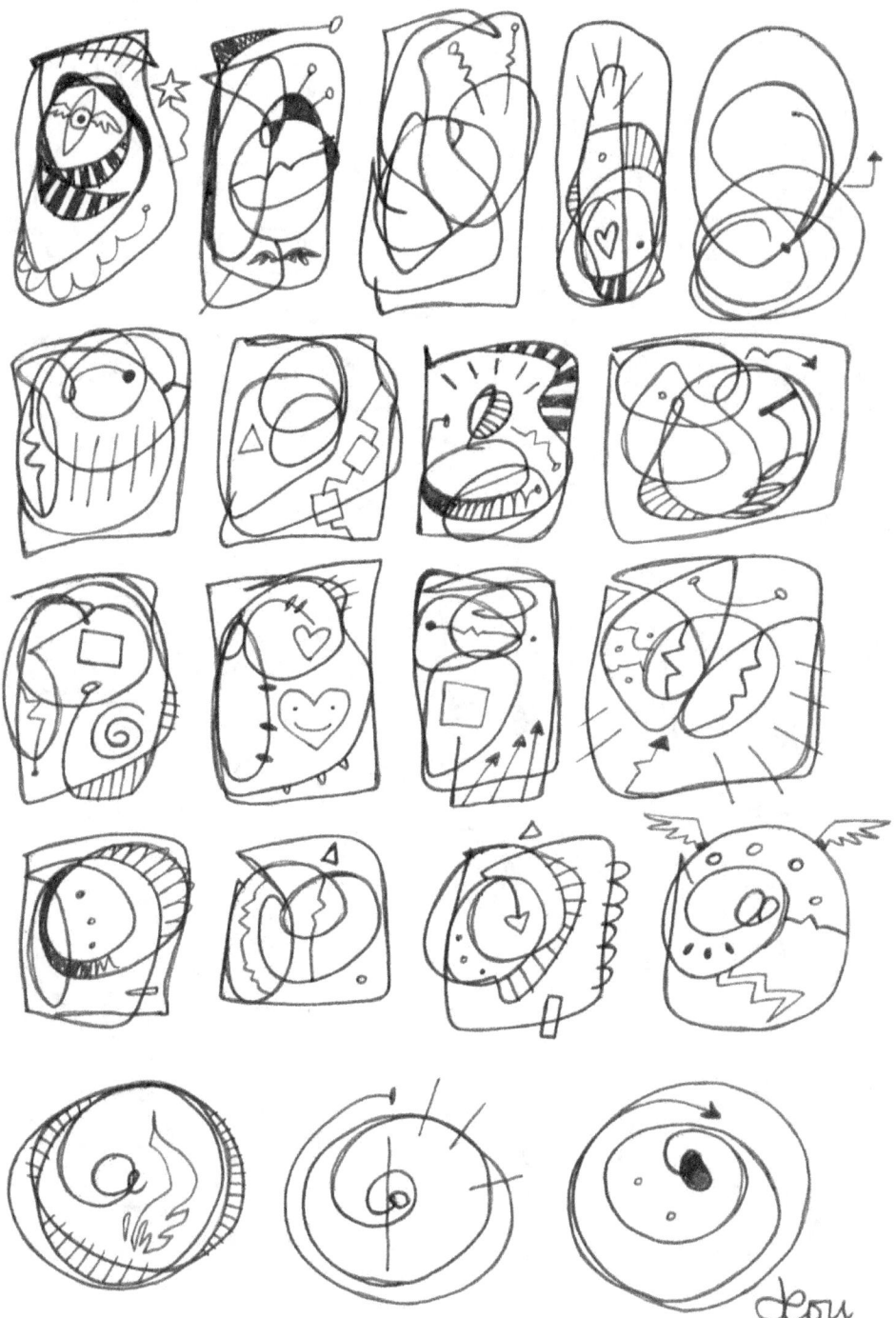

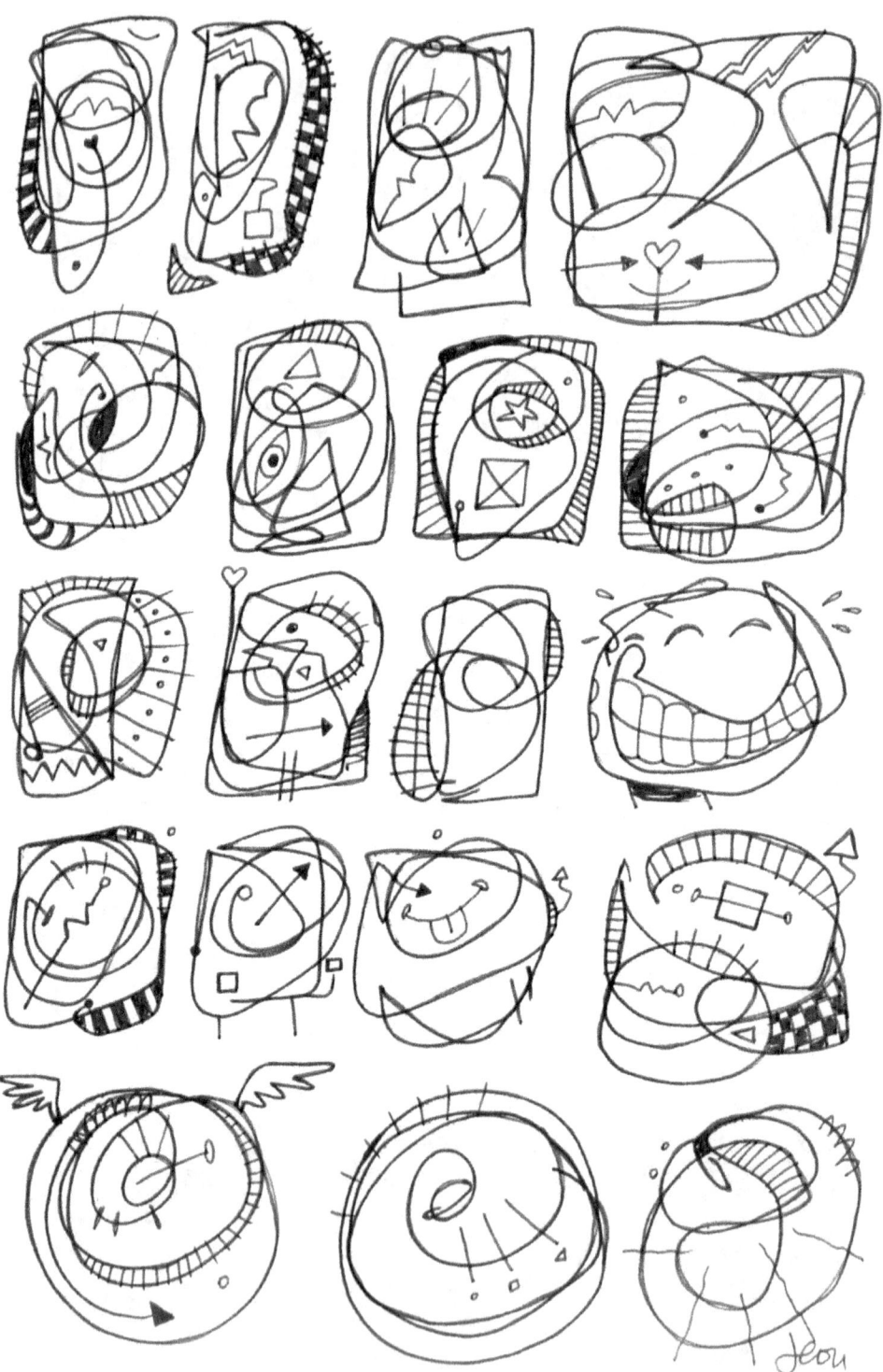

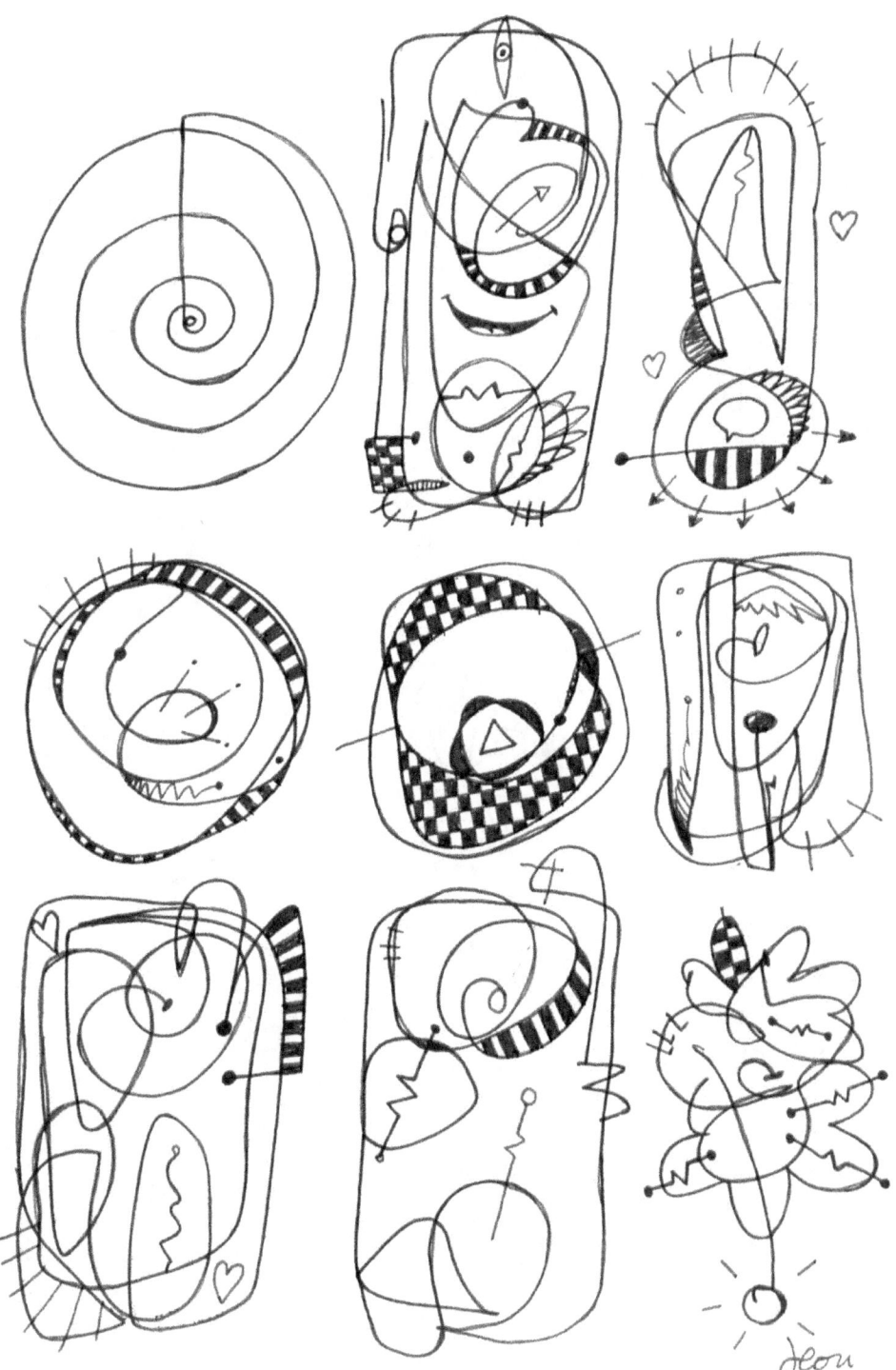

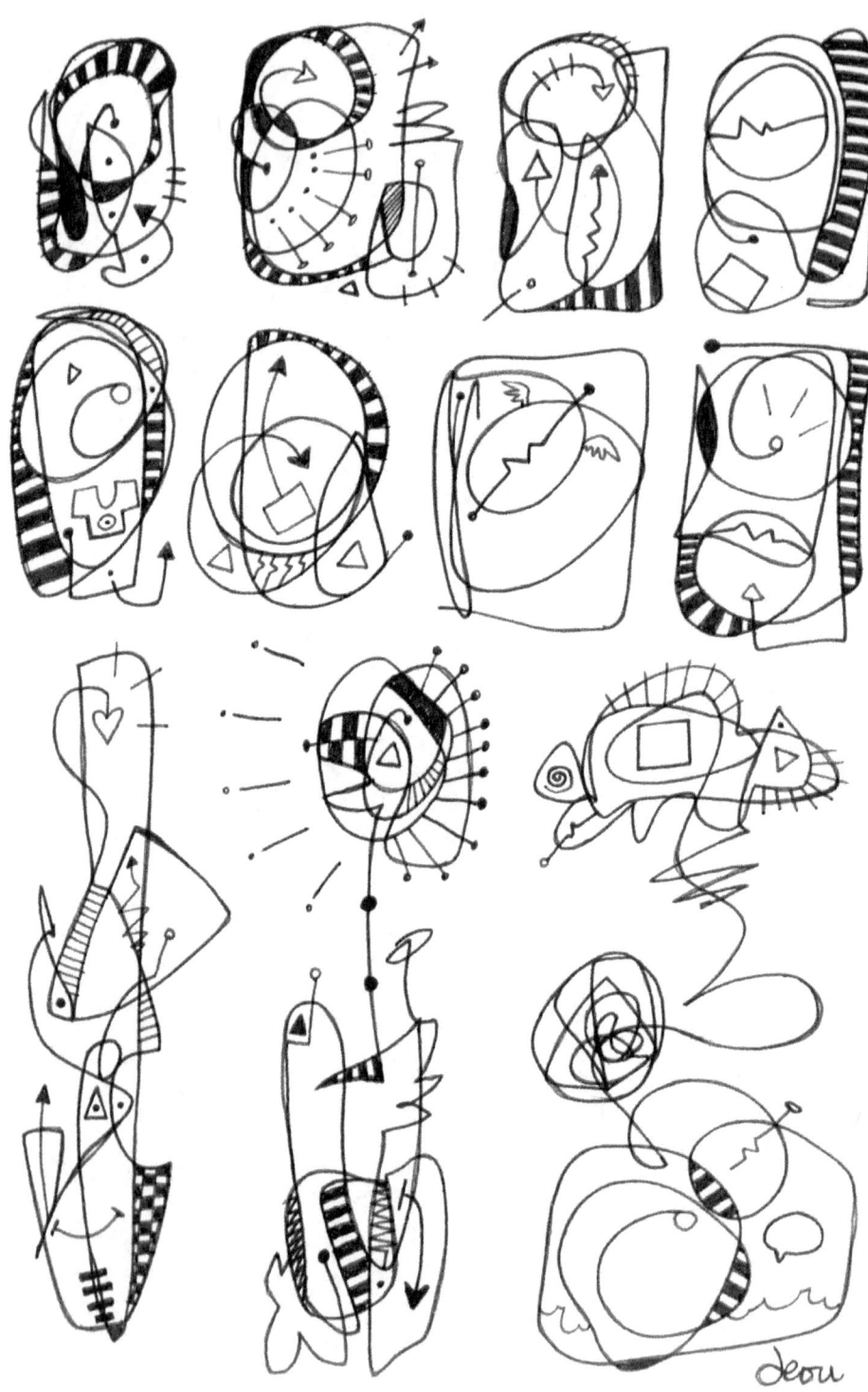

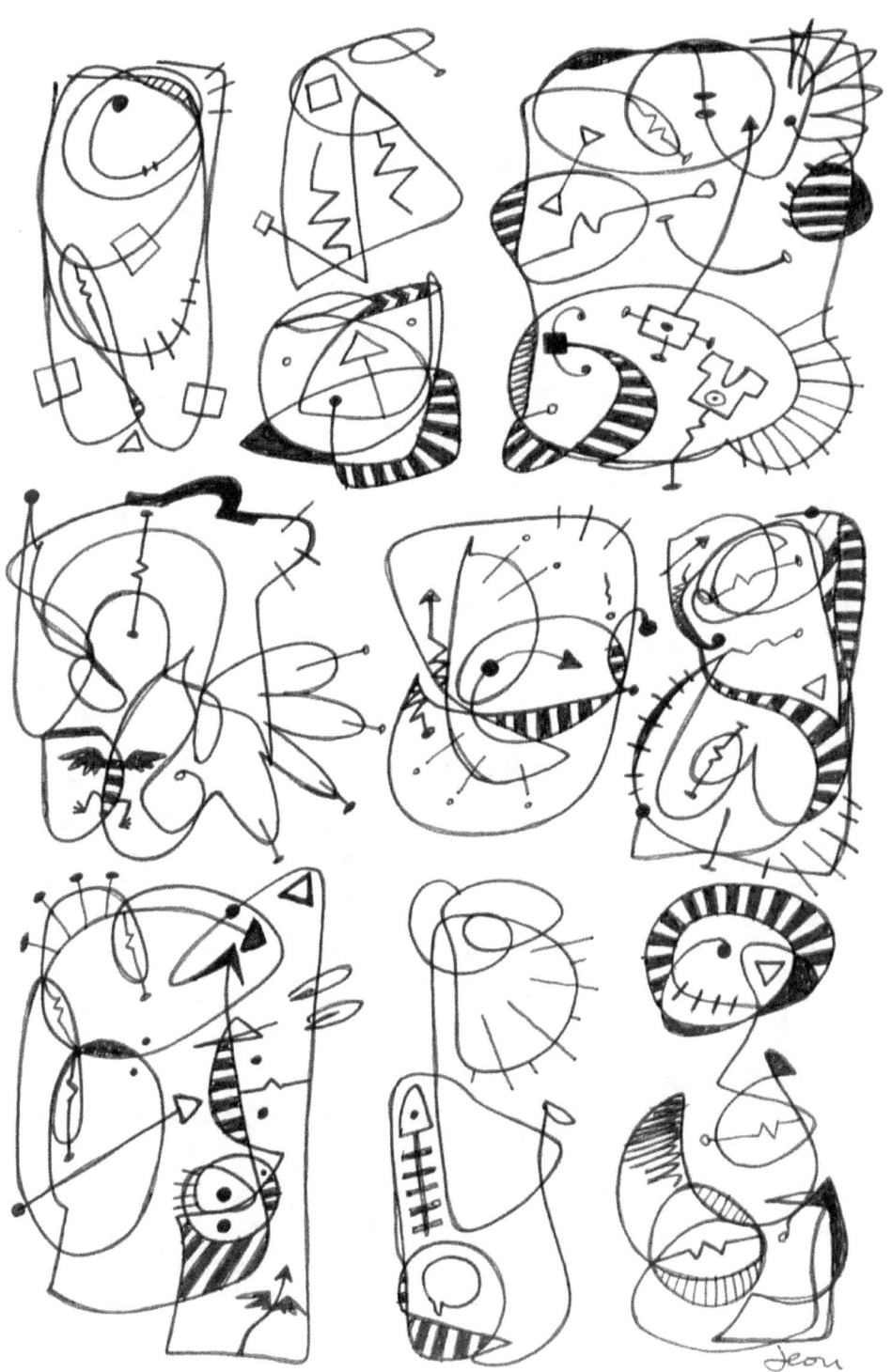

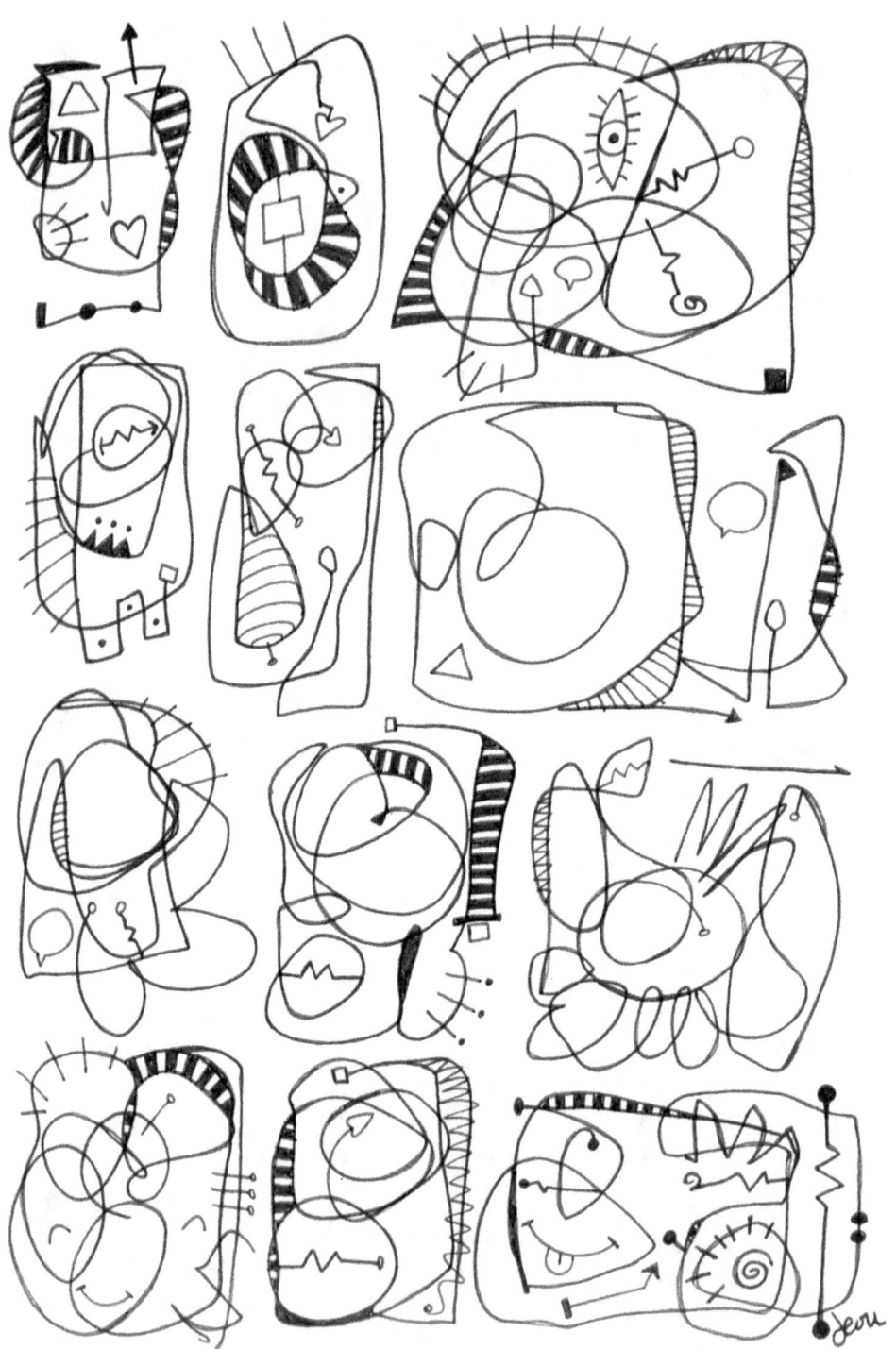

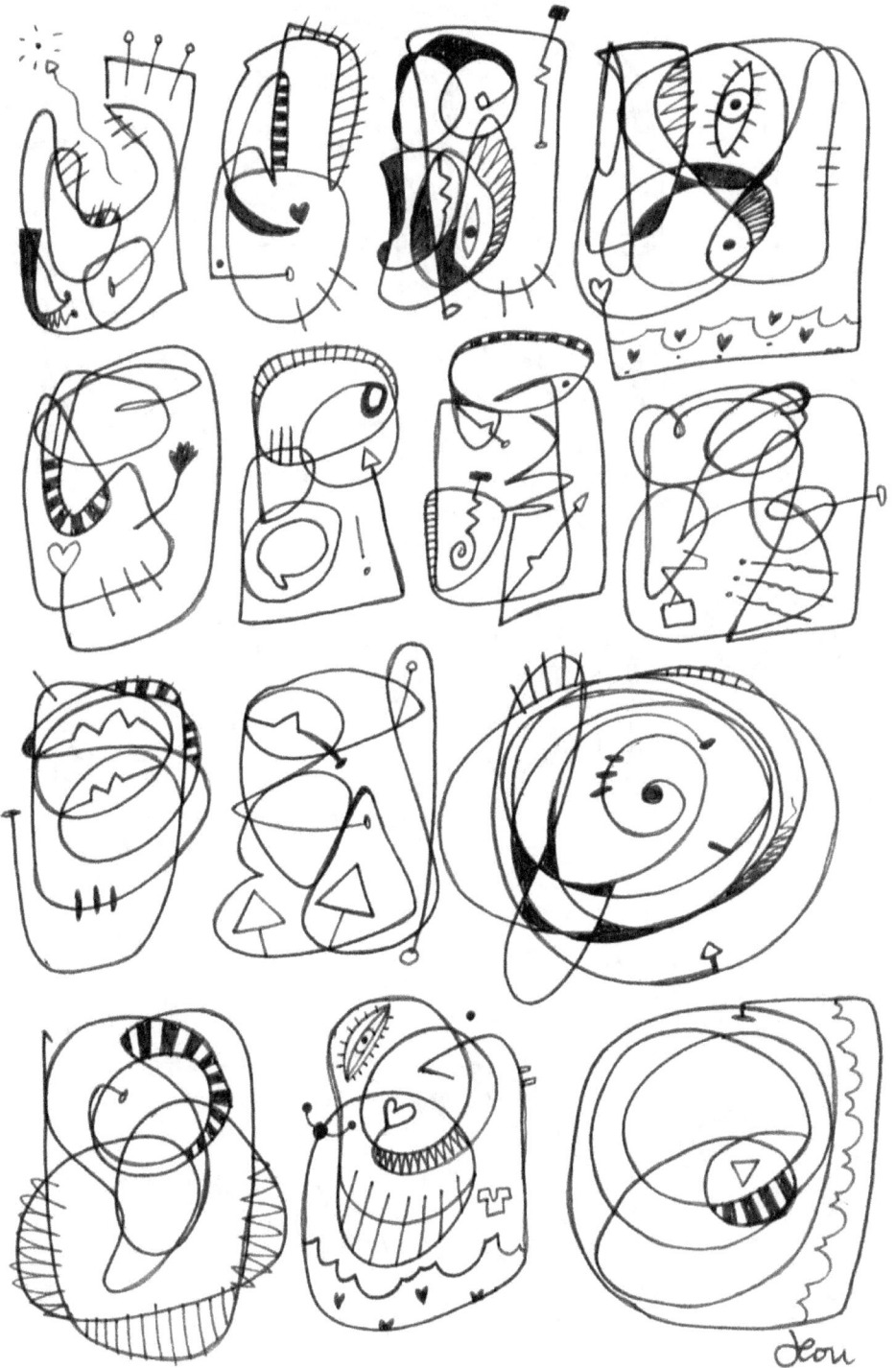

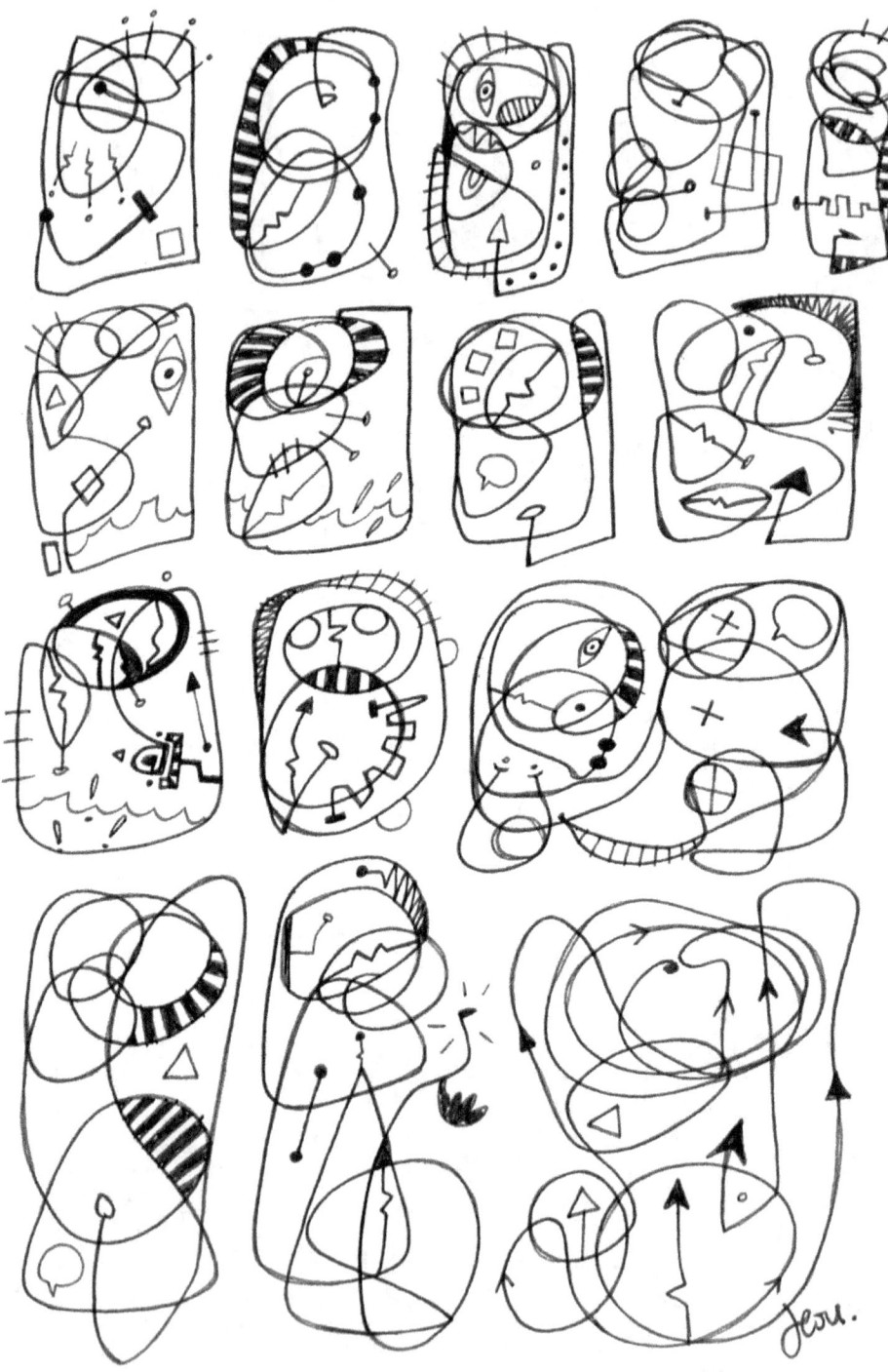

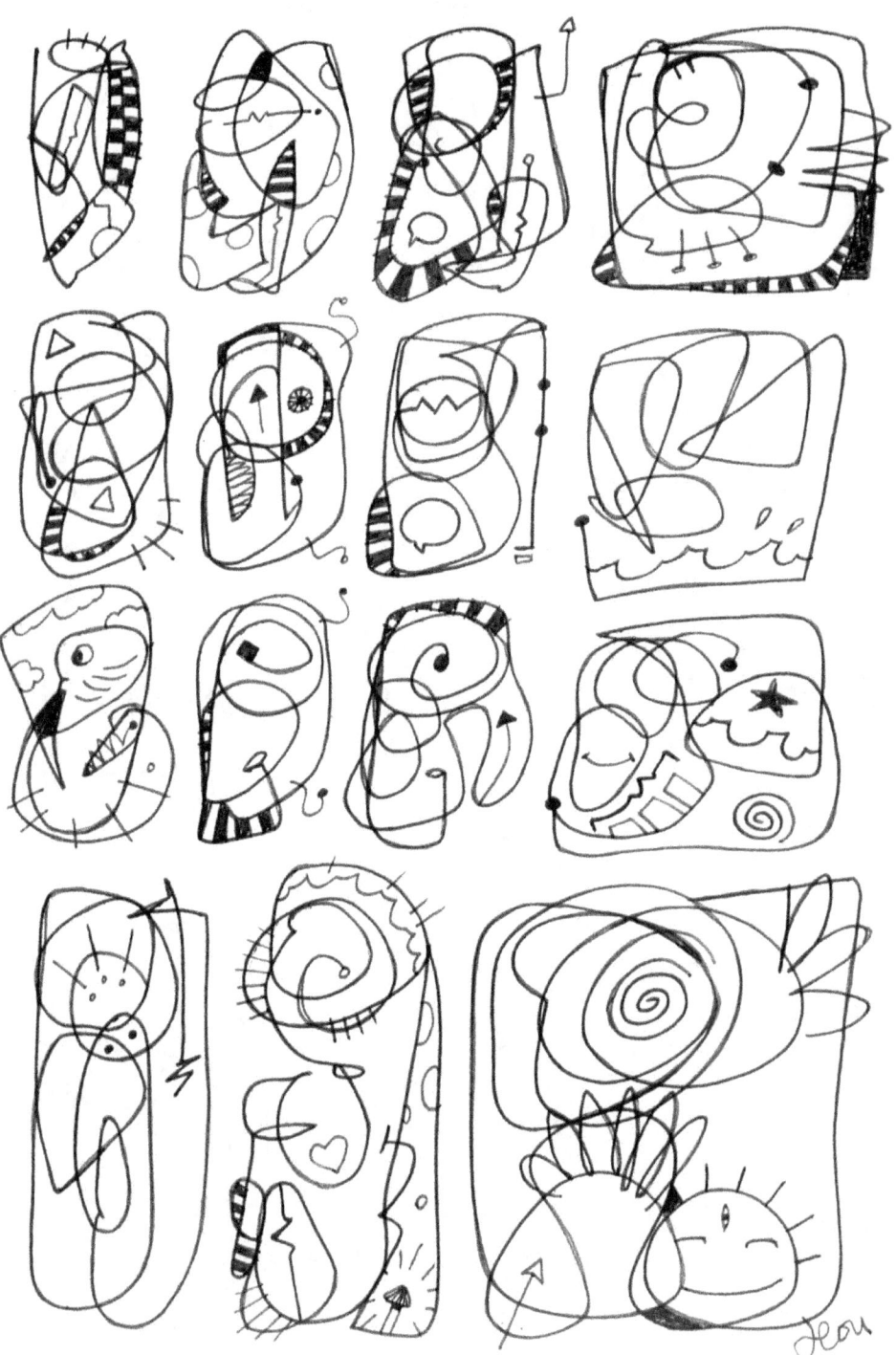

57

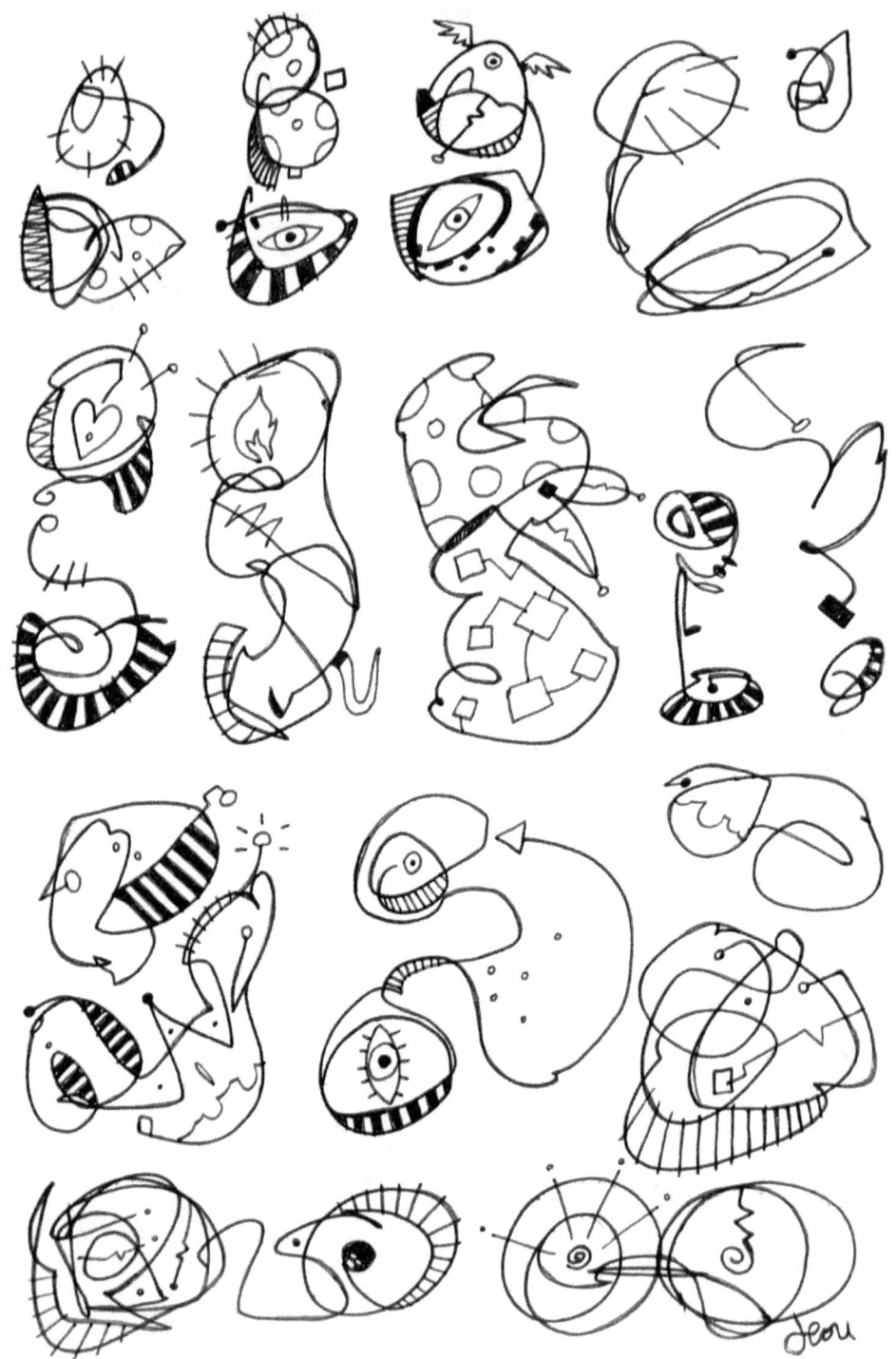

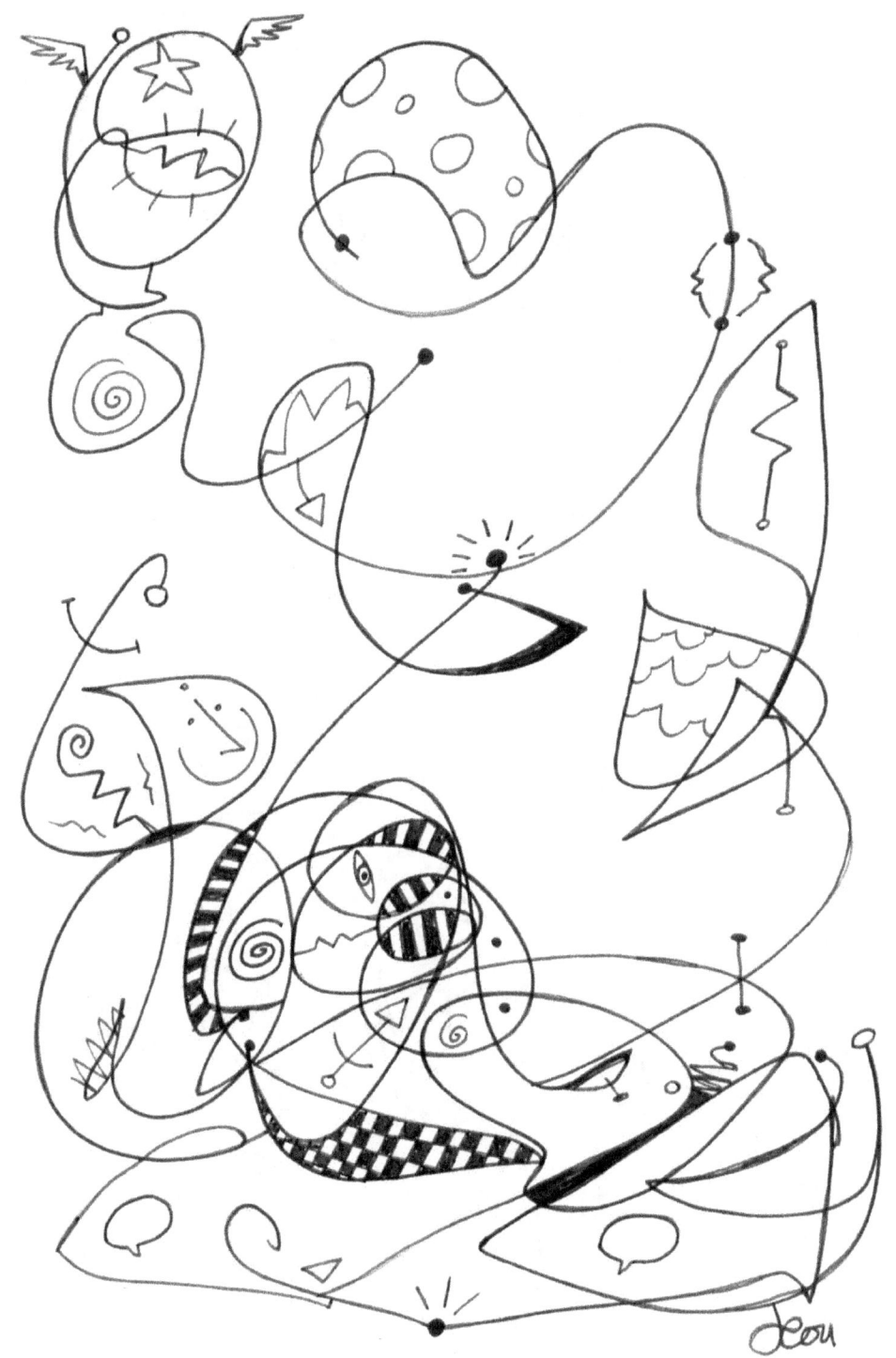

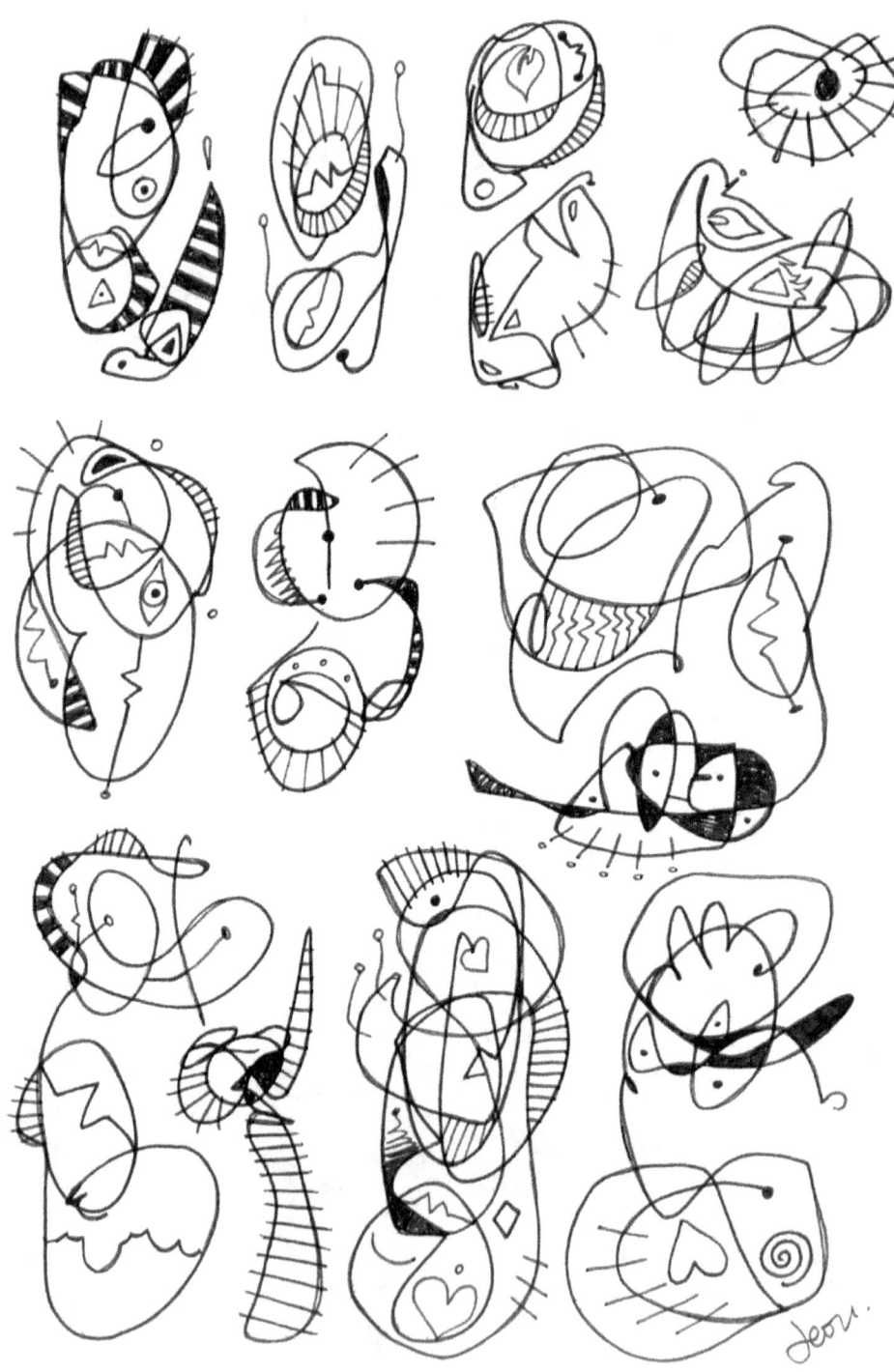

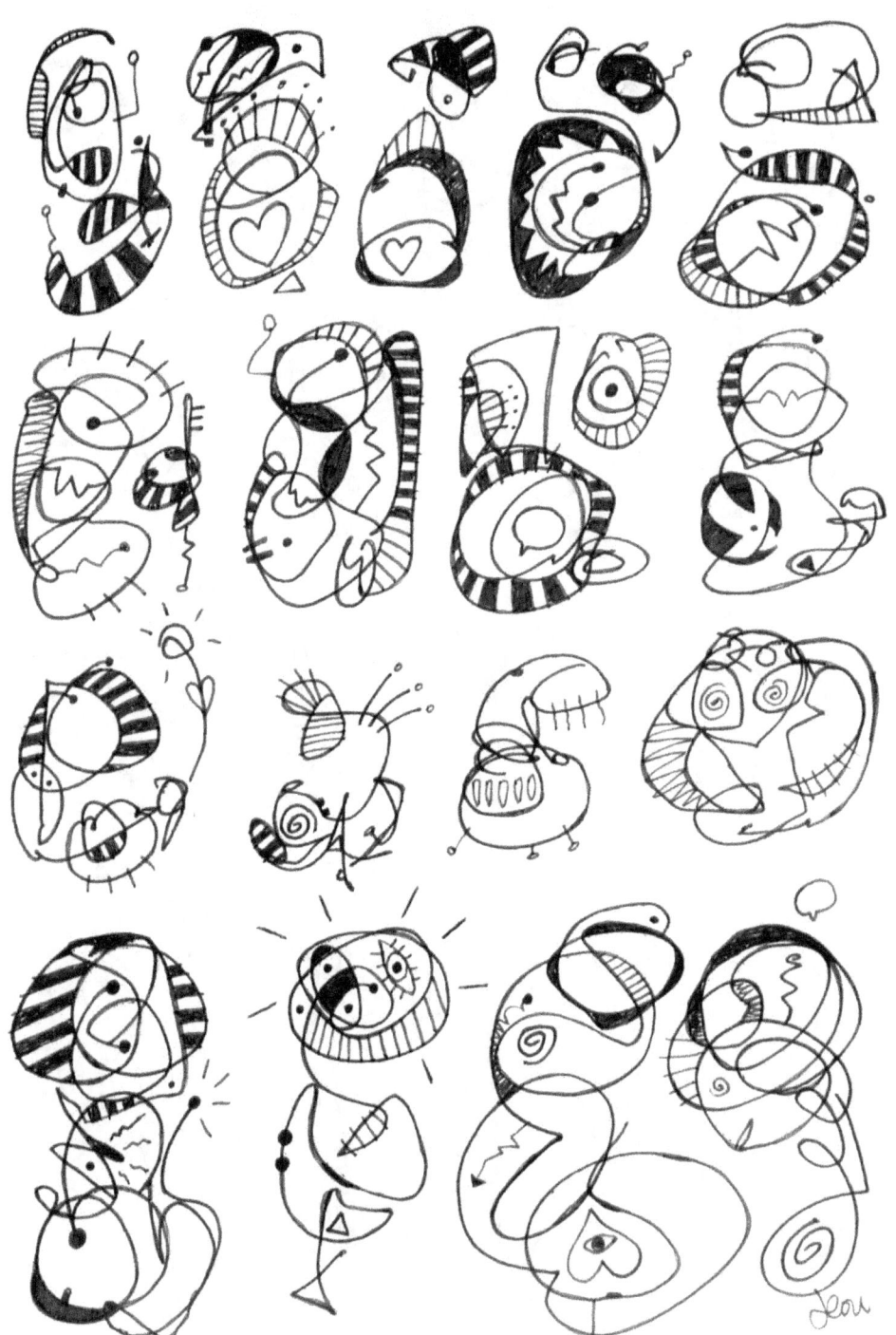

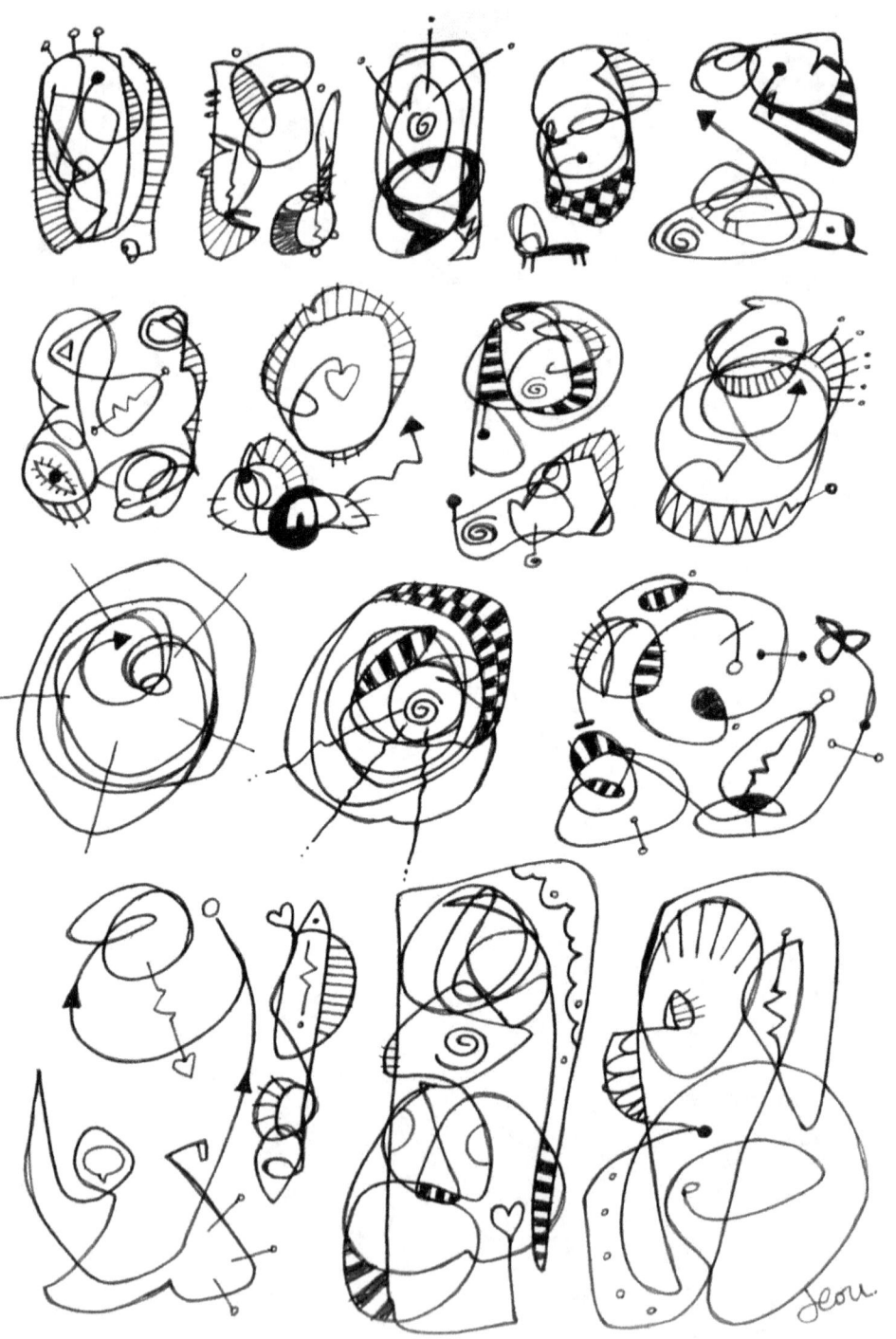

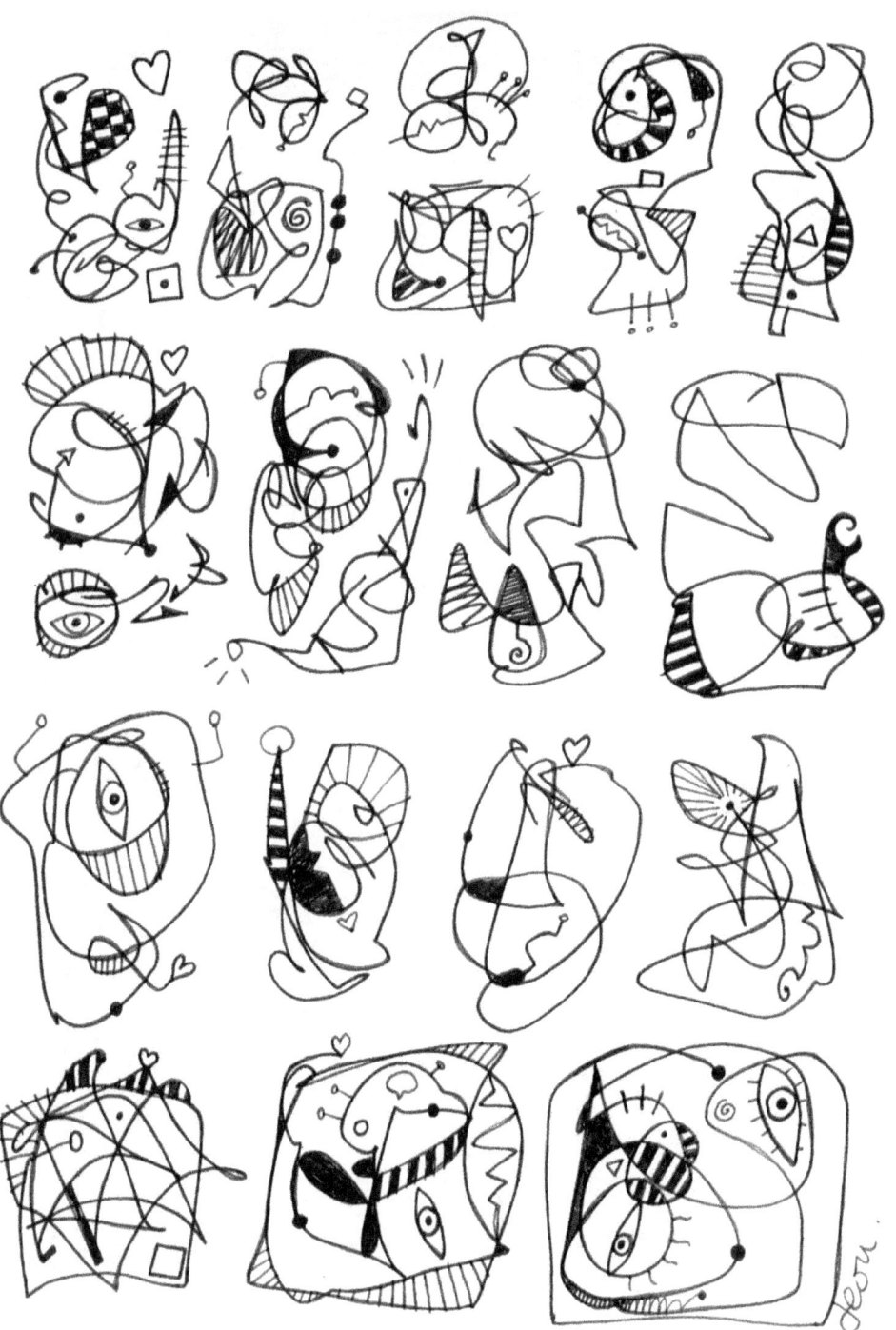

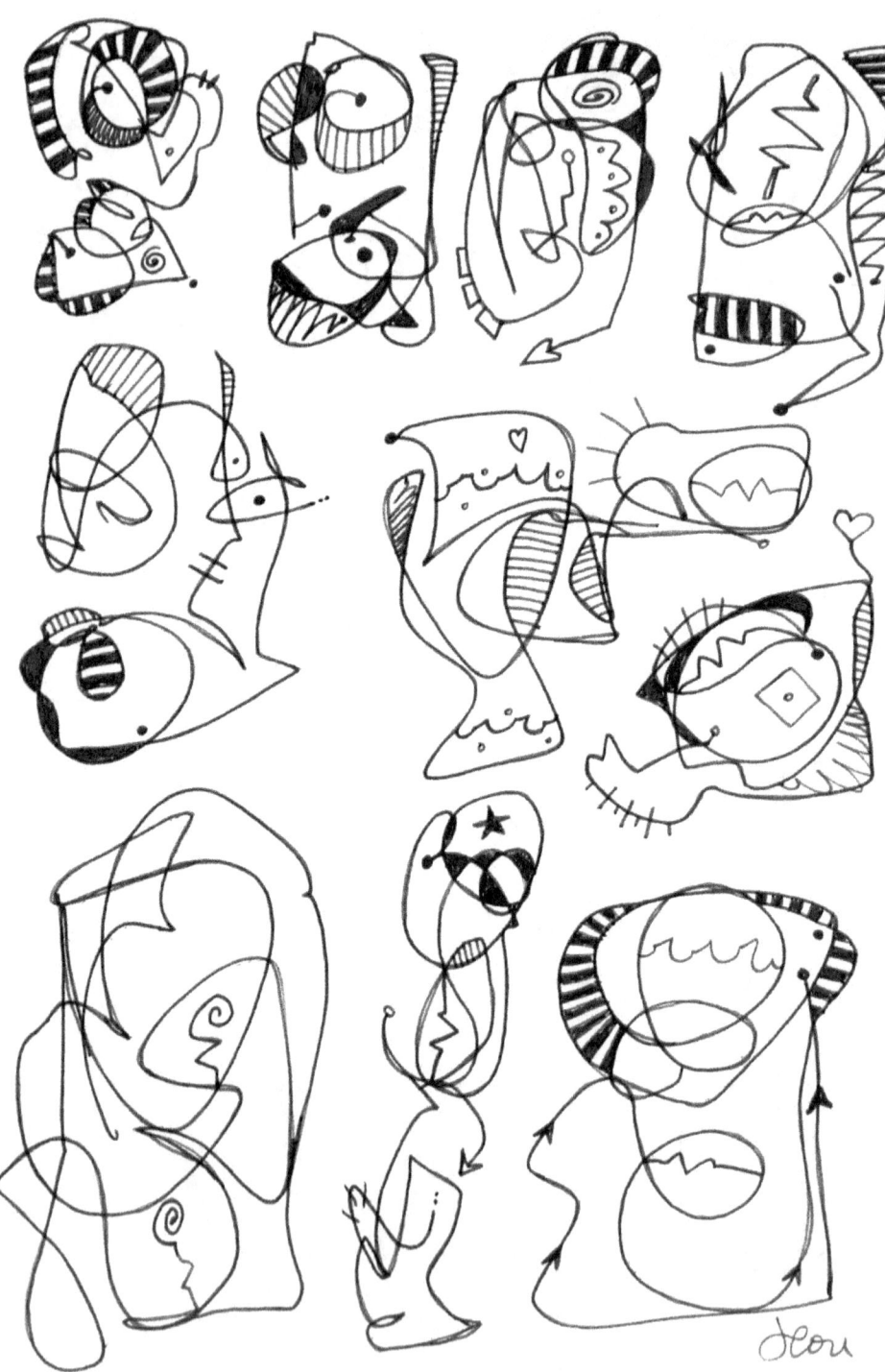

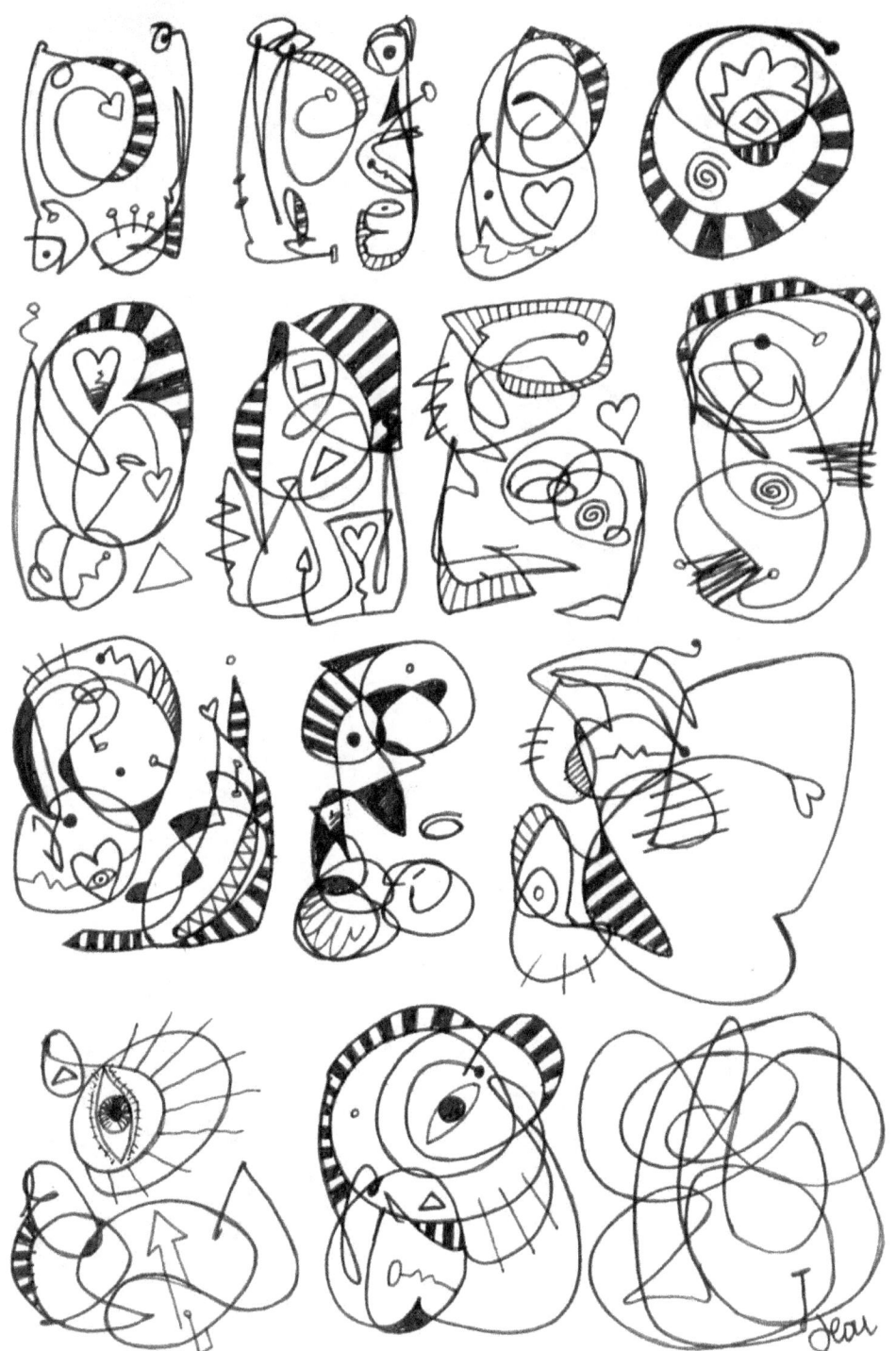

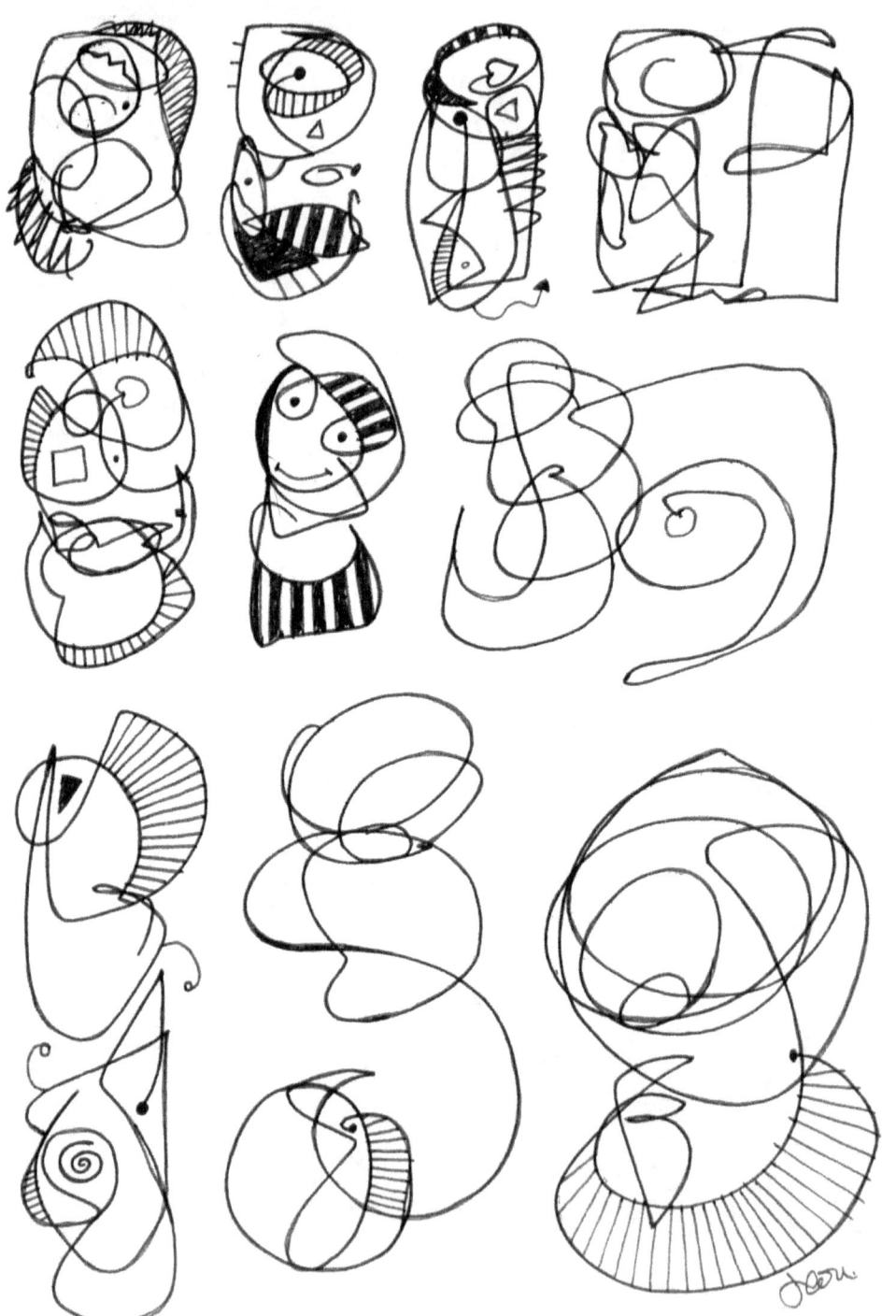

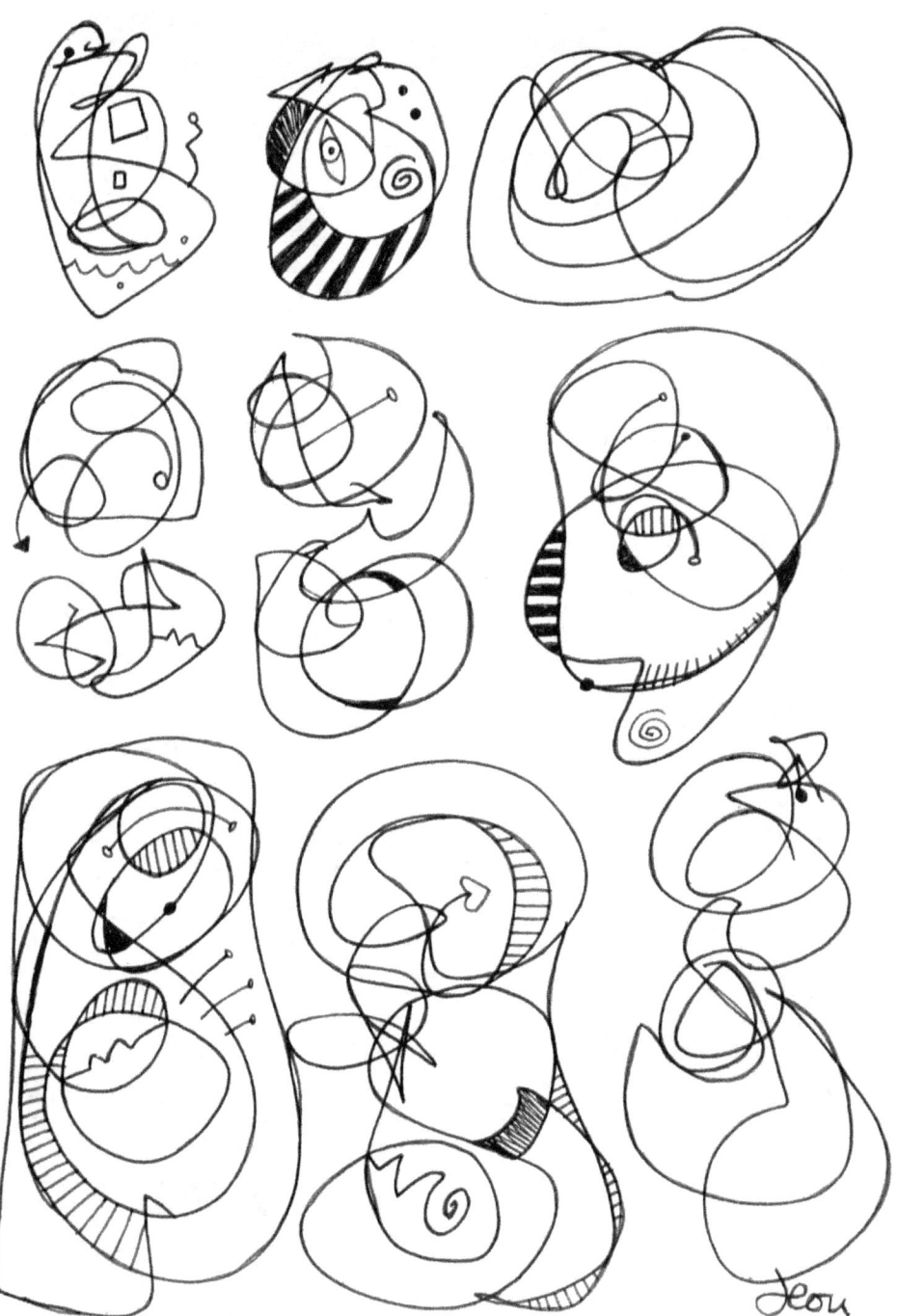

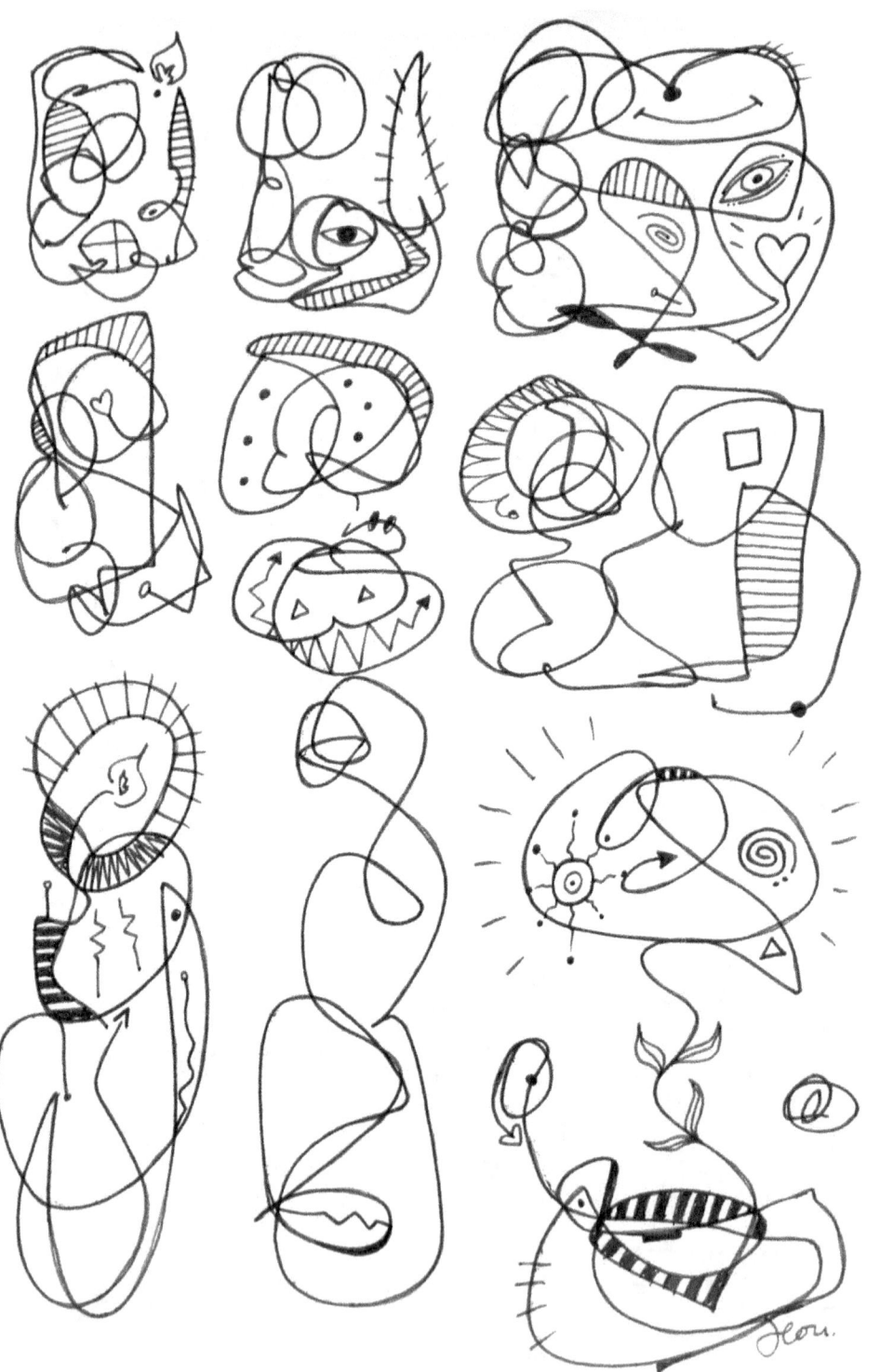

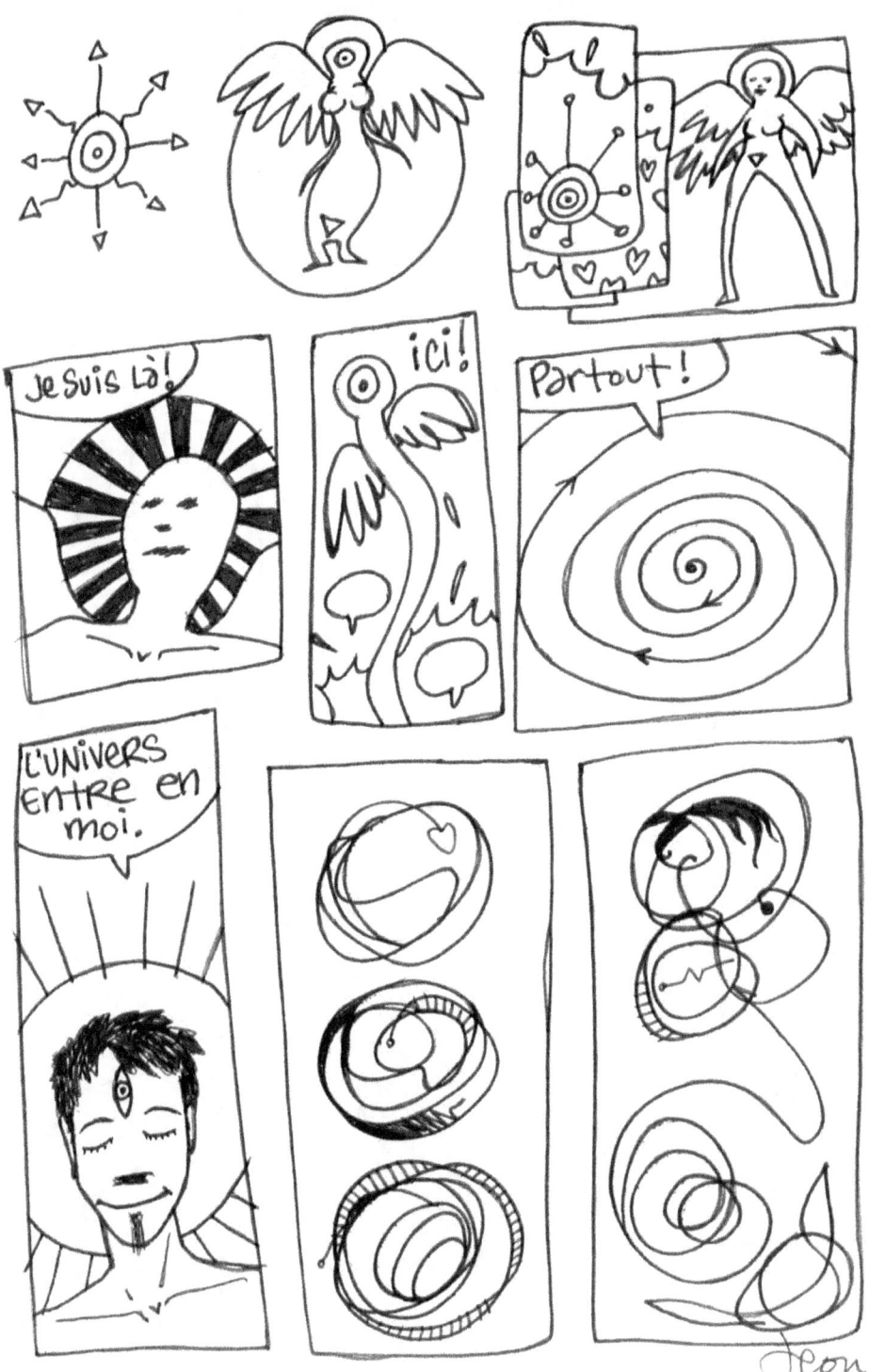

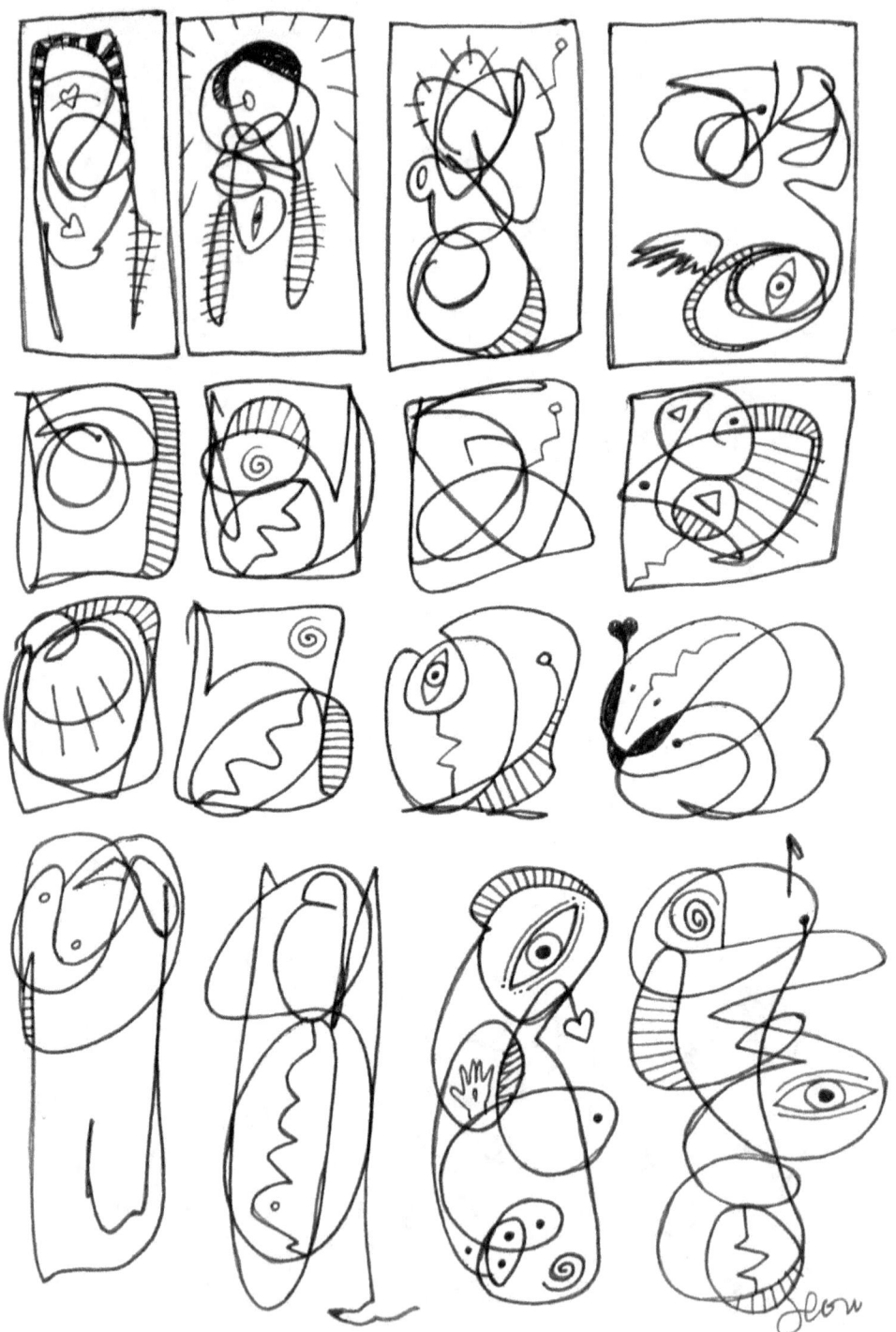

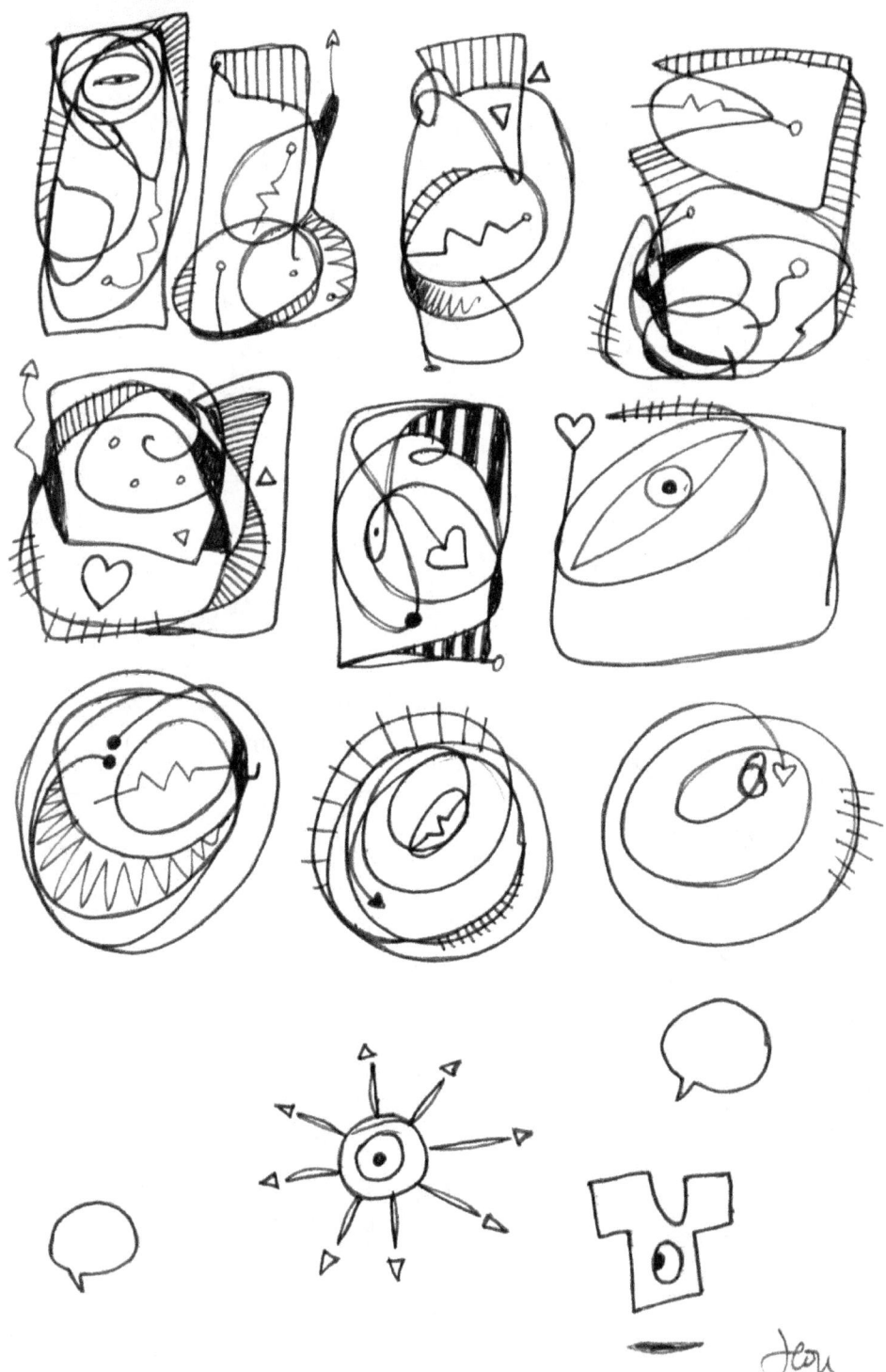

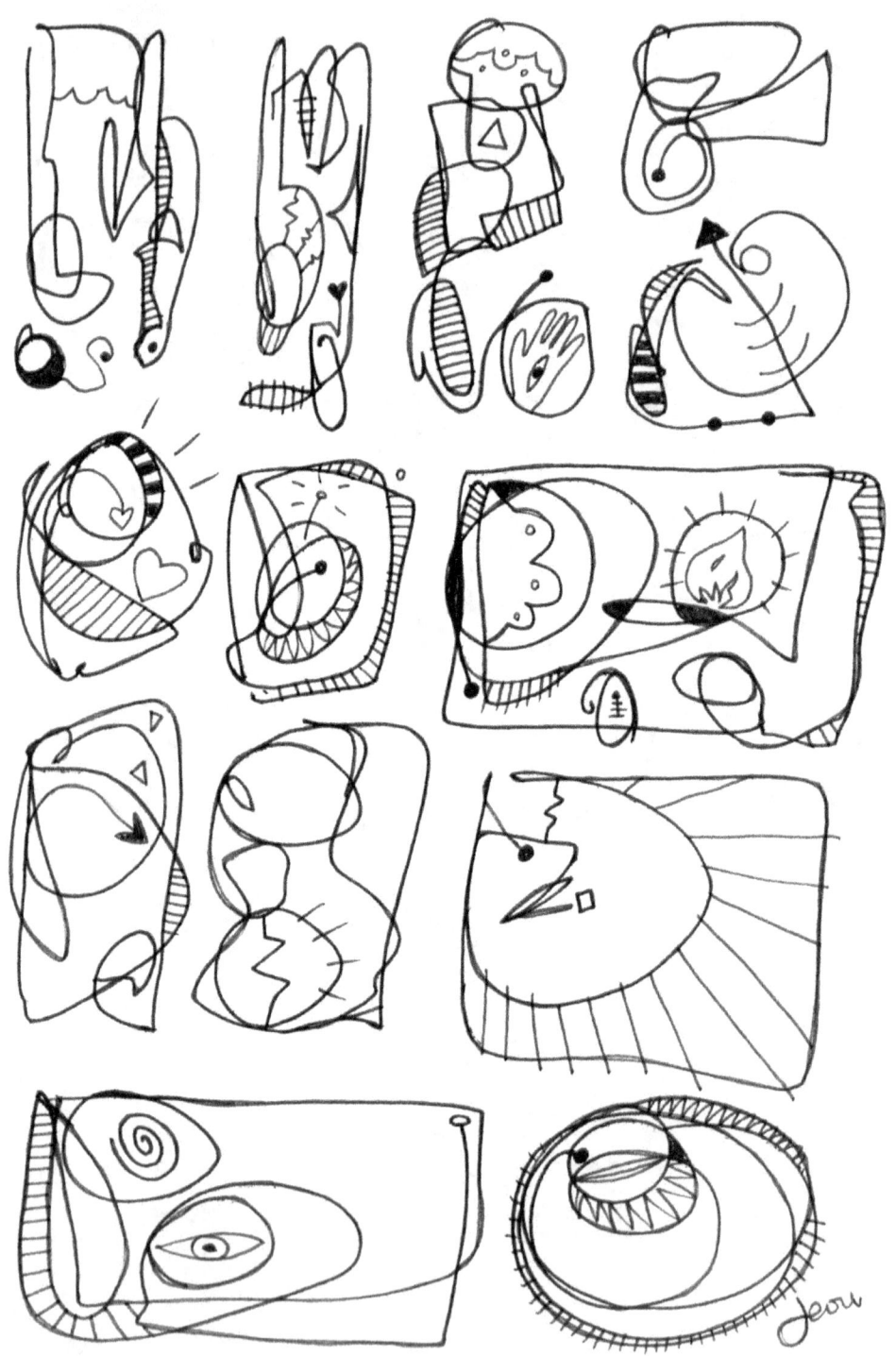

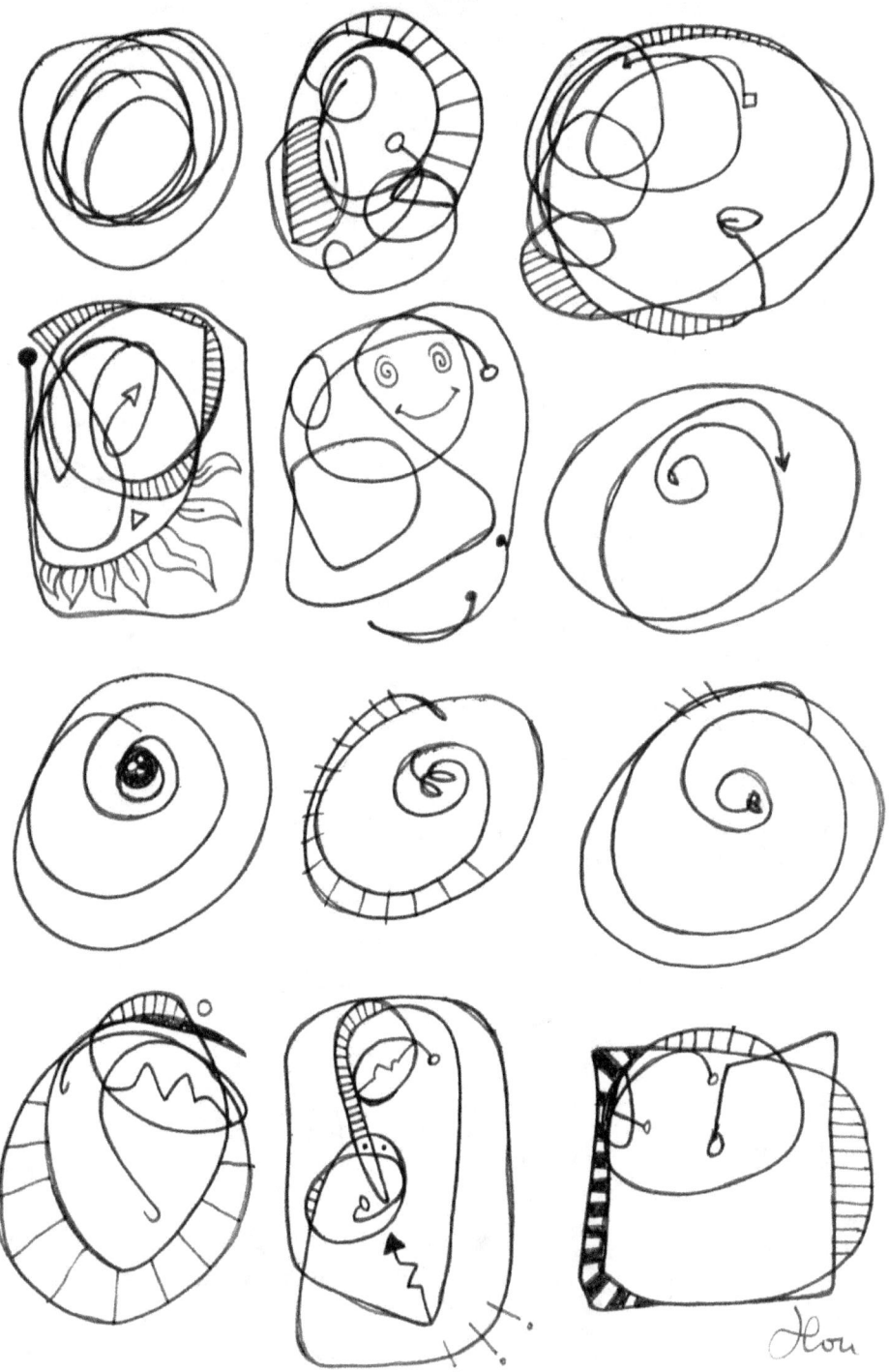

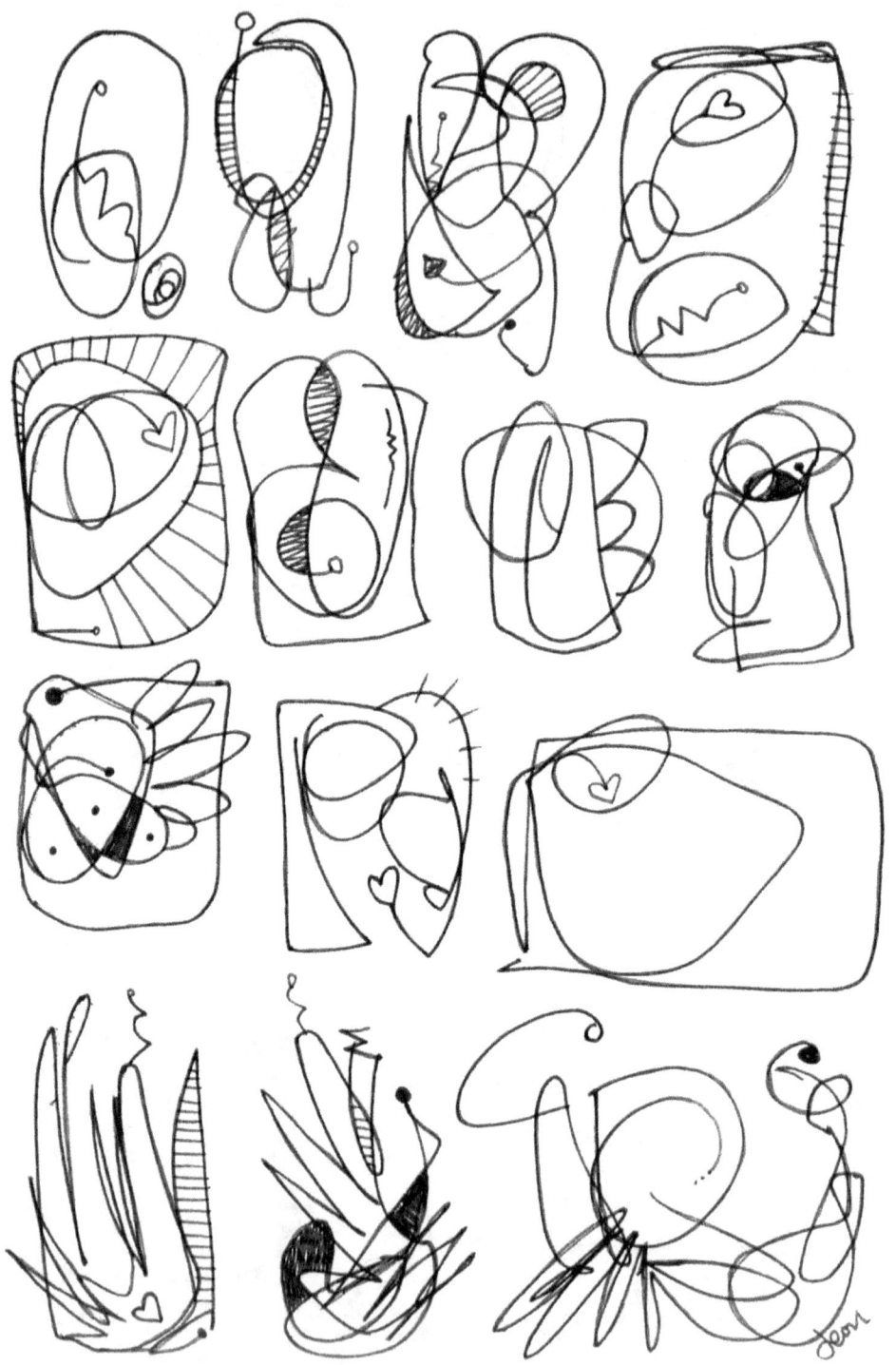

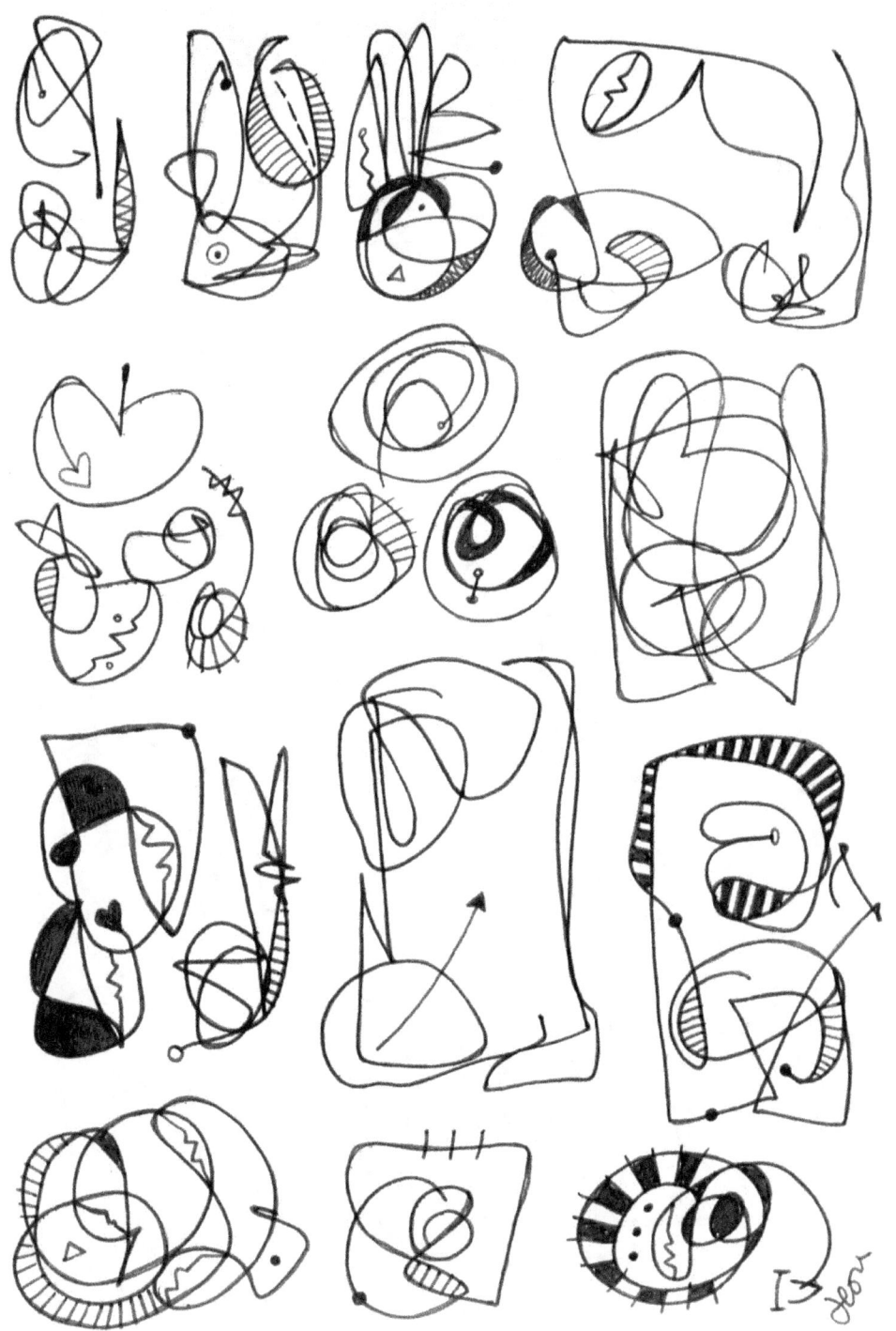

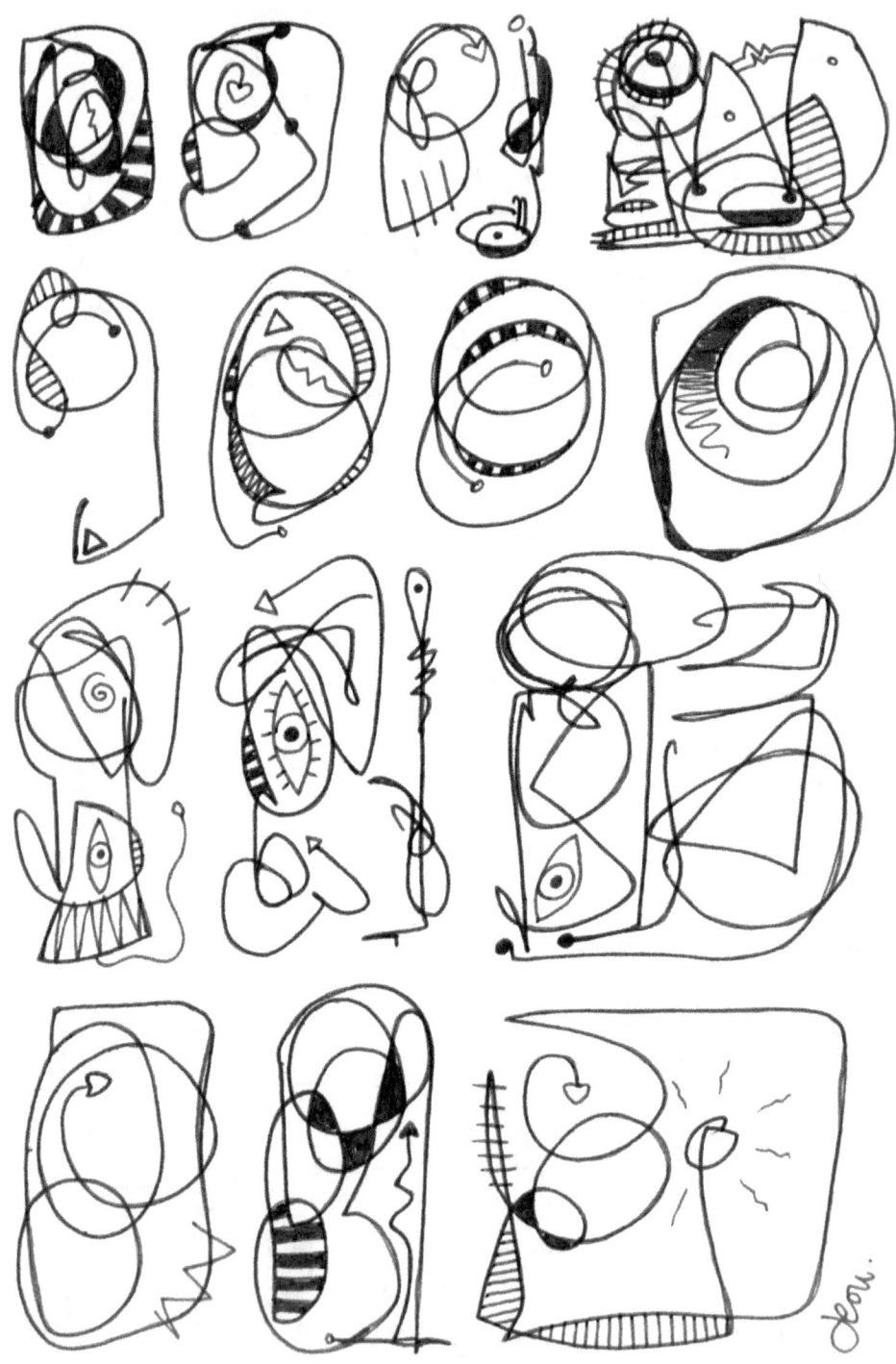

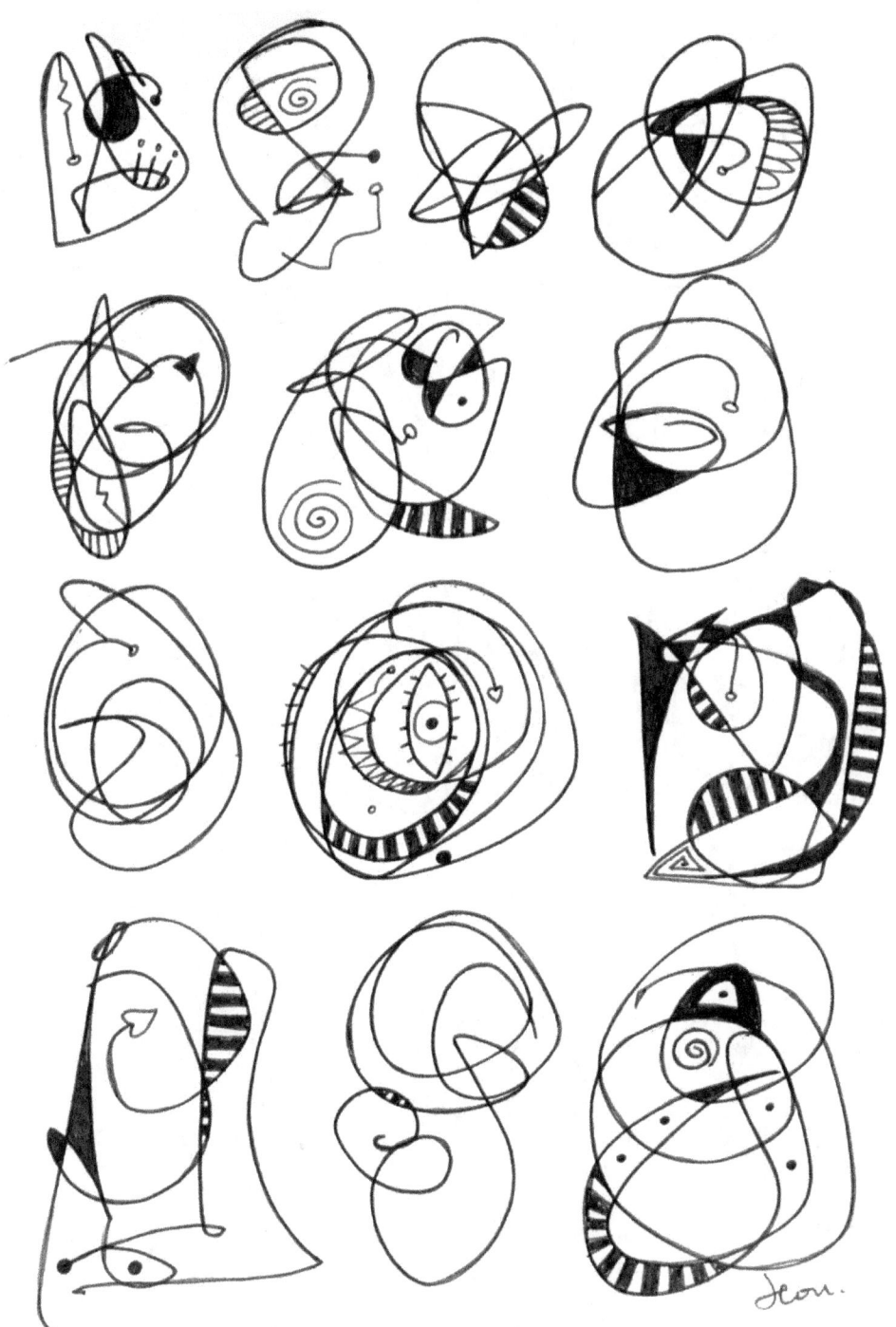

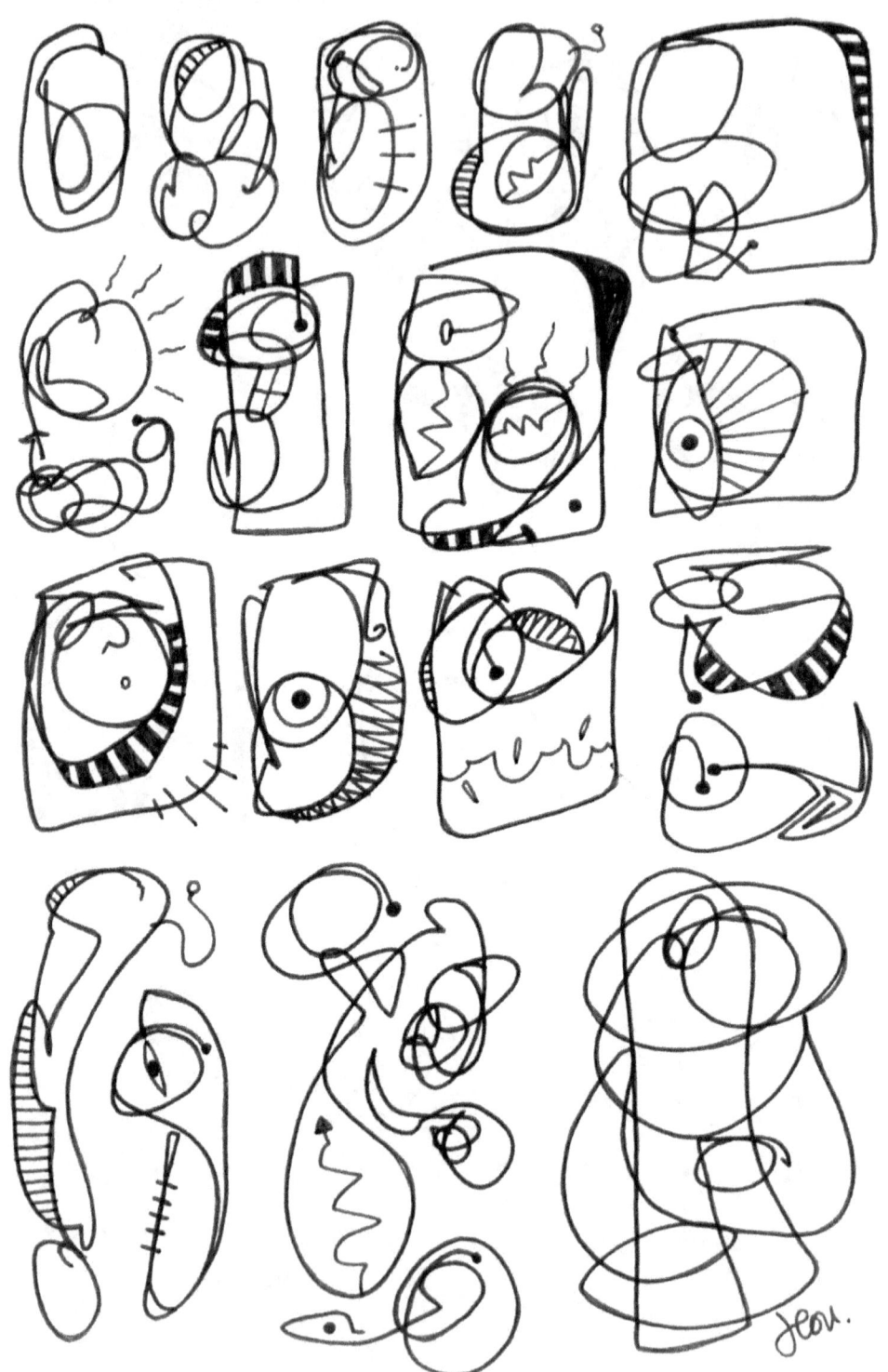

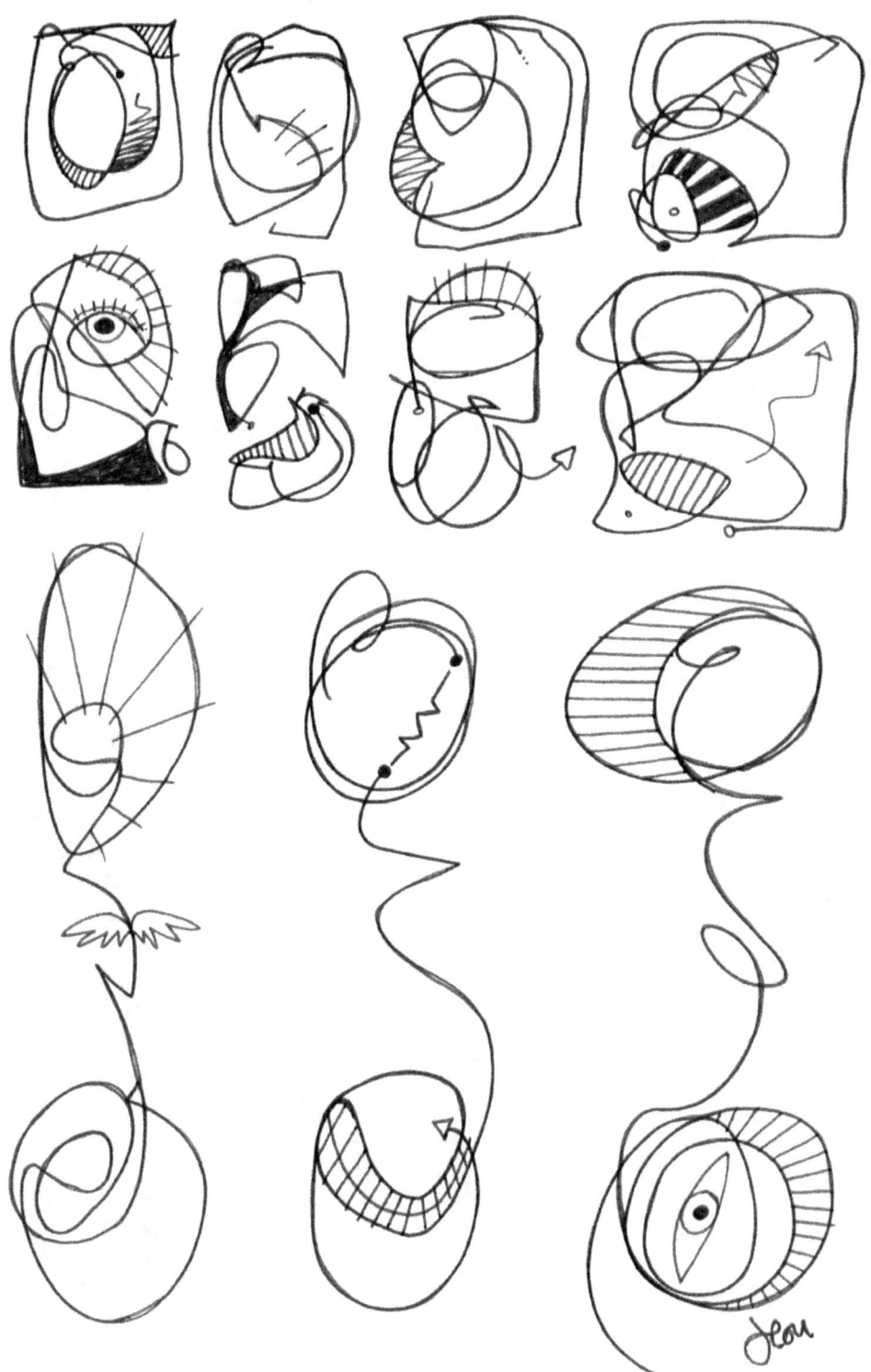

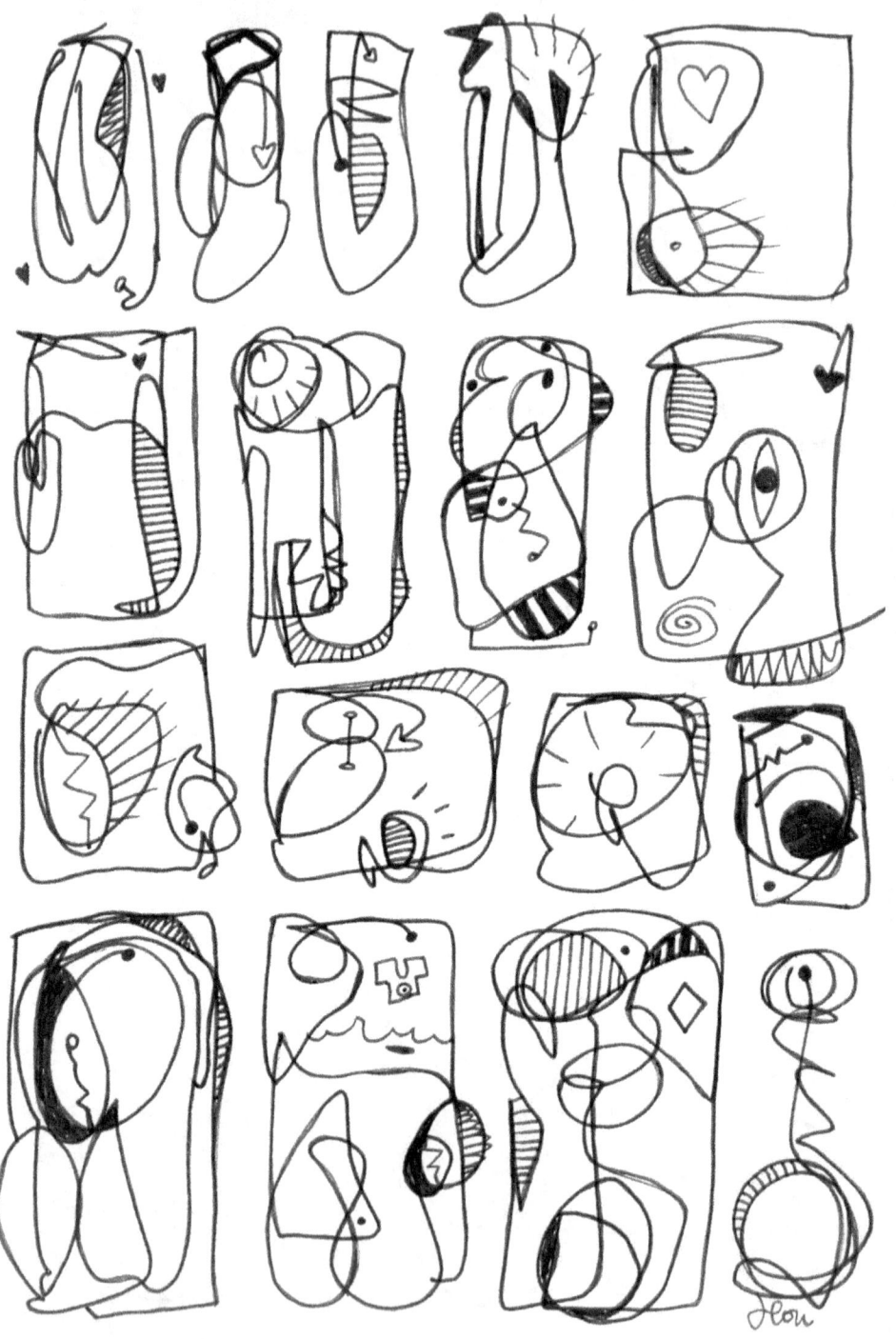

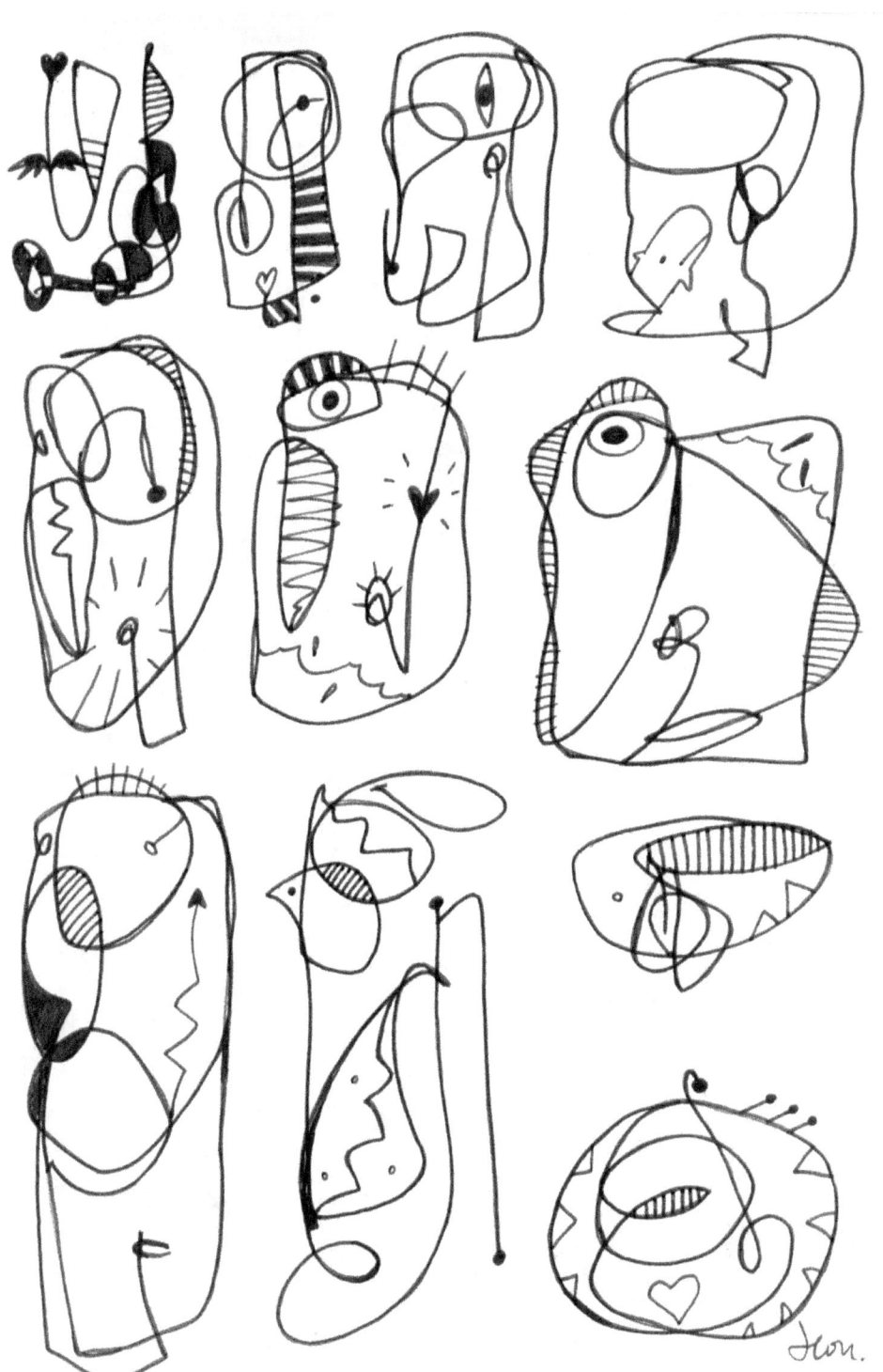

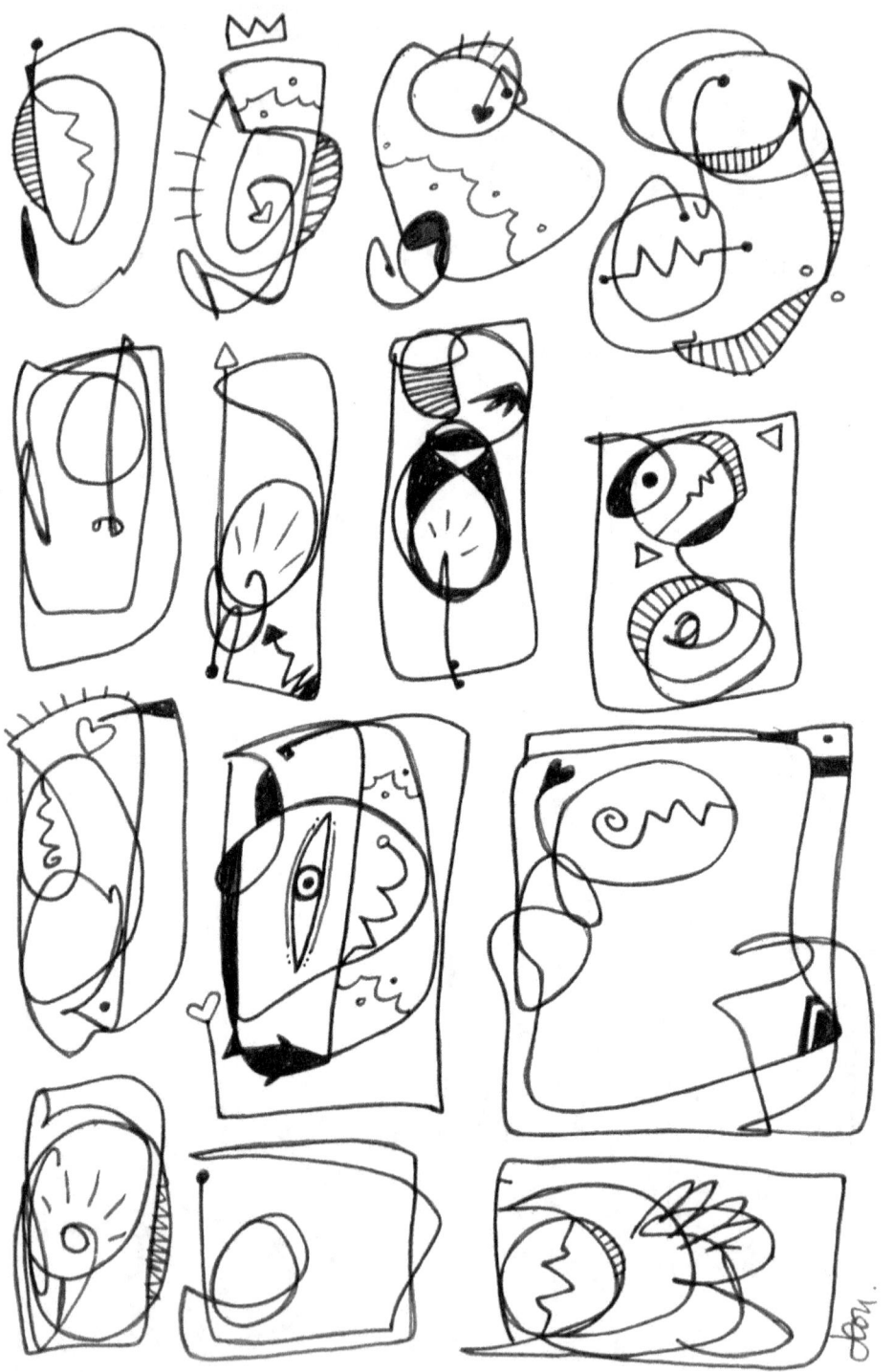

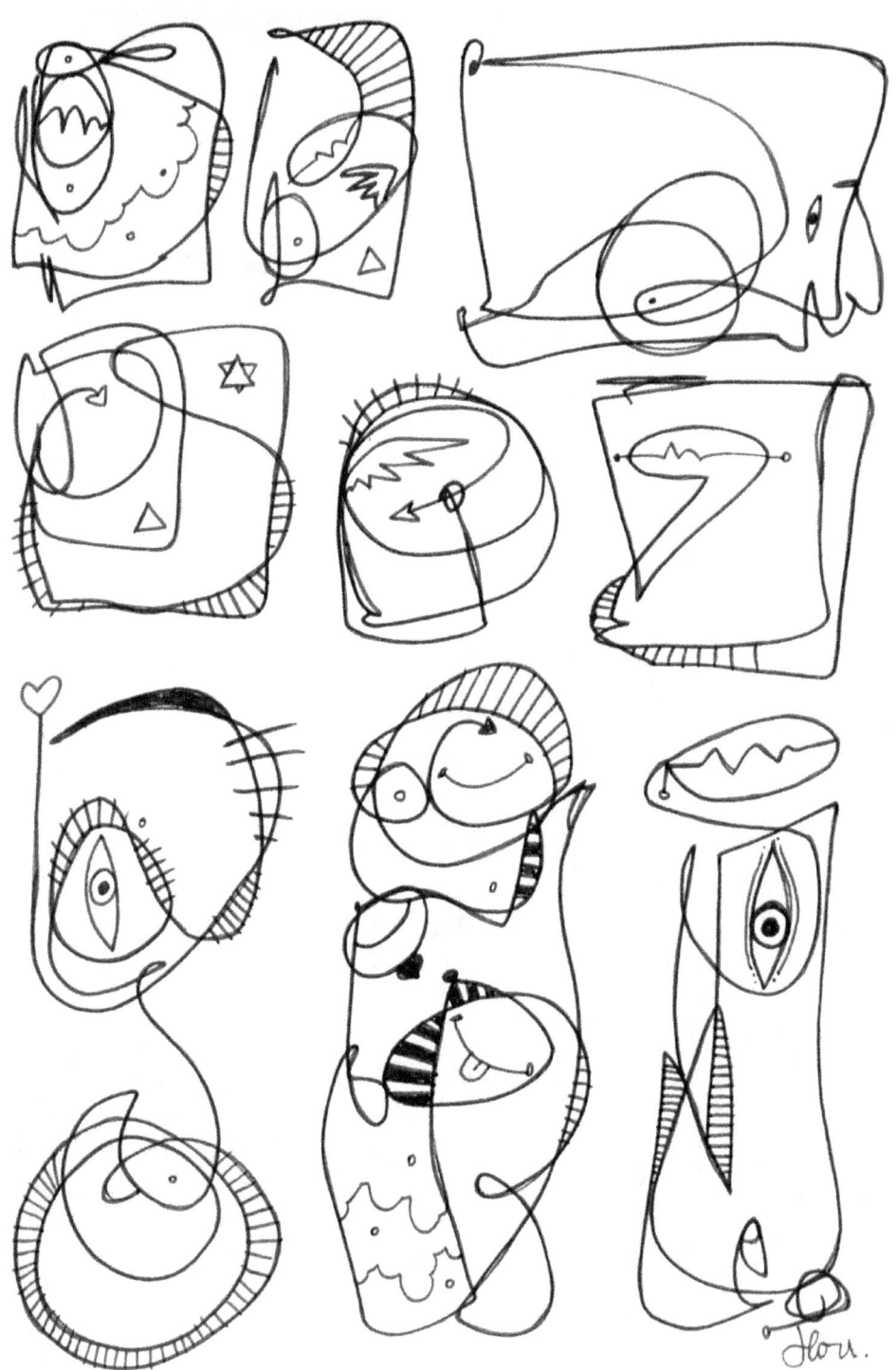

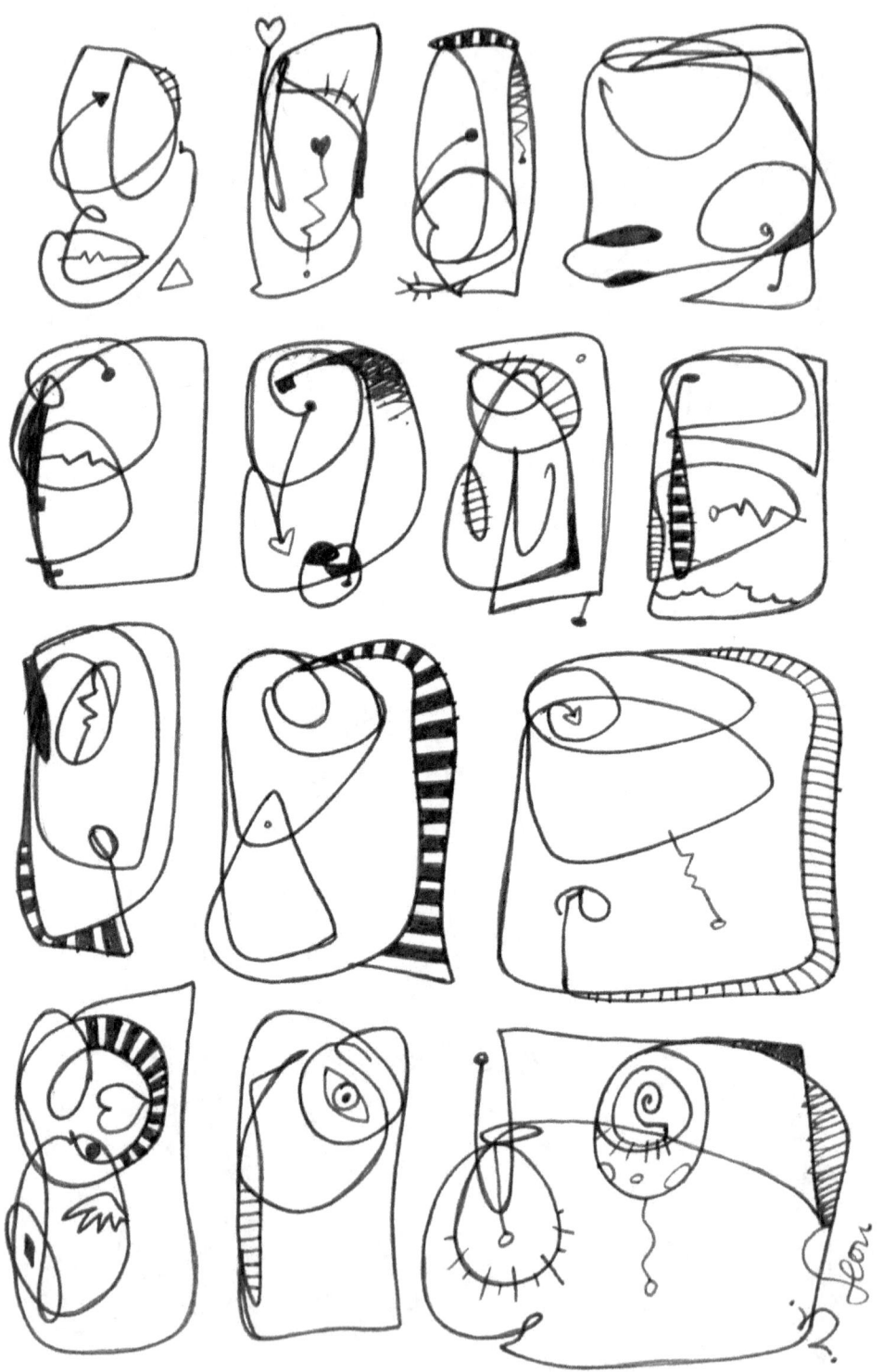

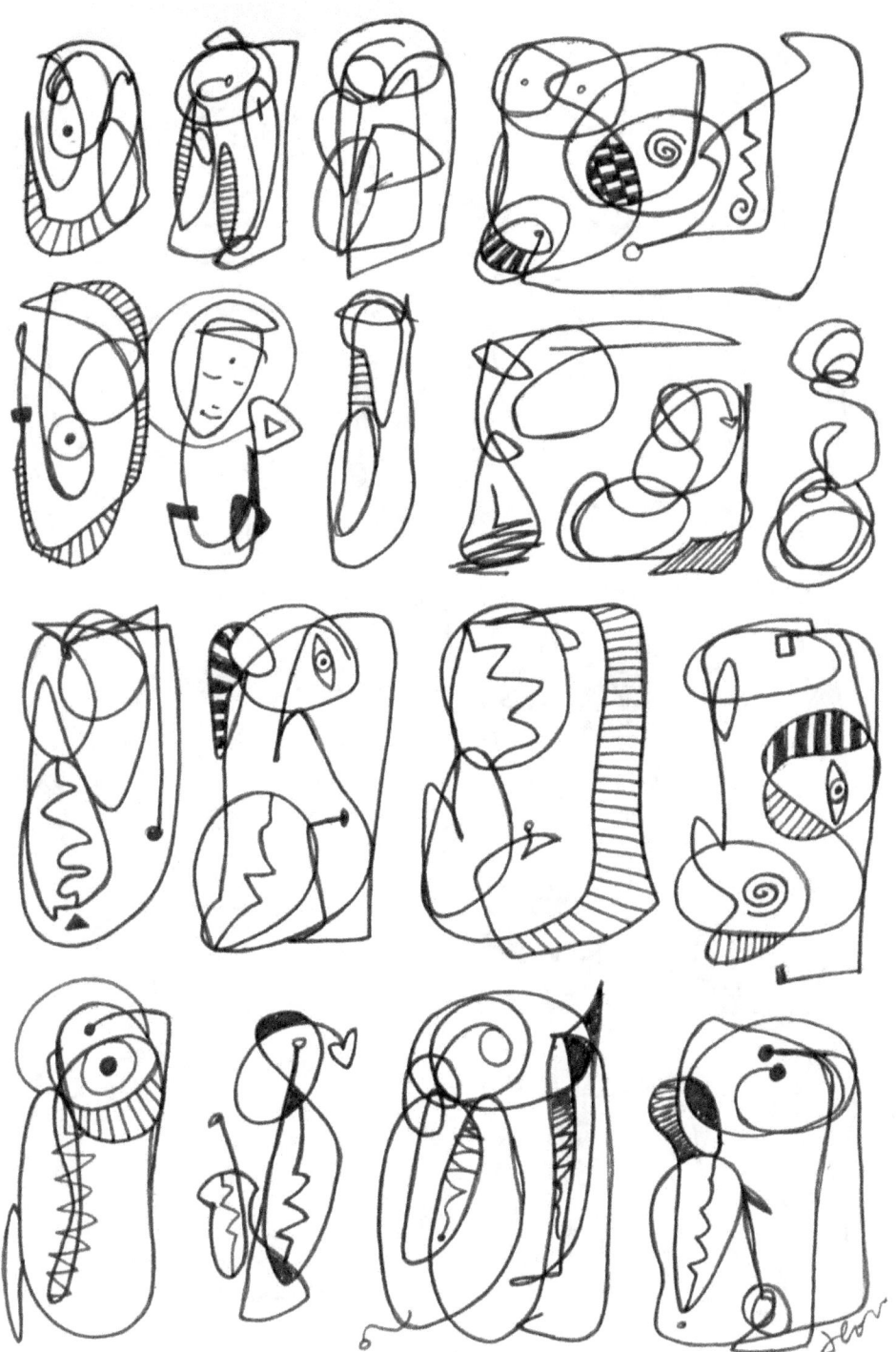

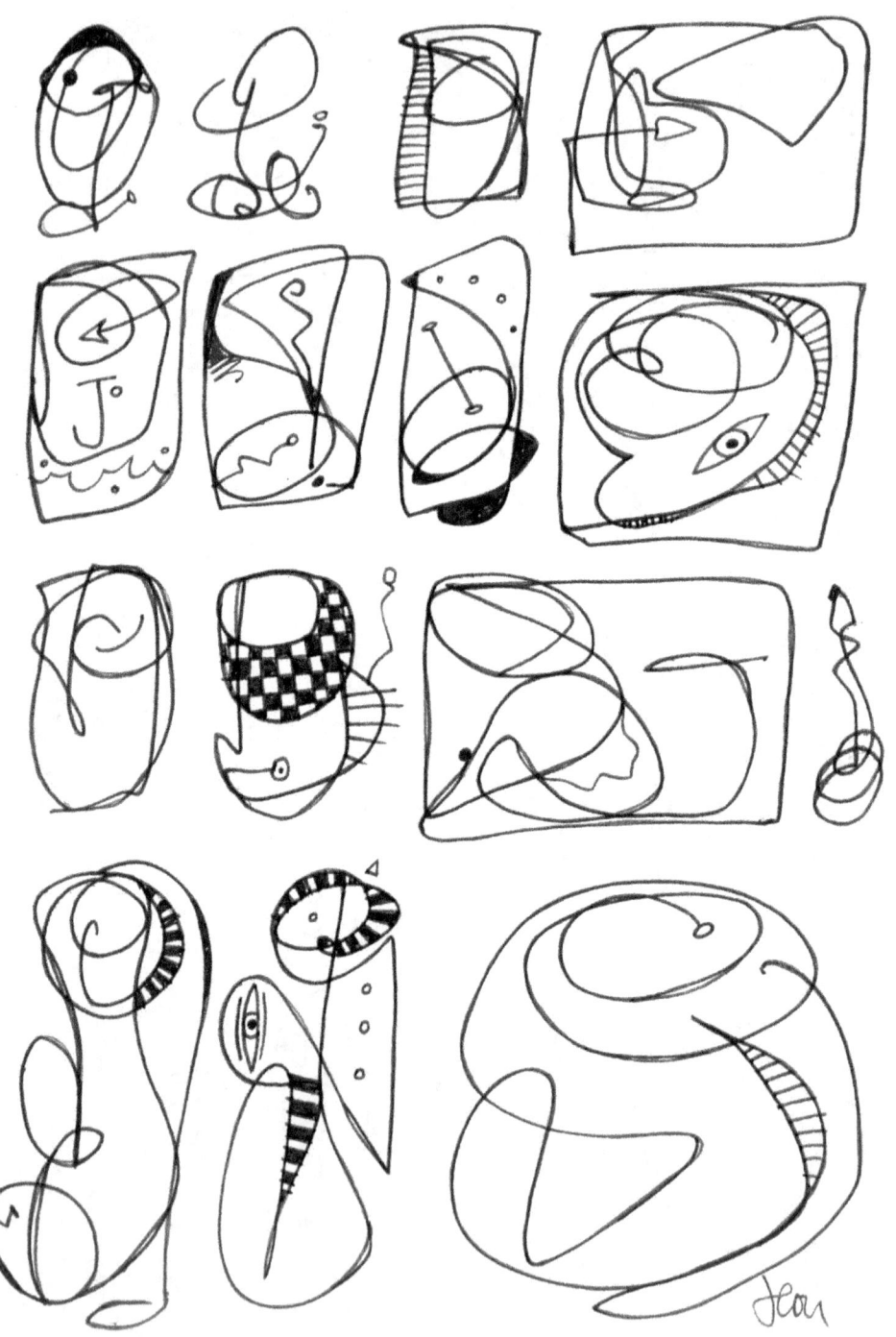

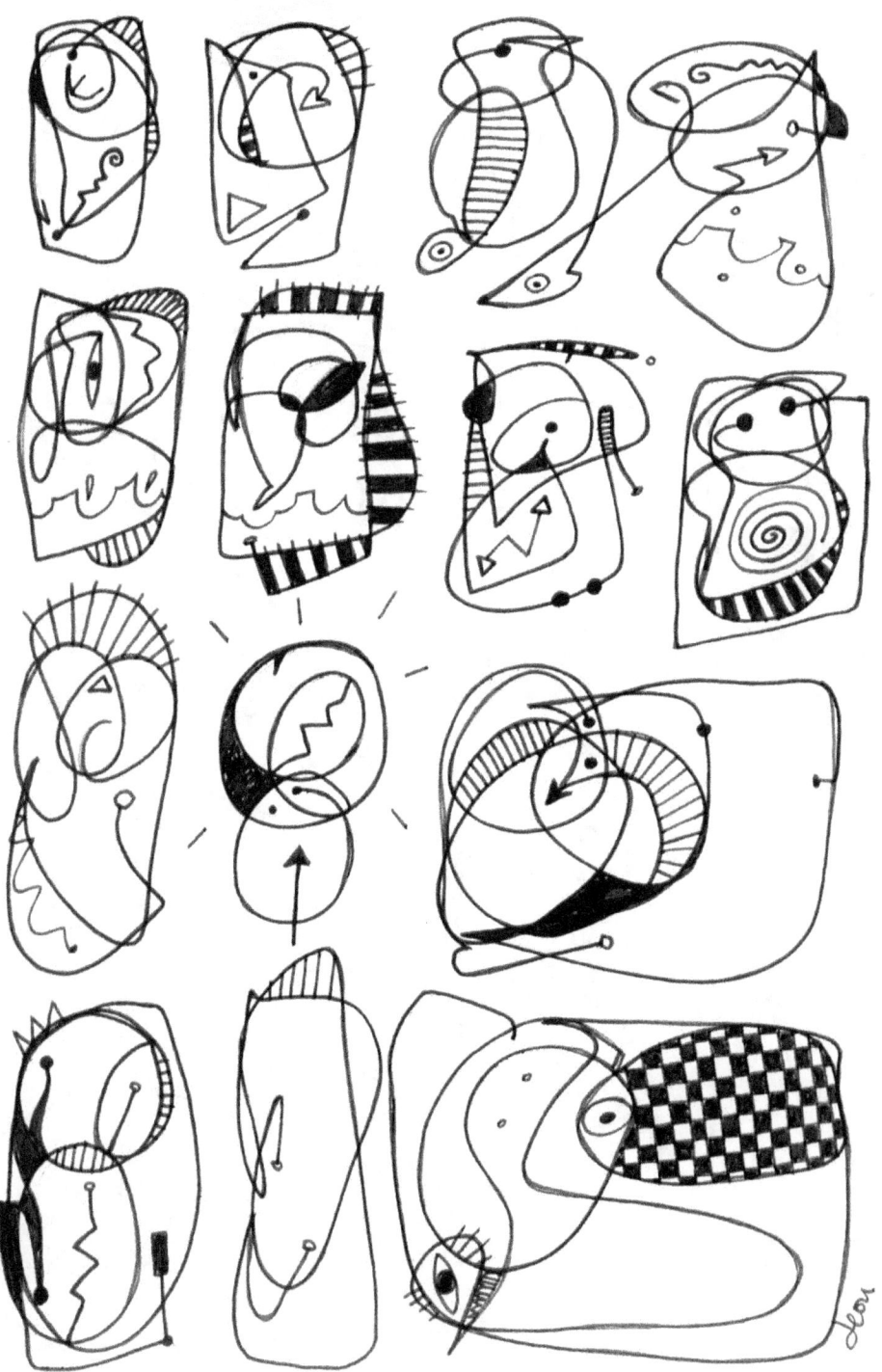

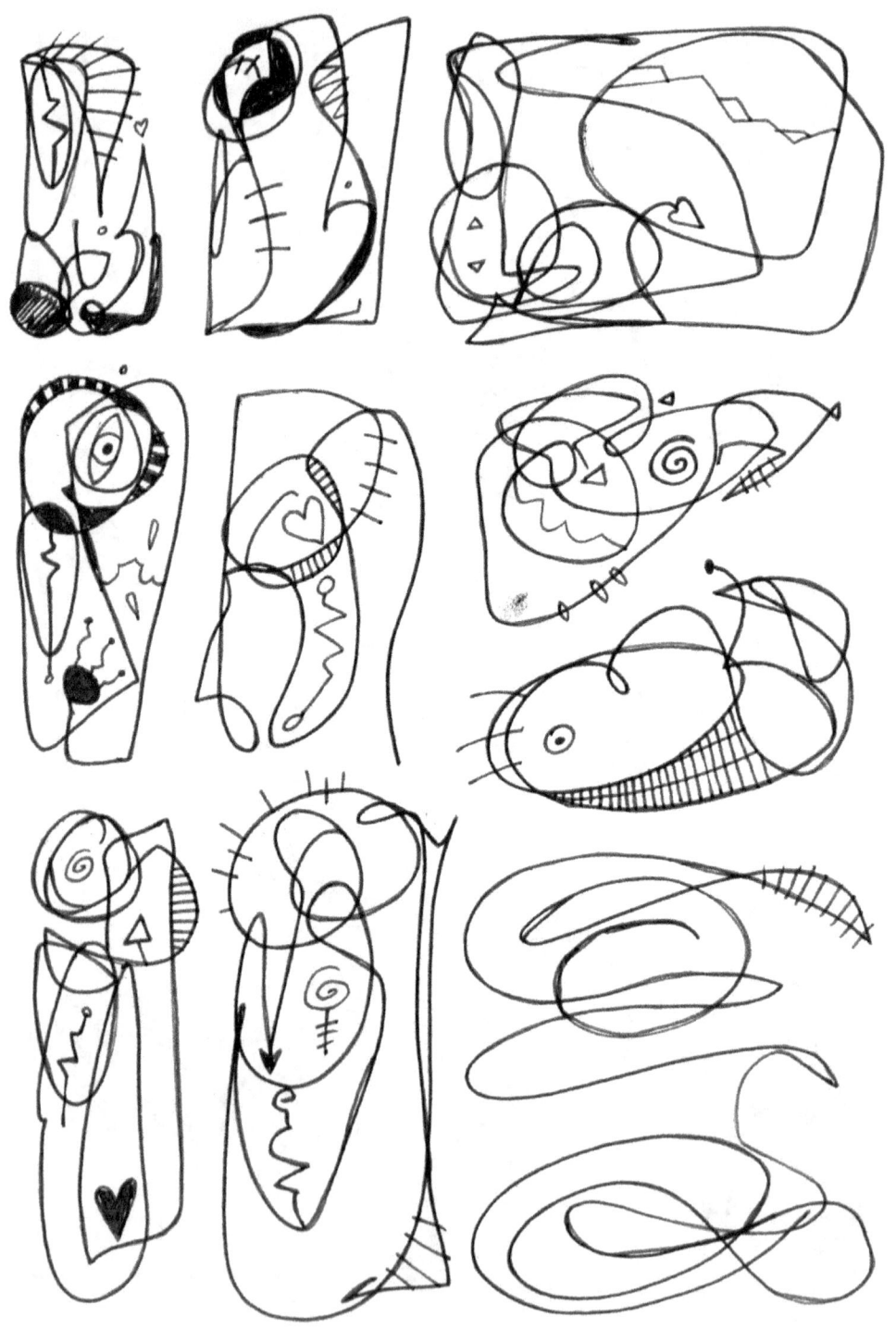

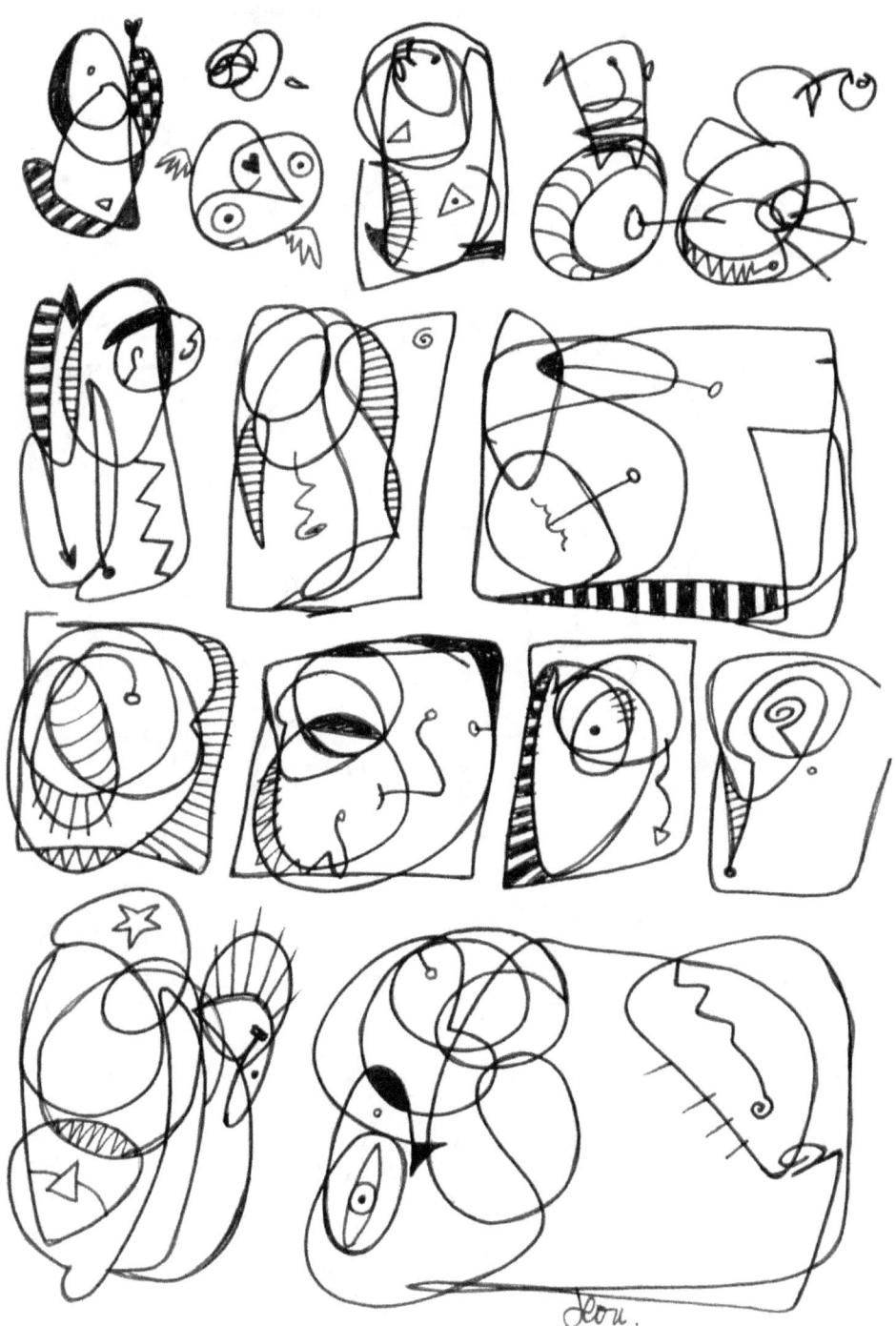

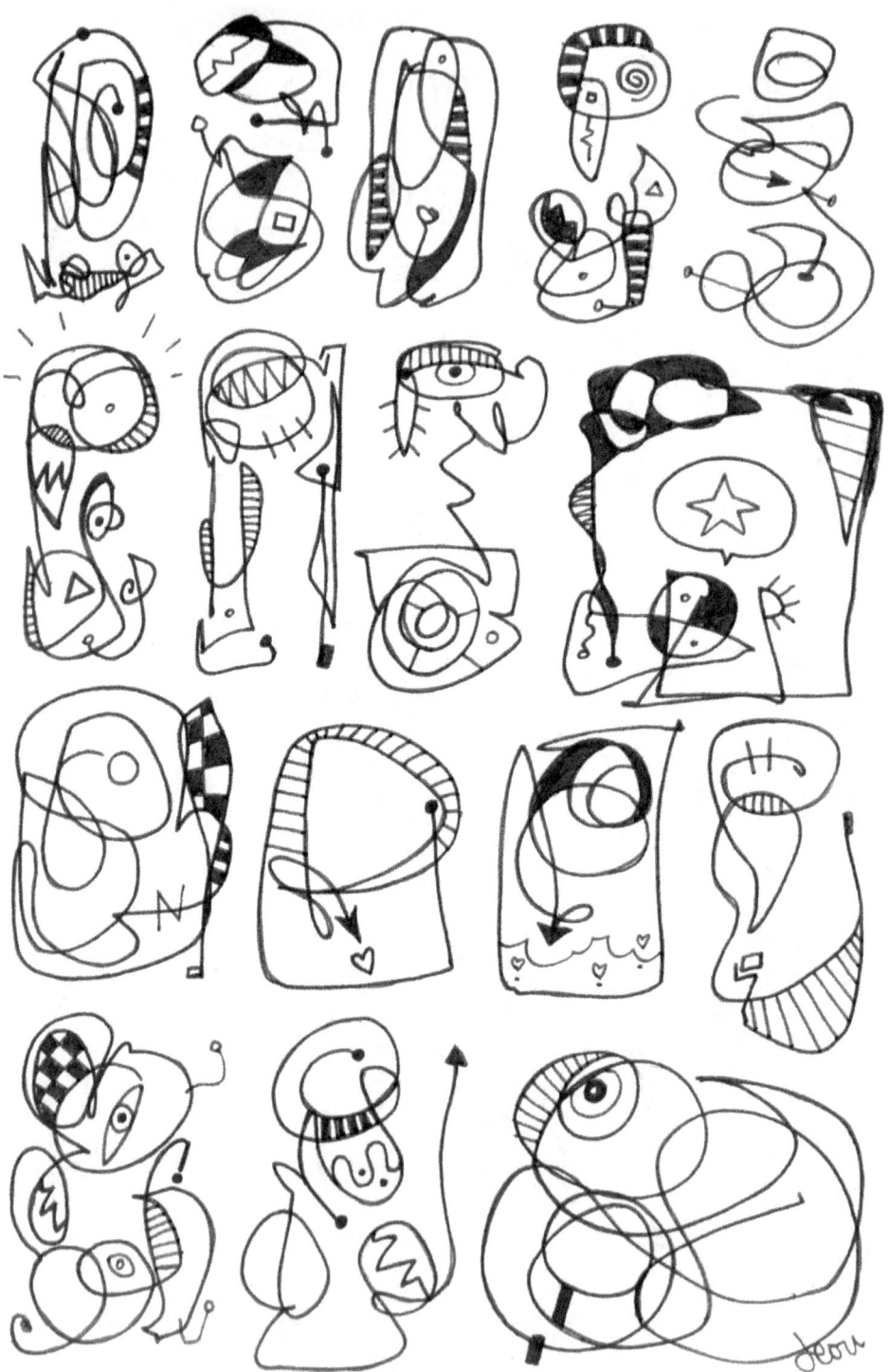

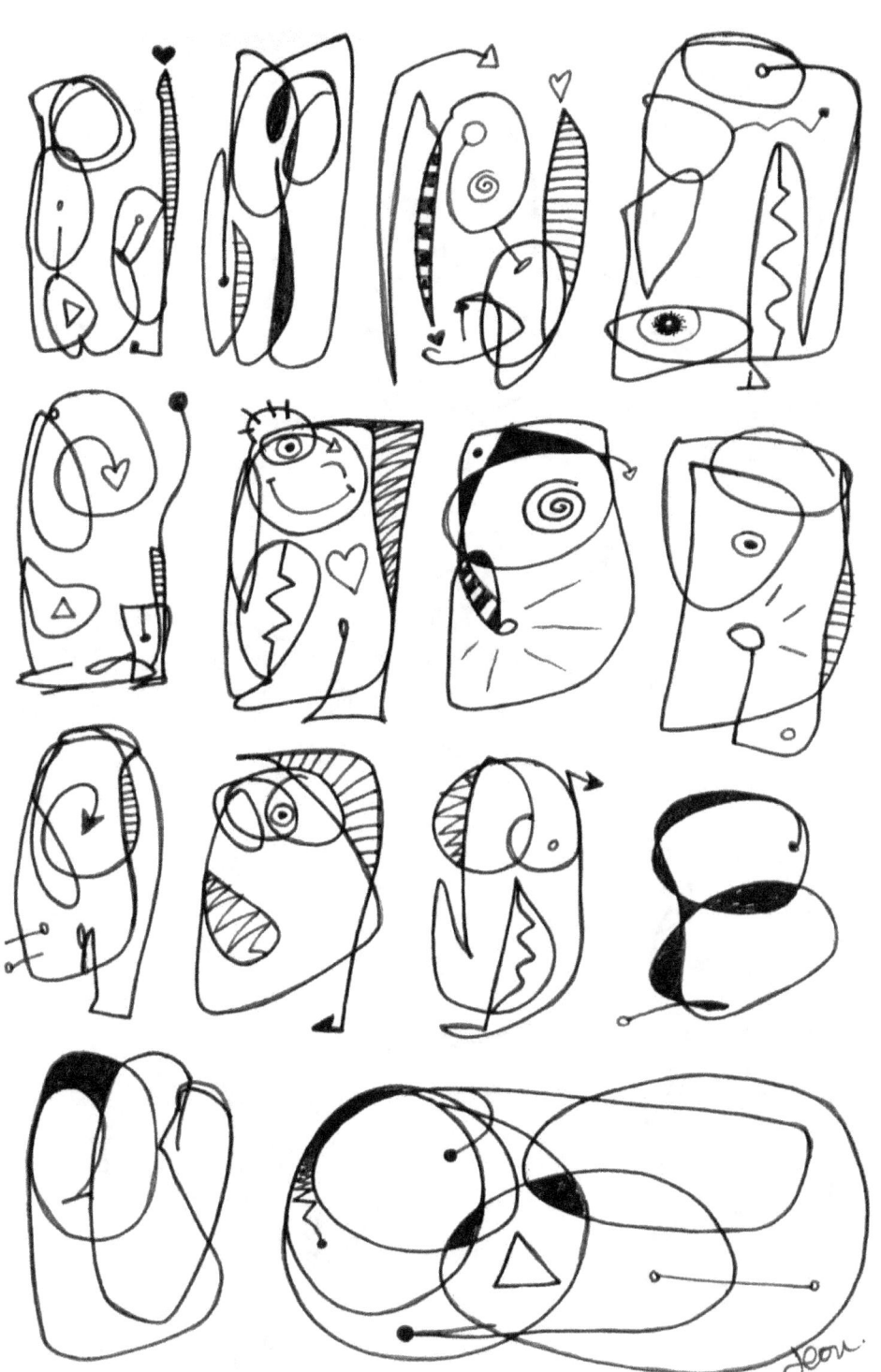

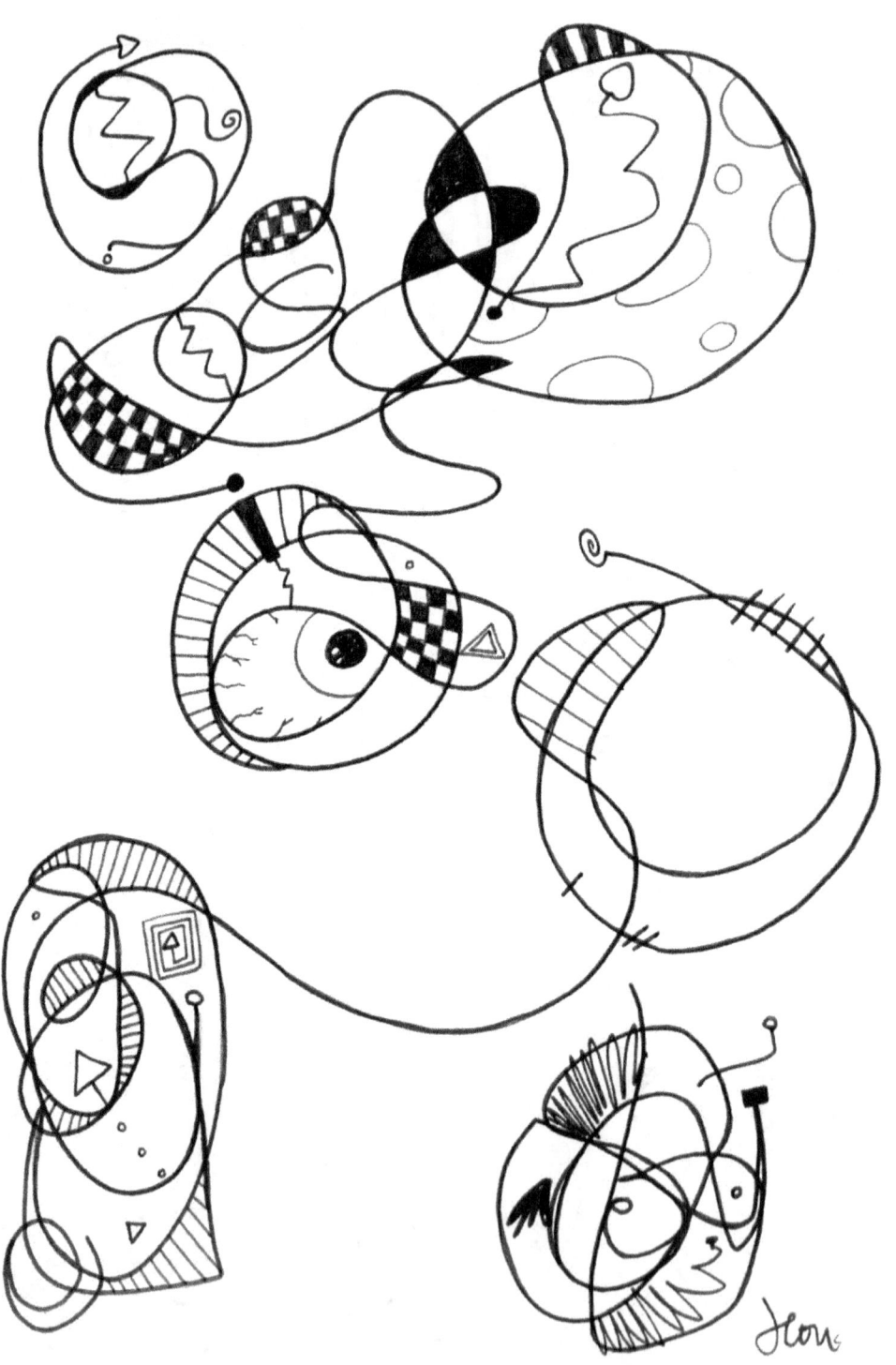

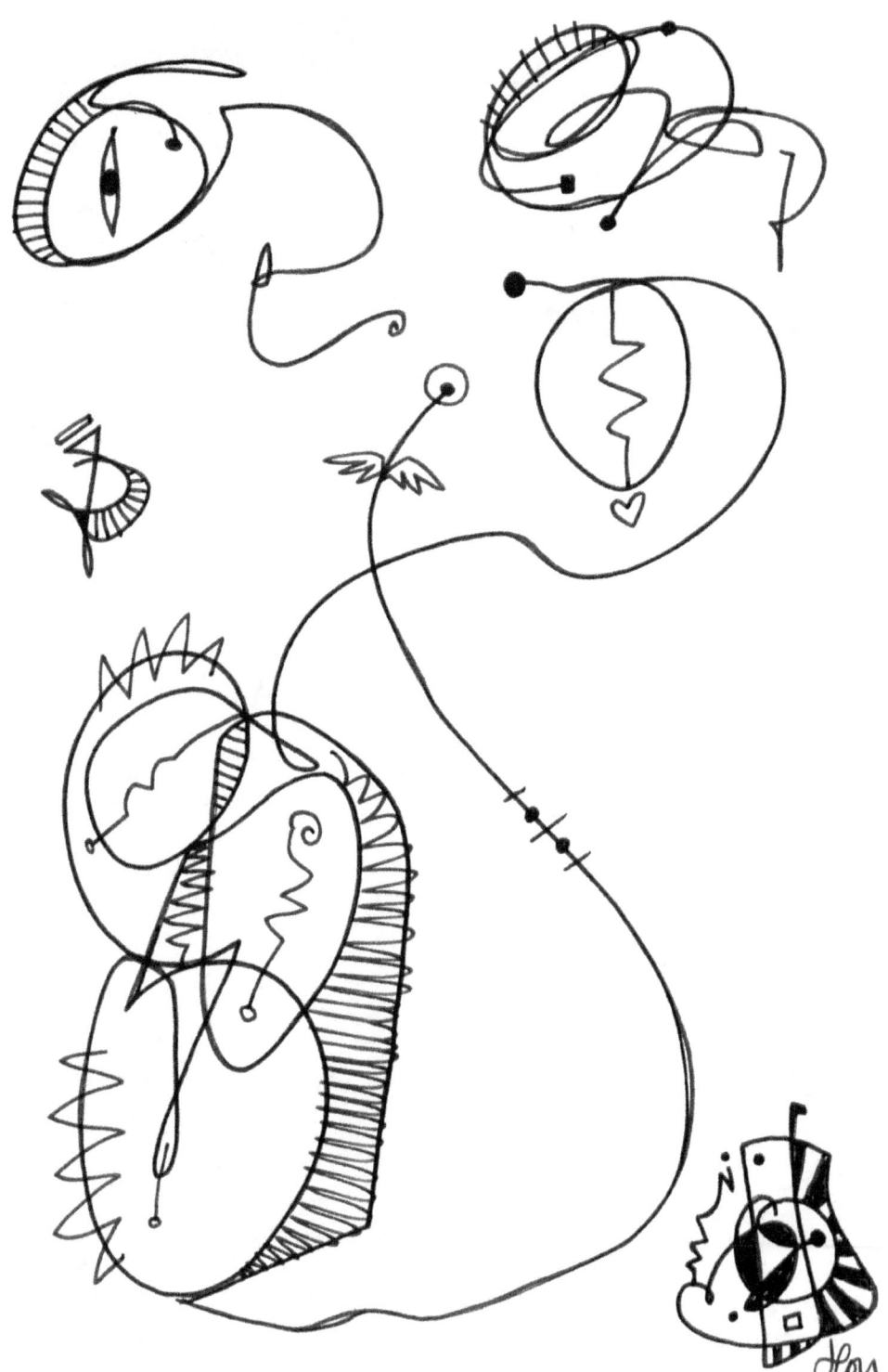

93

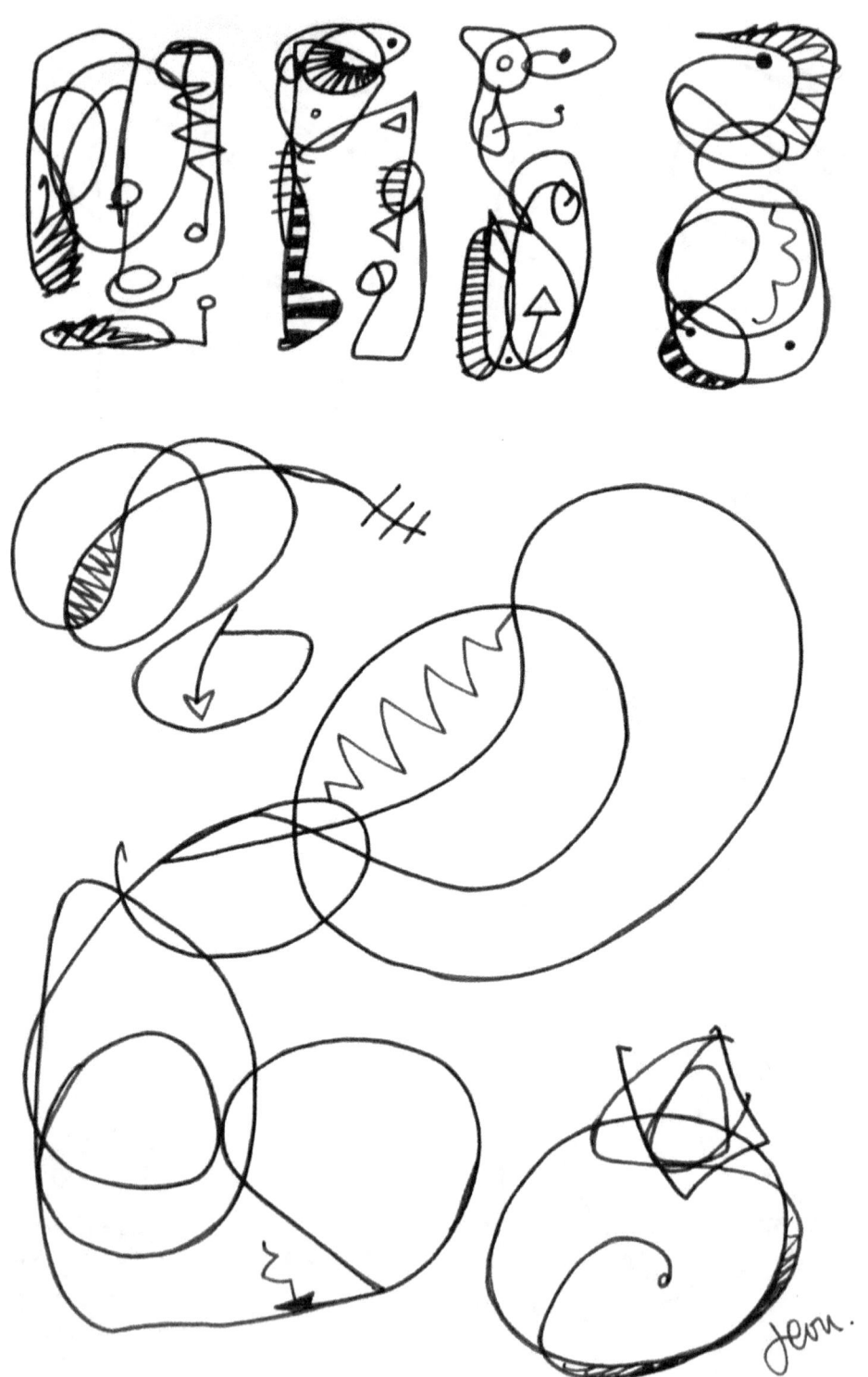

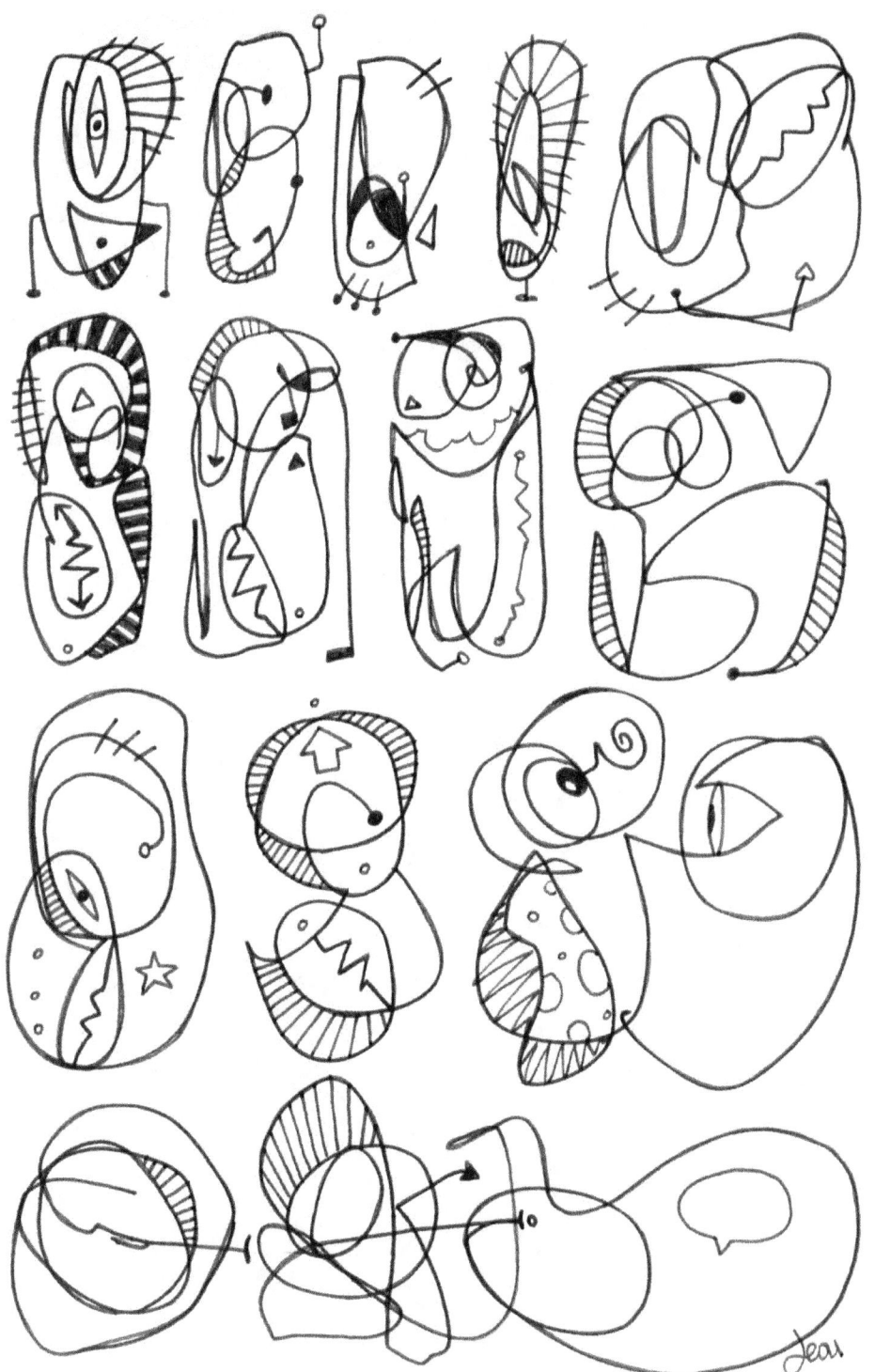

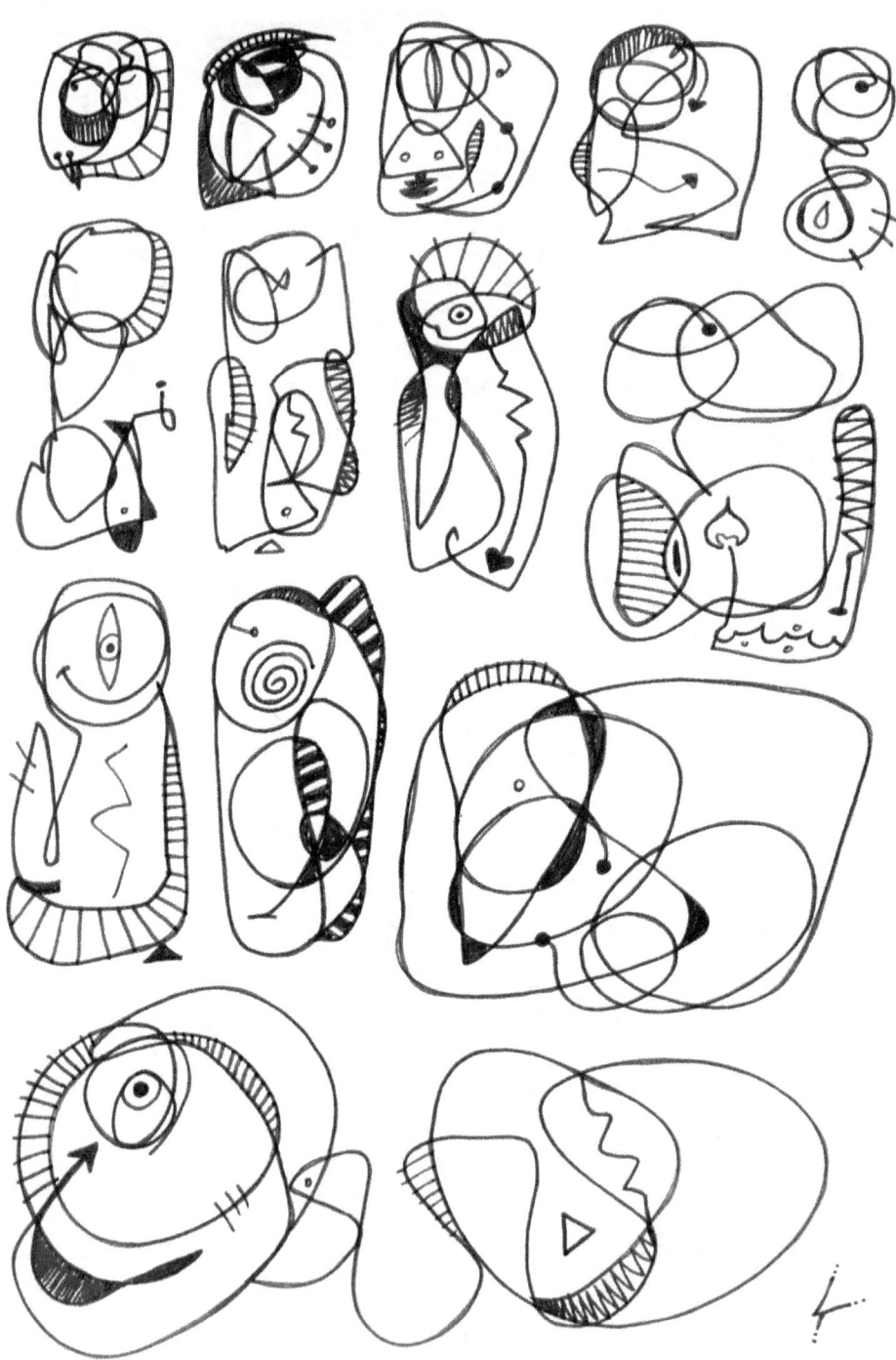

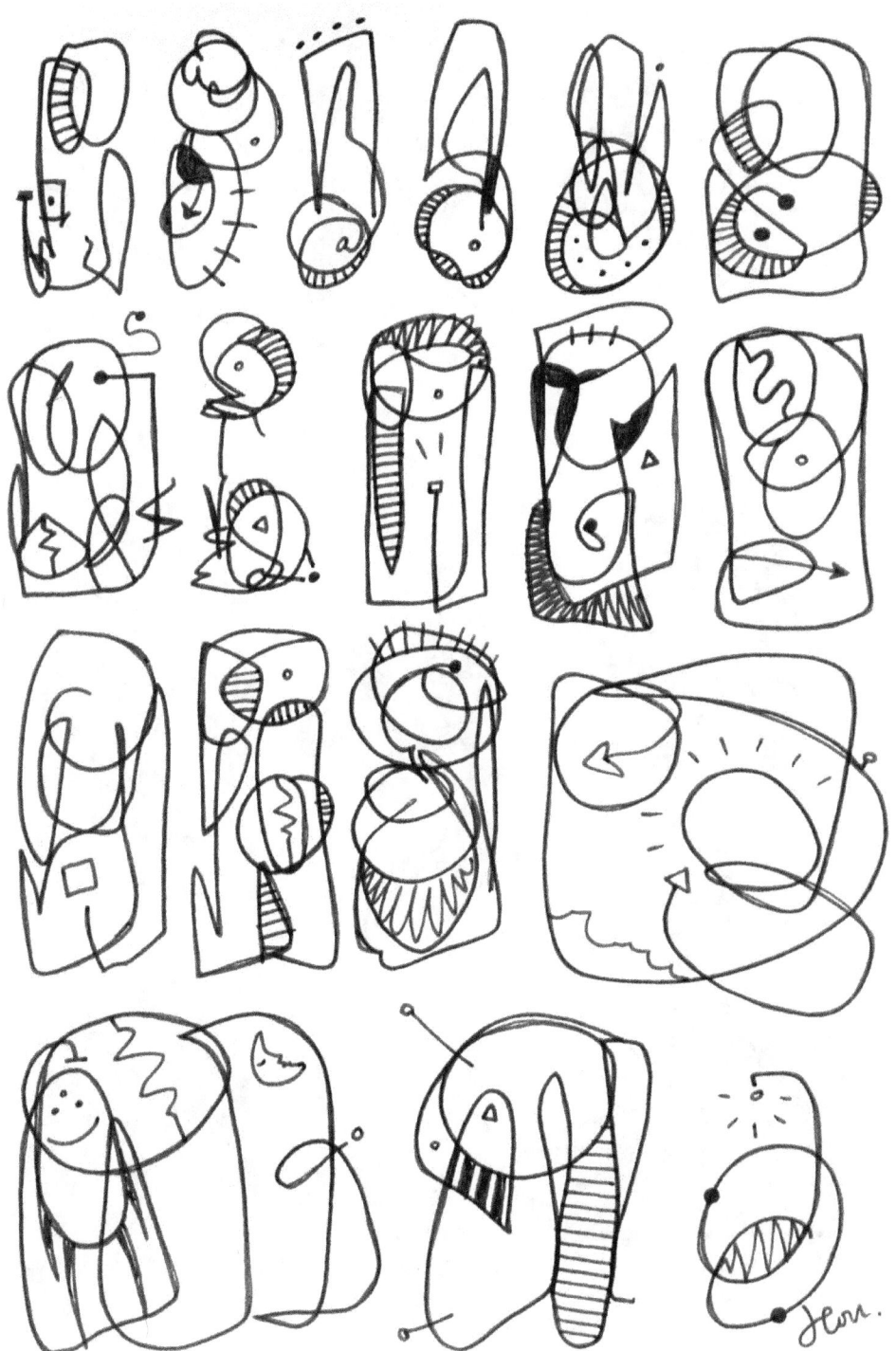

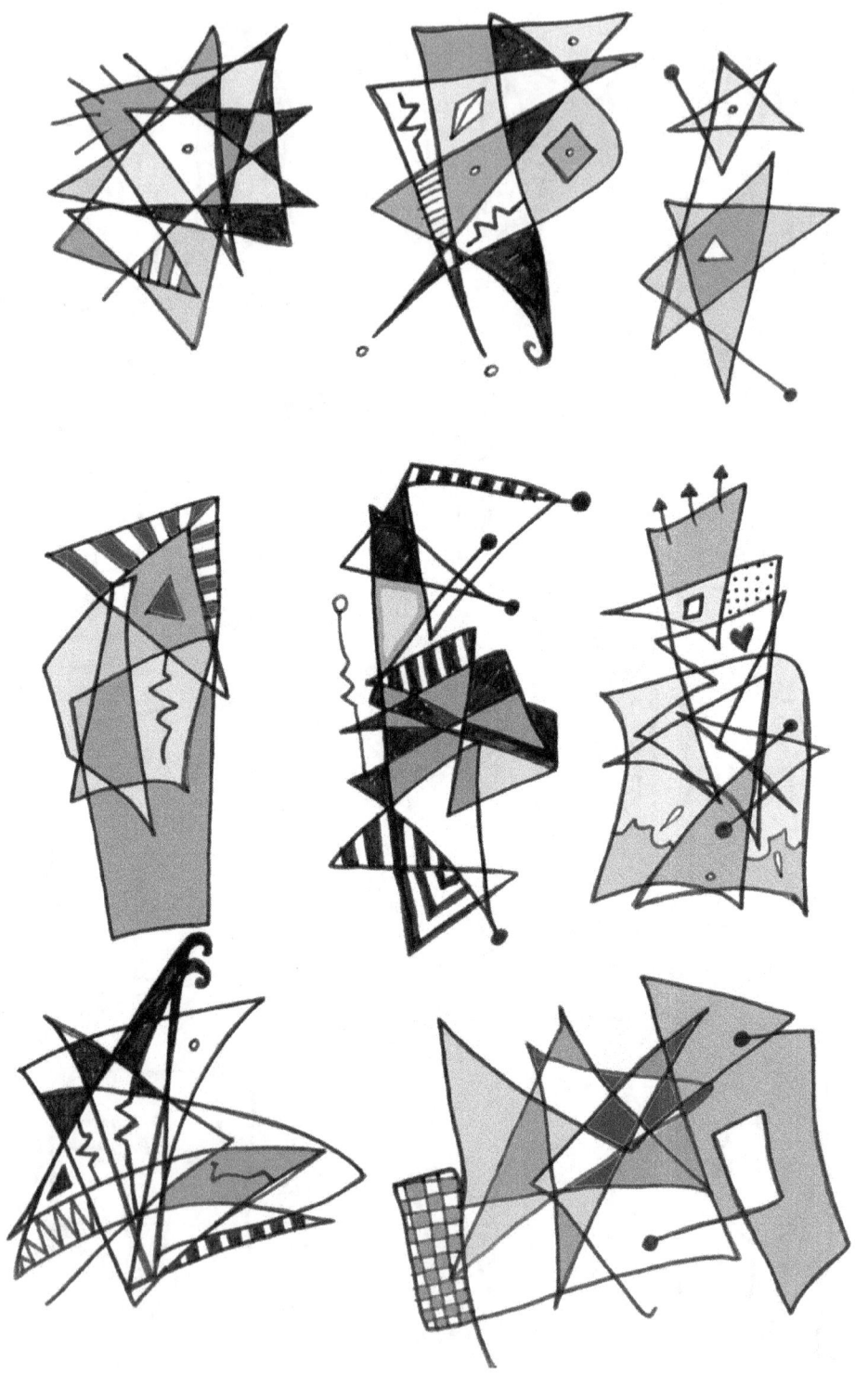

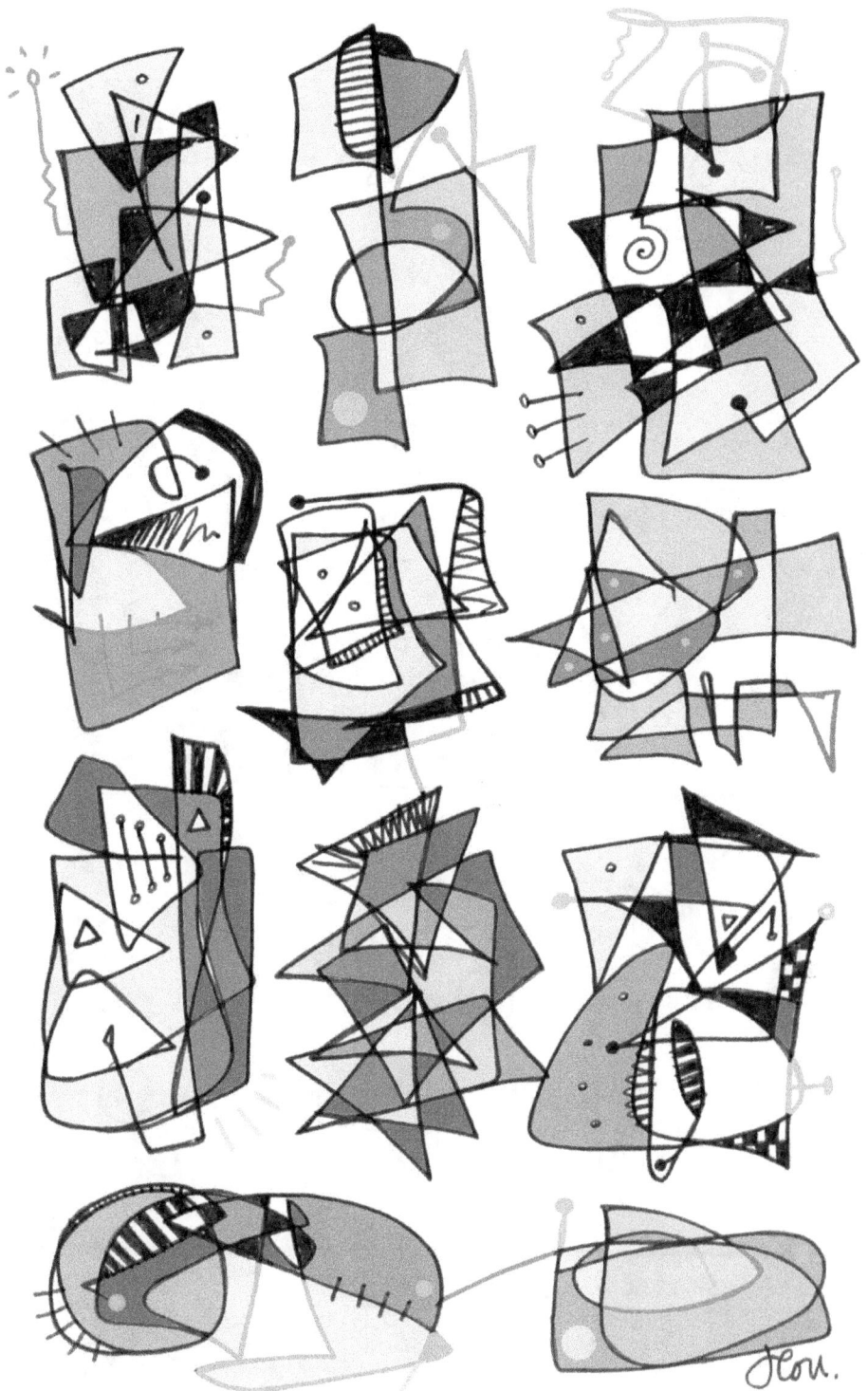

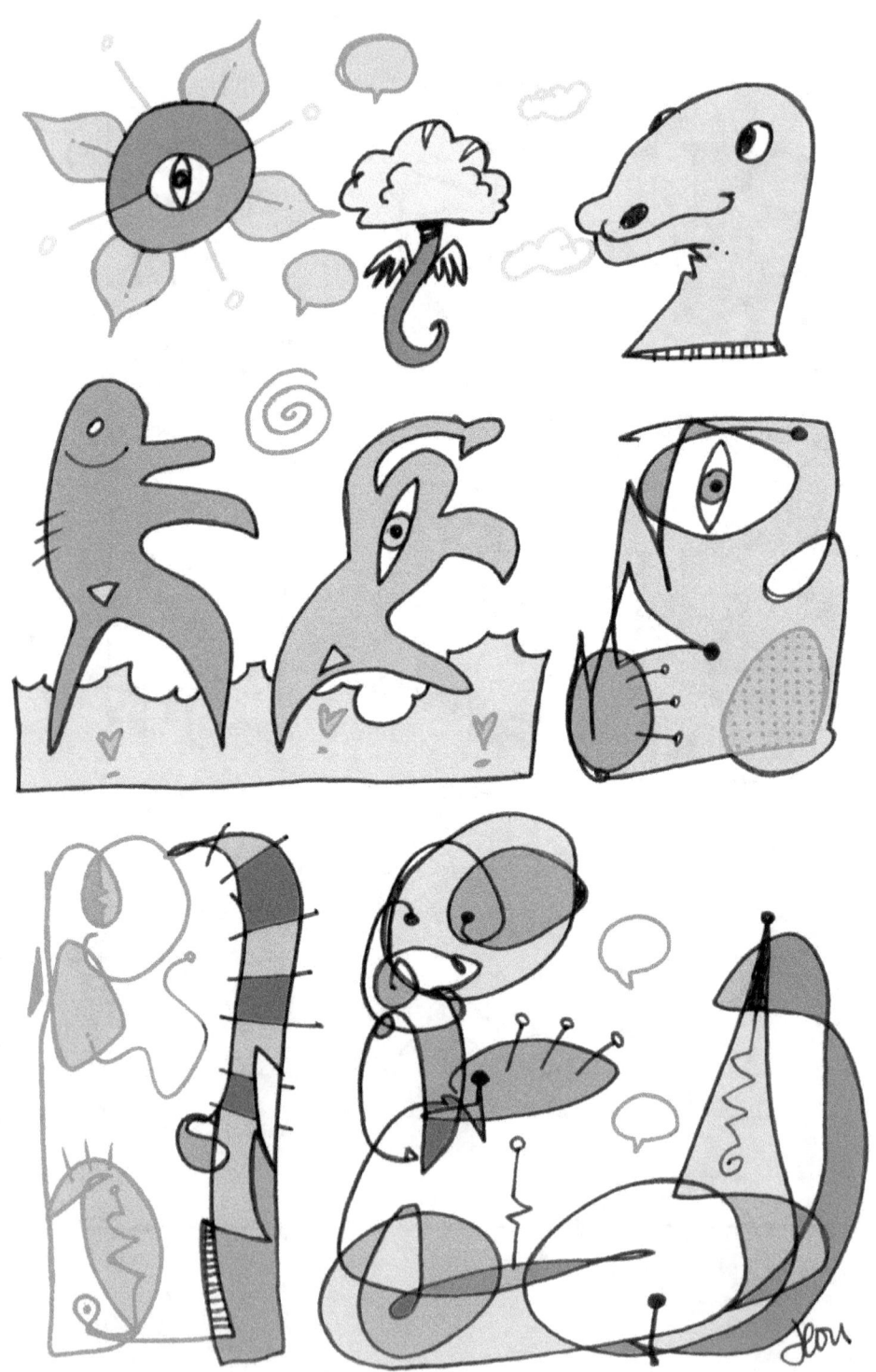

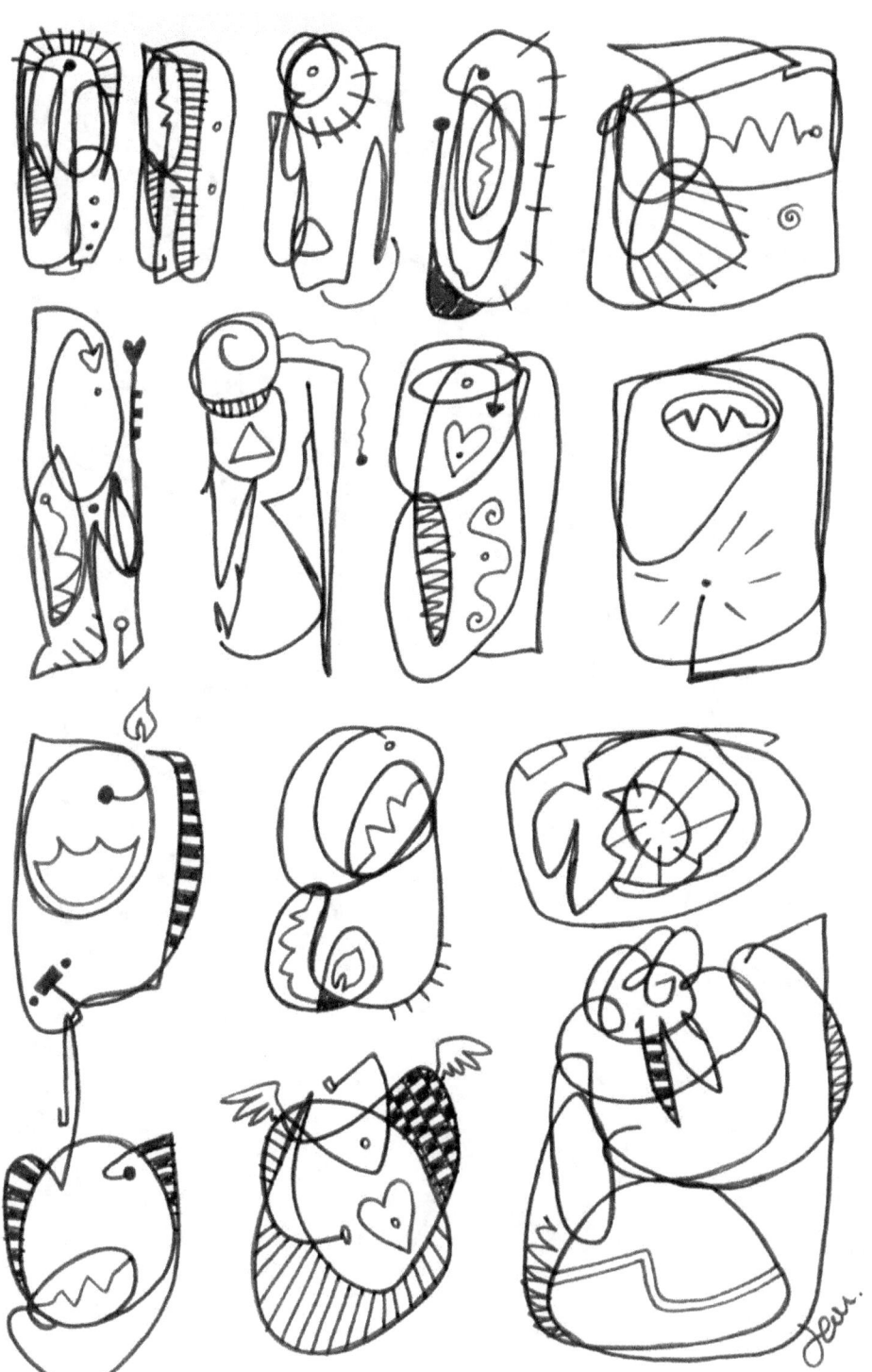

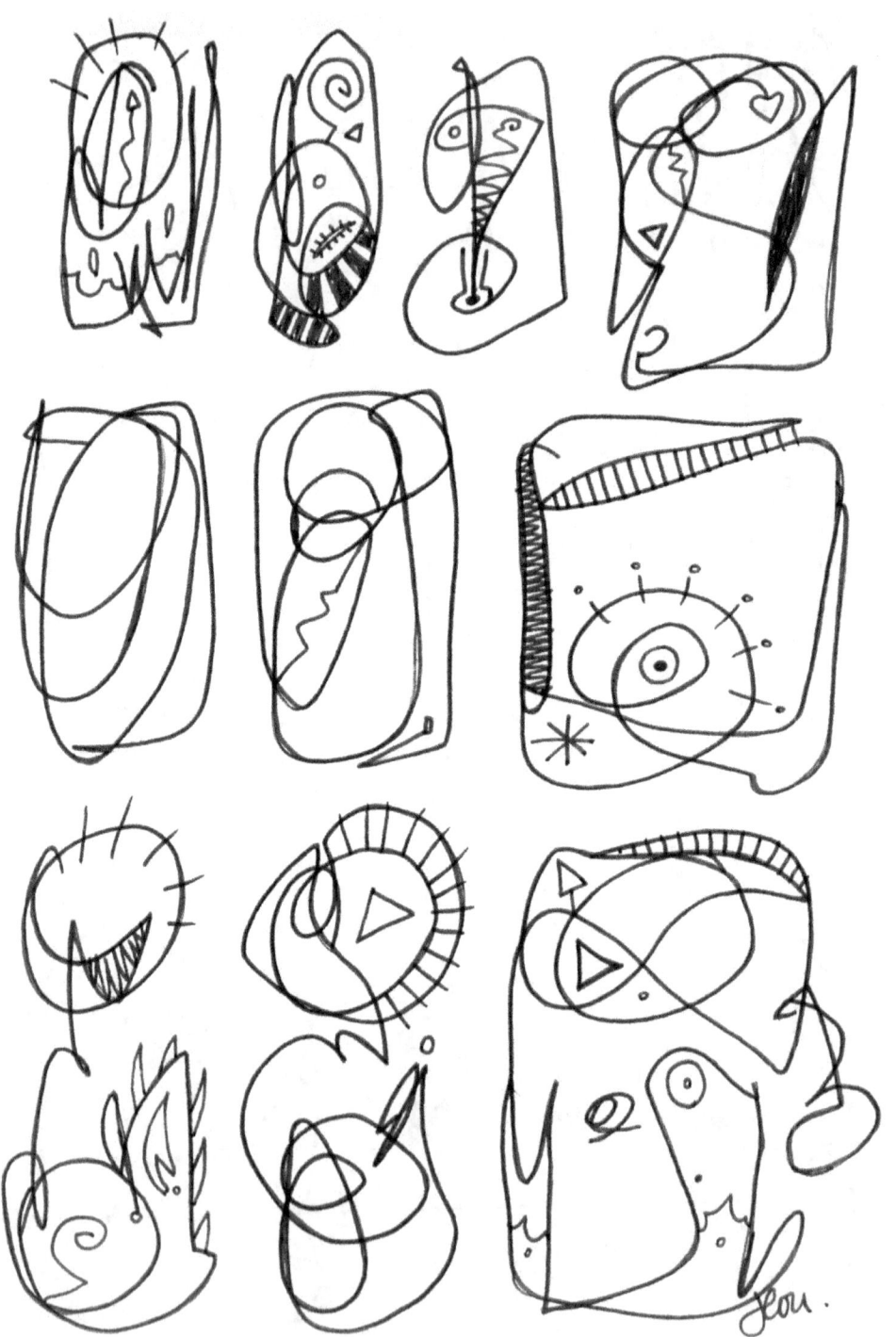

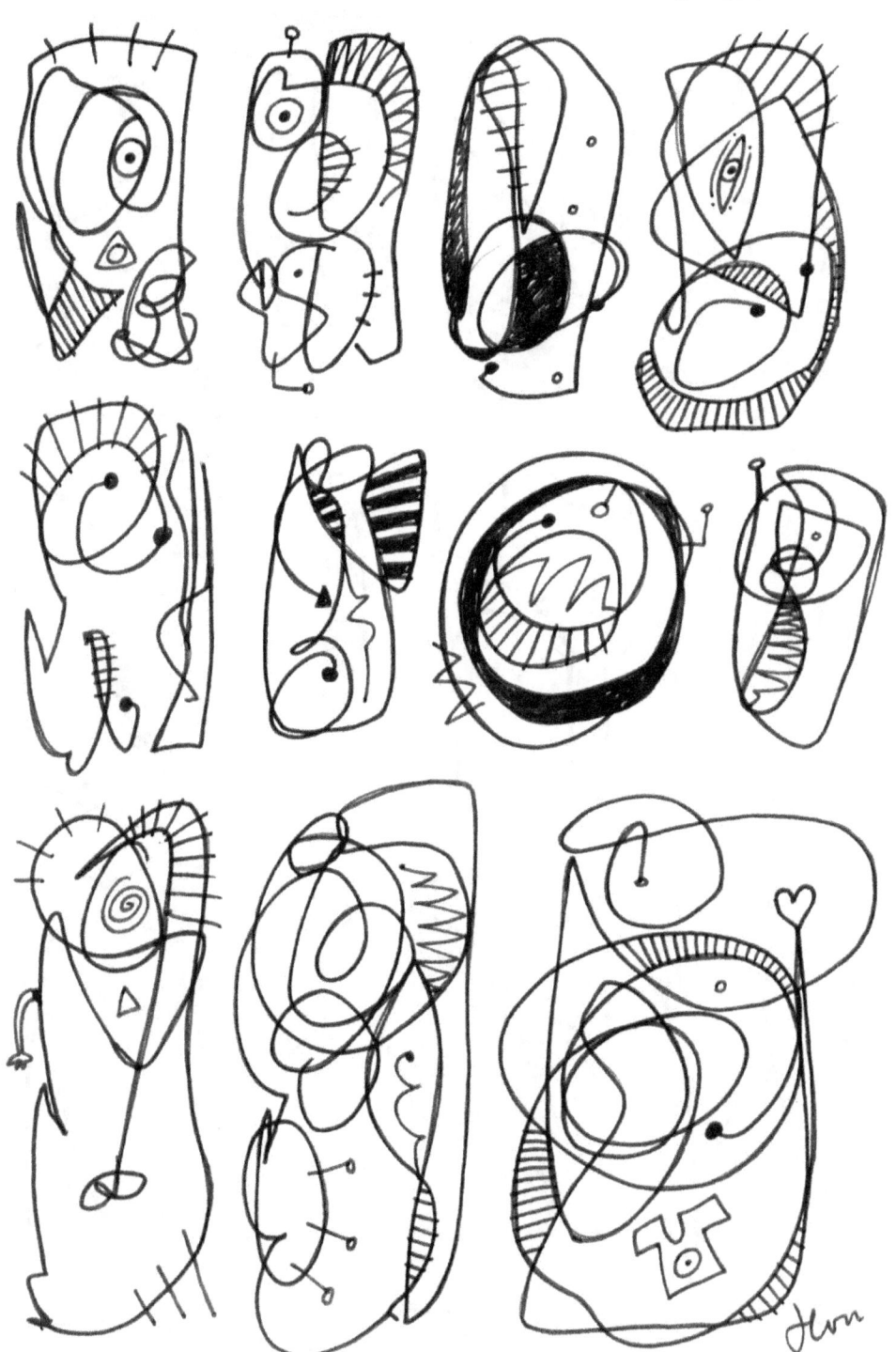

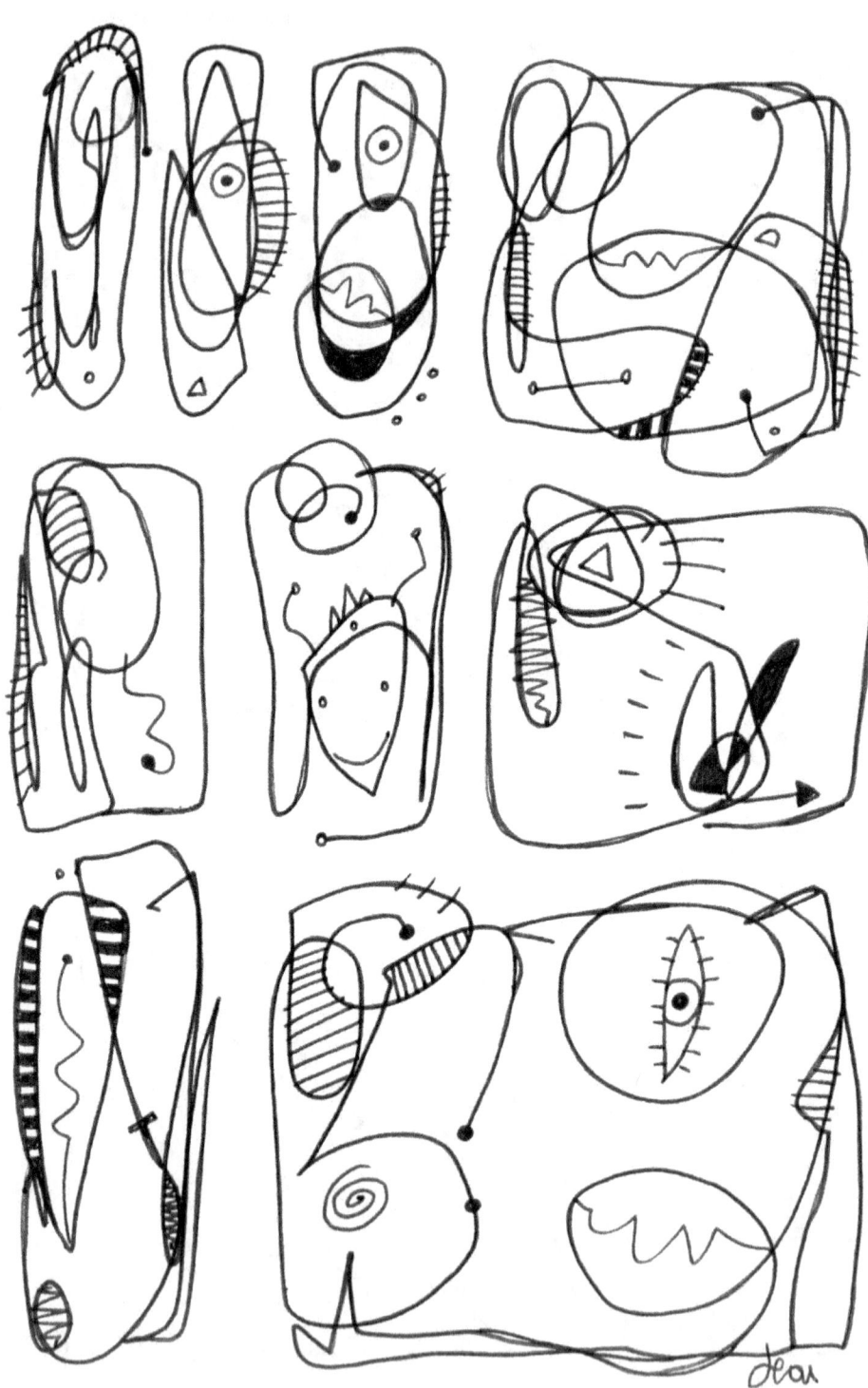

104

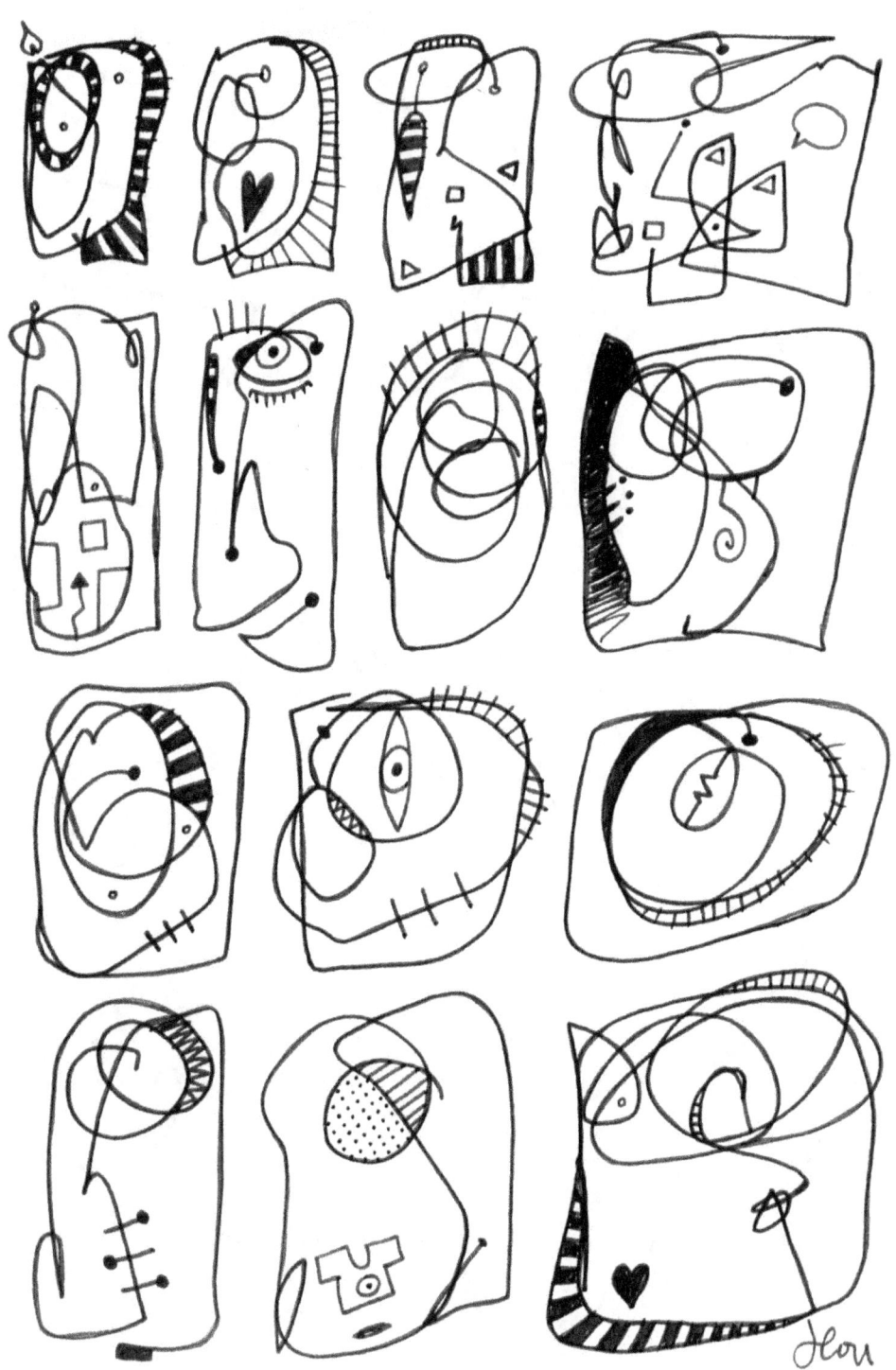

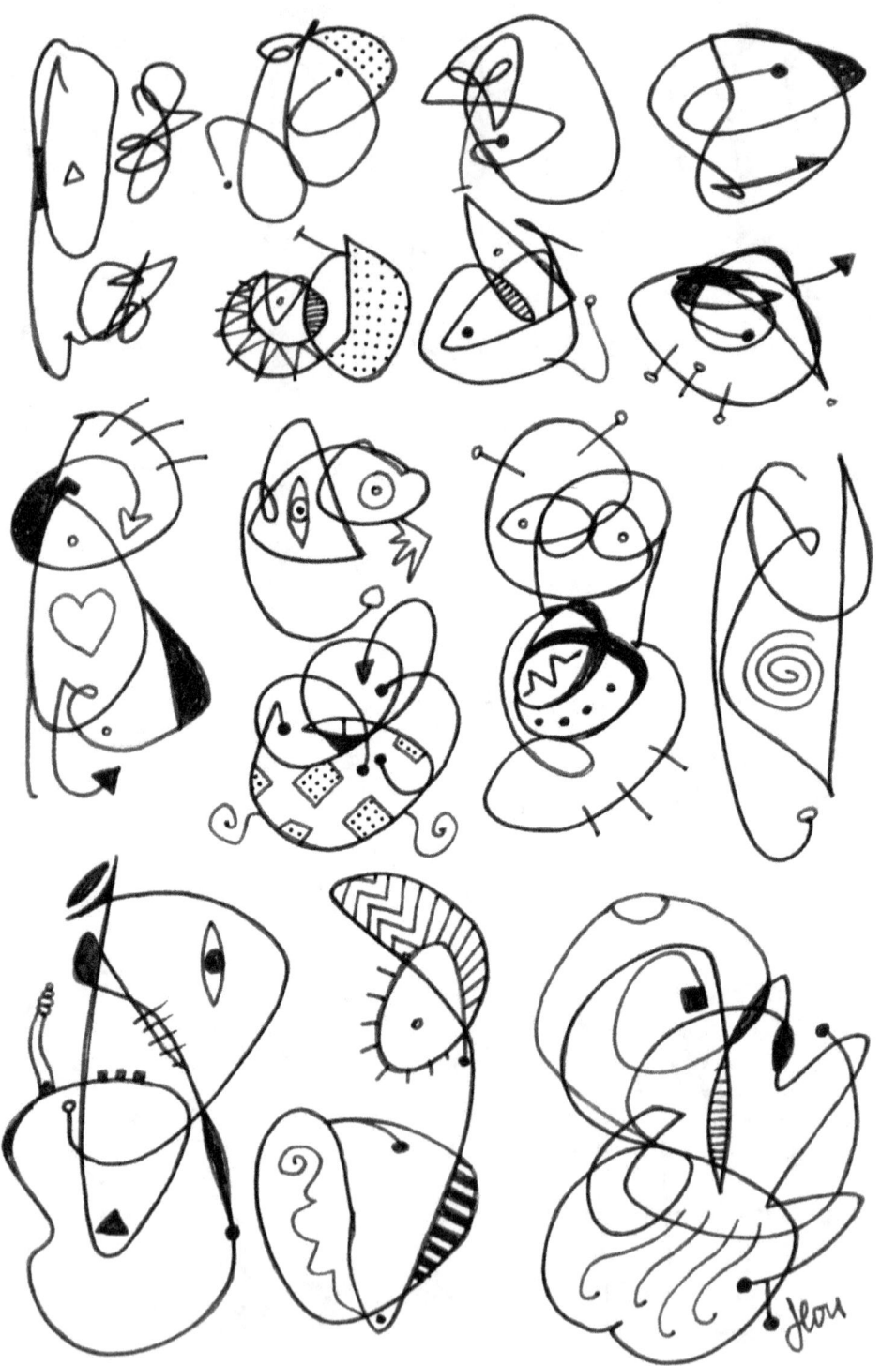

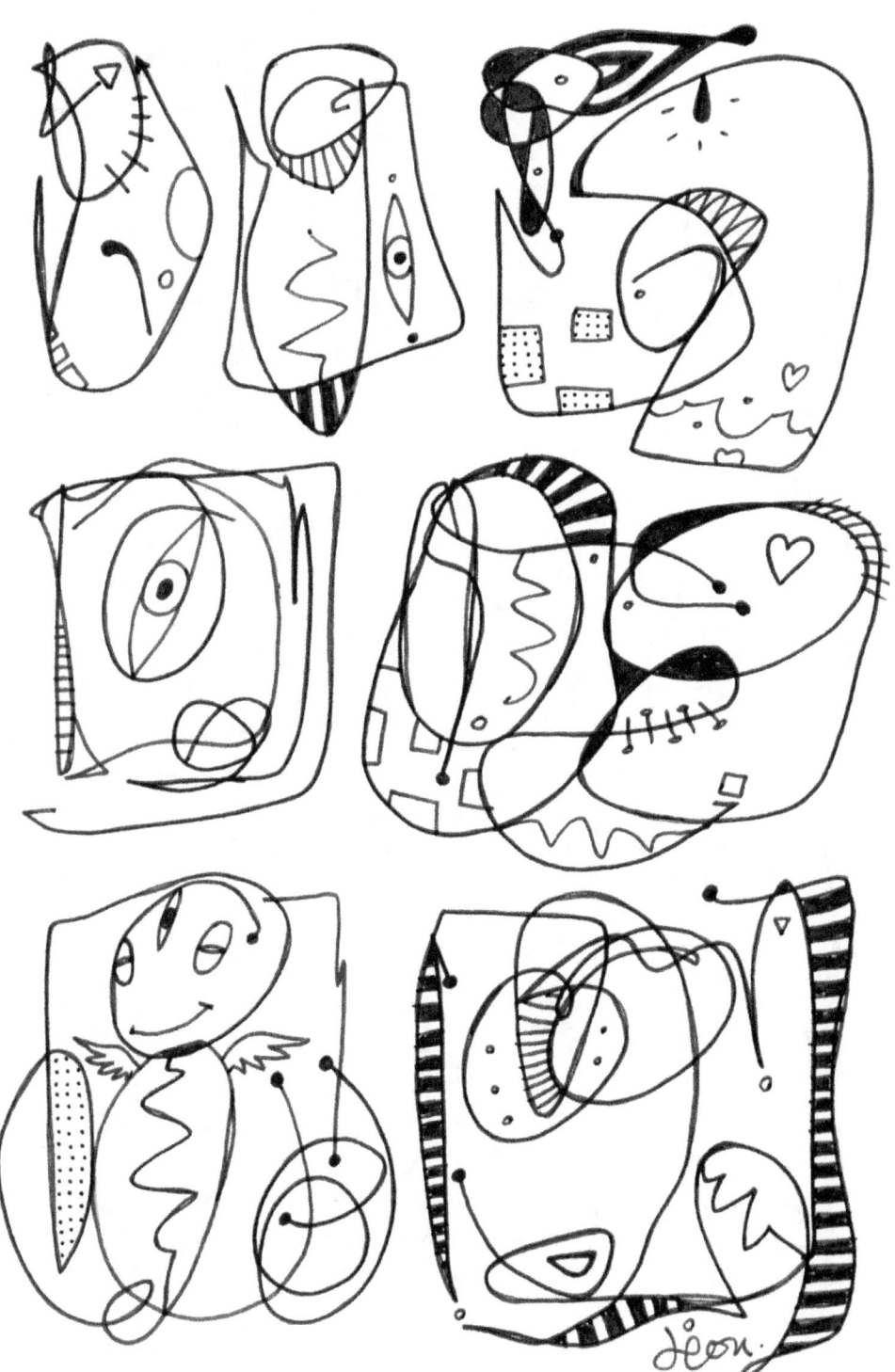

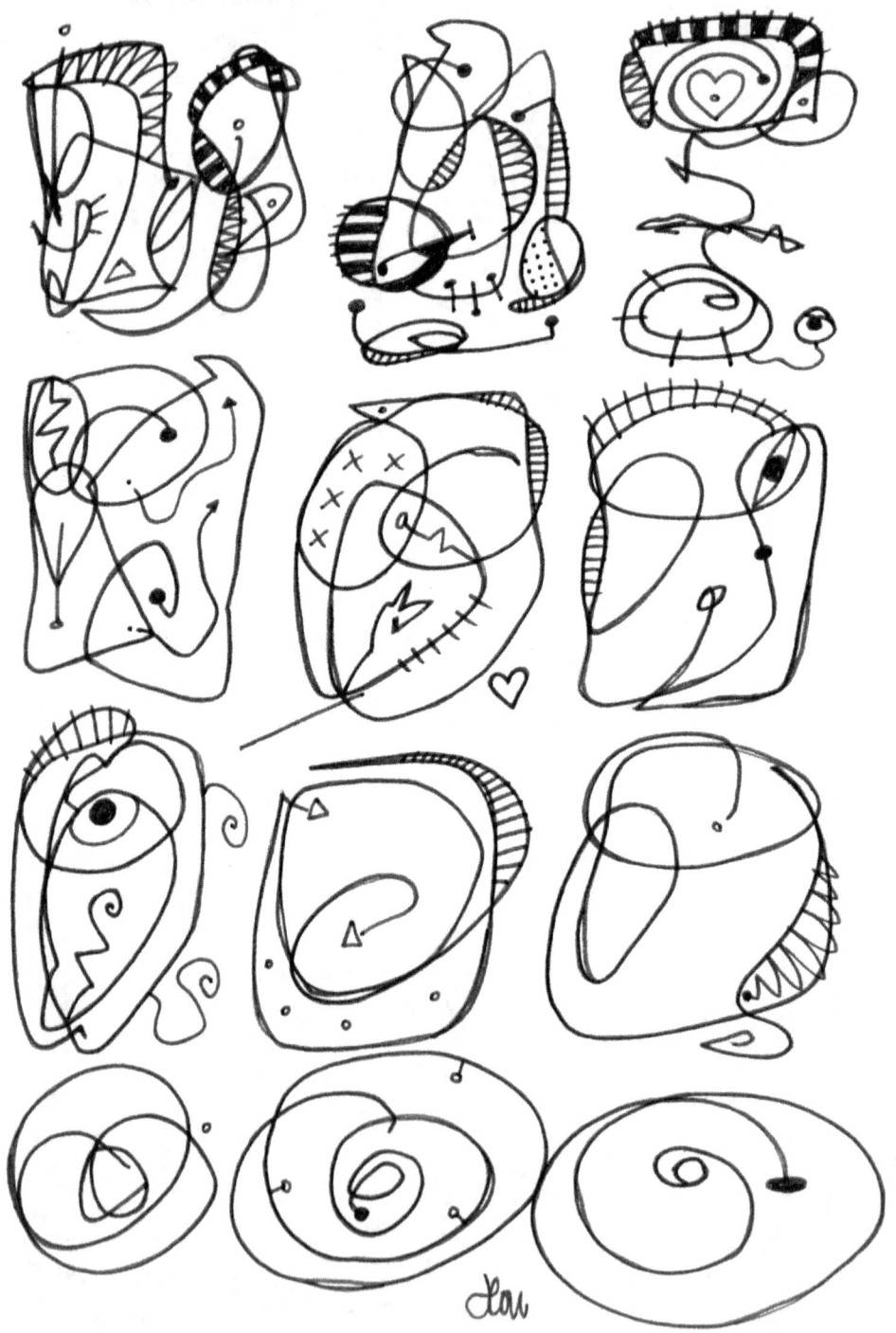

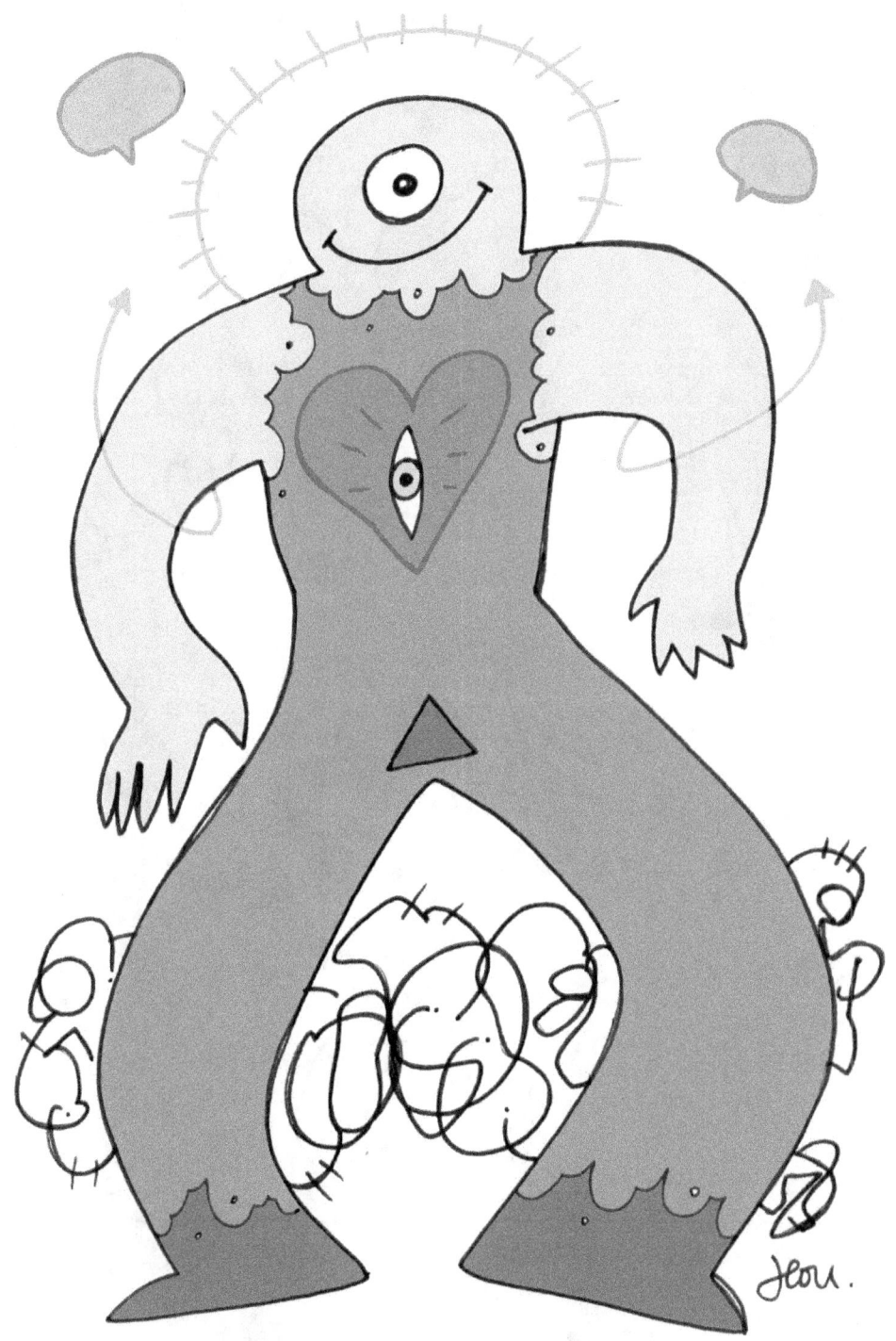

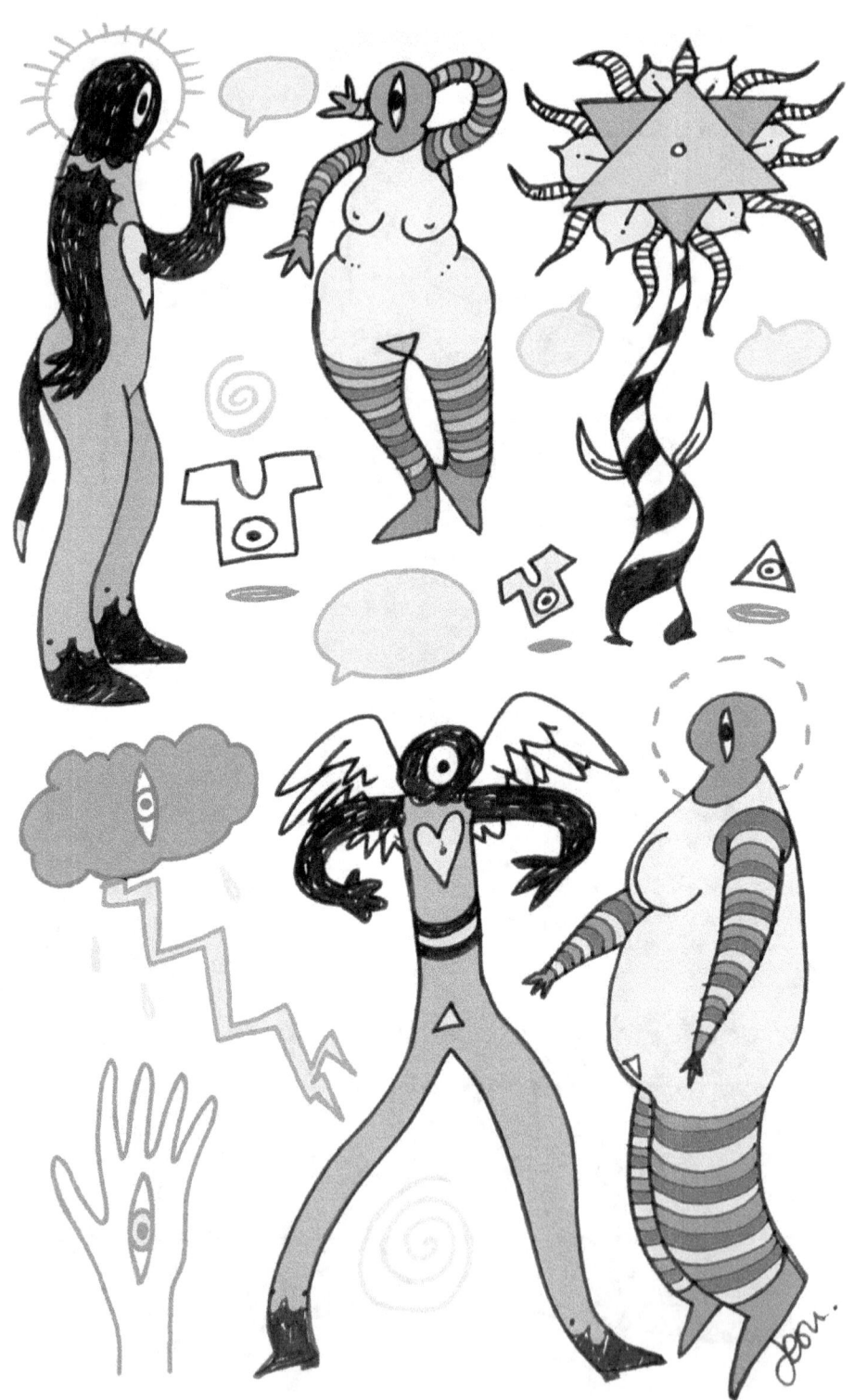

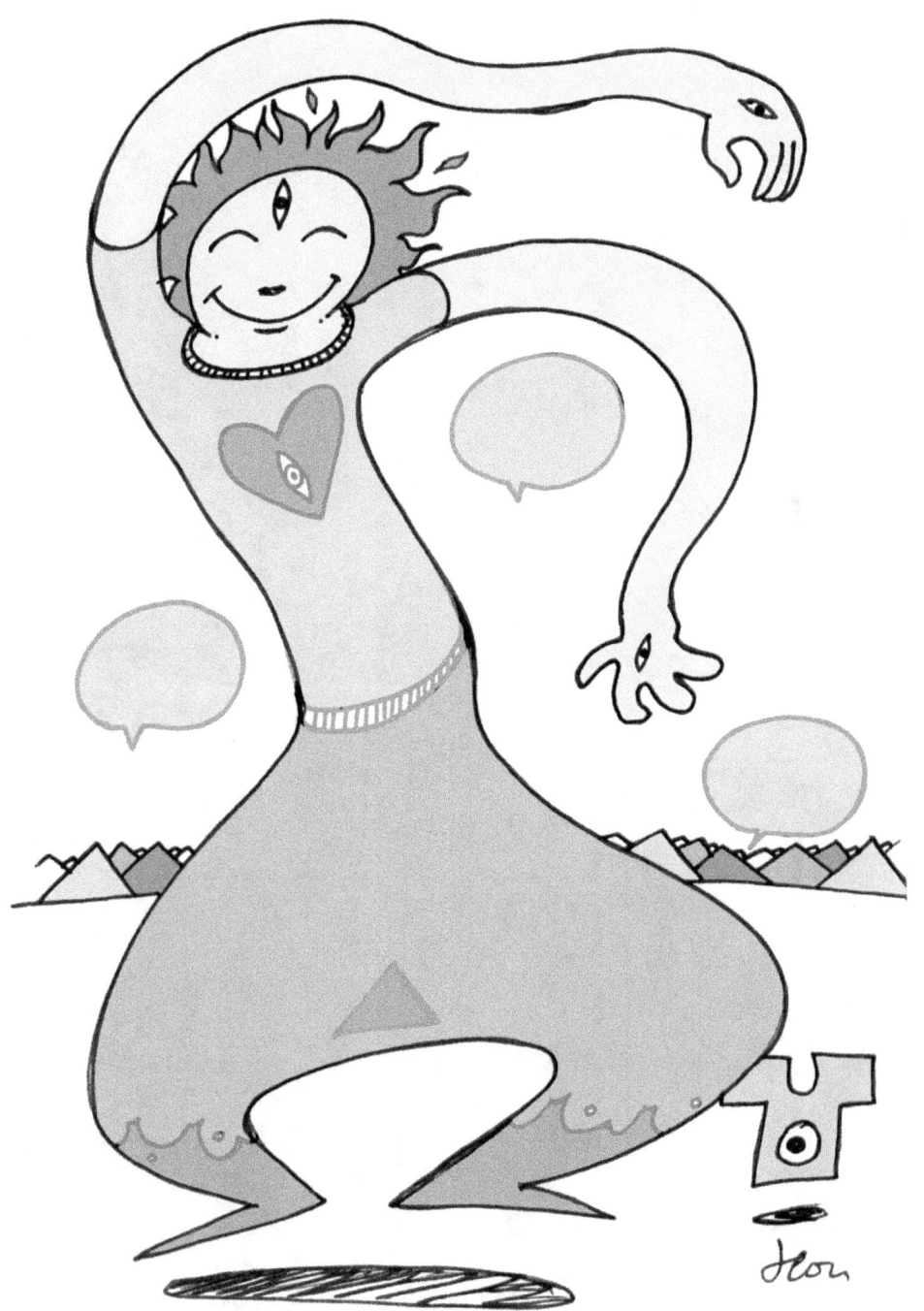

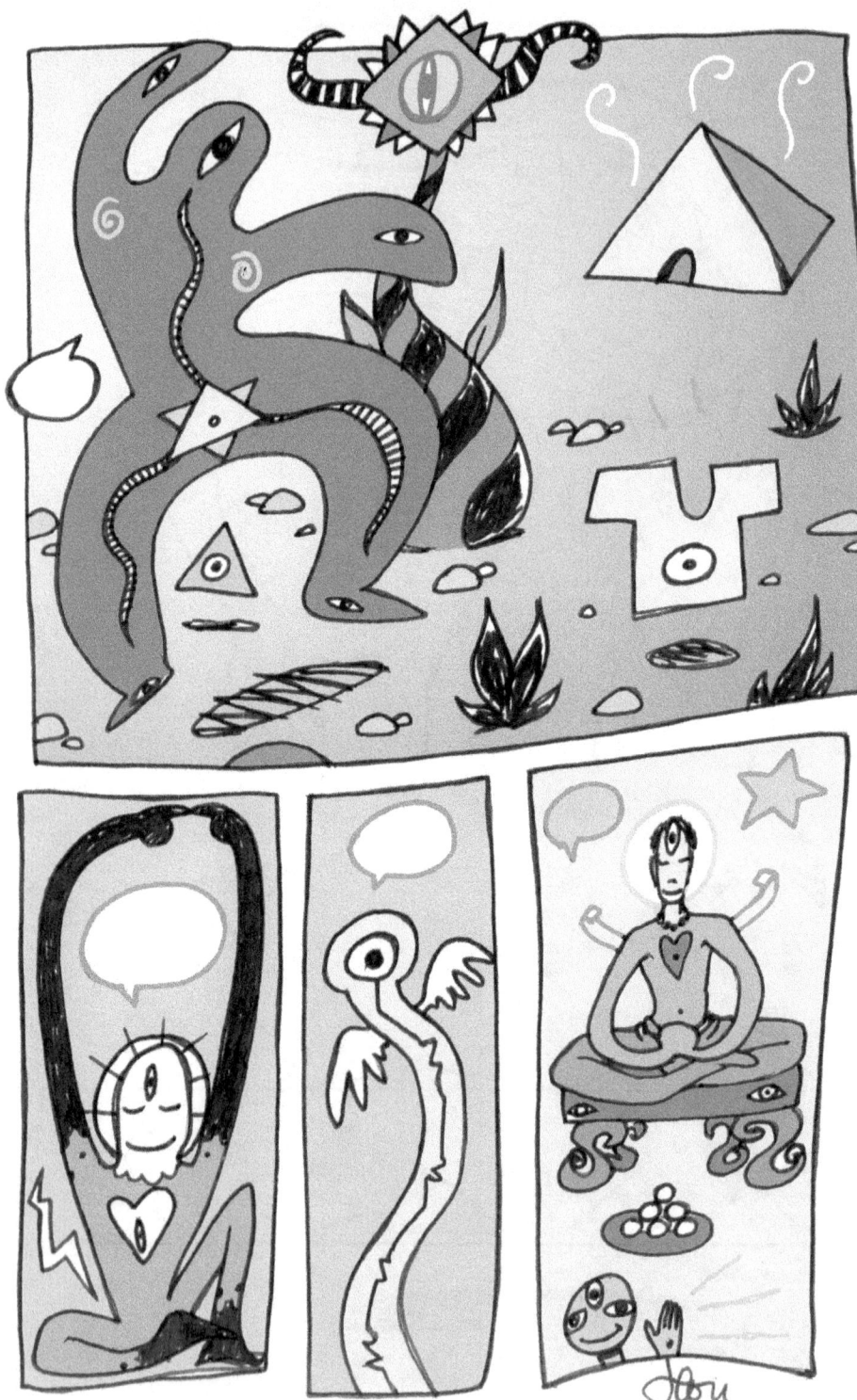

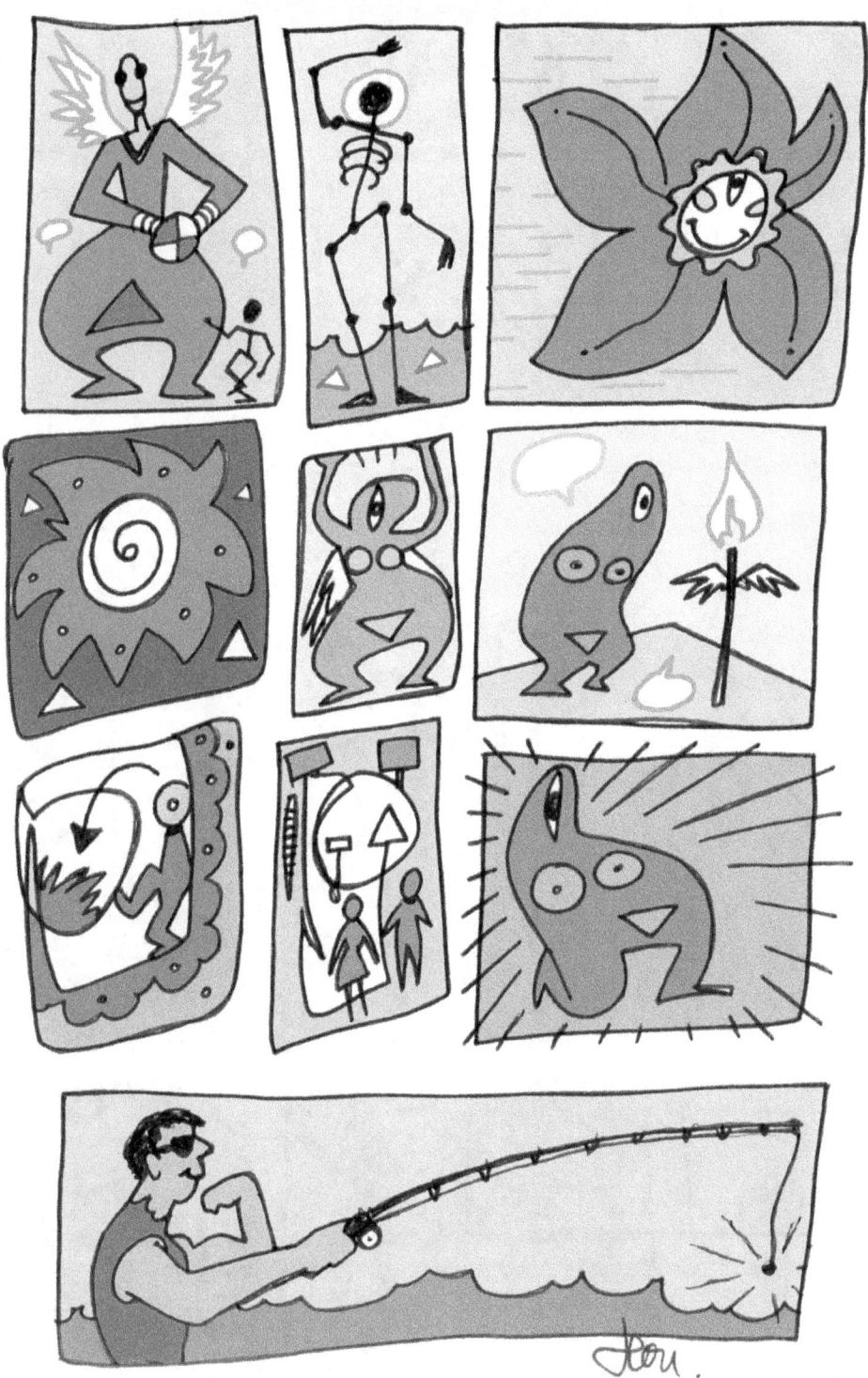

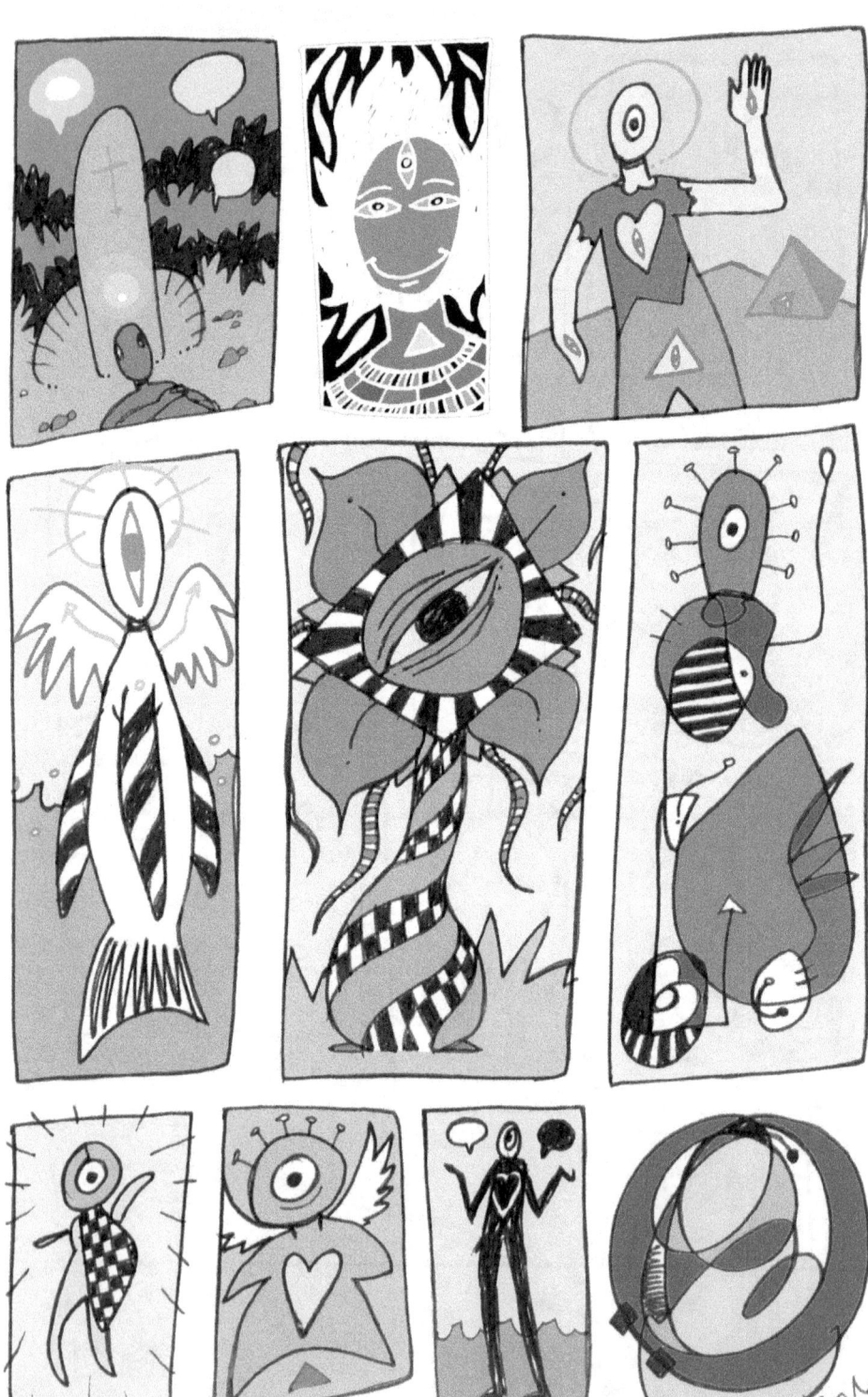

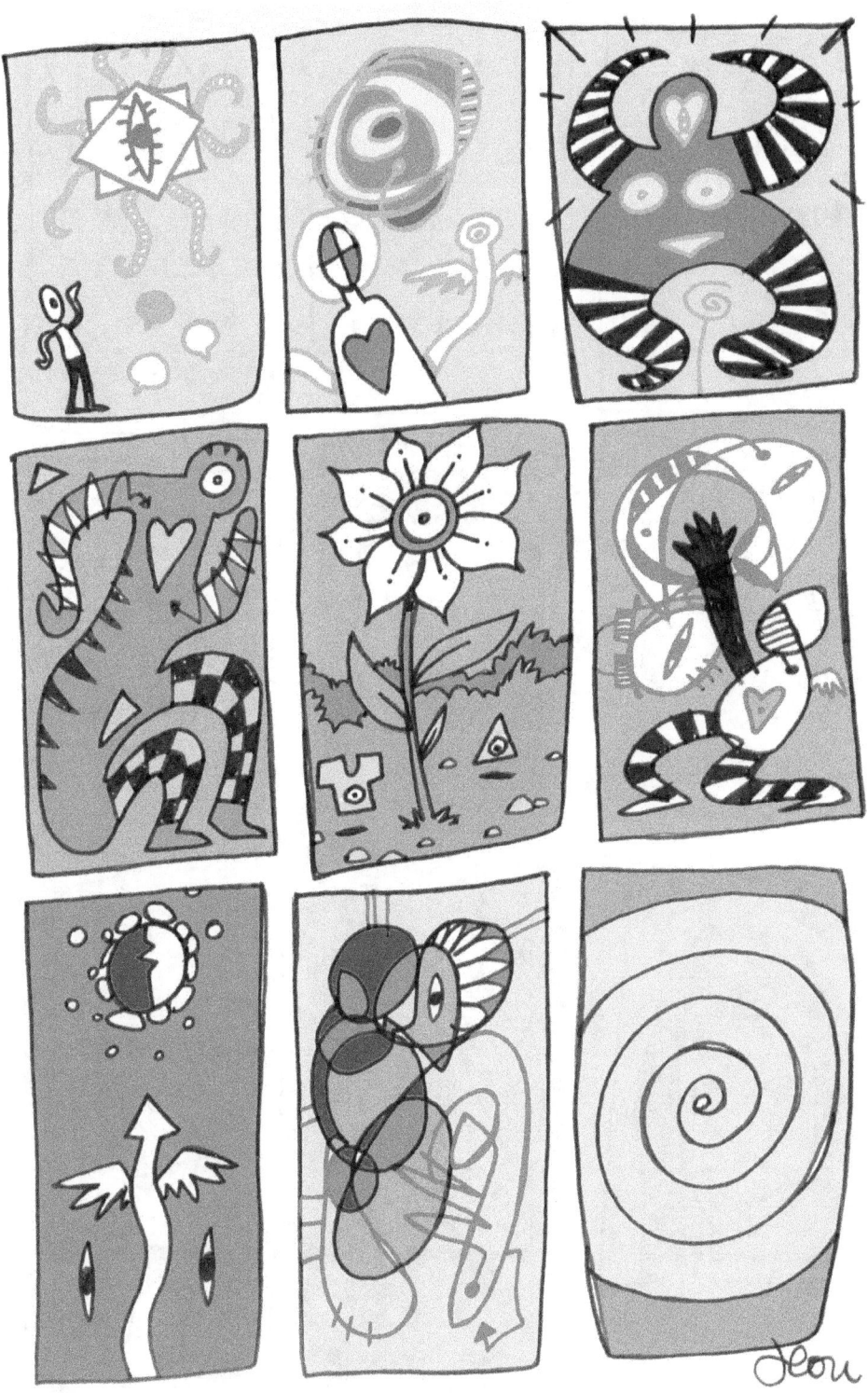

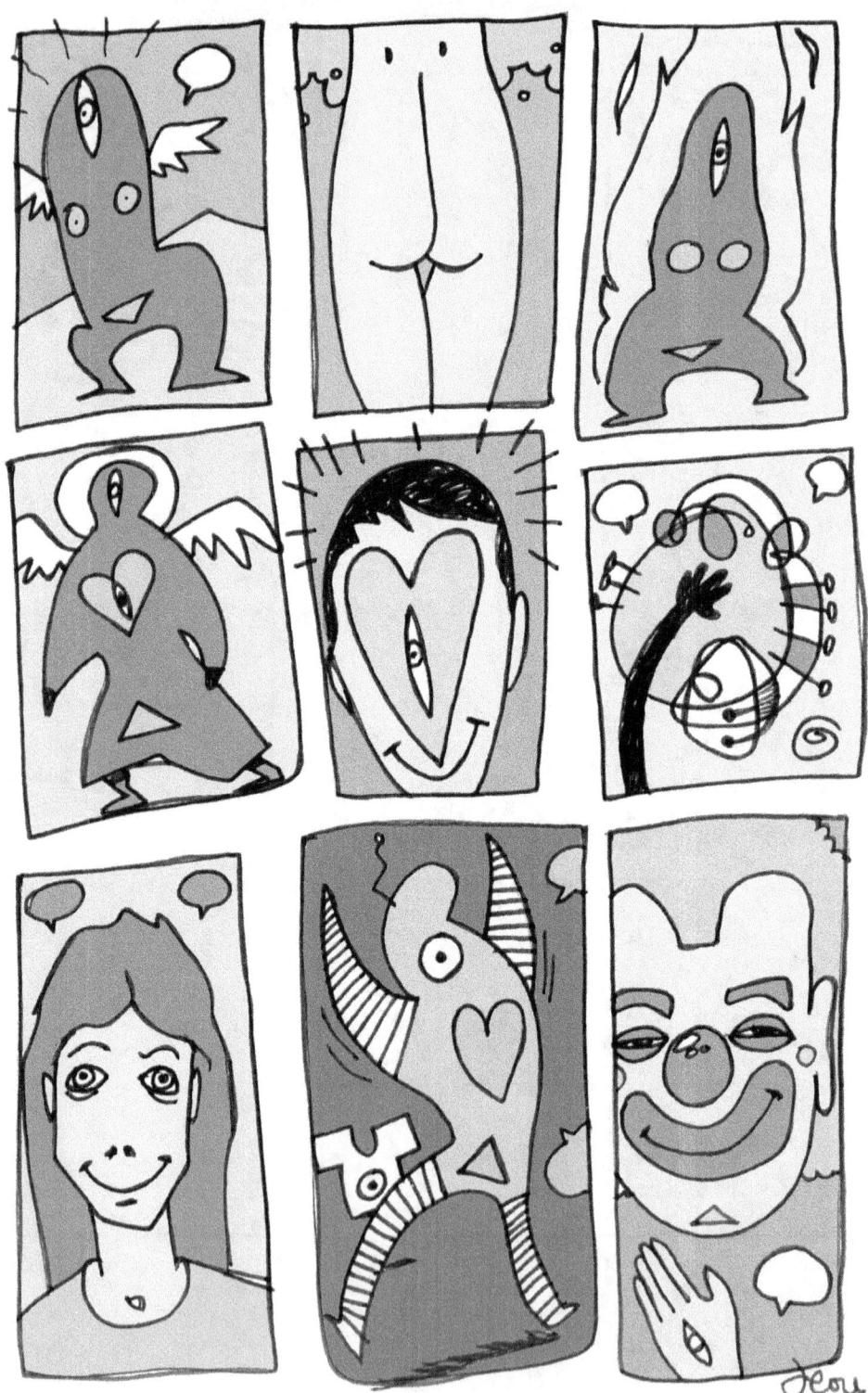

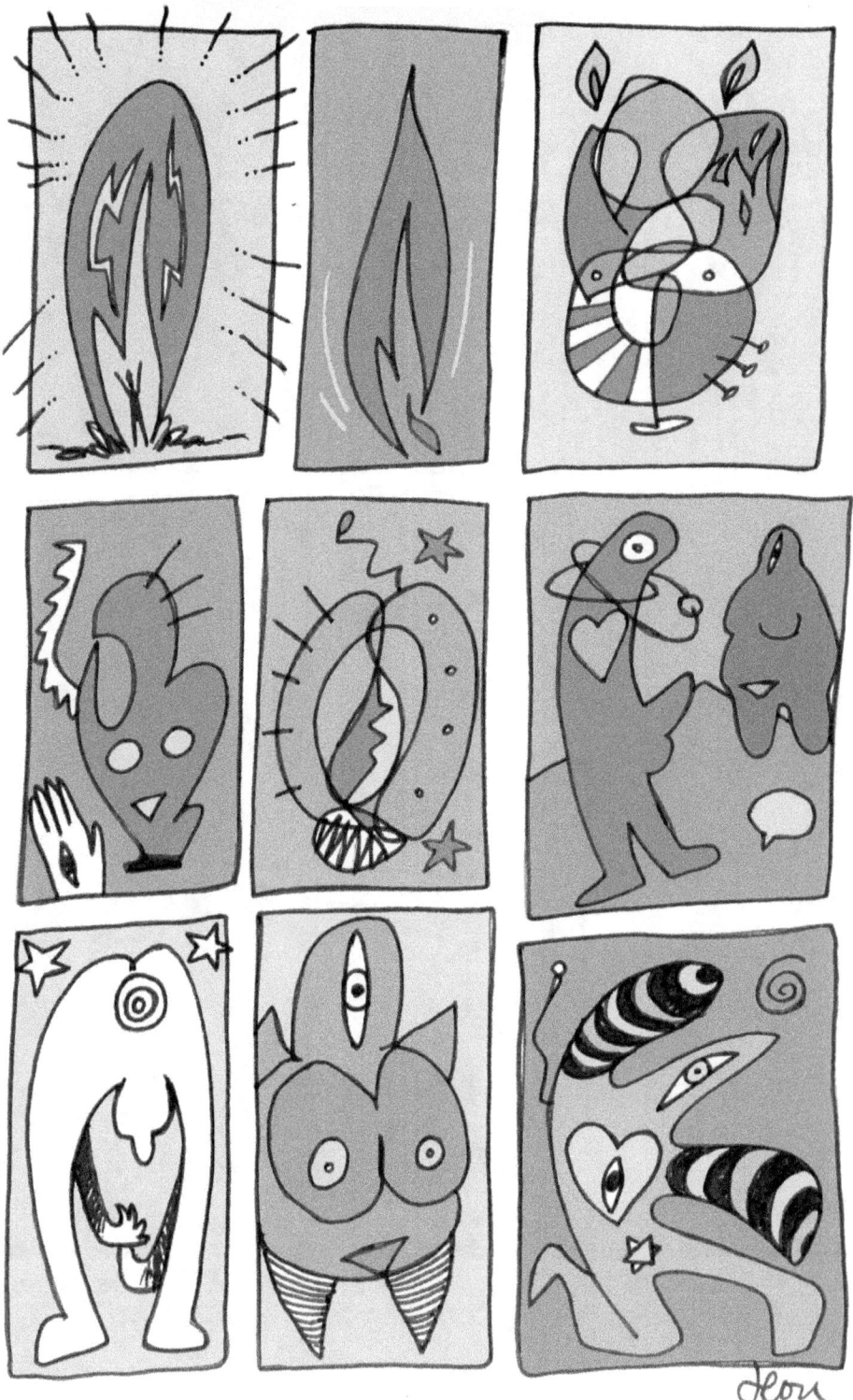

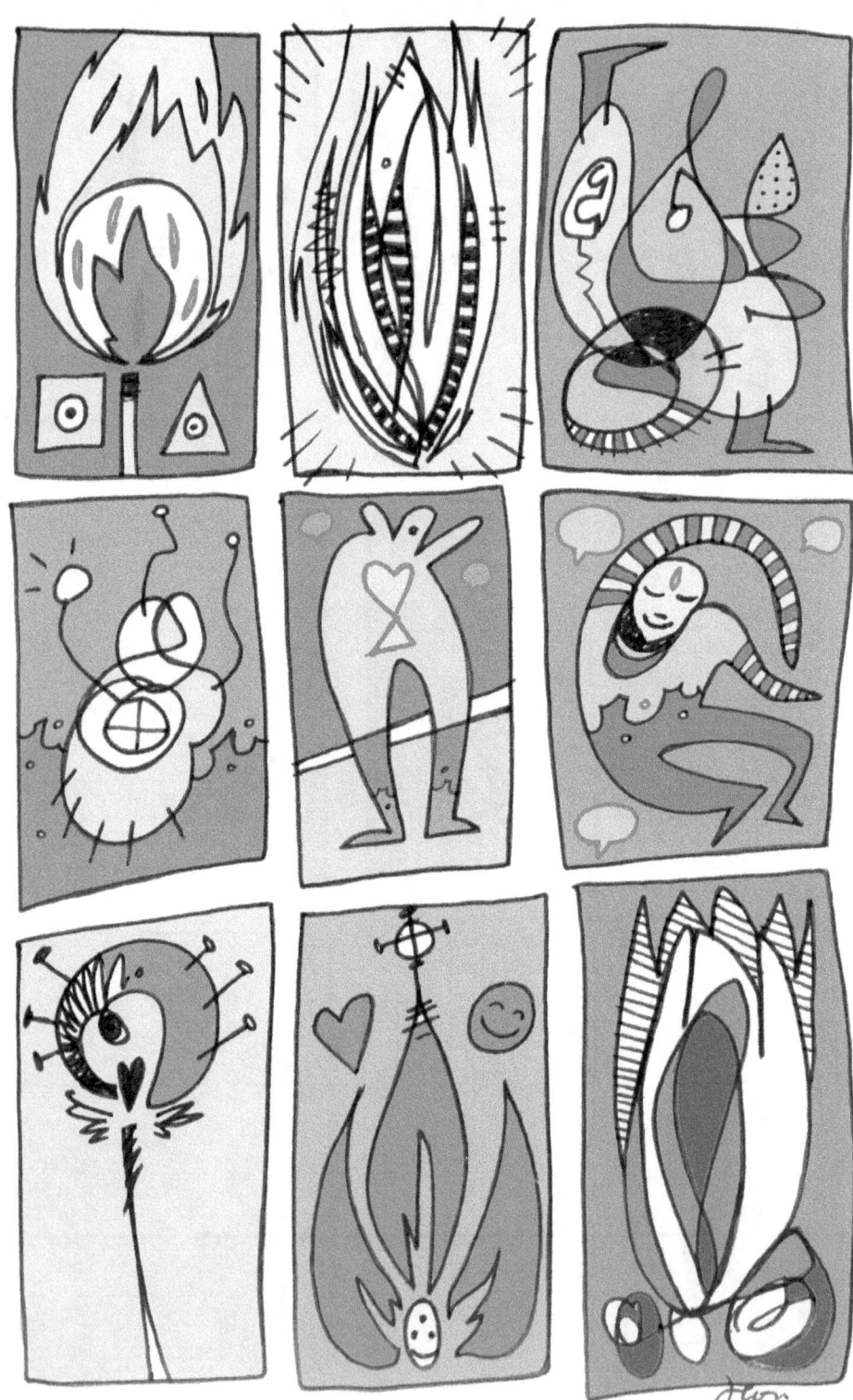

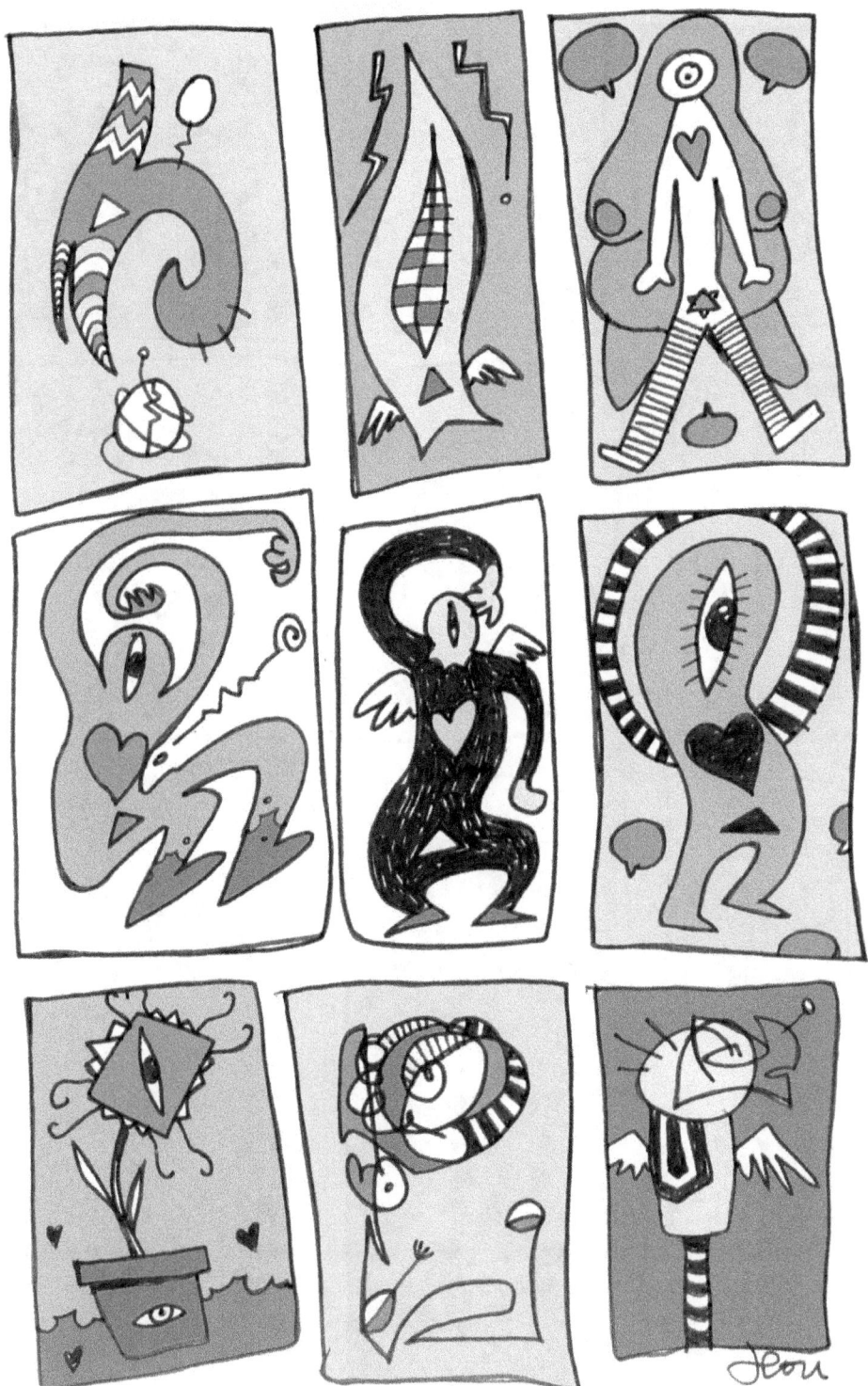

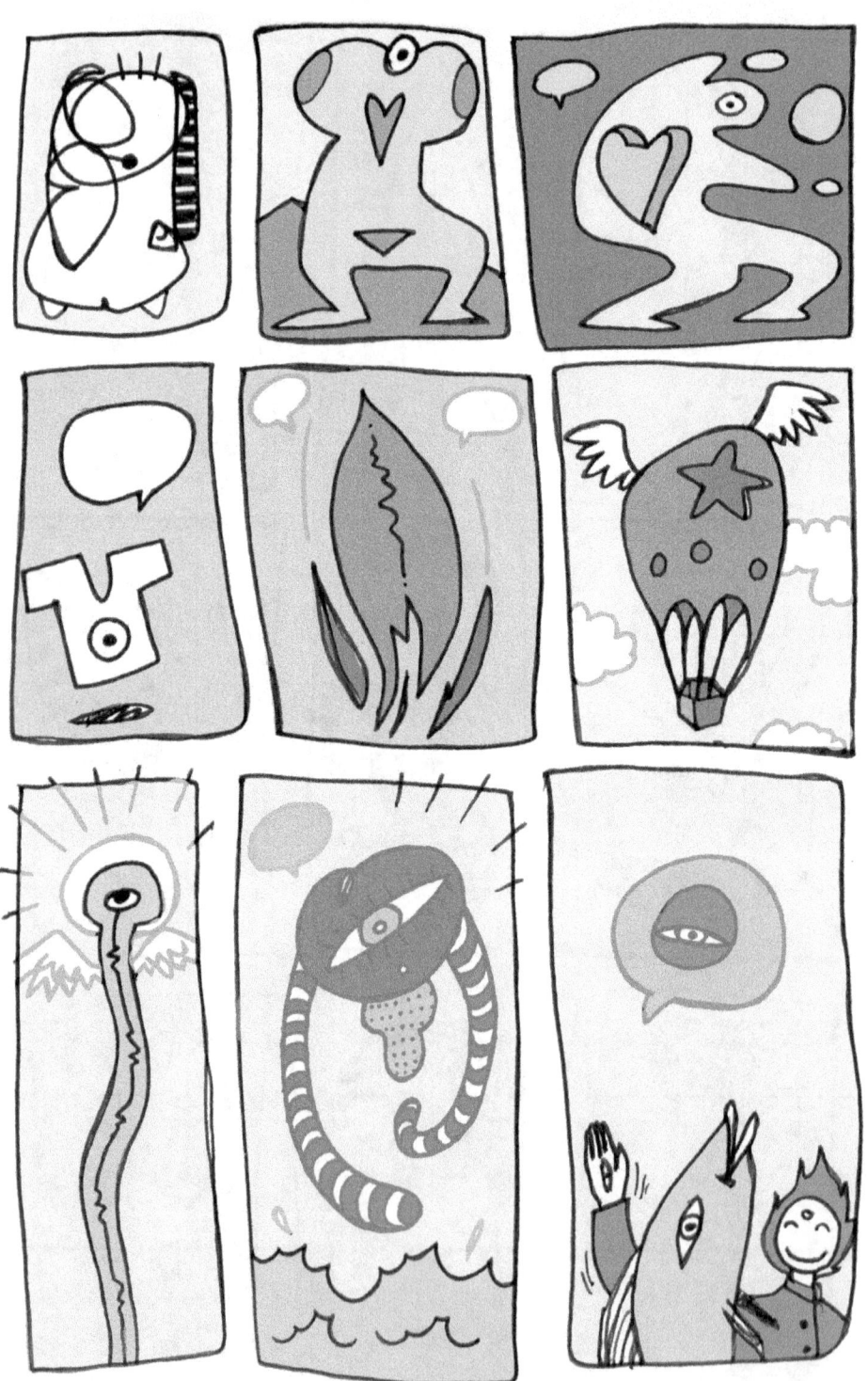

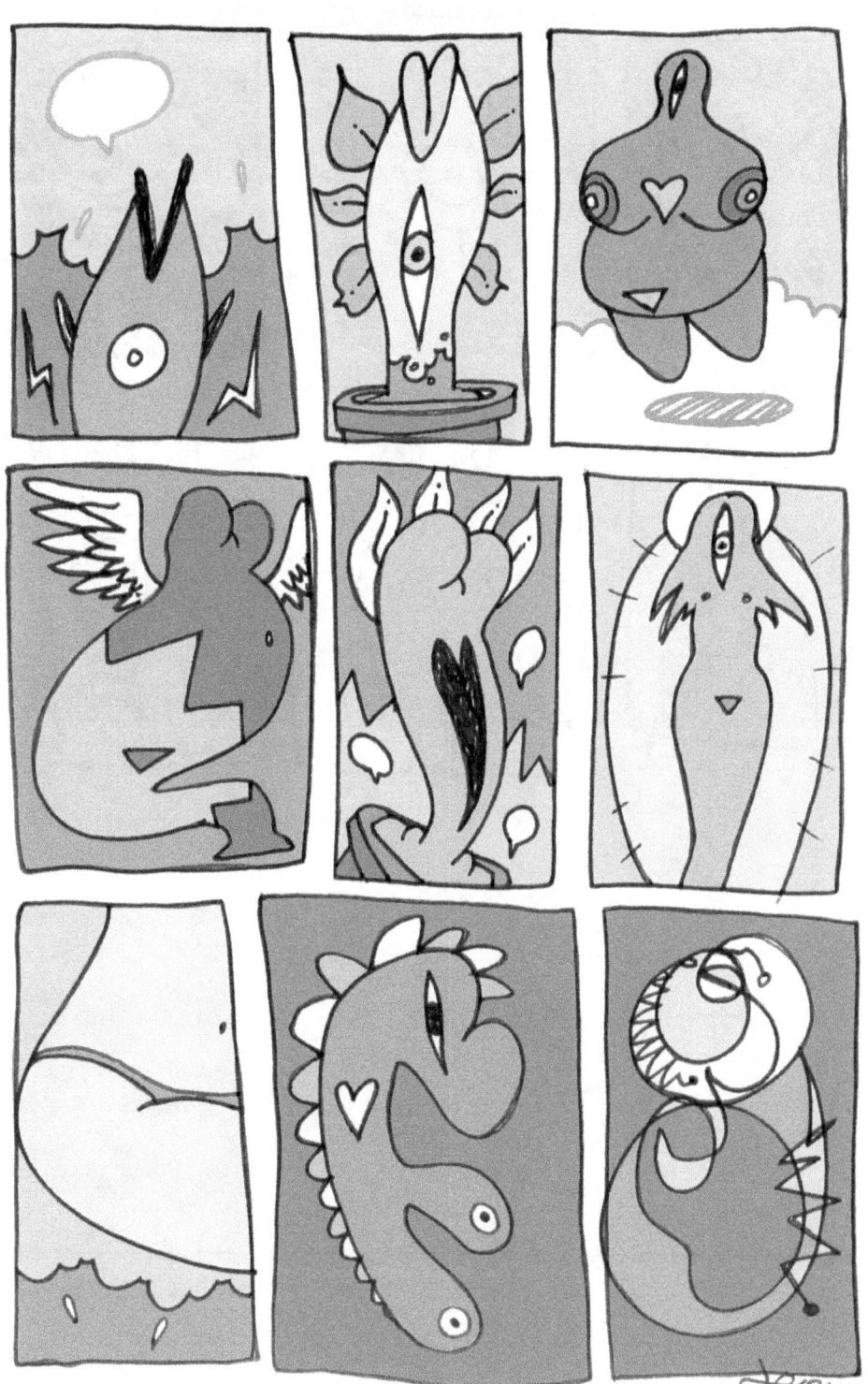

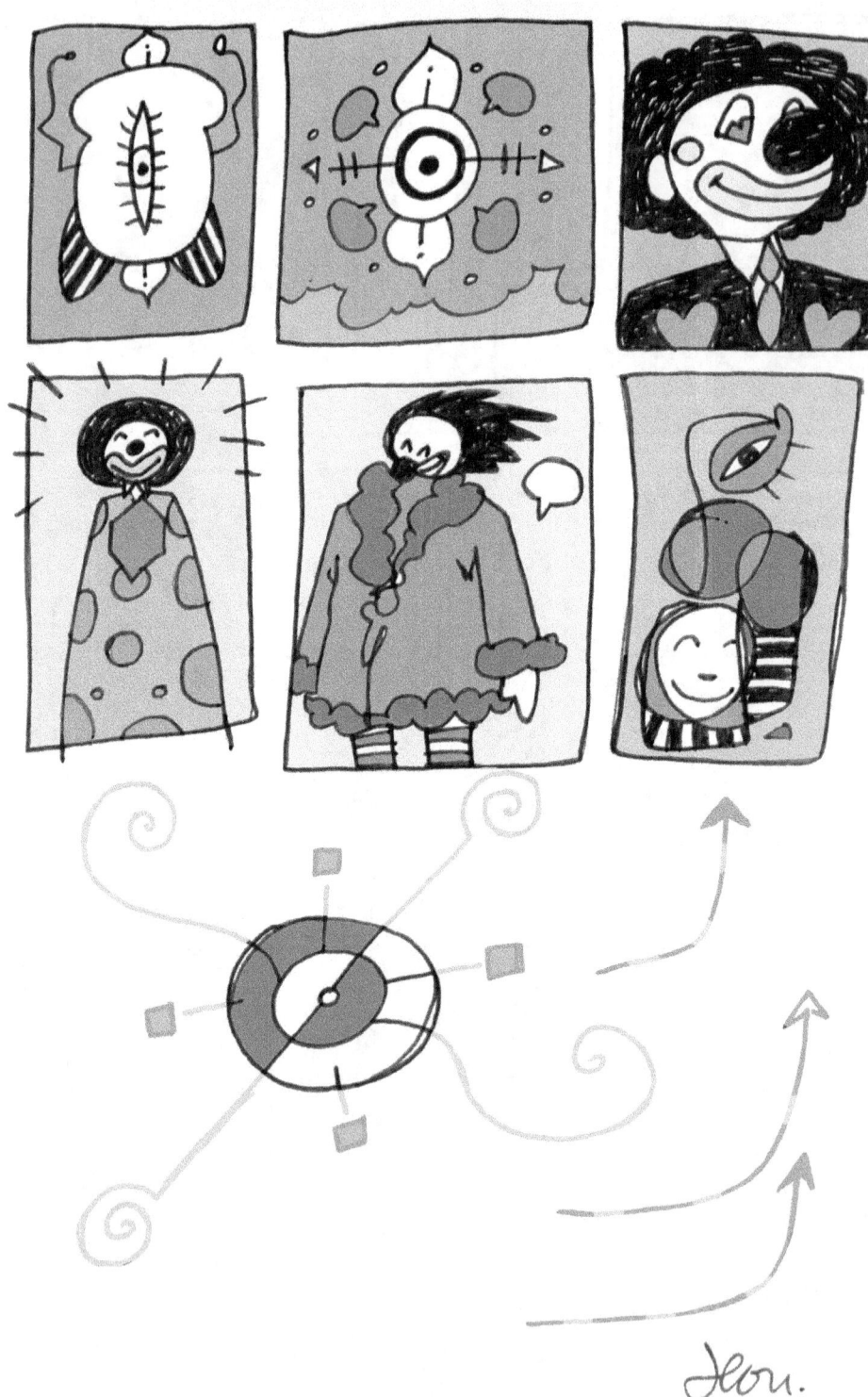

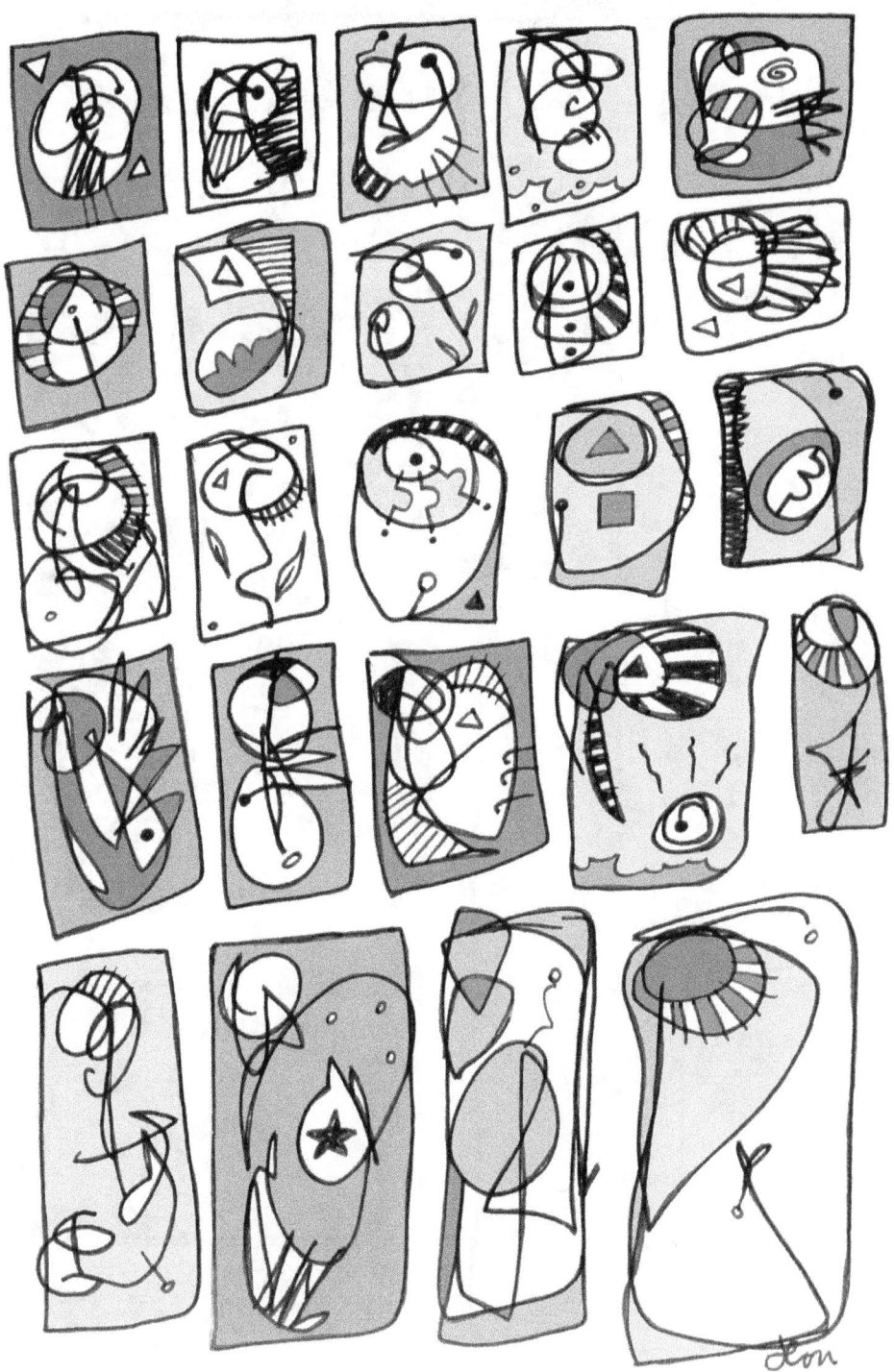

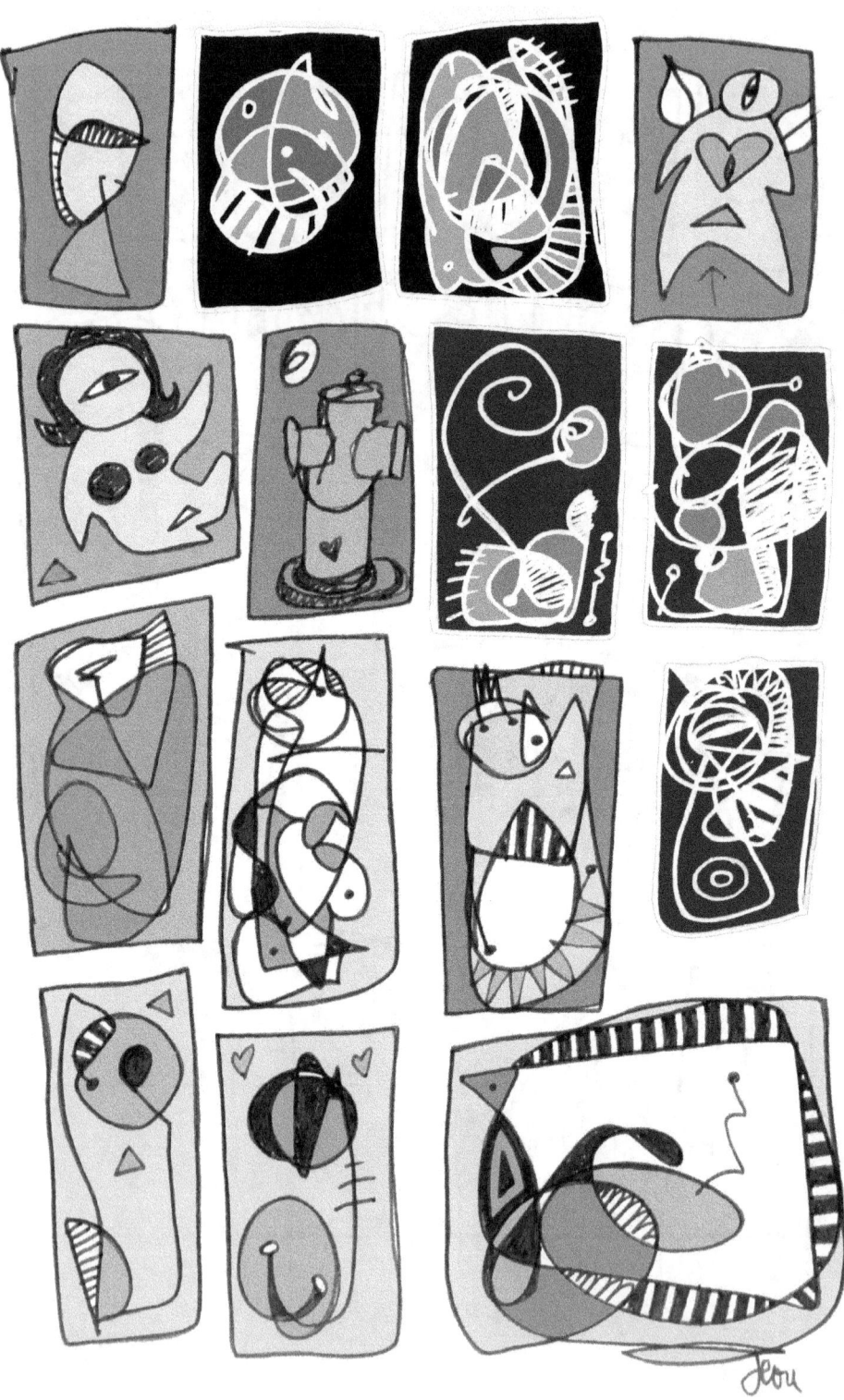

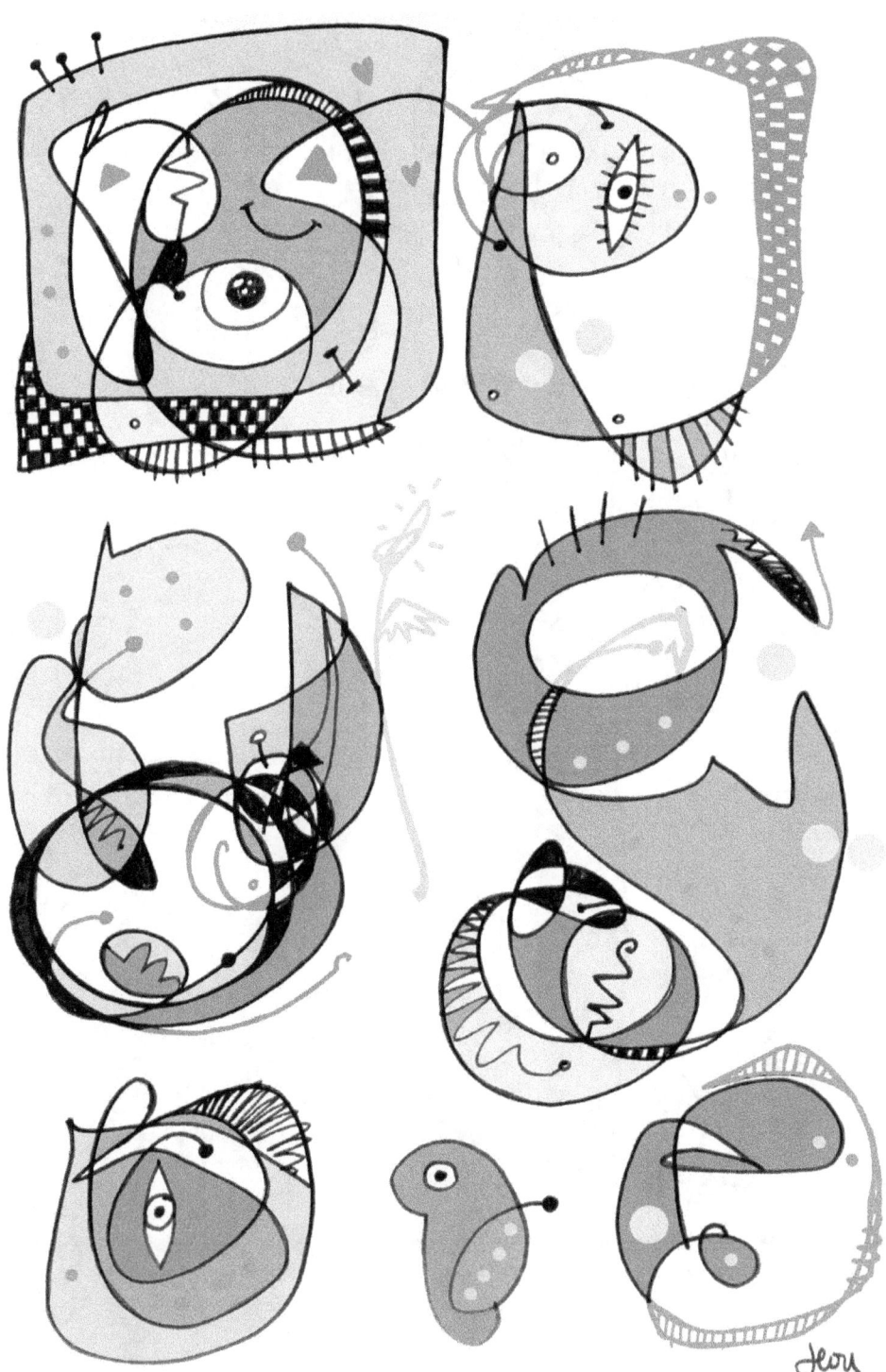

125

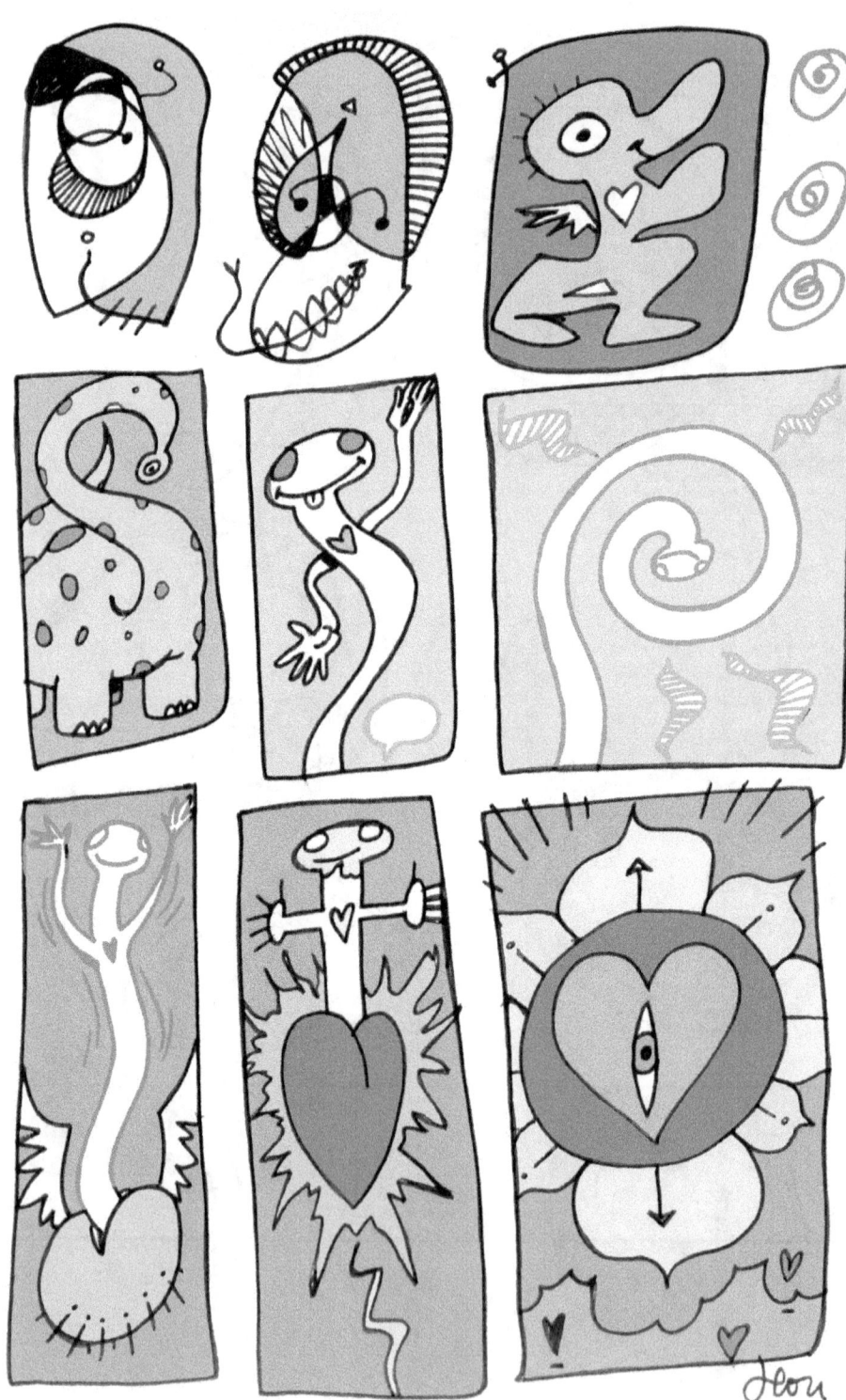

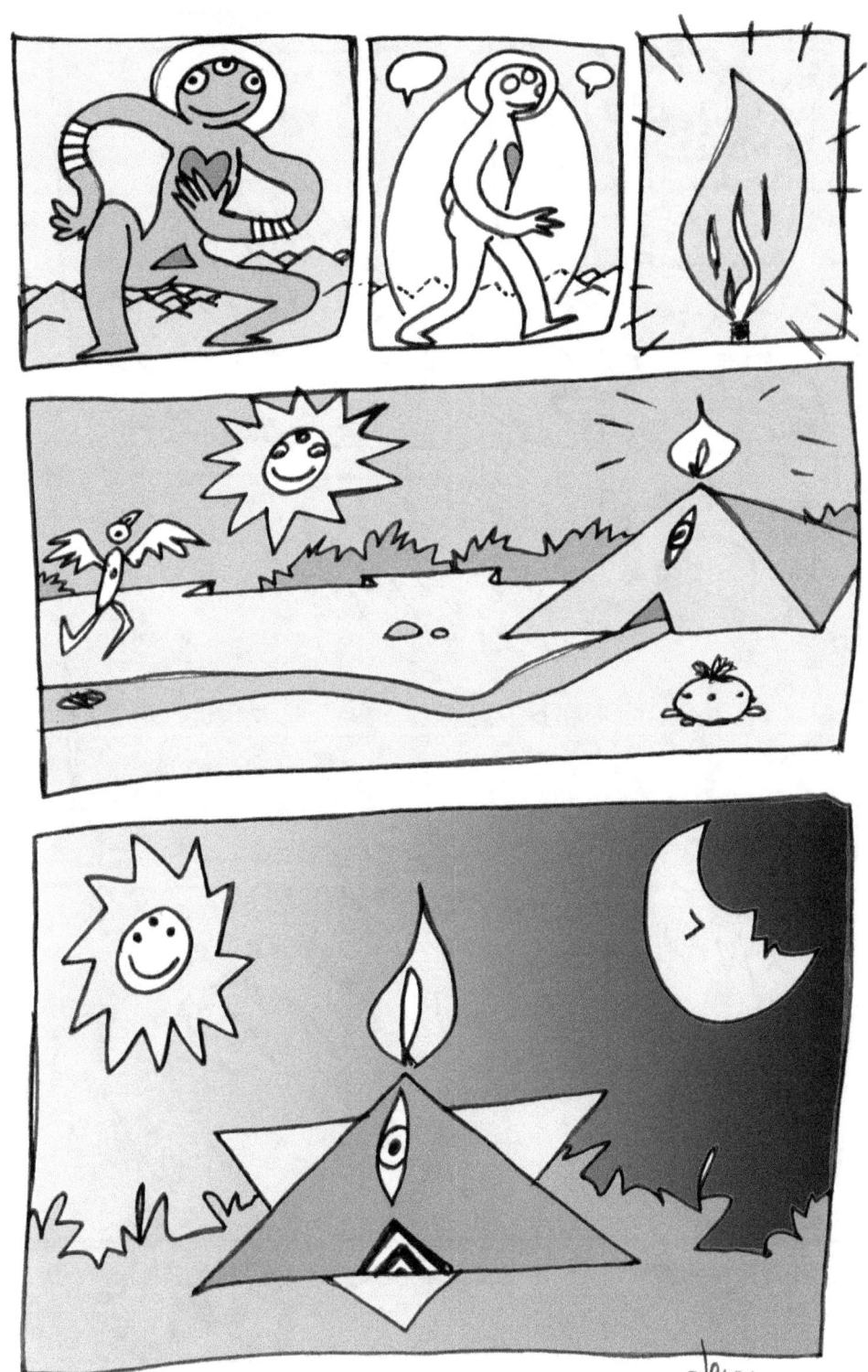

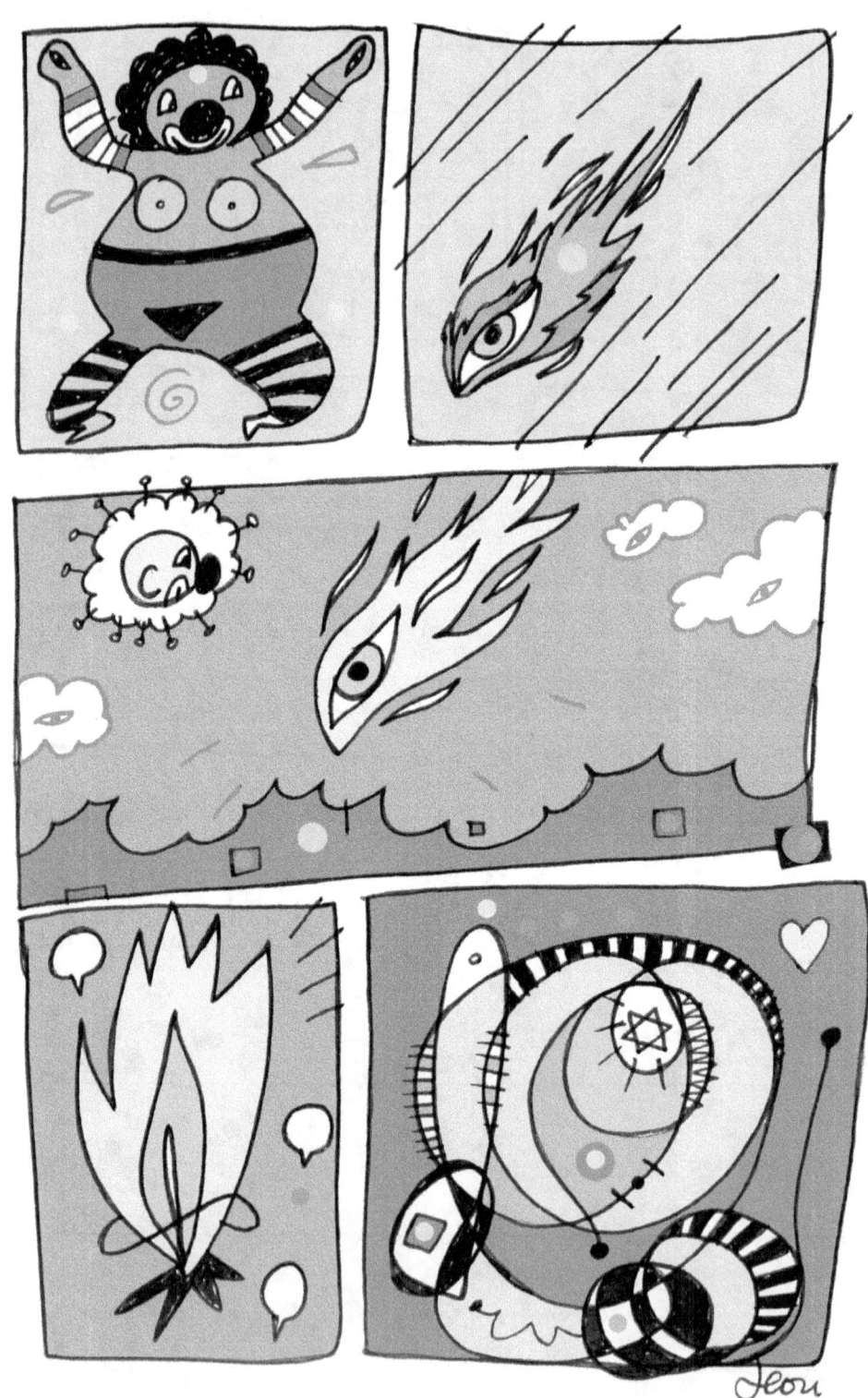

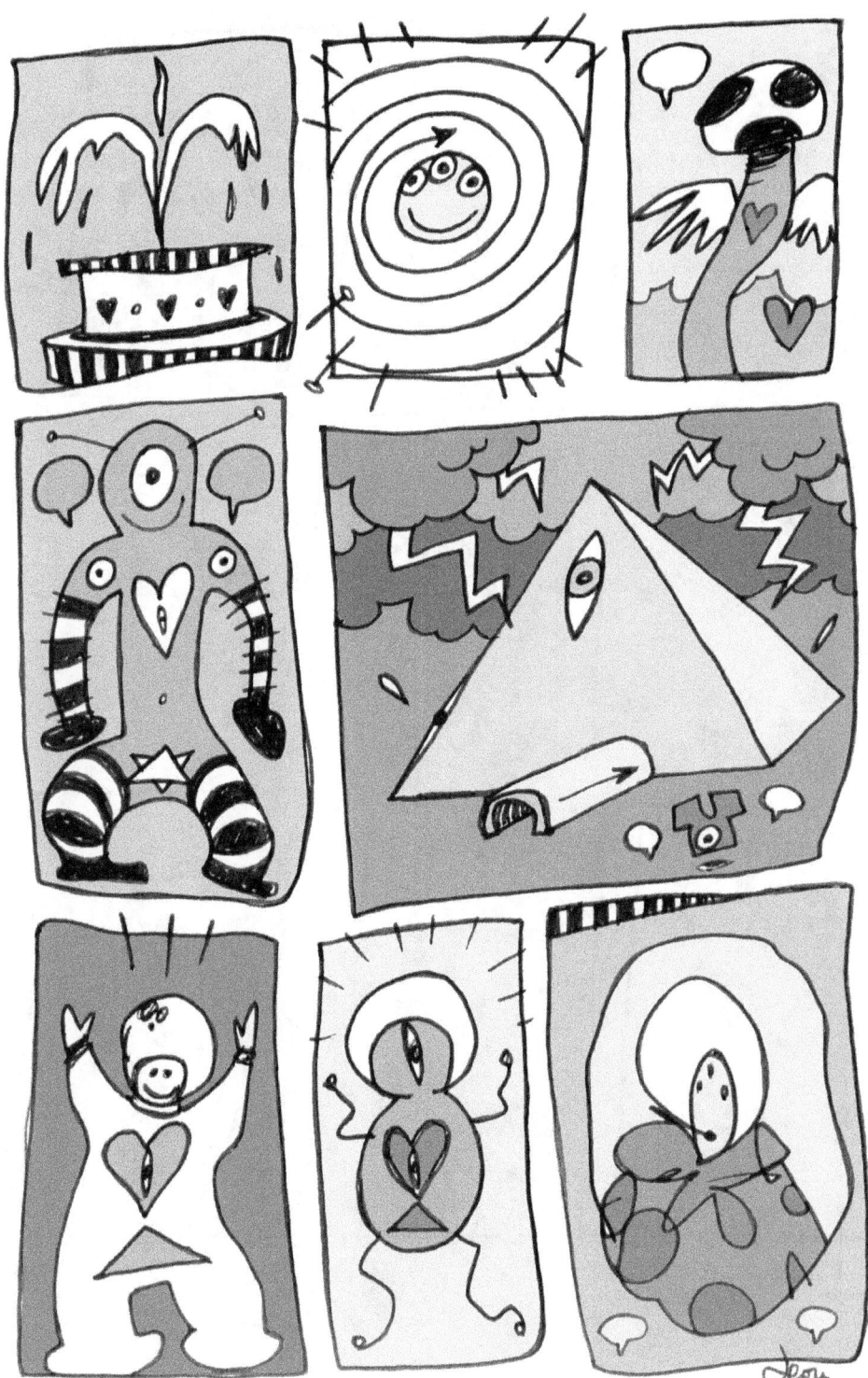

129

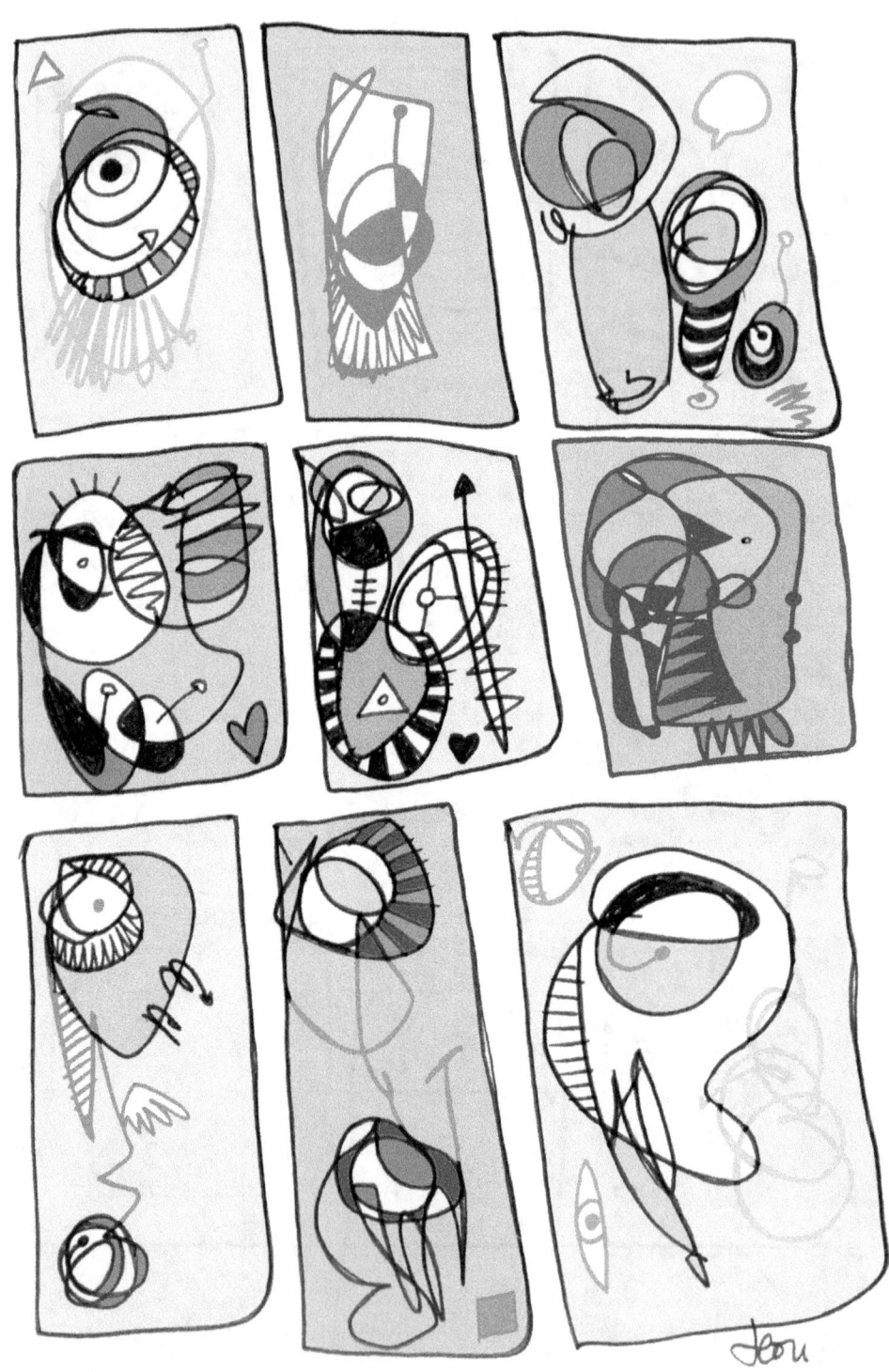

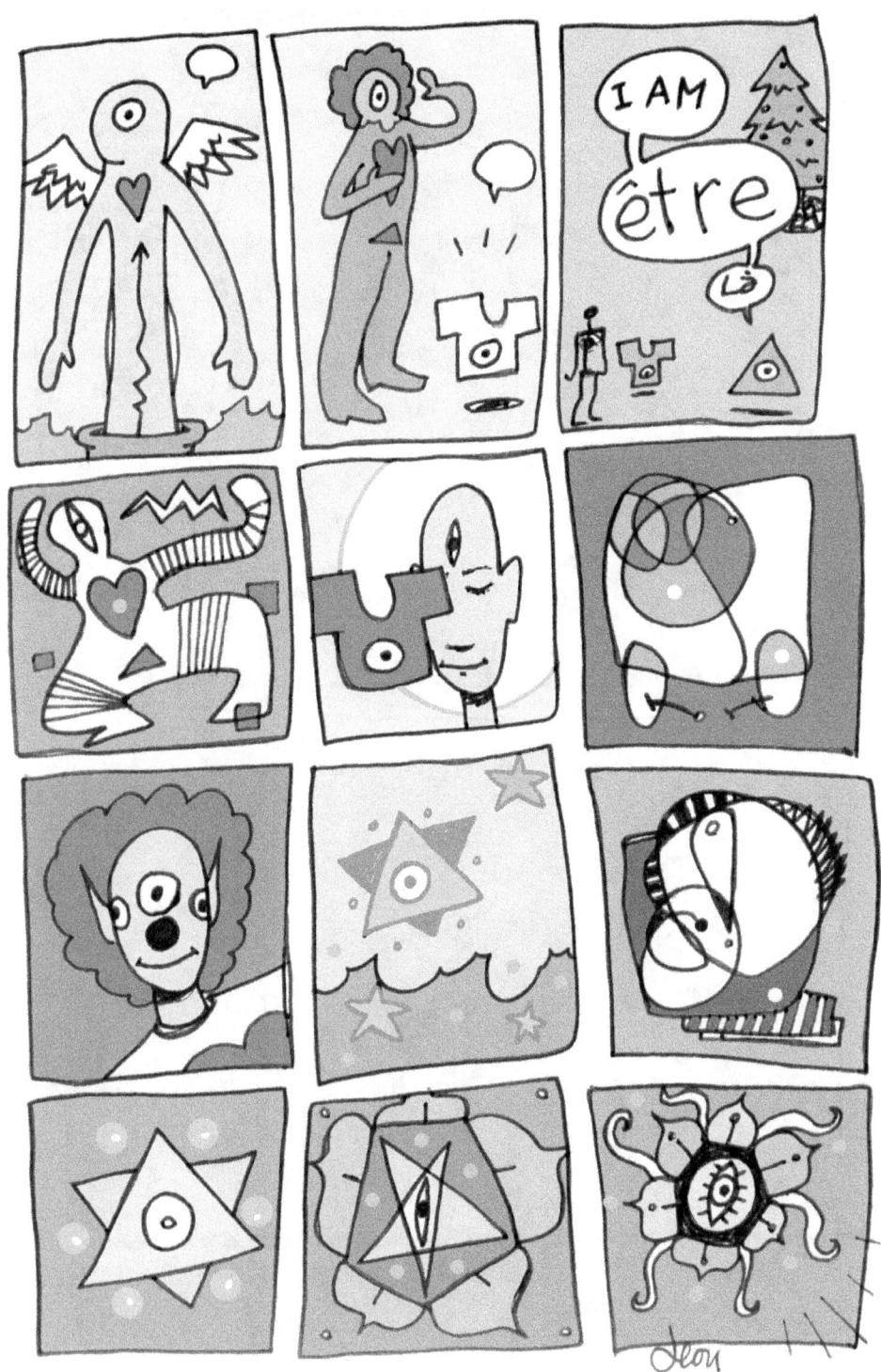

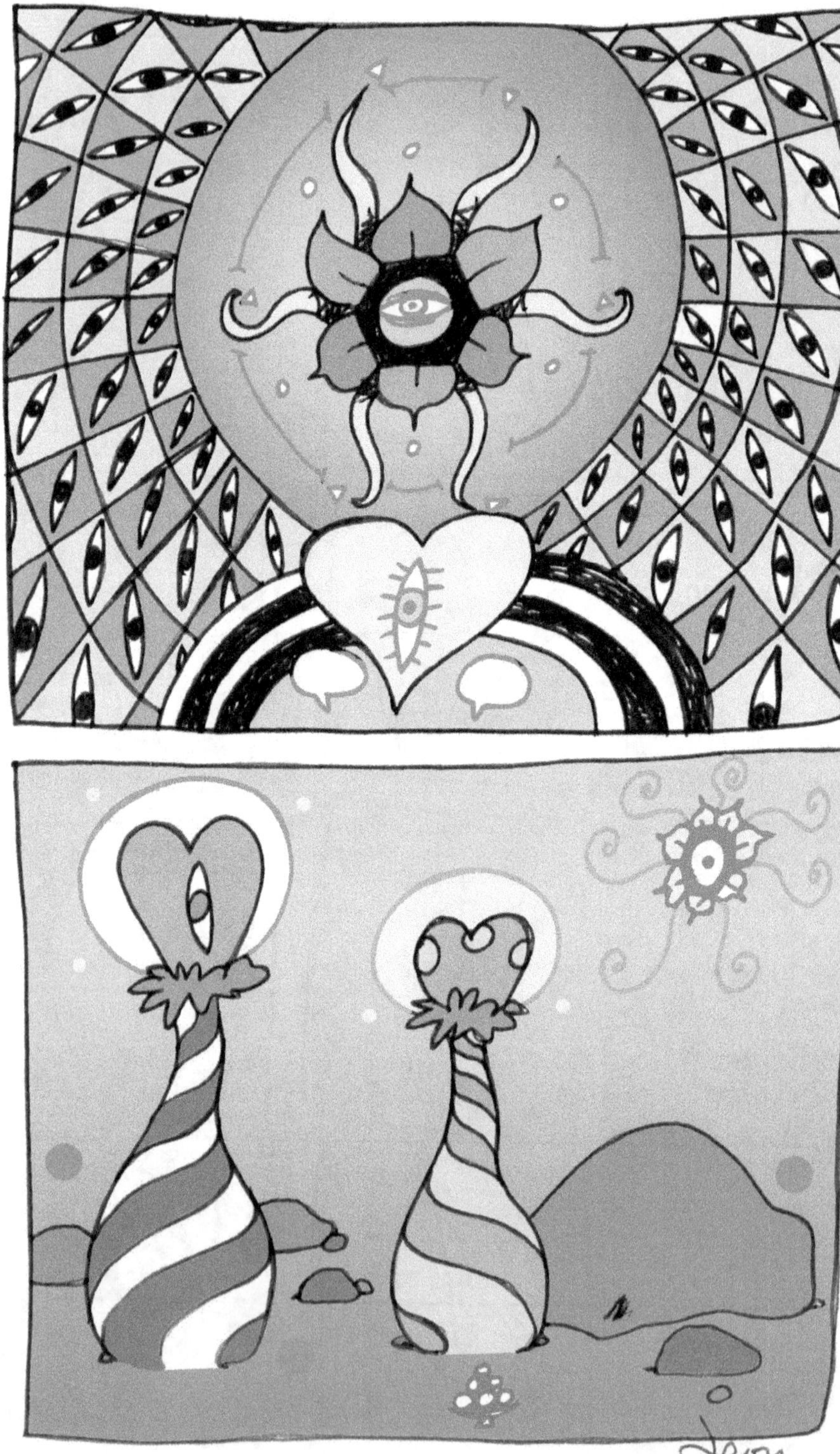

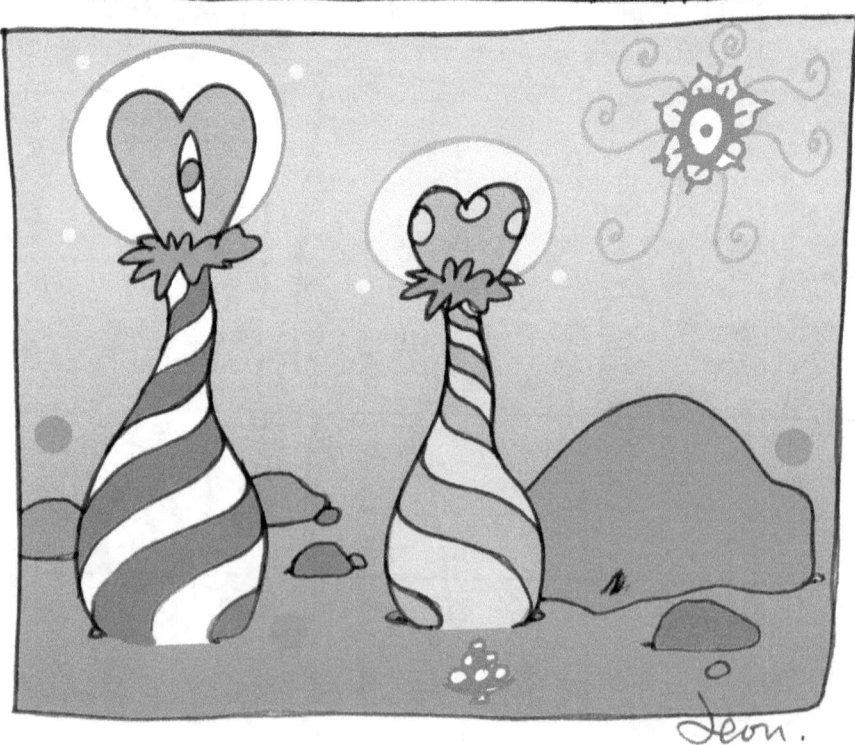

Leon.

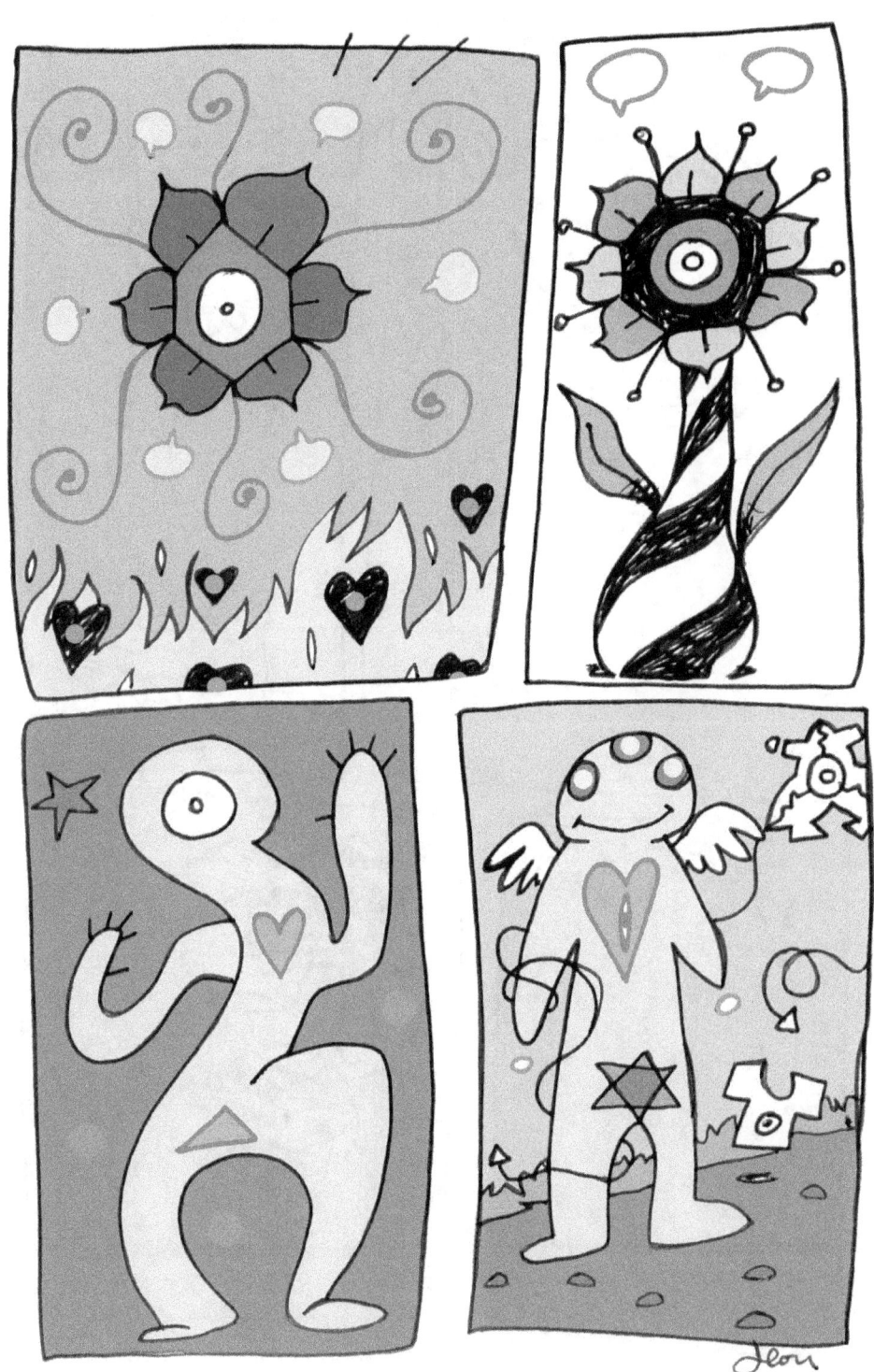

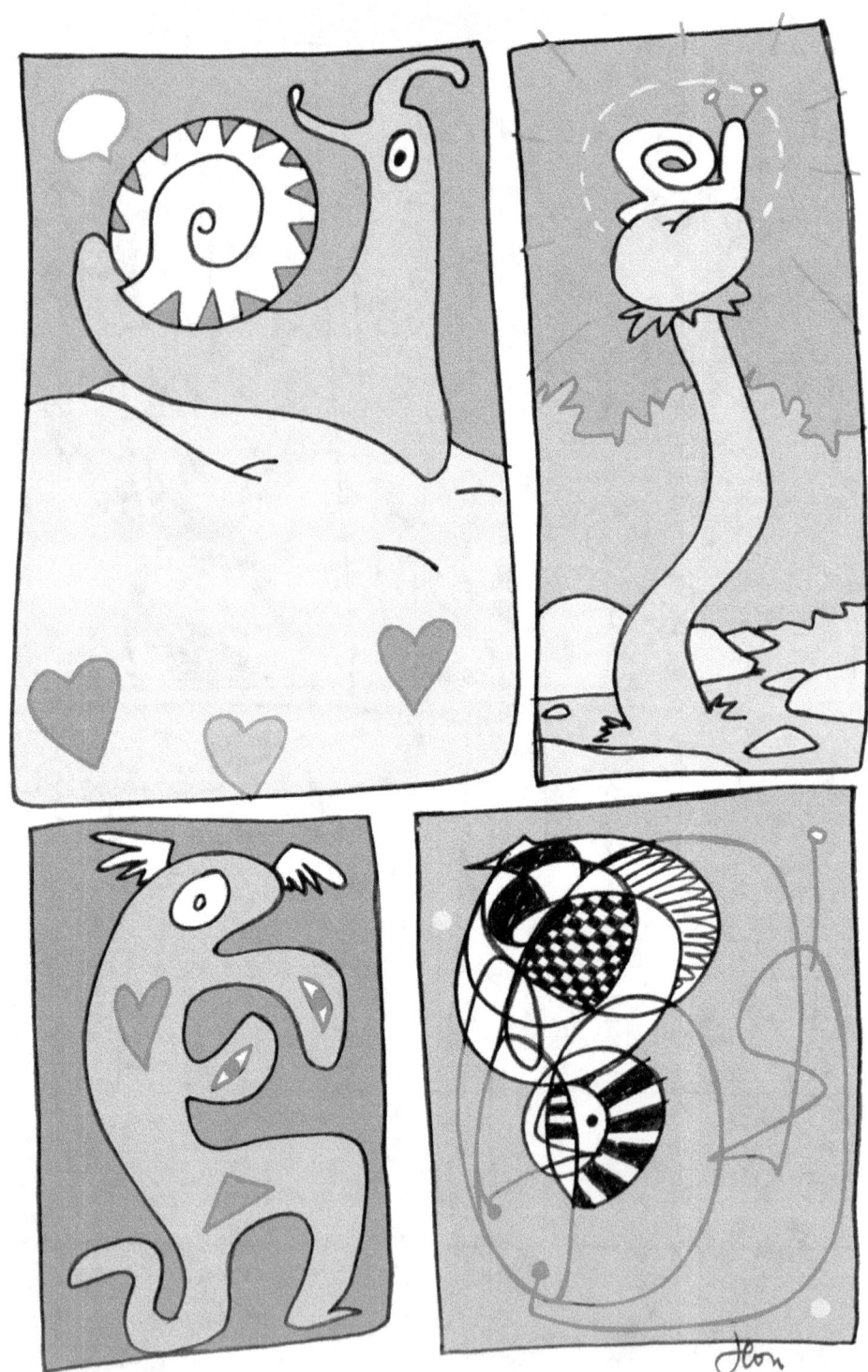

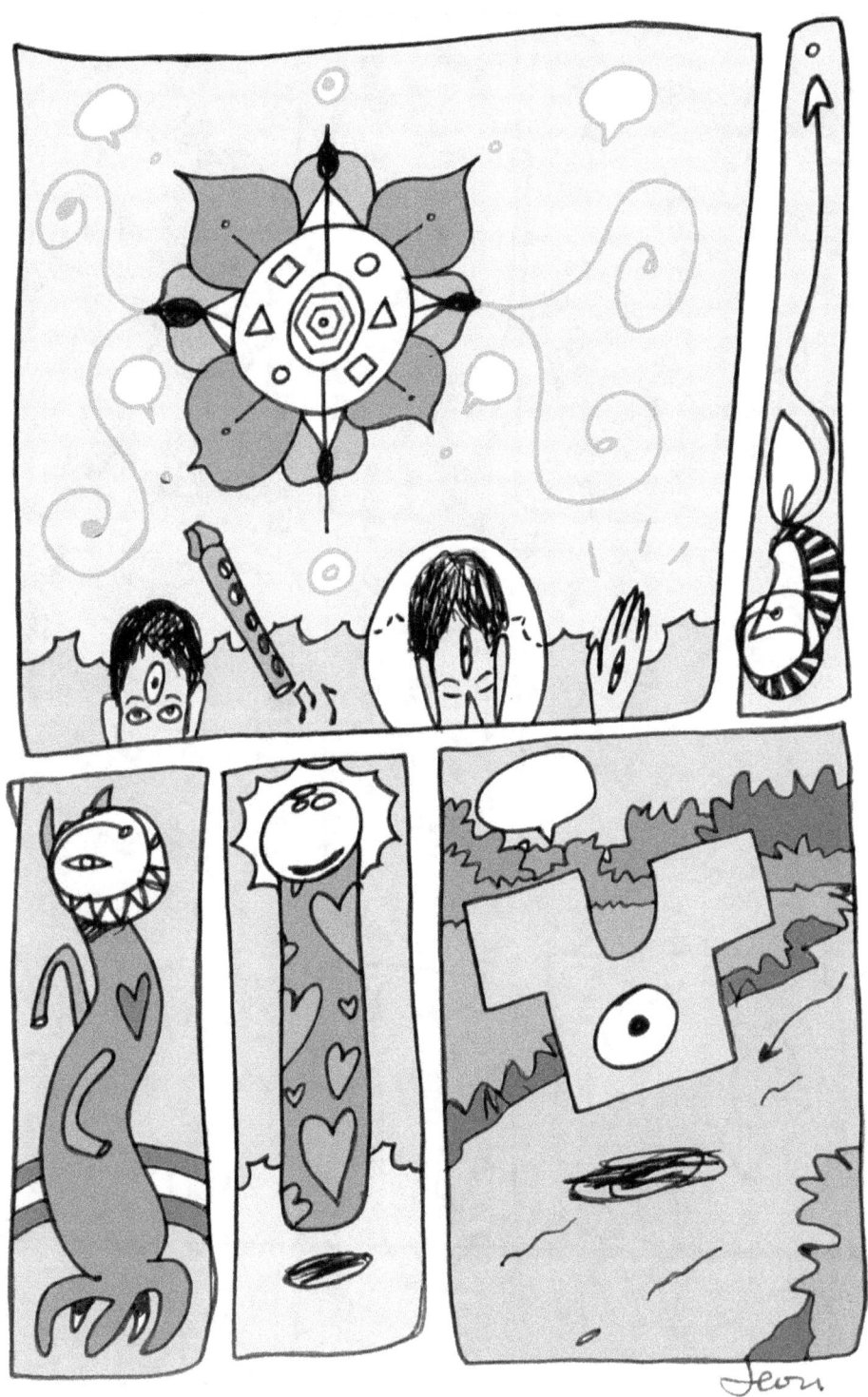

135

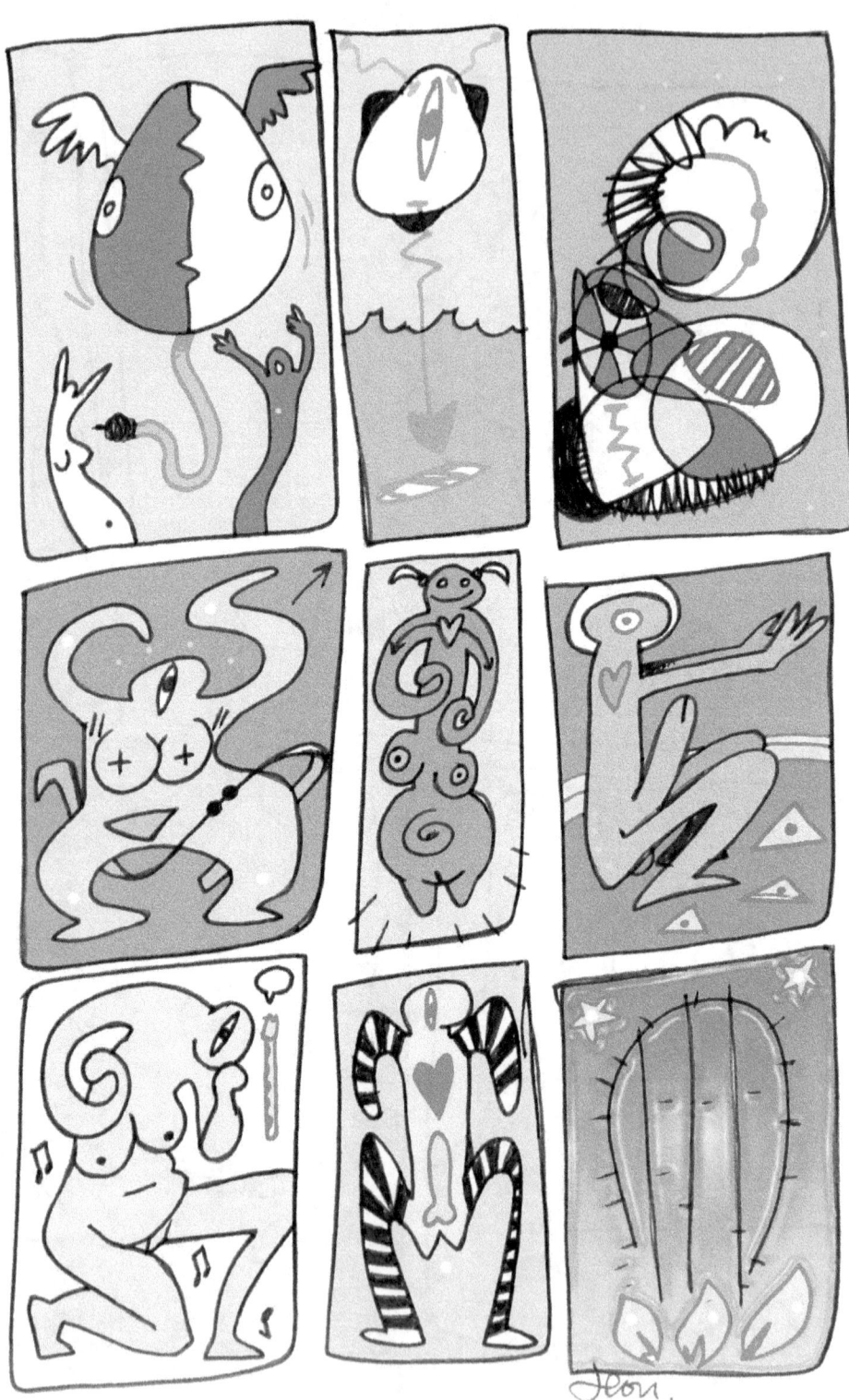

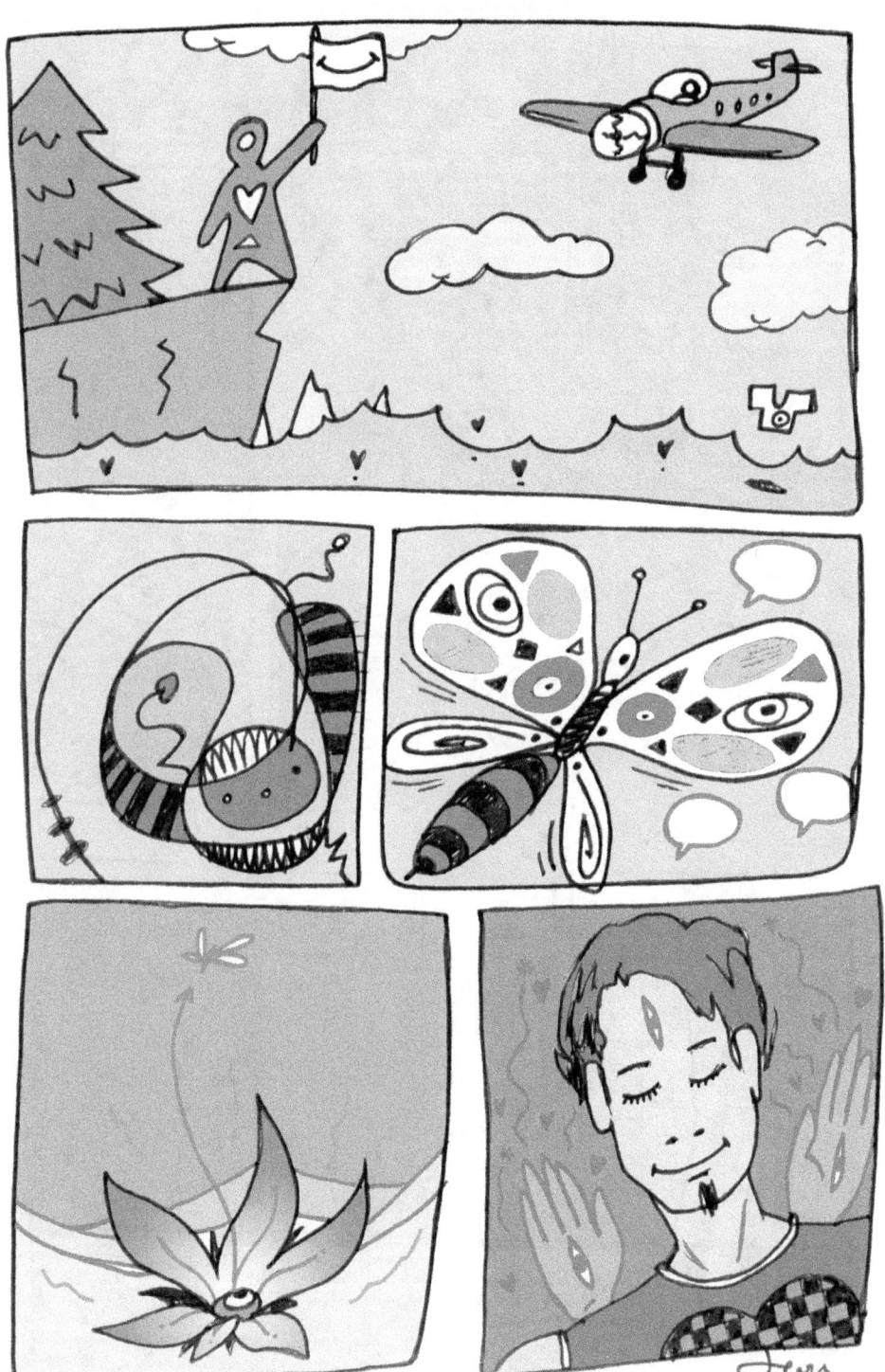

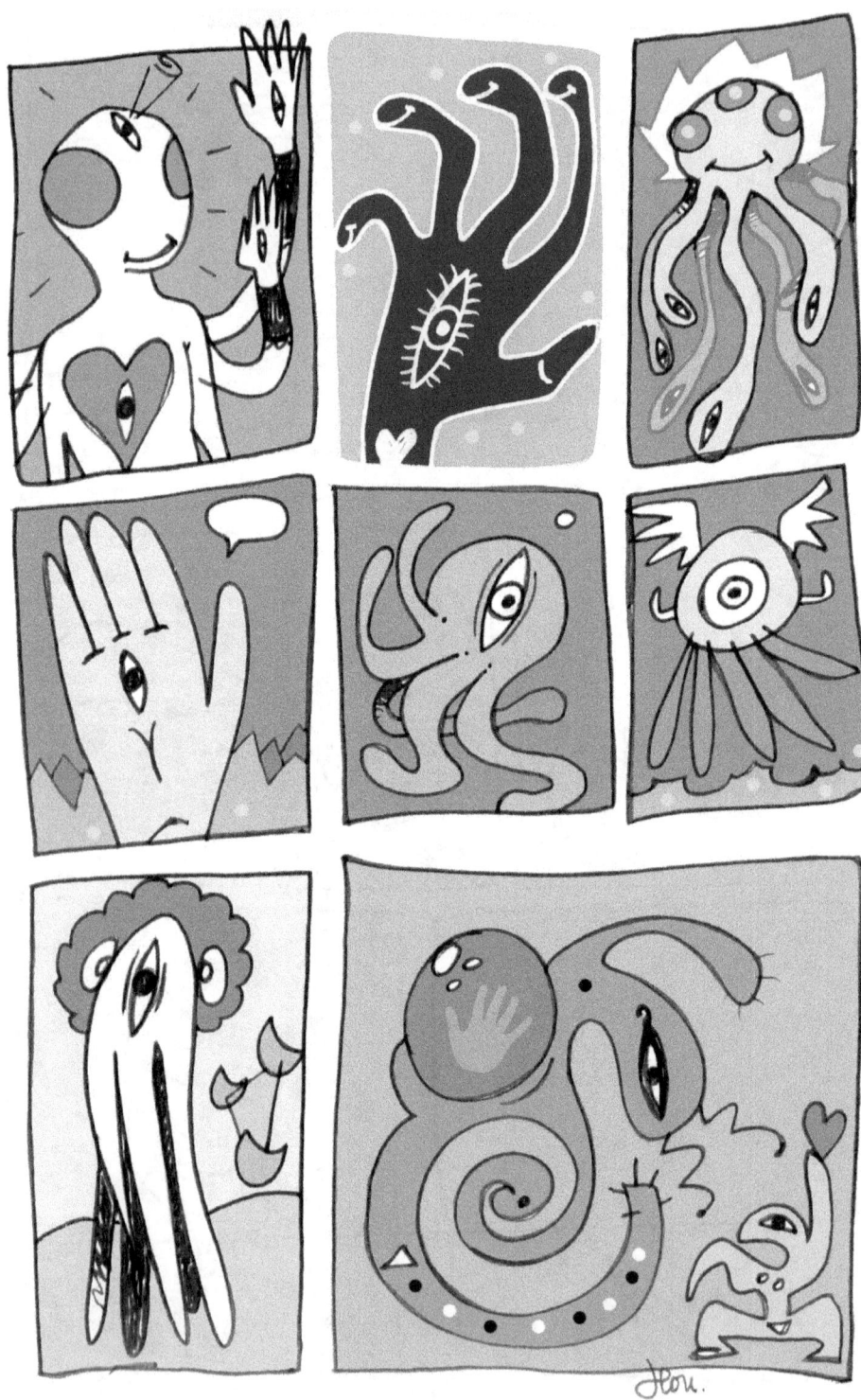

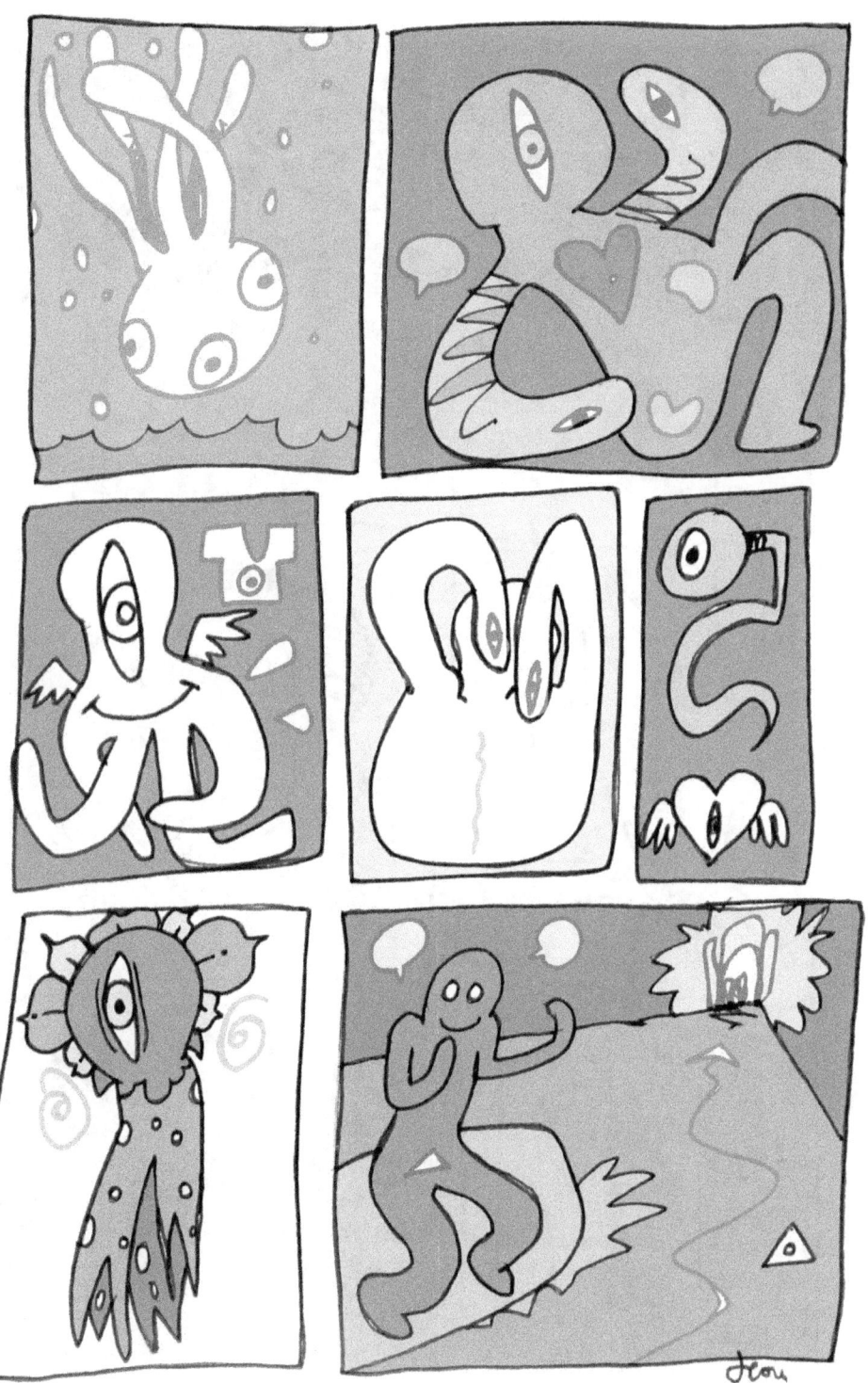

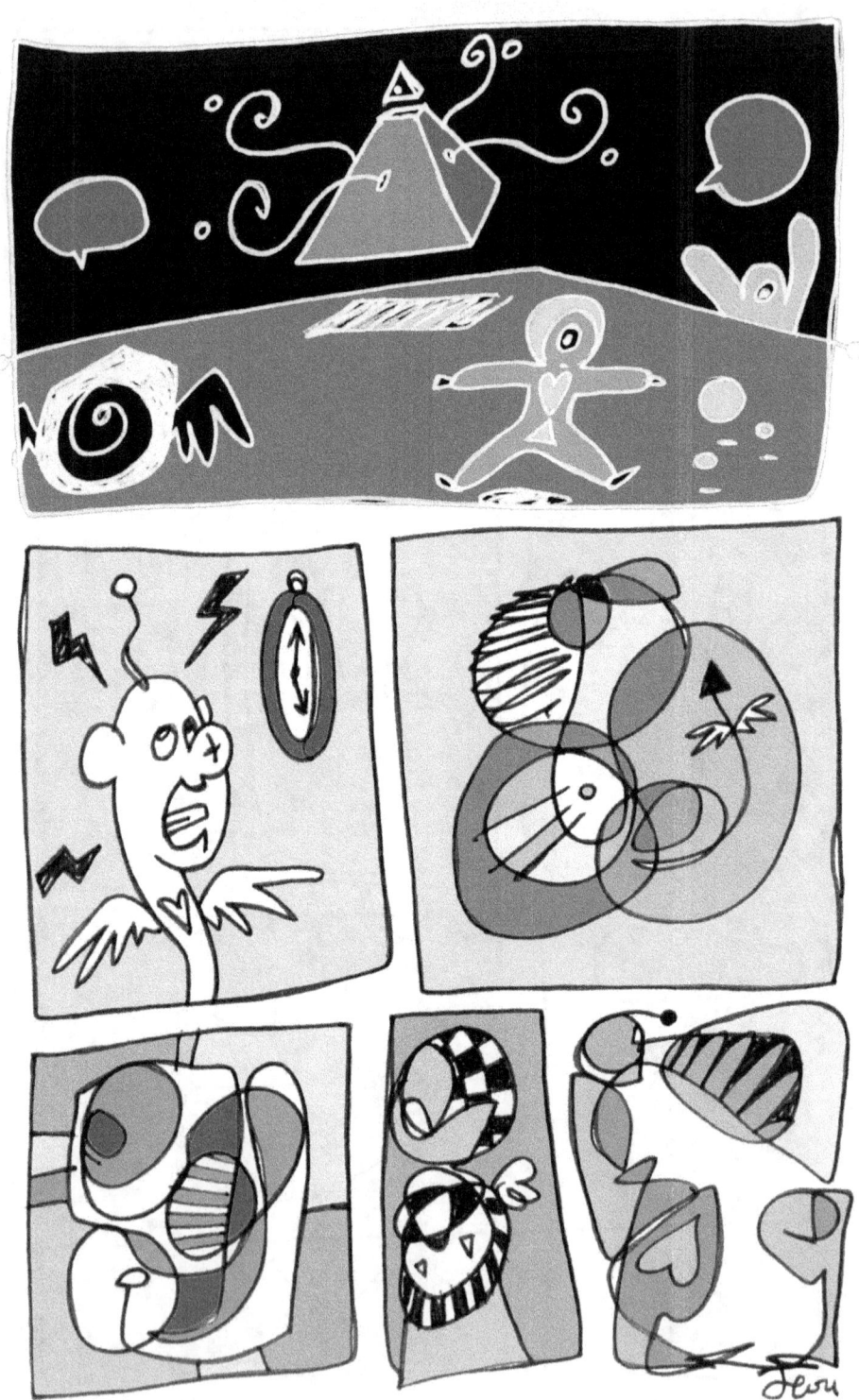

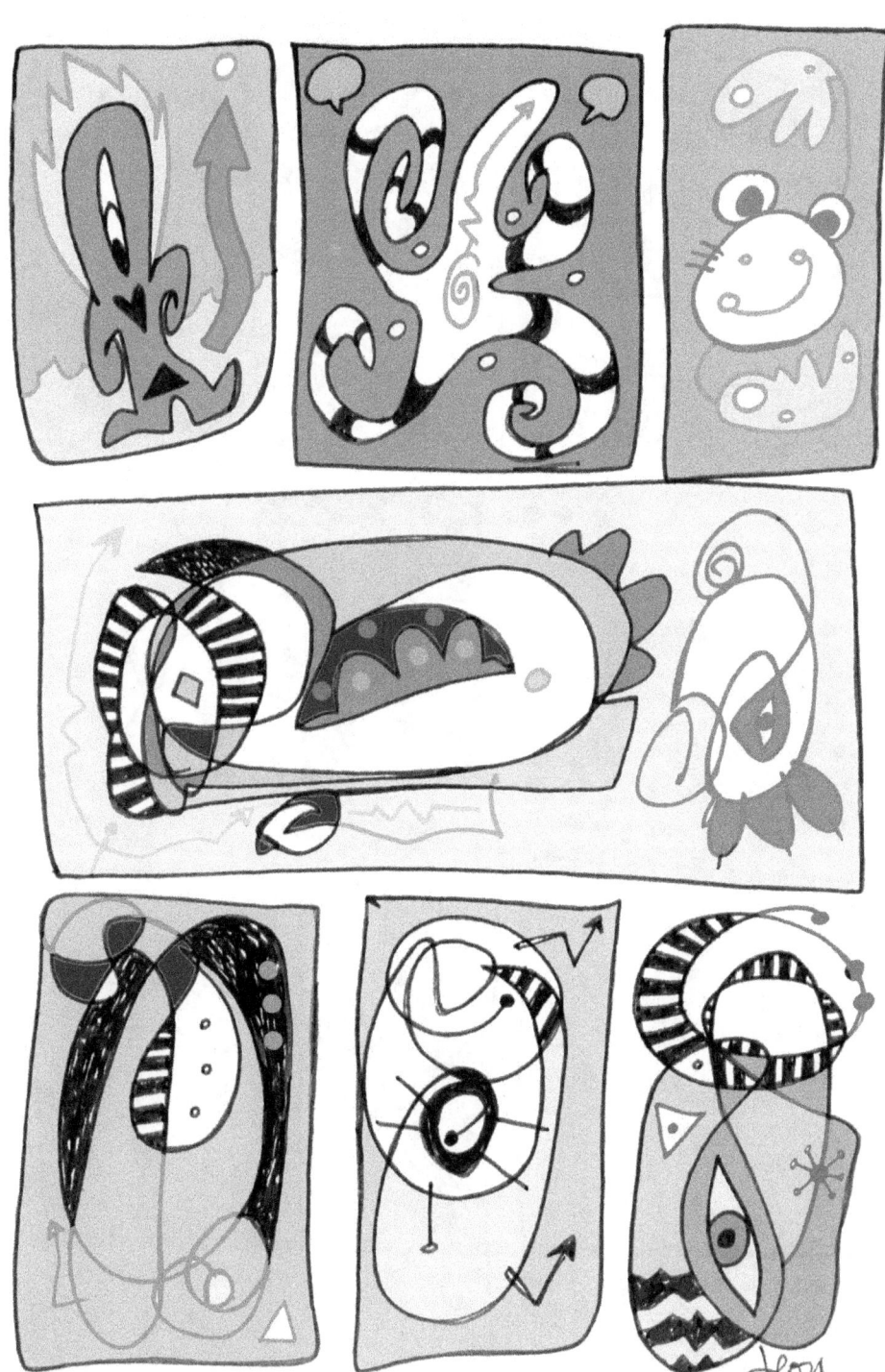

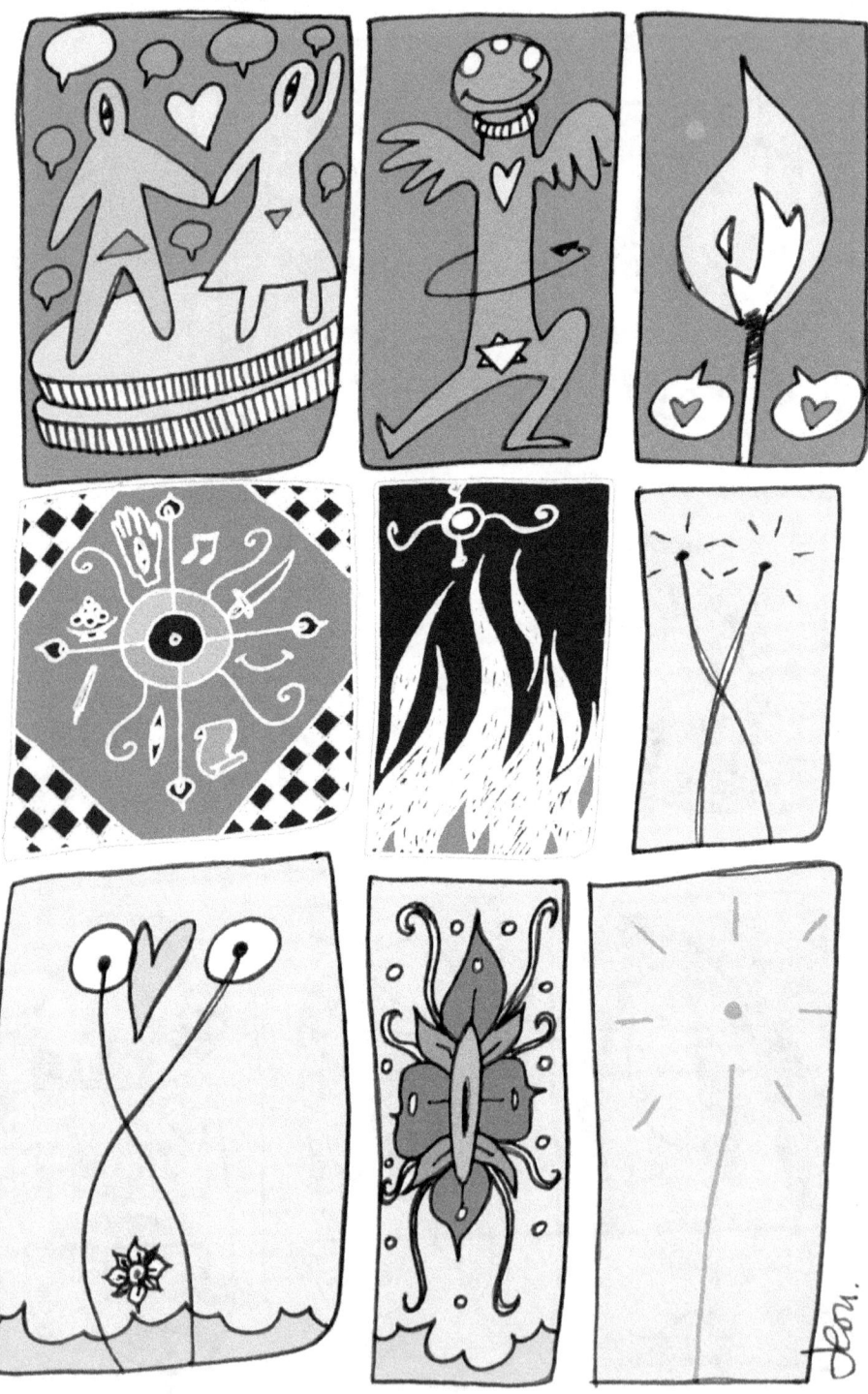

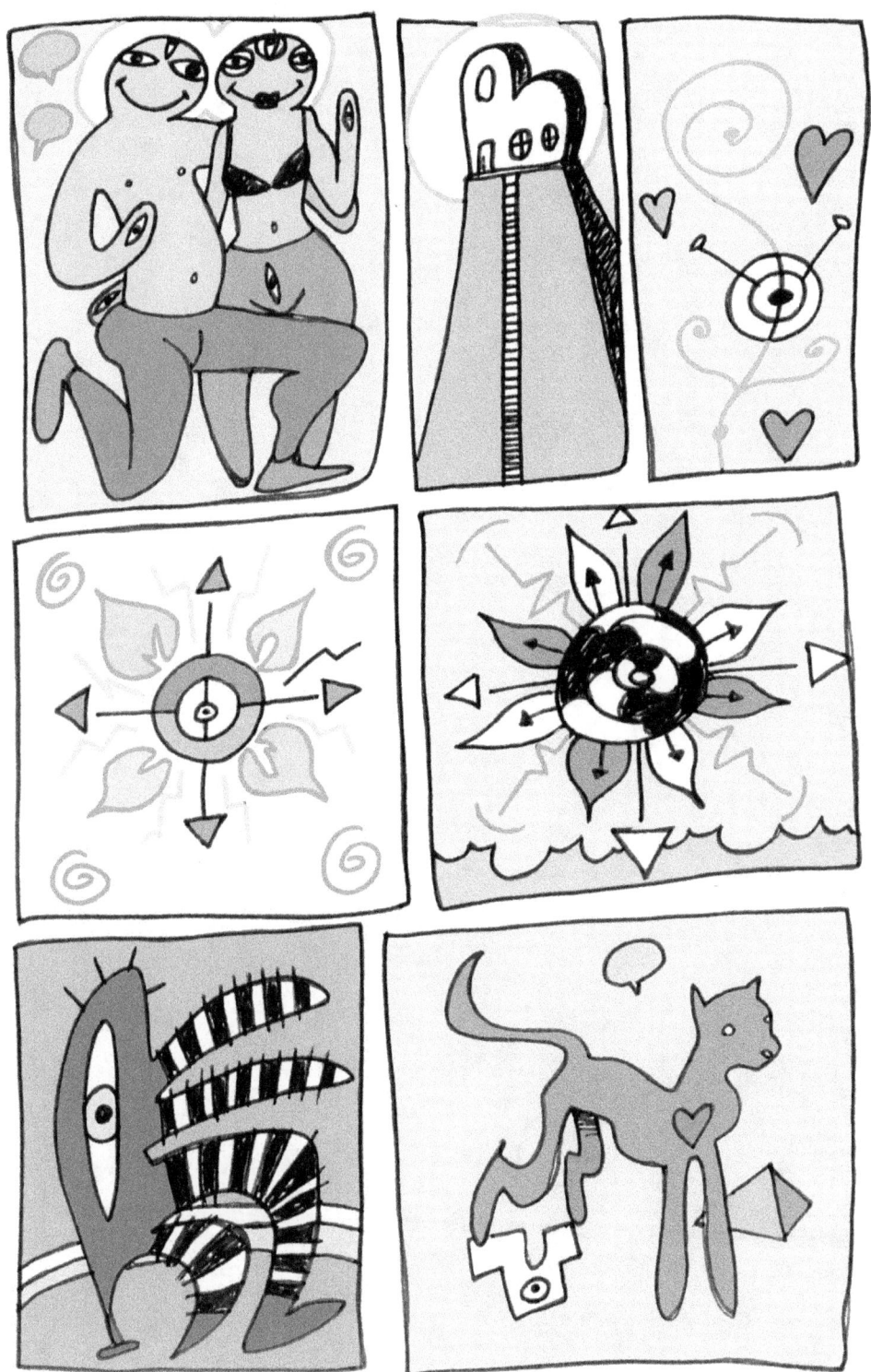

libre

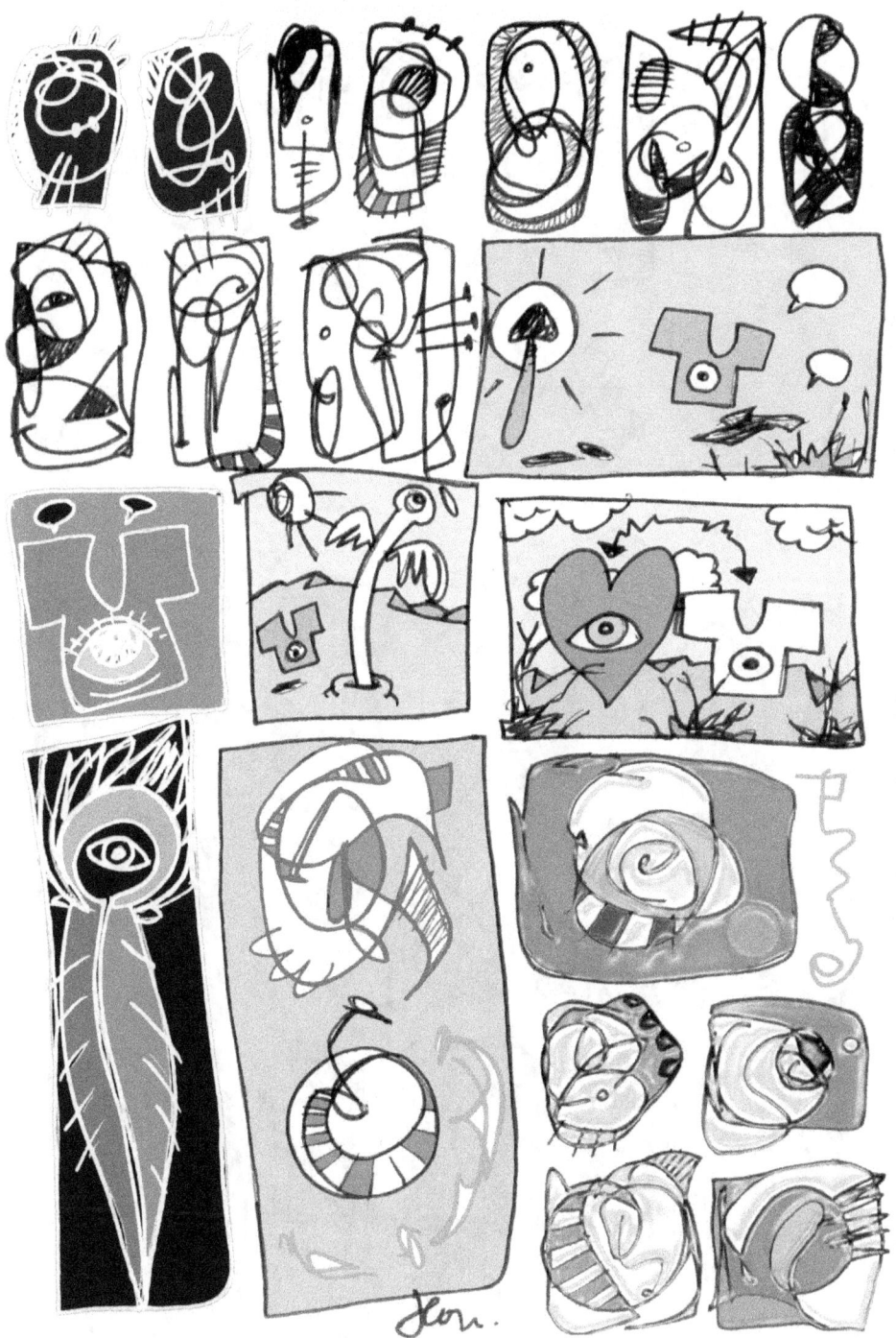

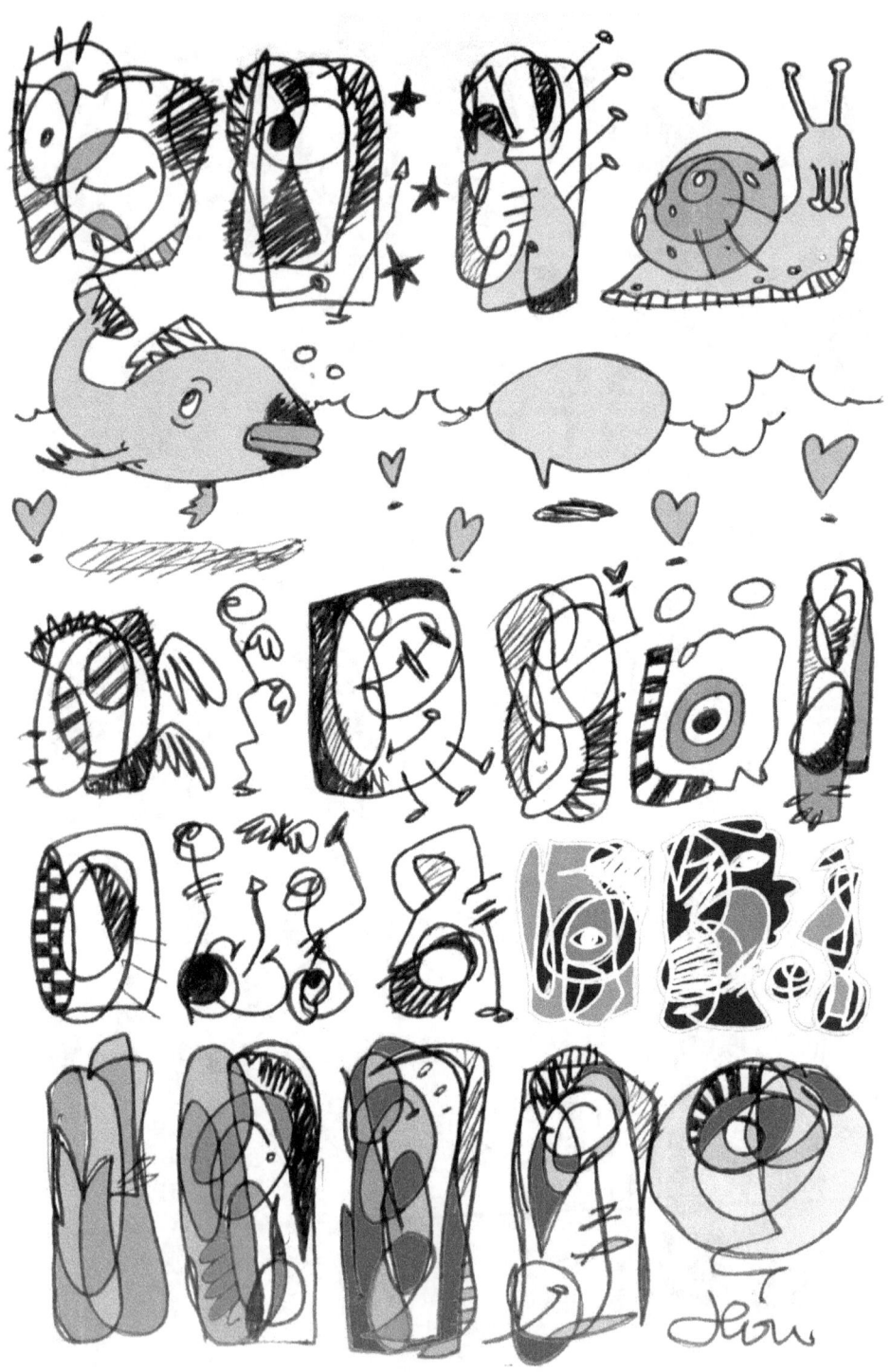

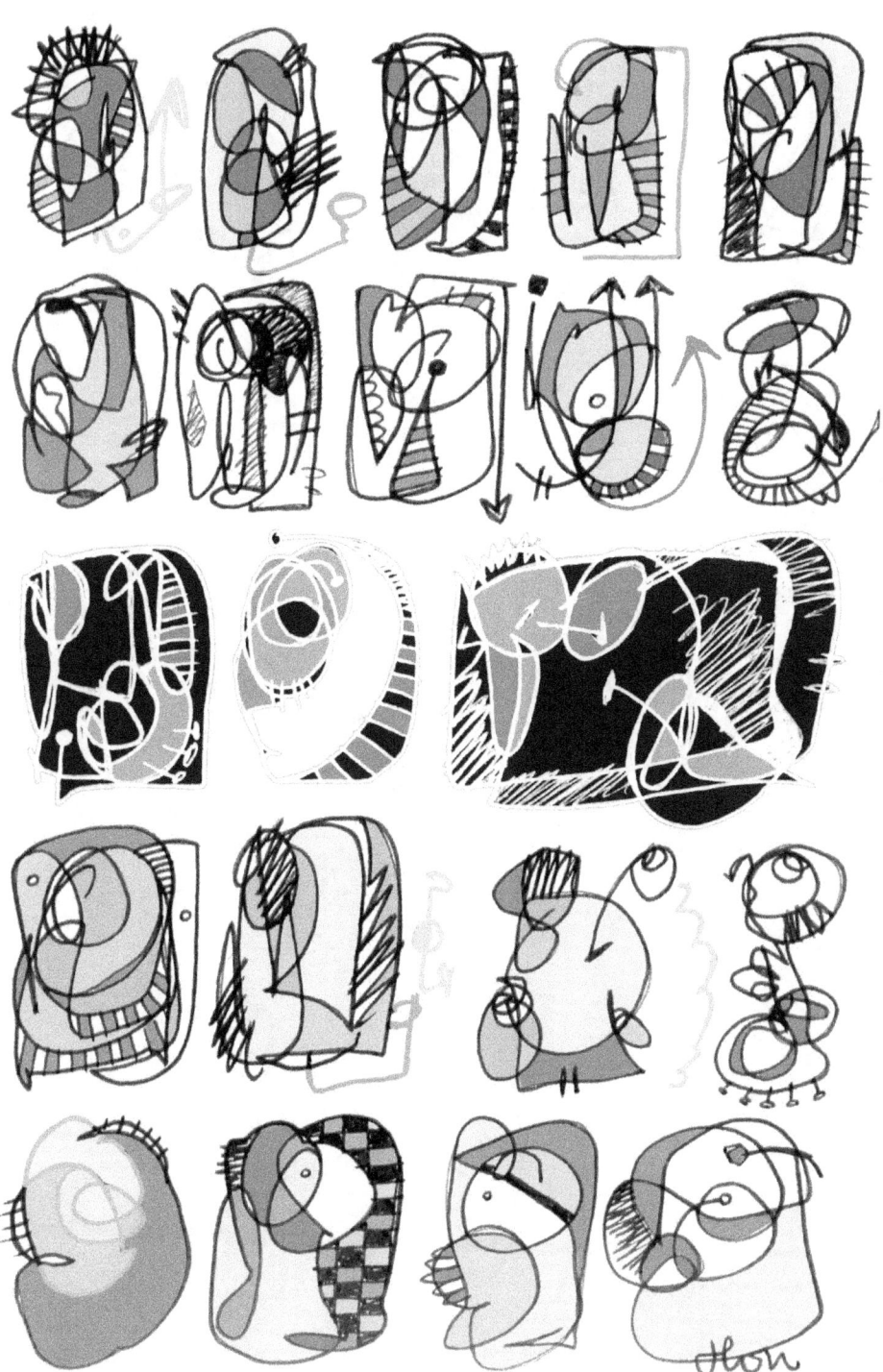

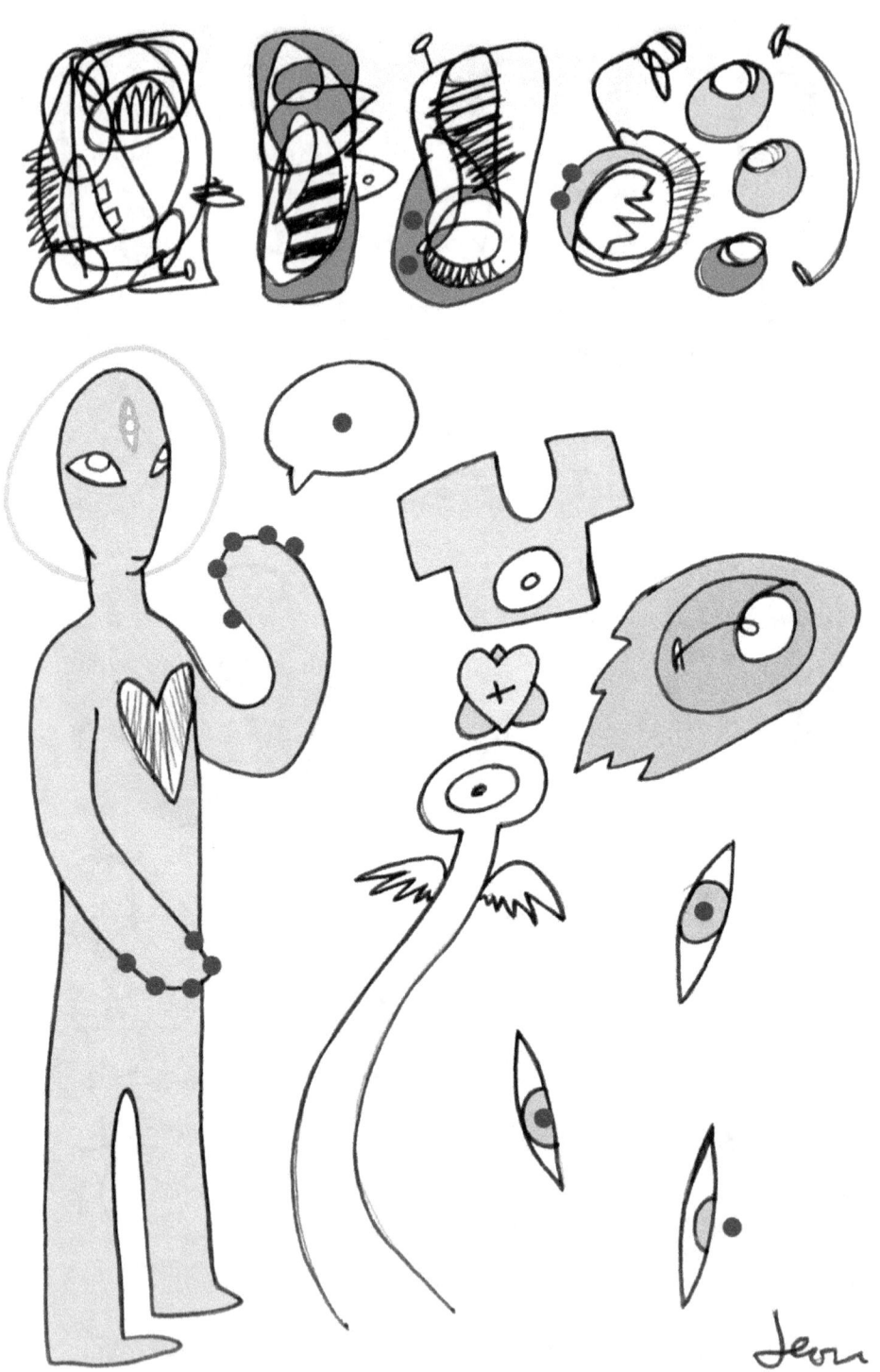

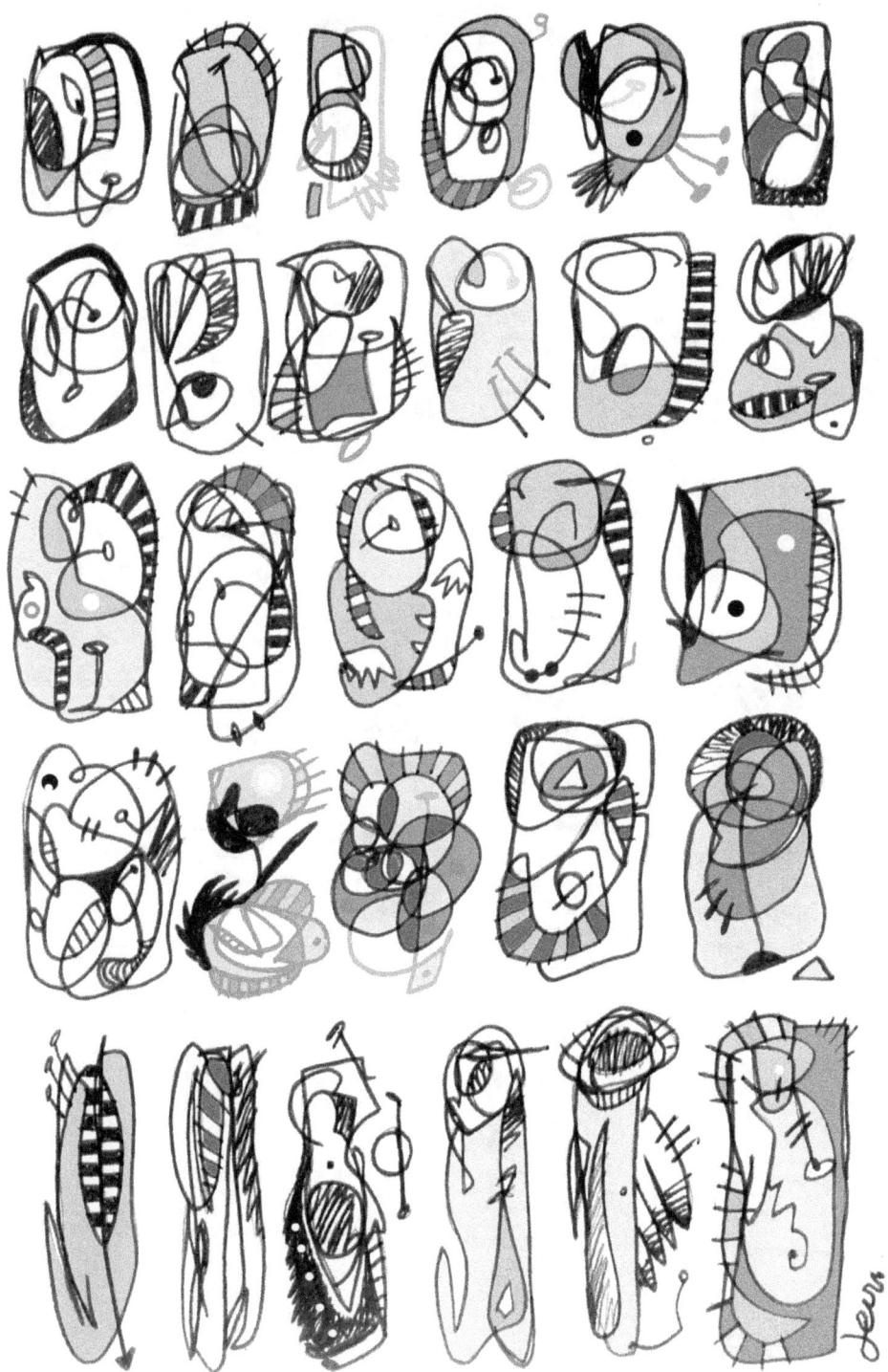

149

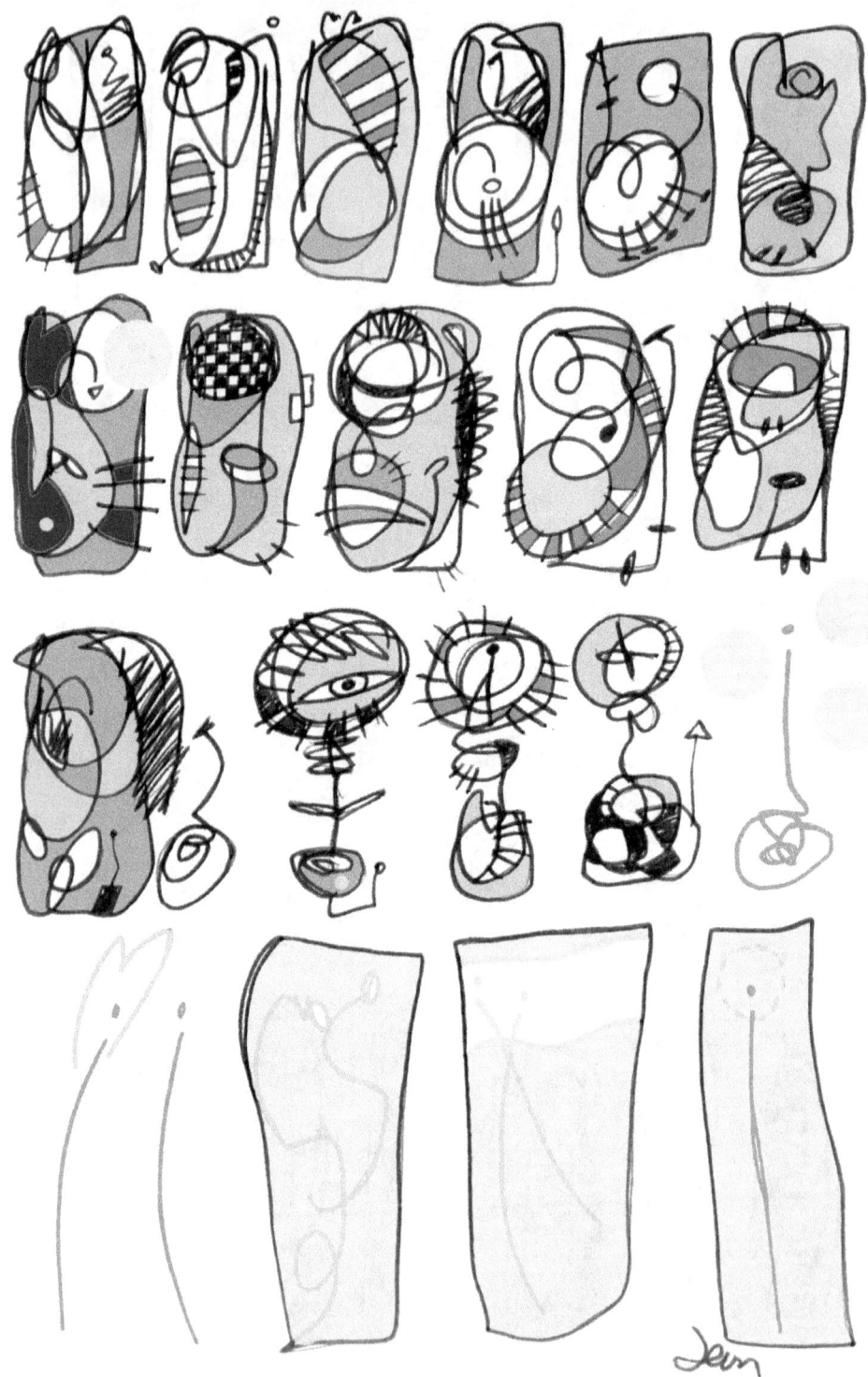

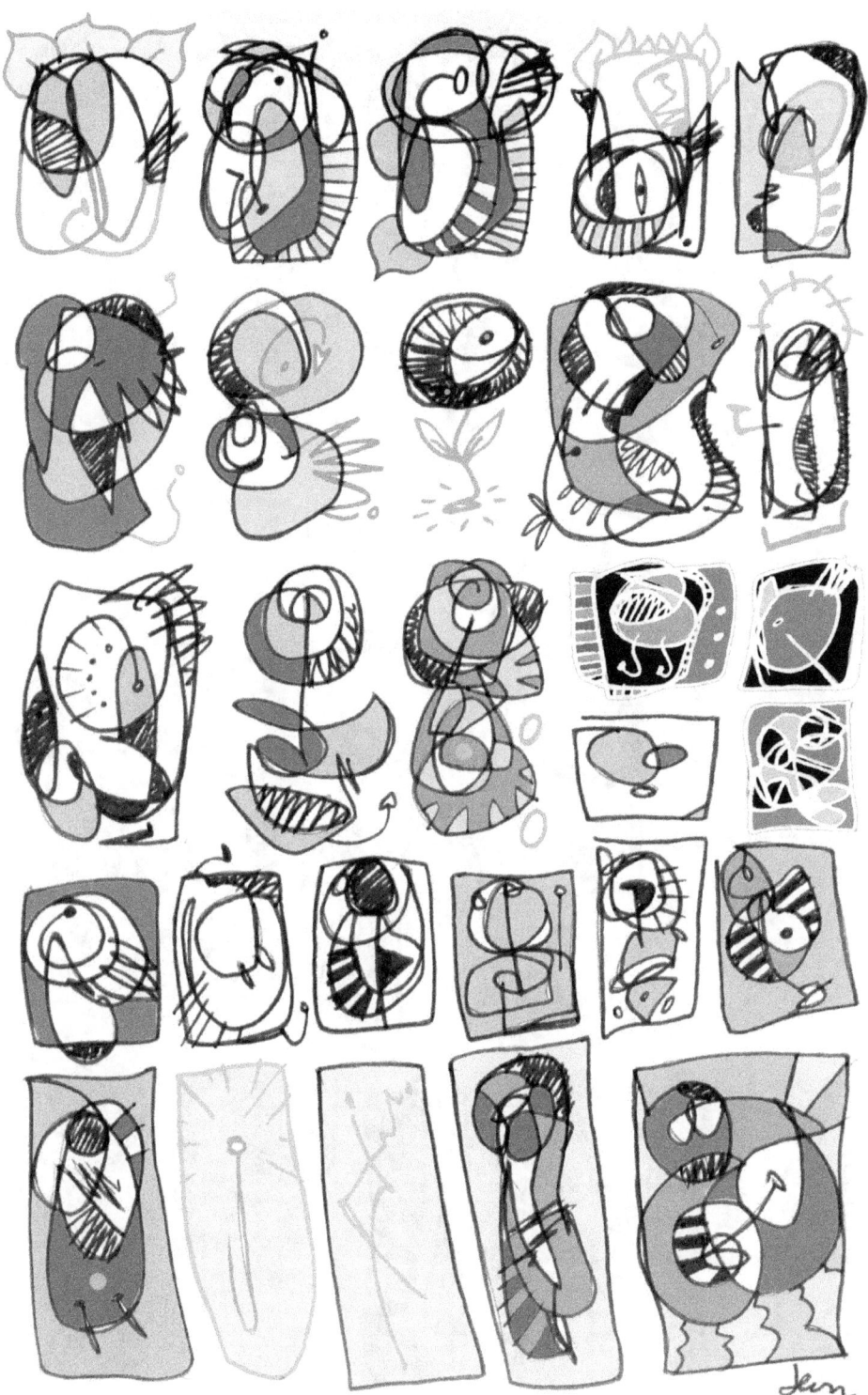

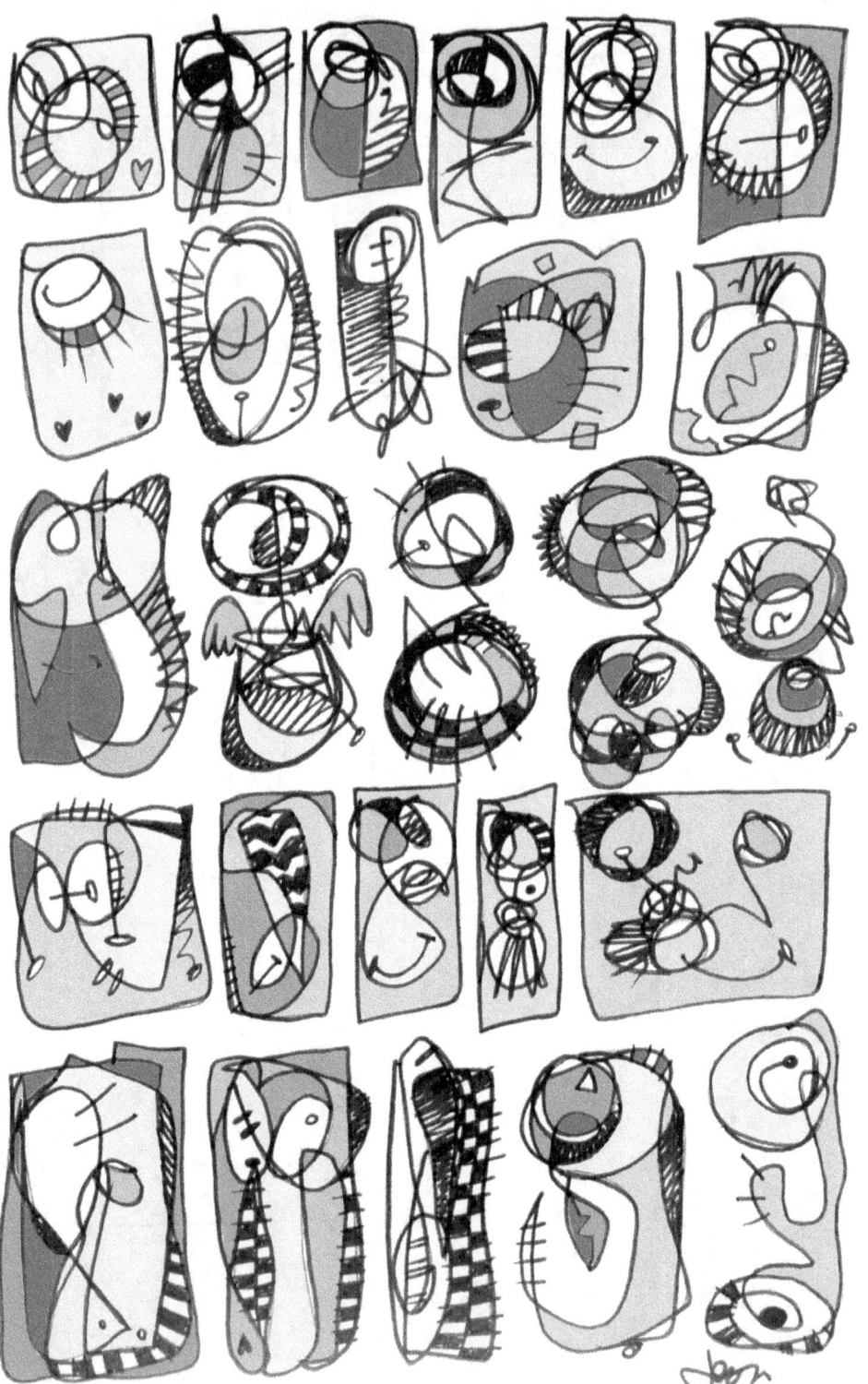

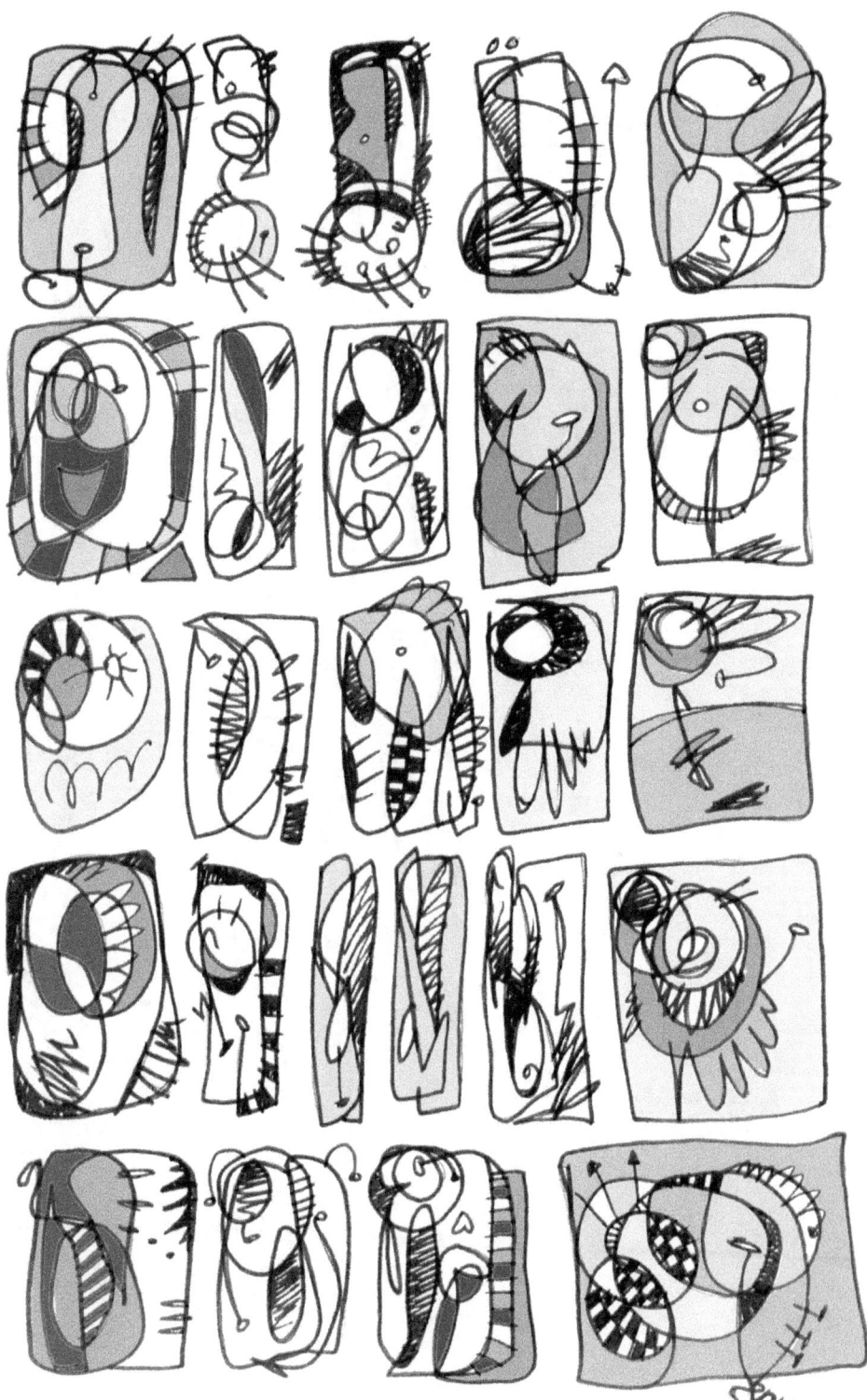

153

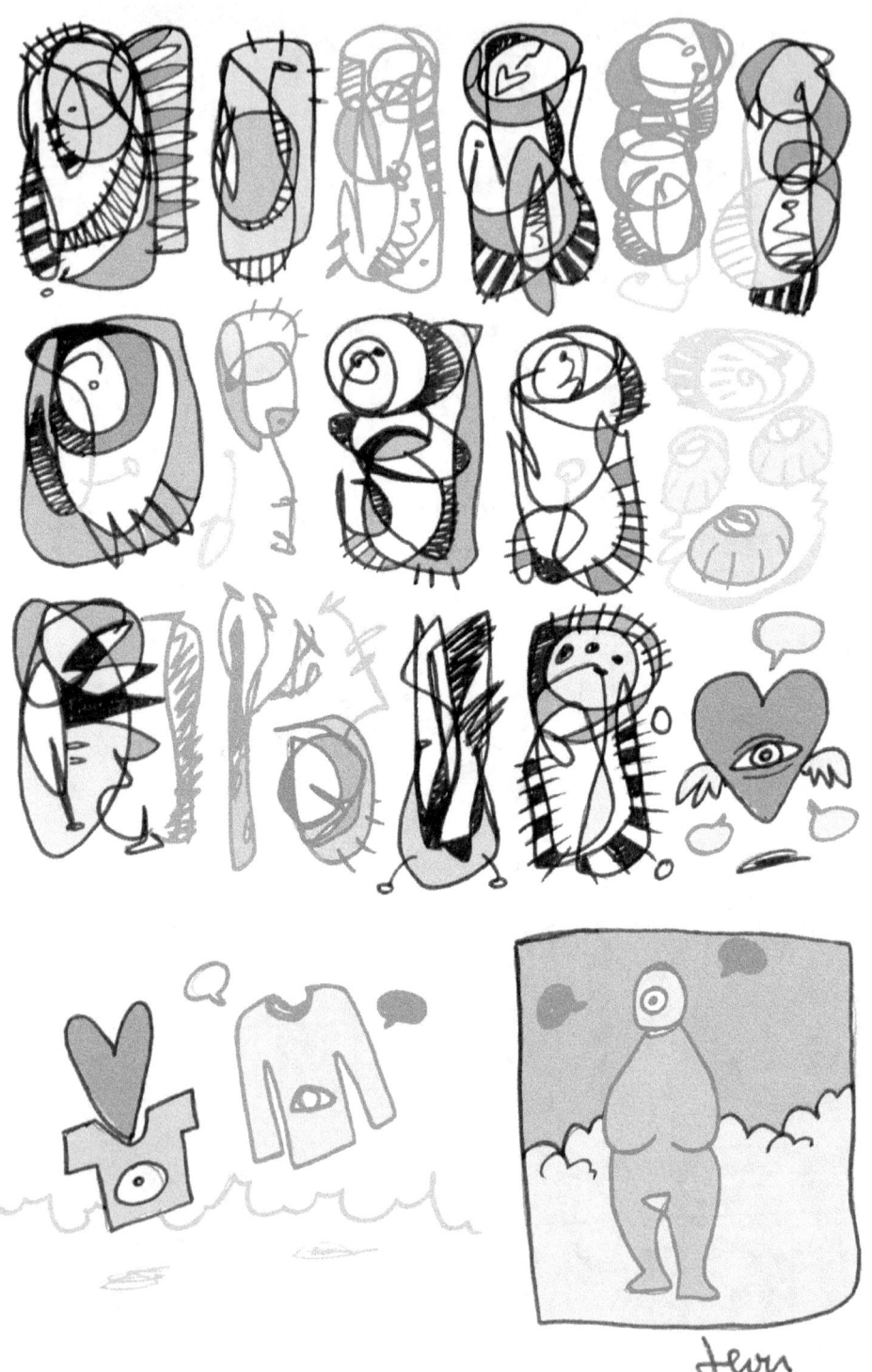

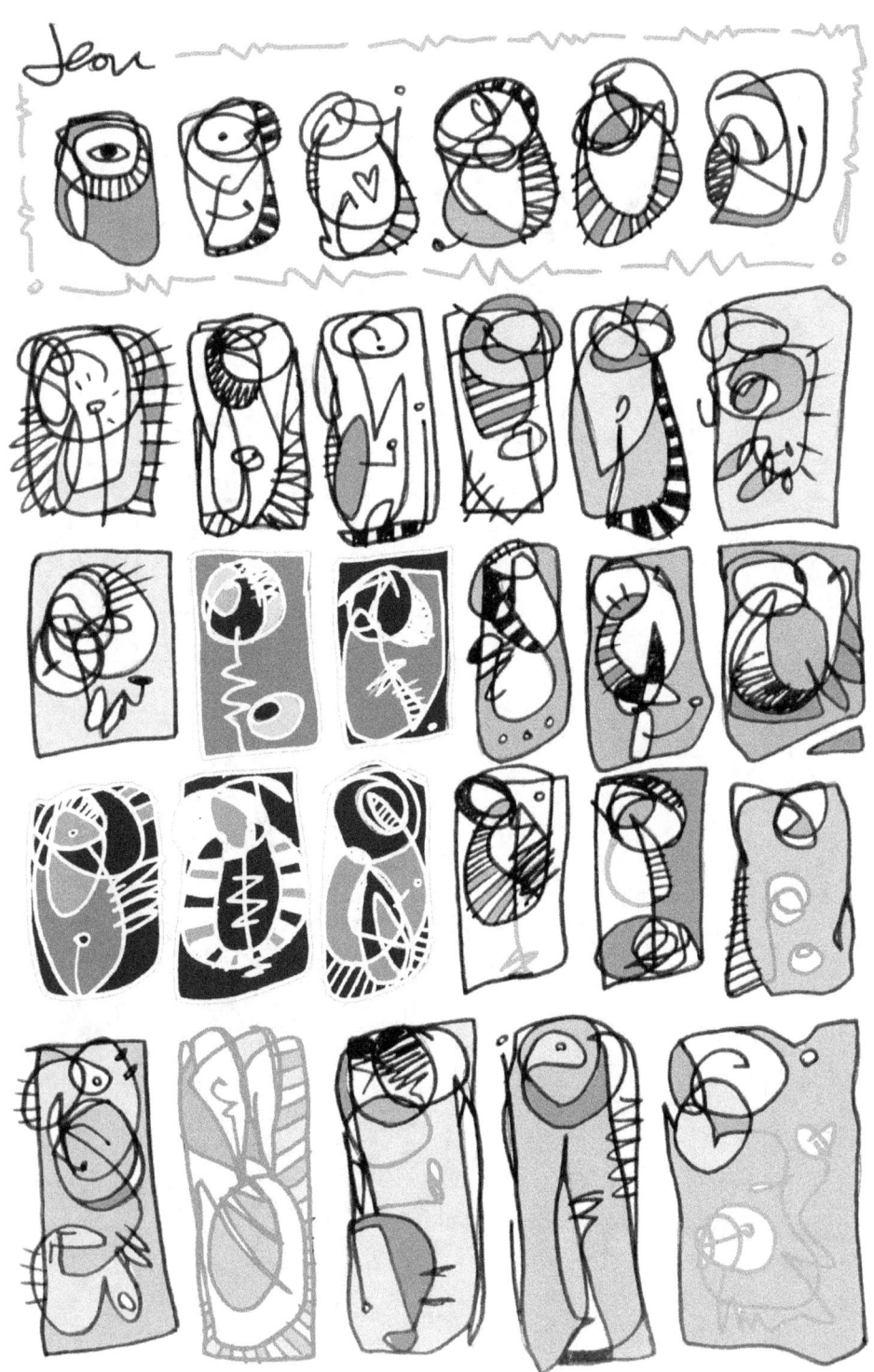

155

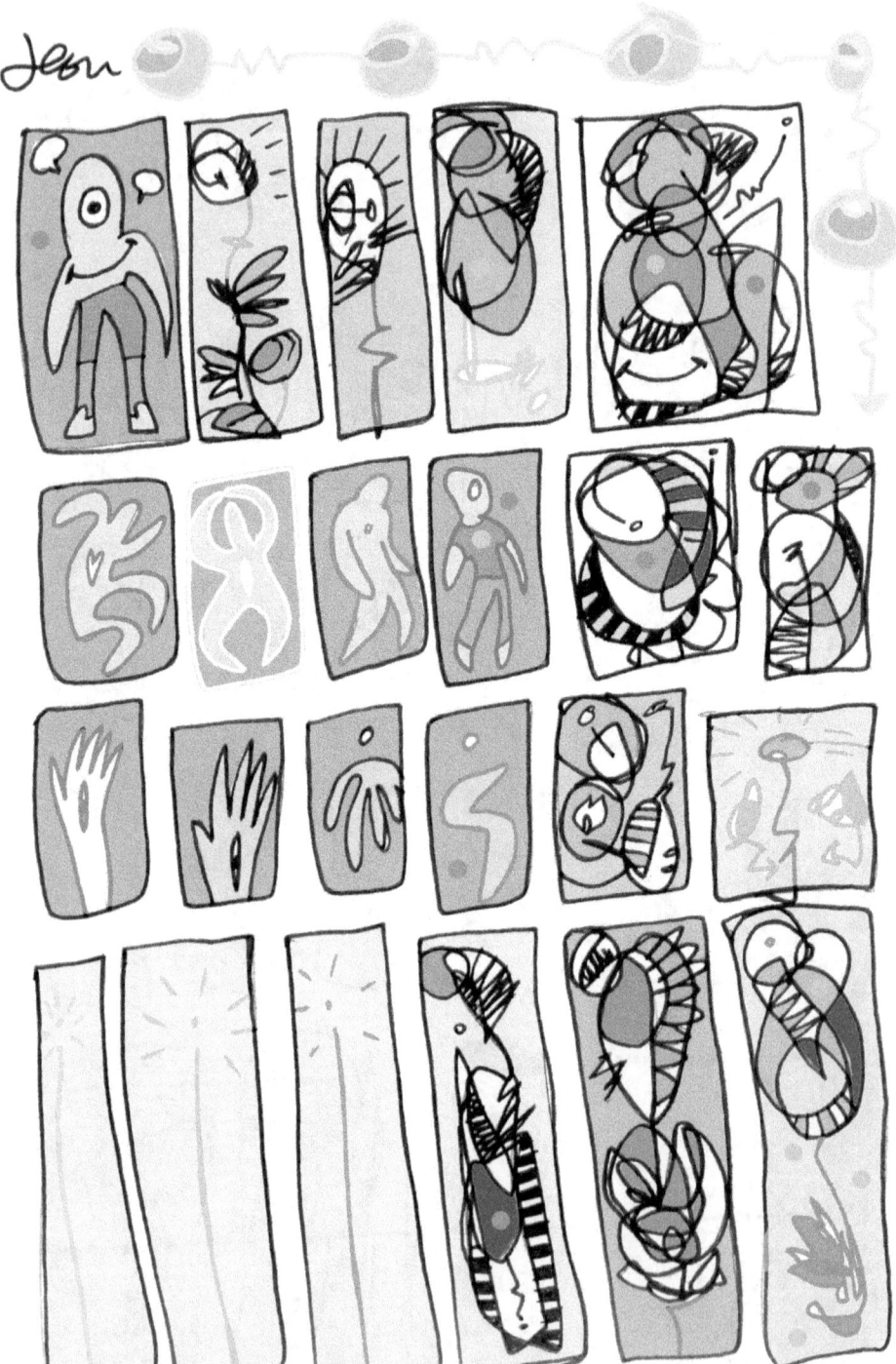

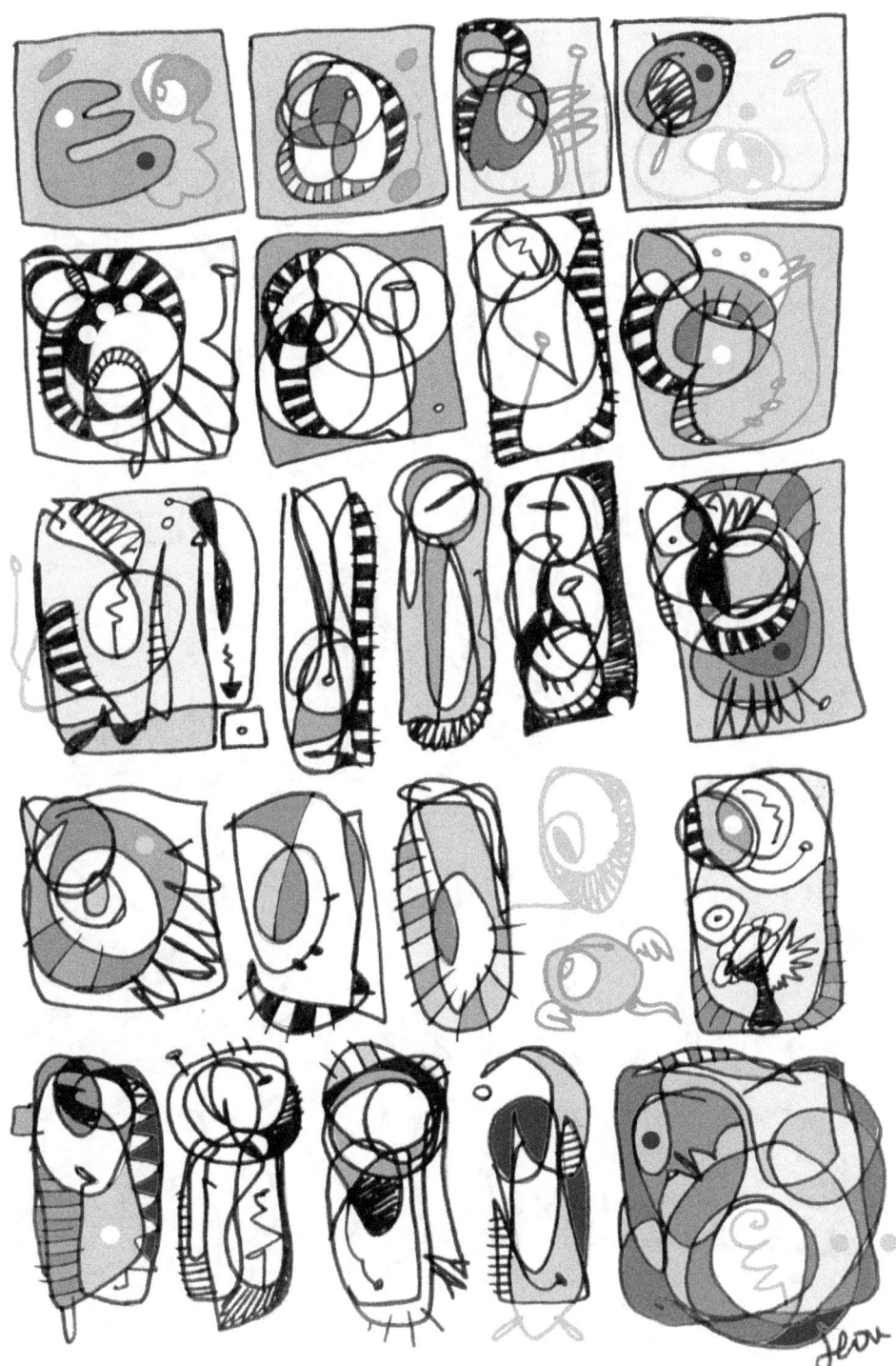

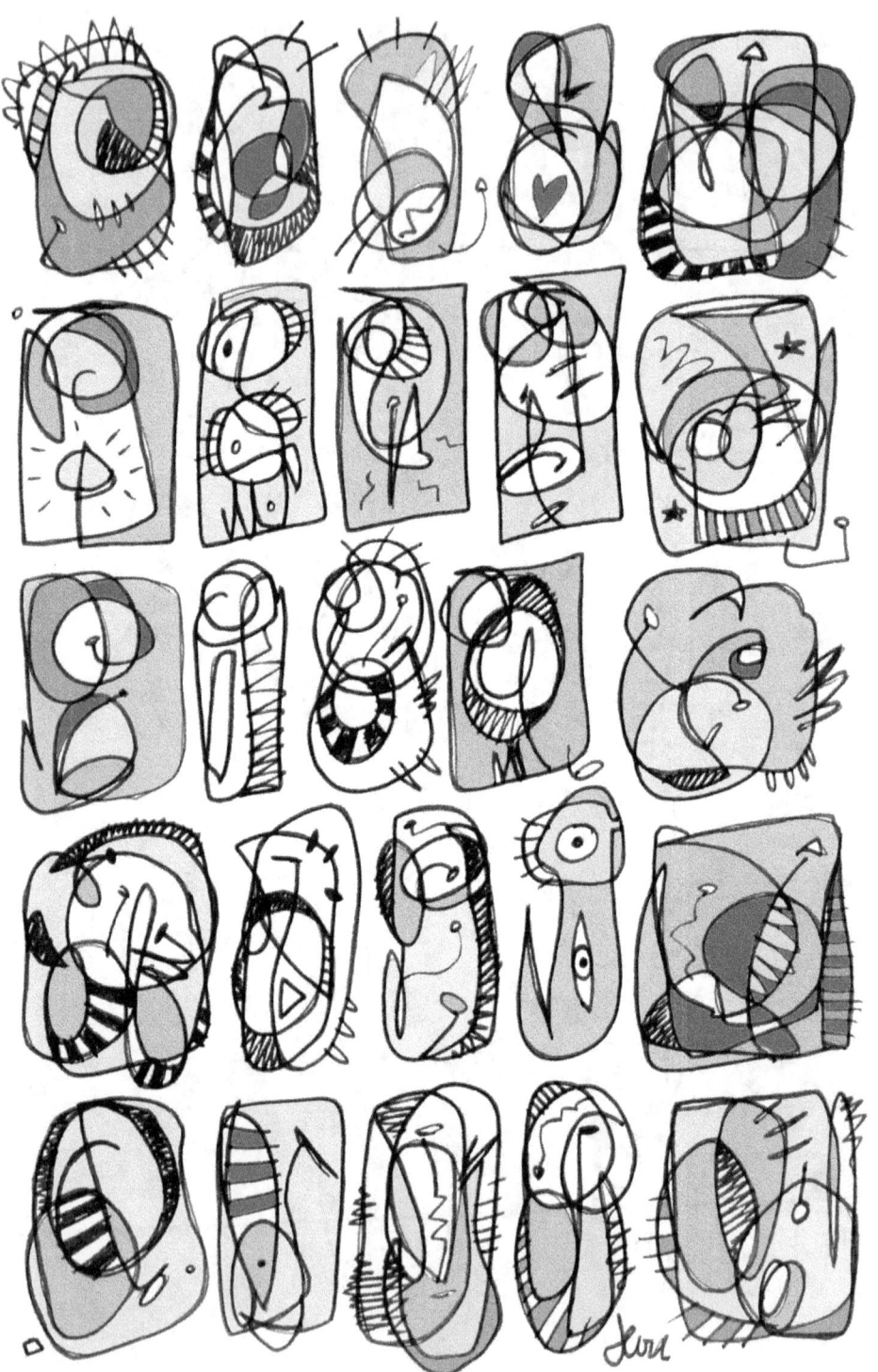

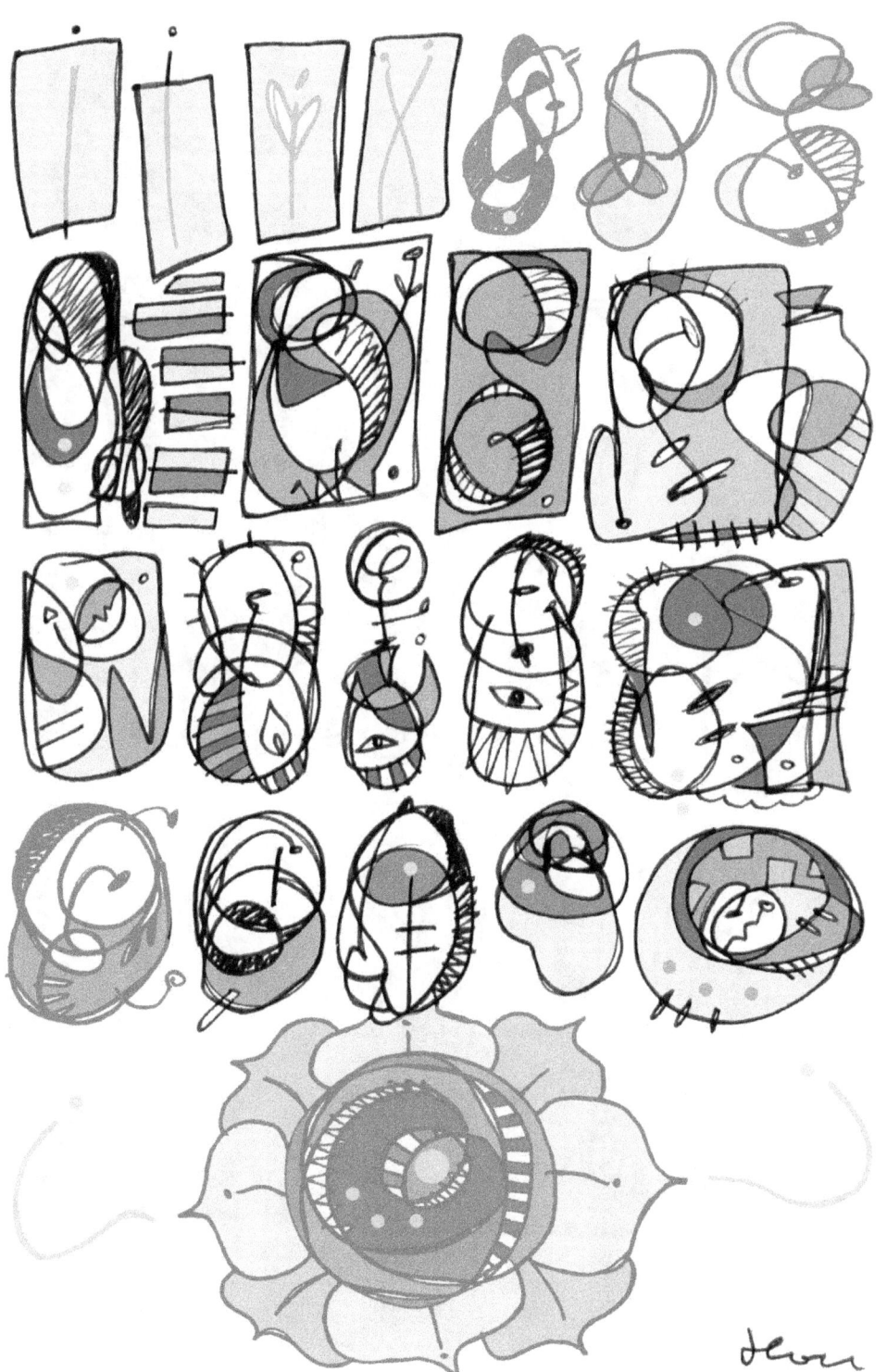

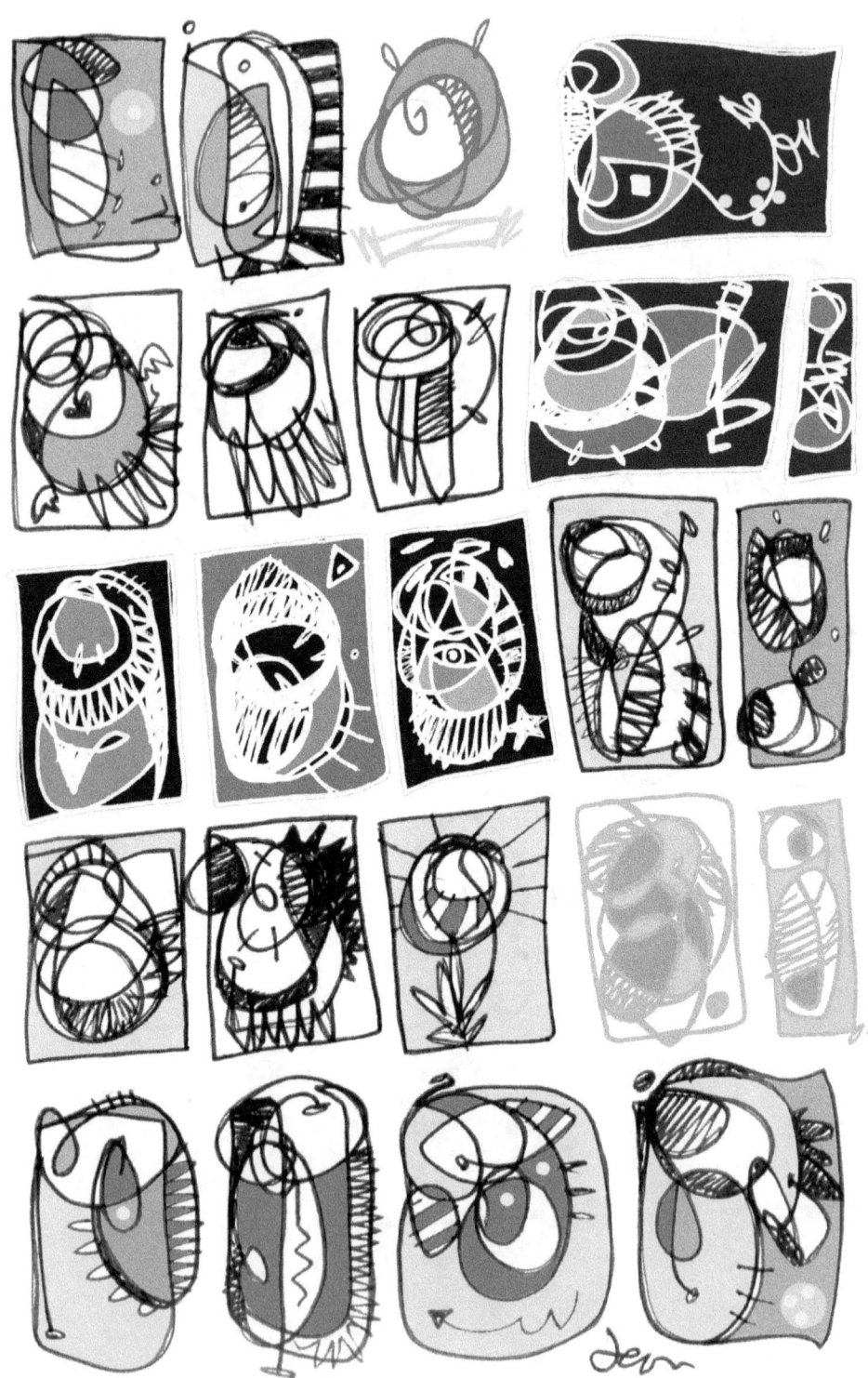

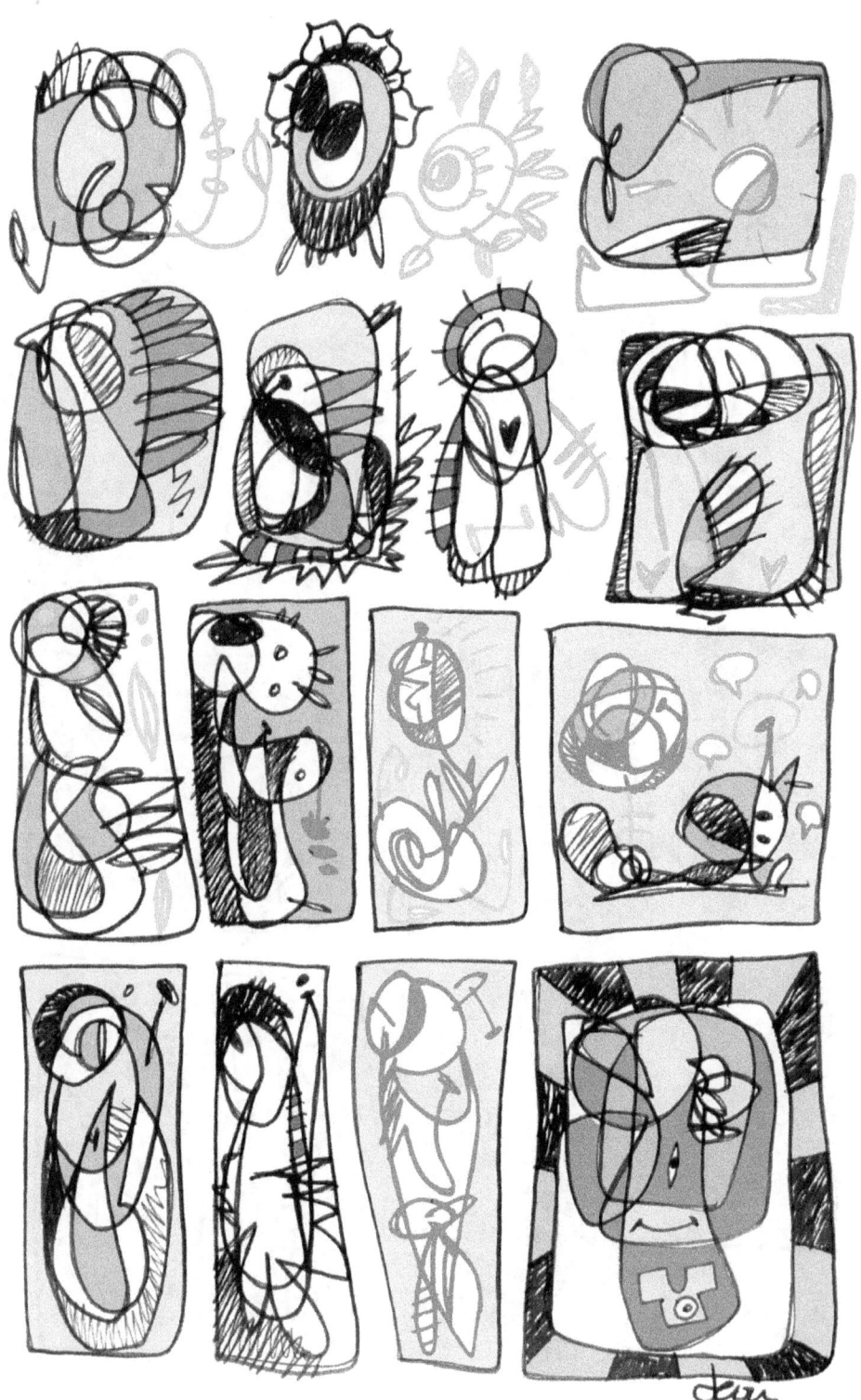

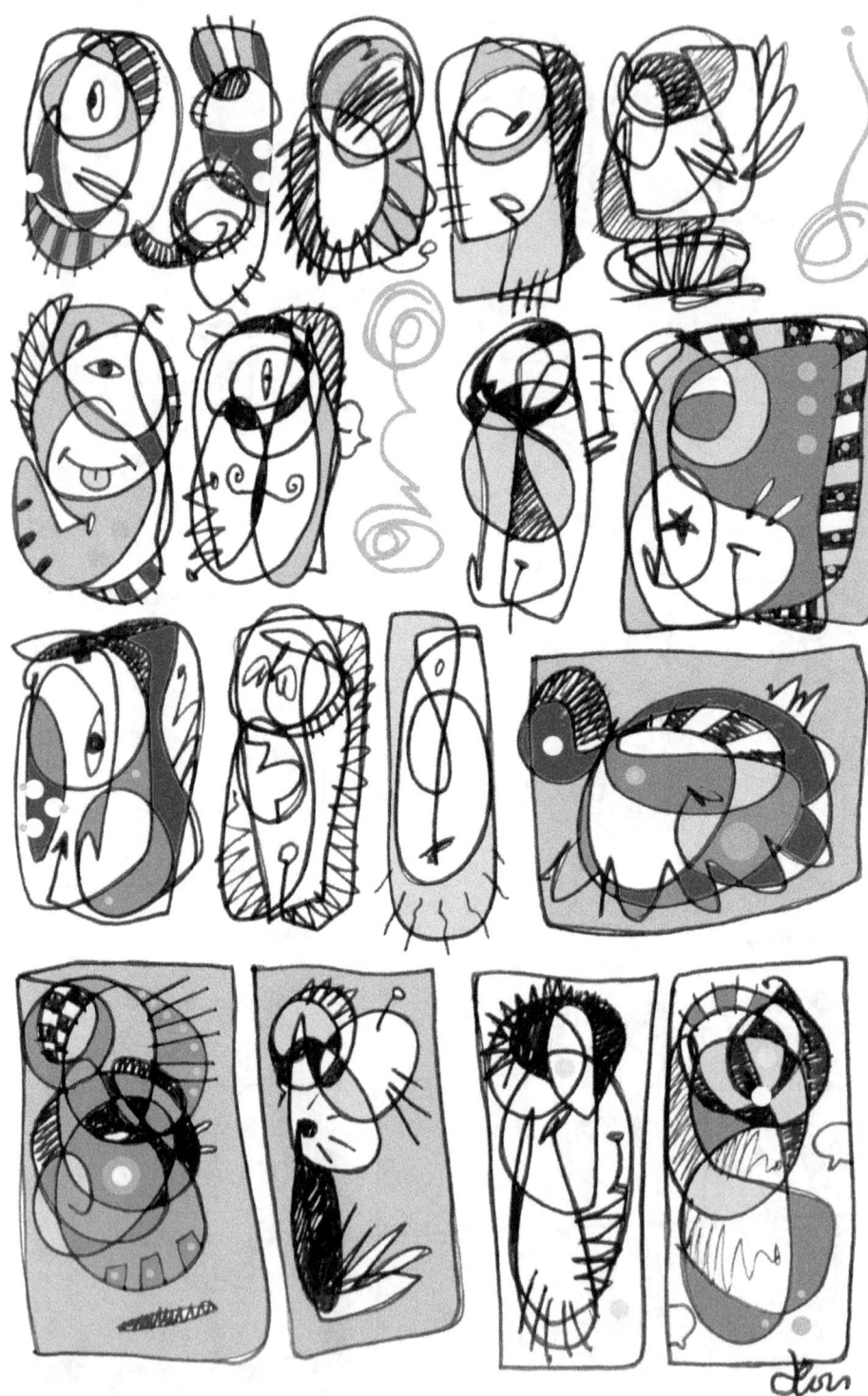

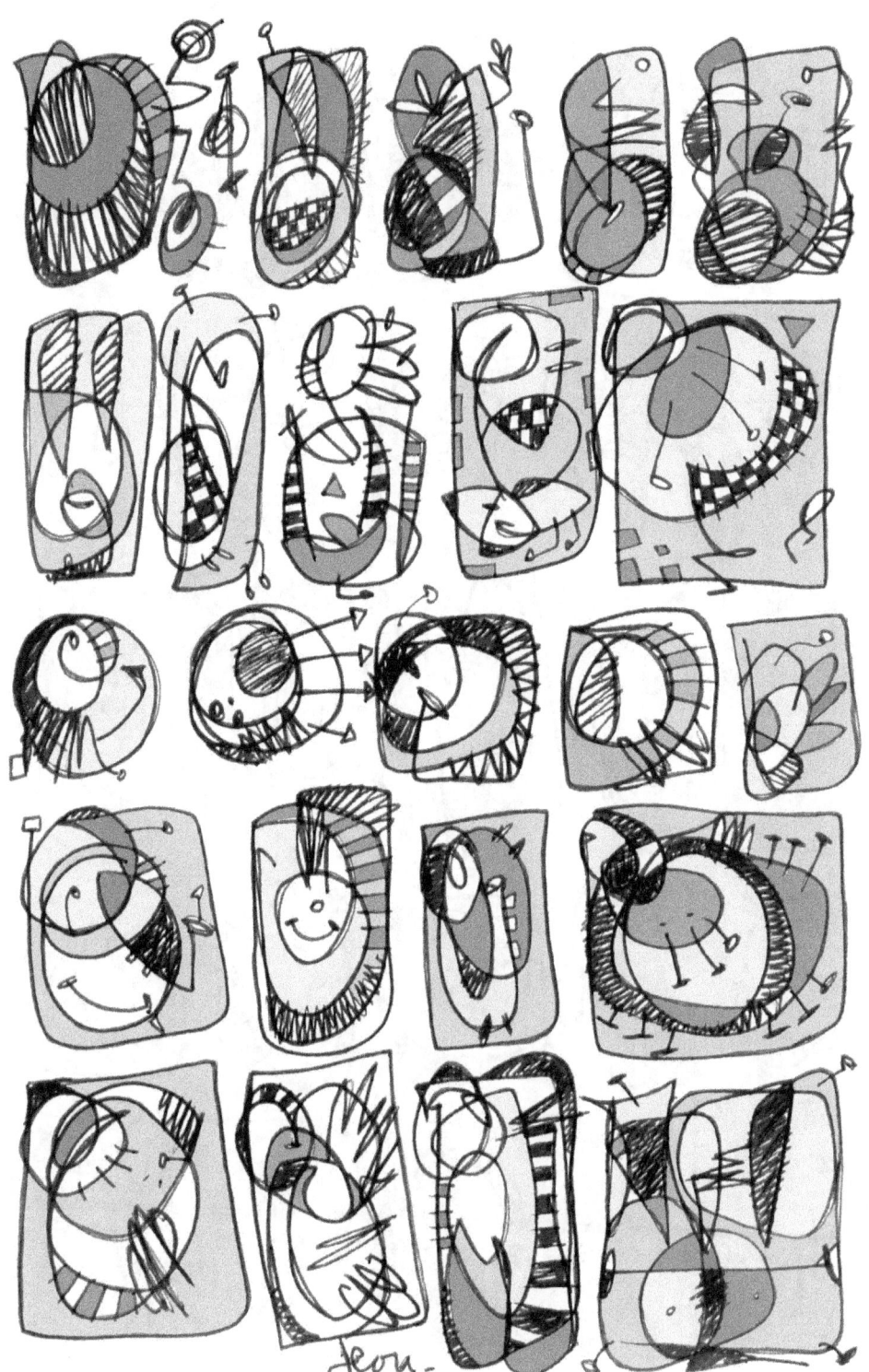

163

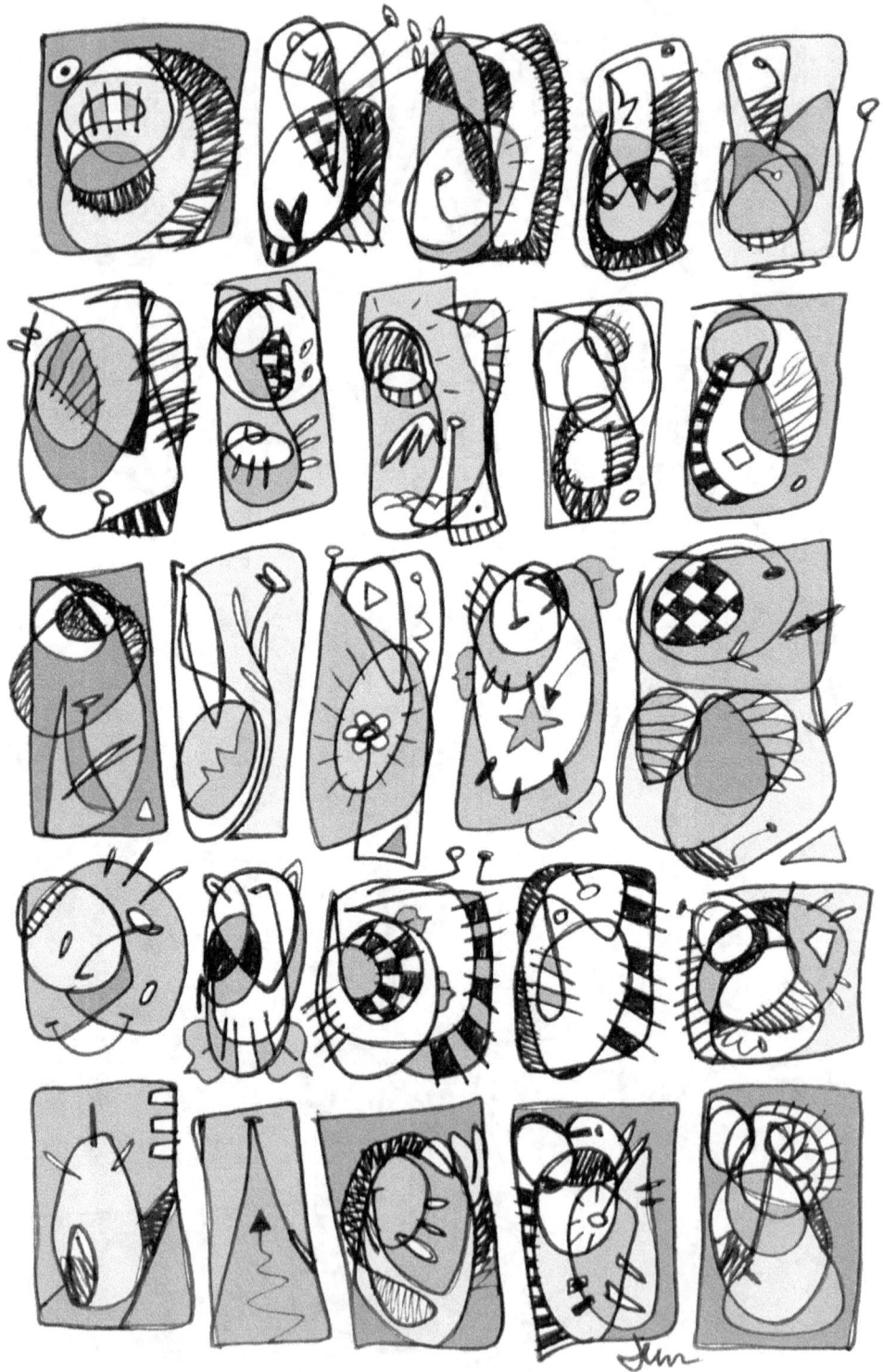

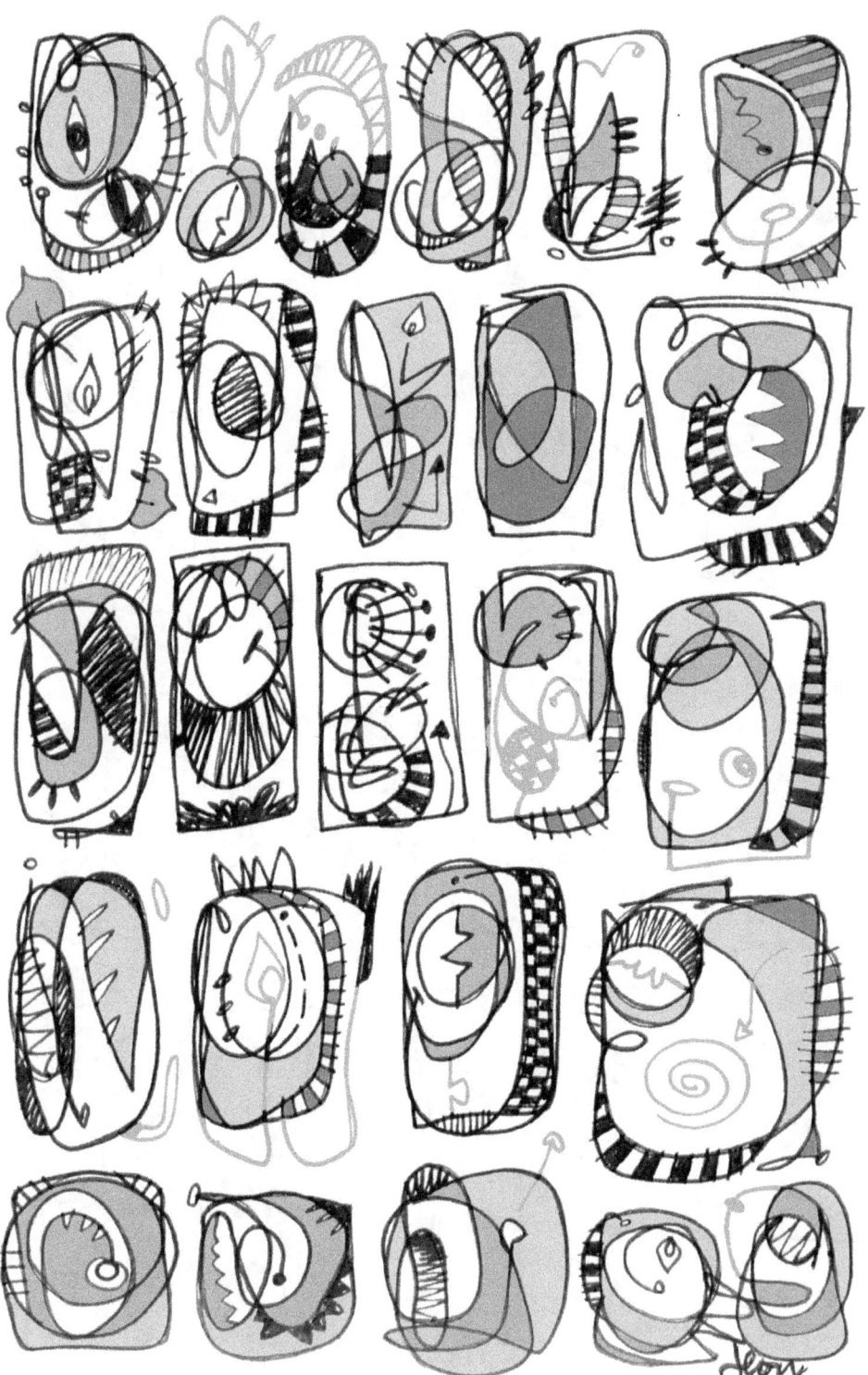

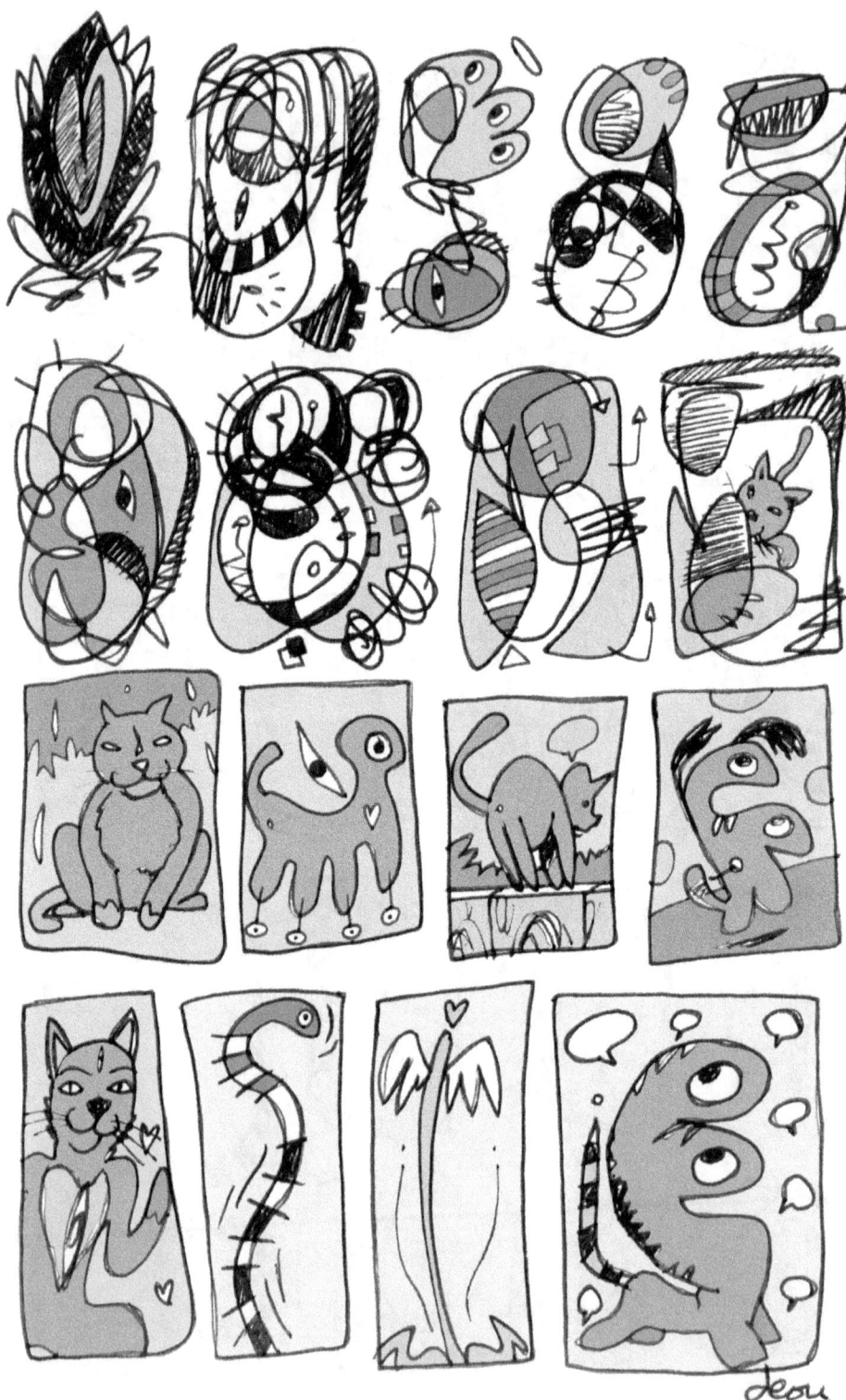

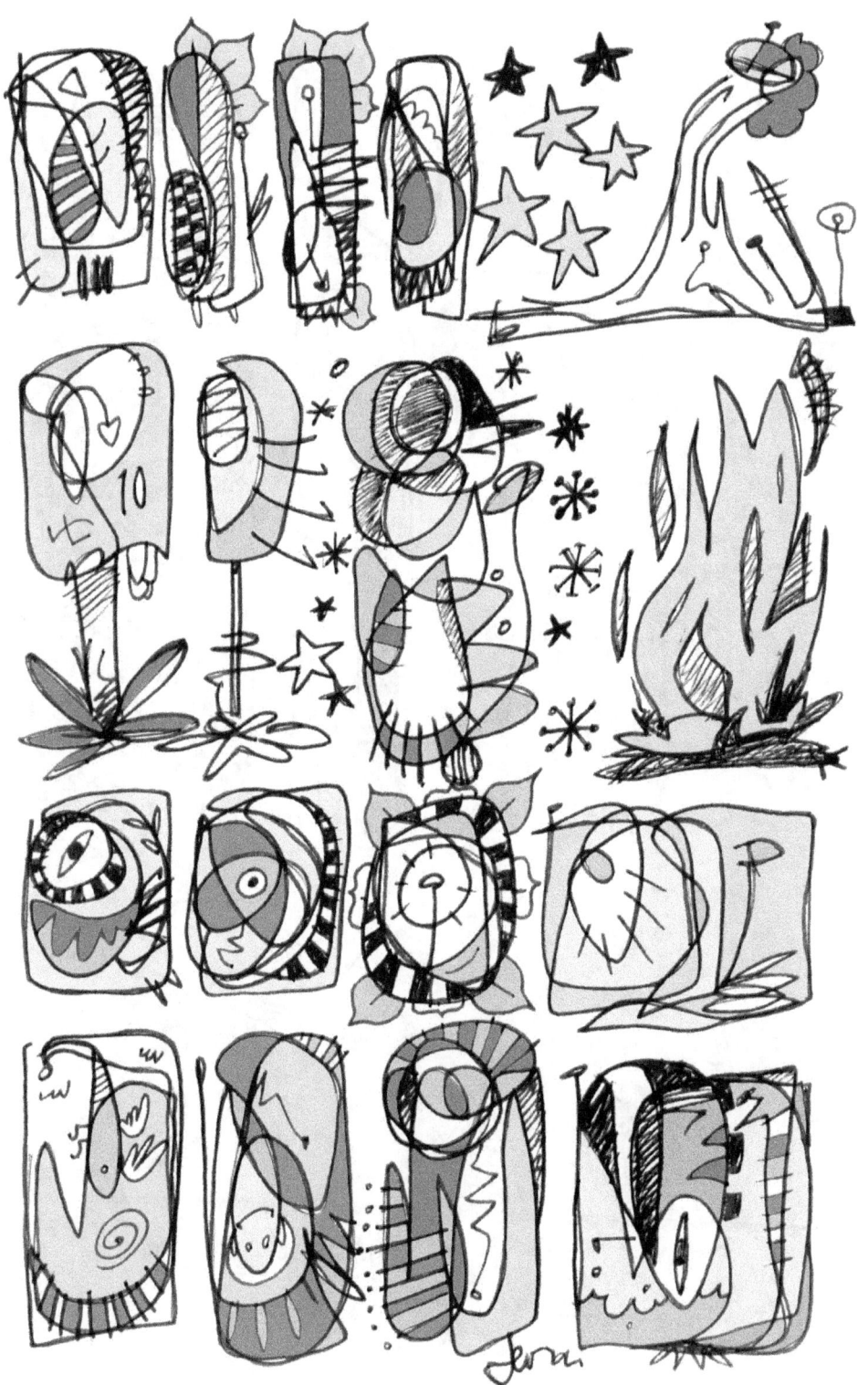

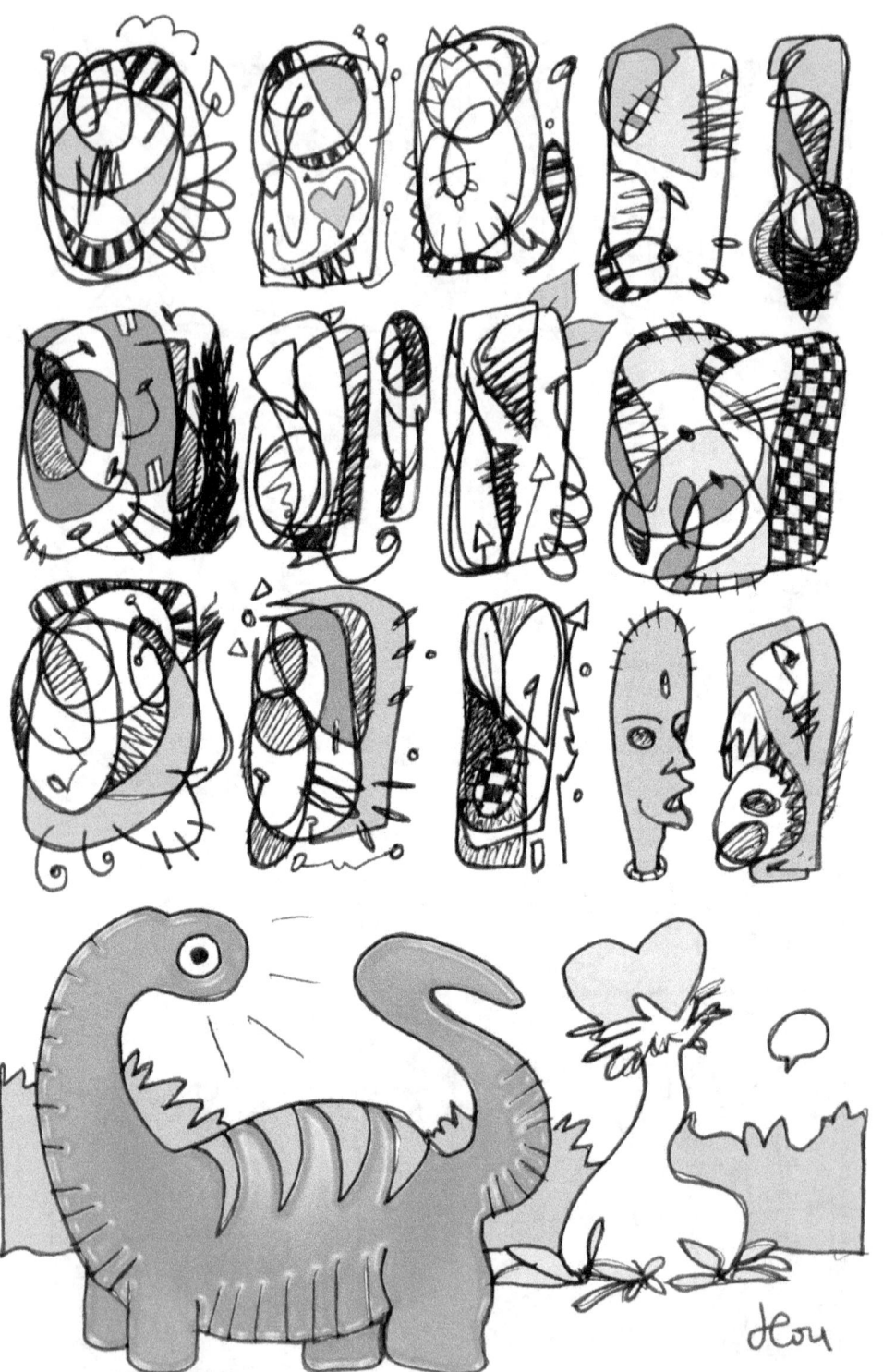

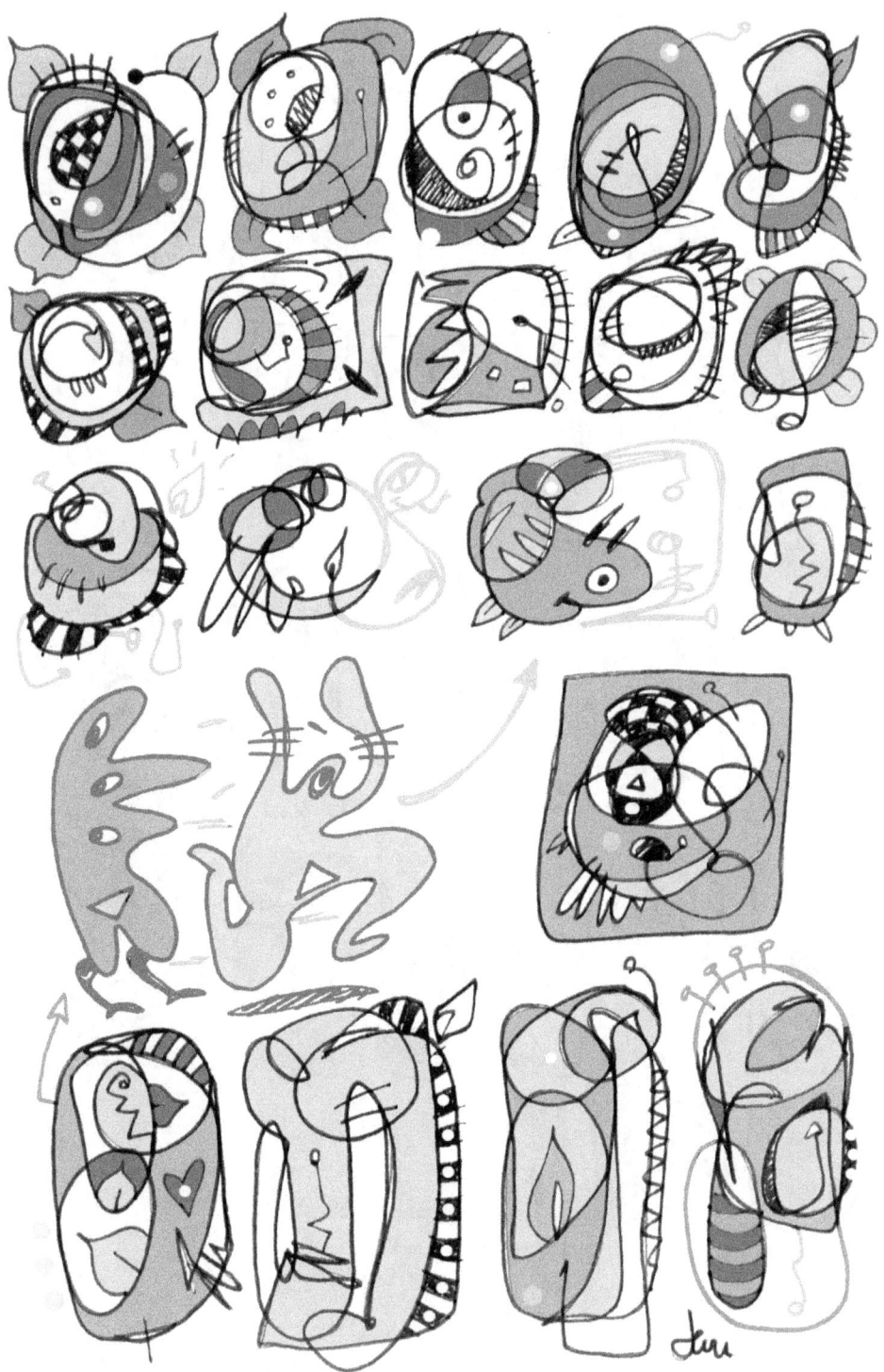

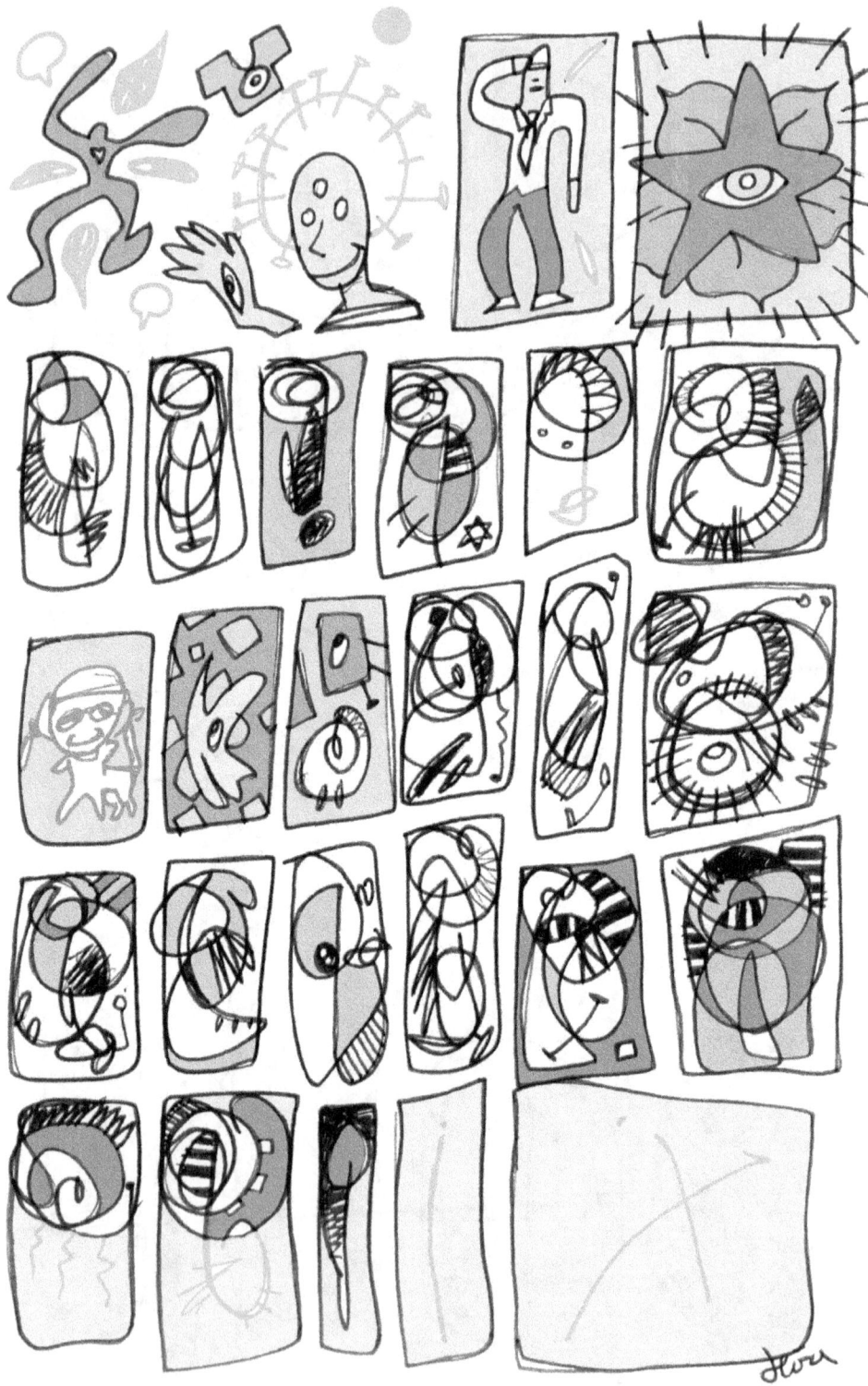

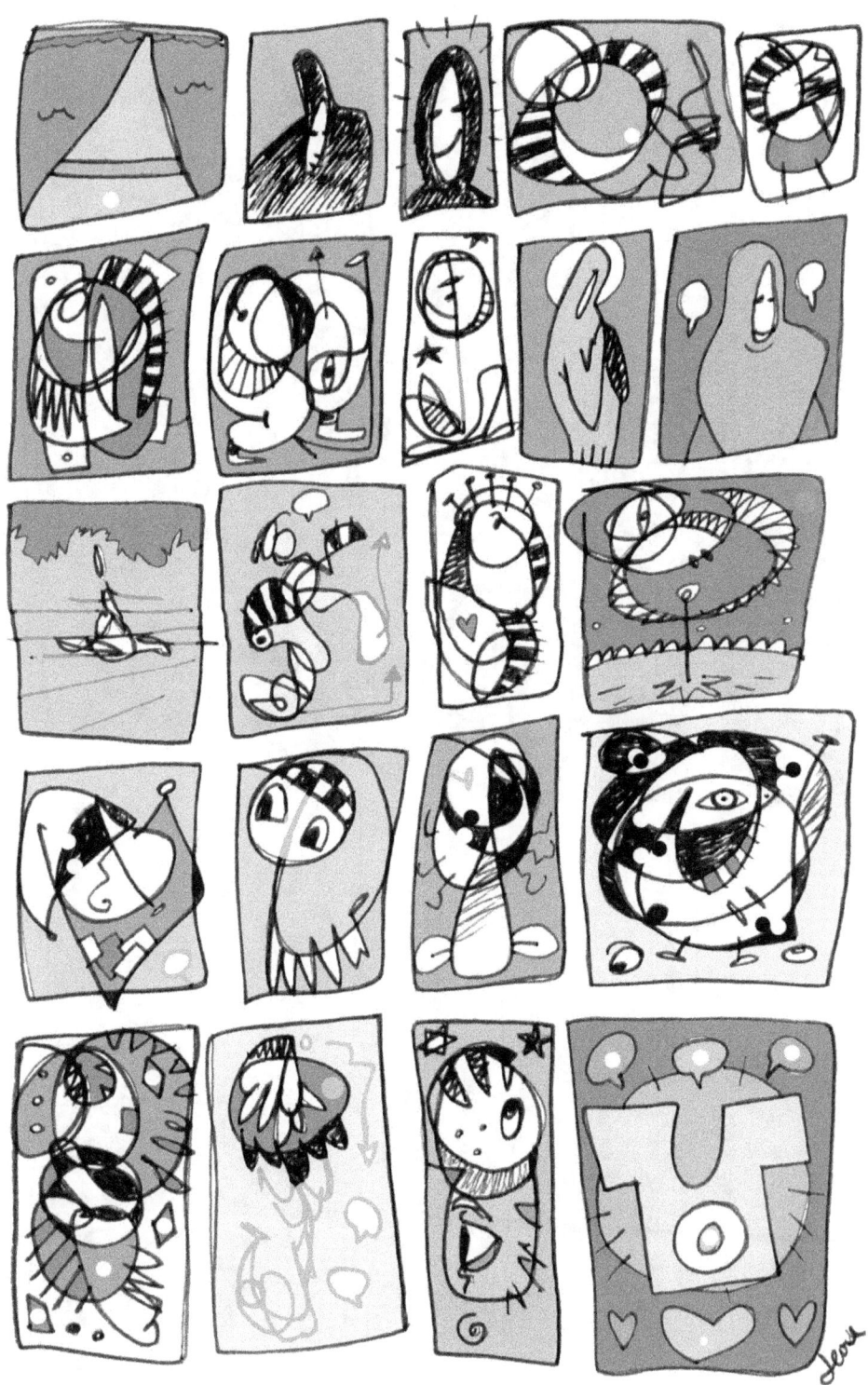

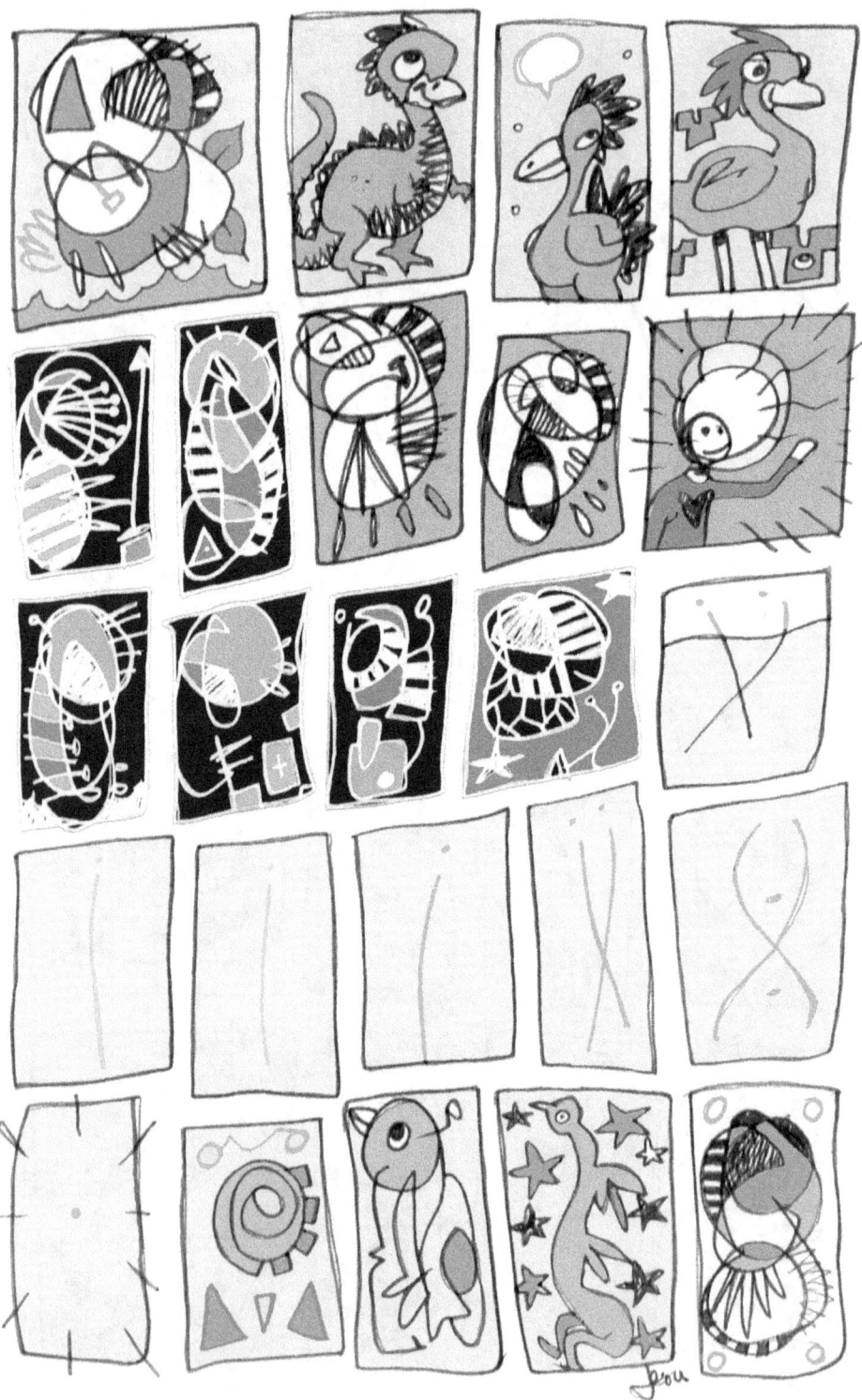

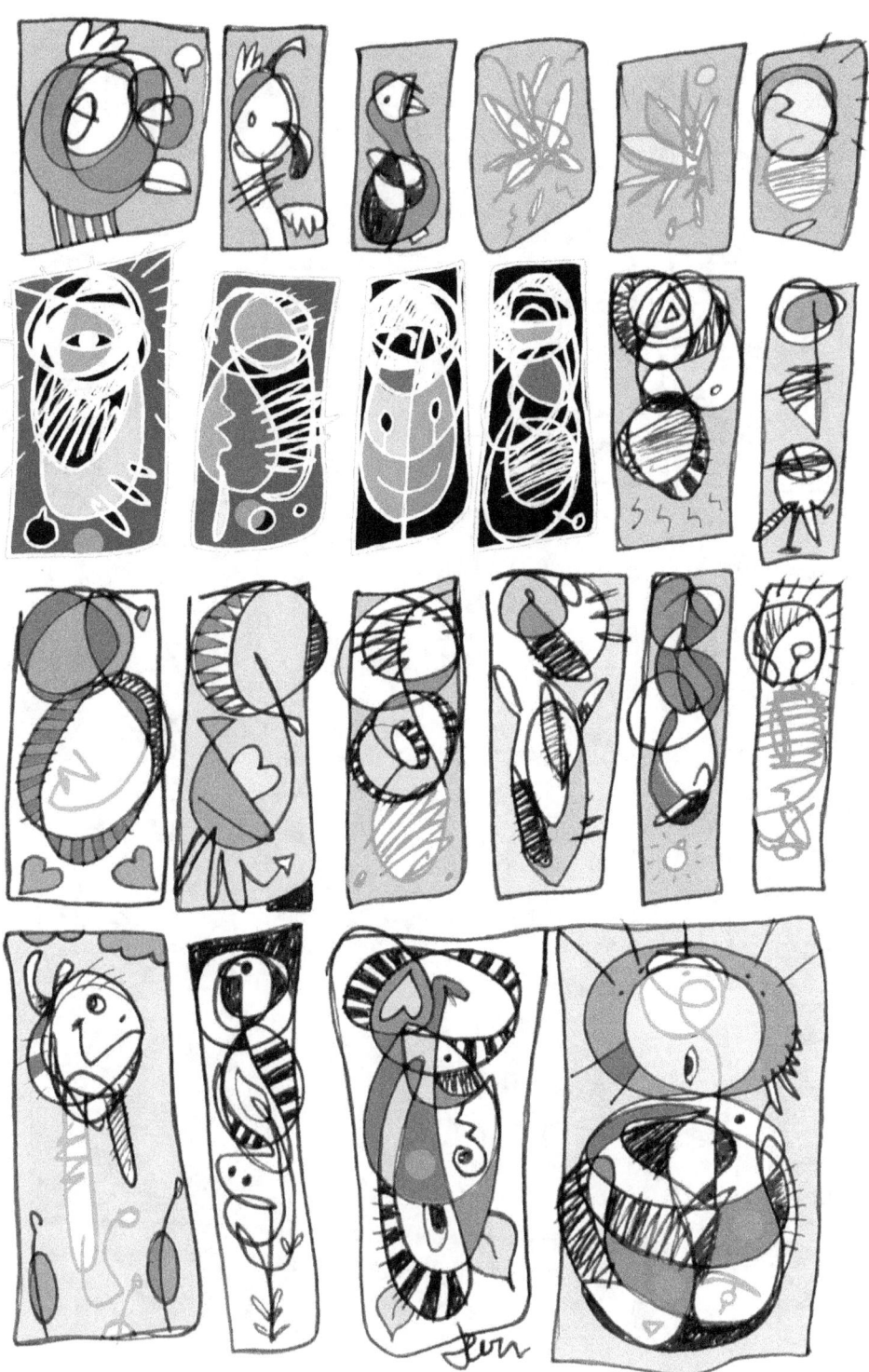

173

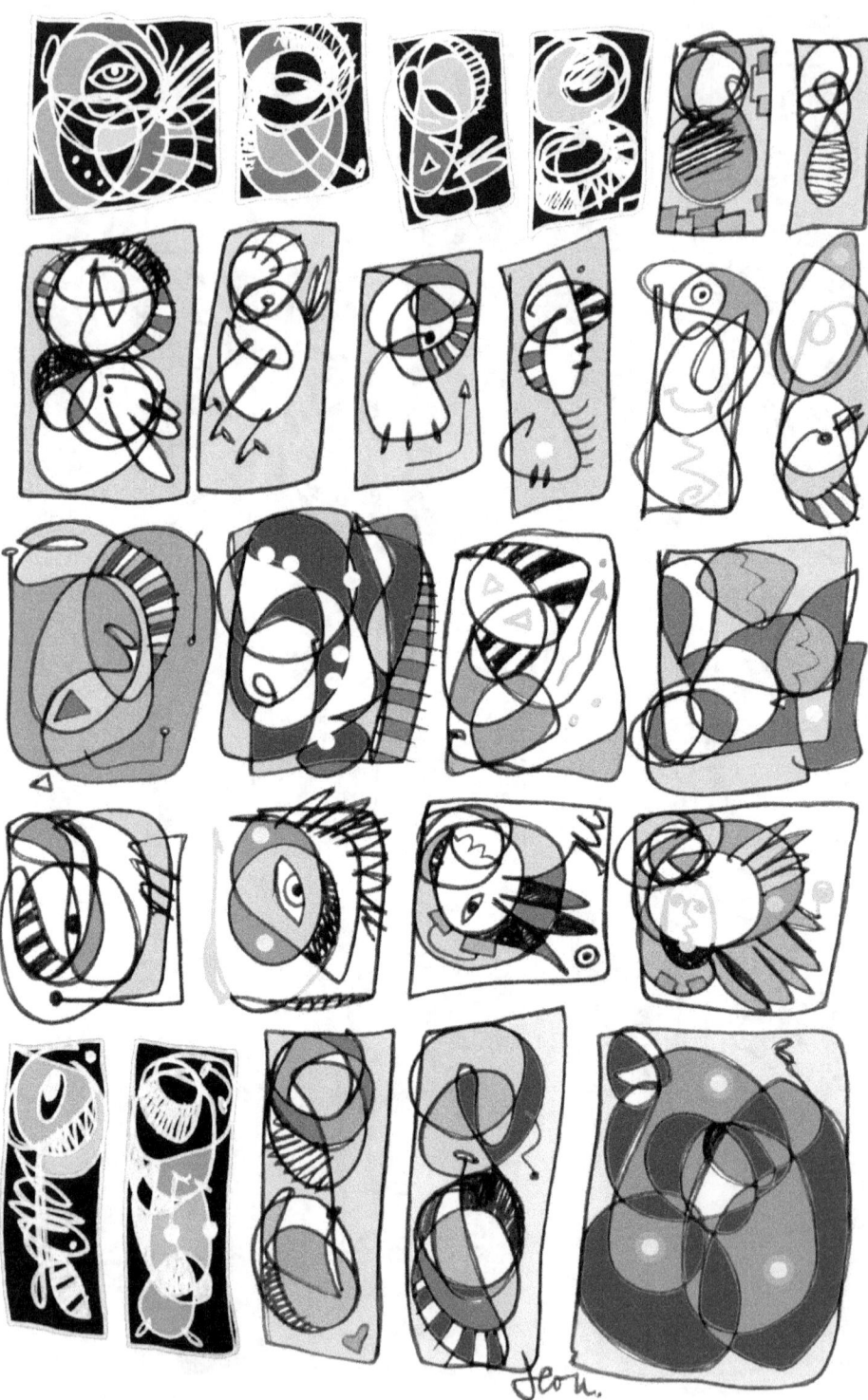

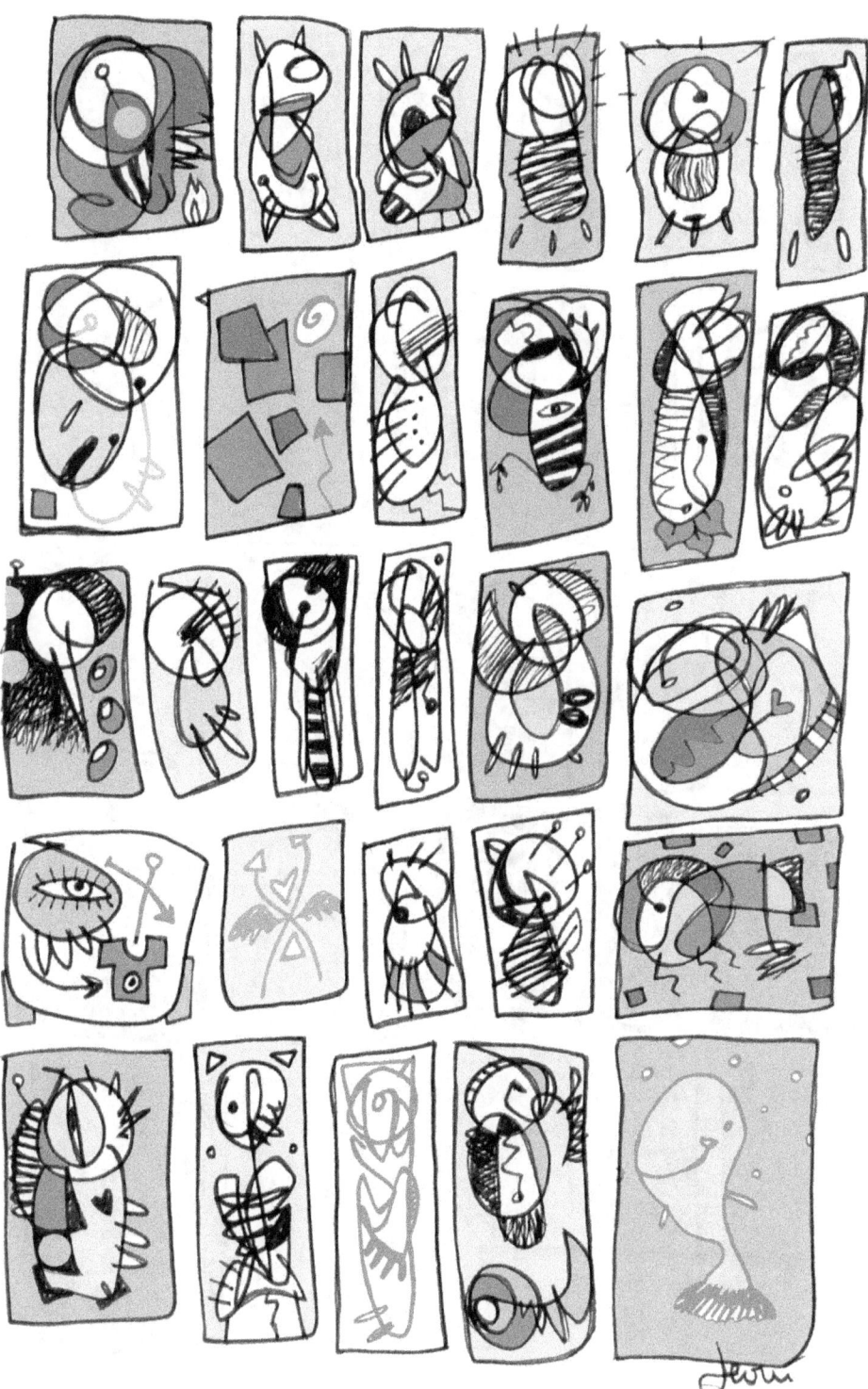

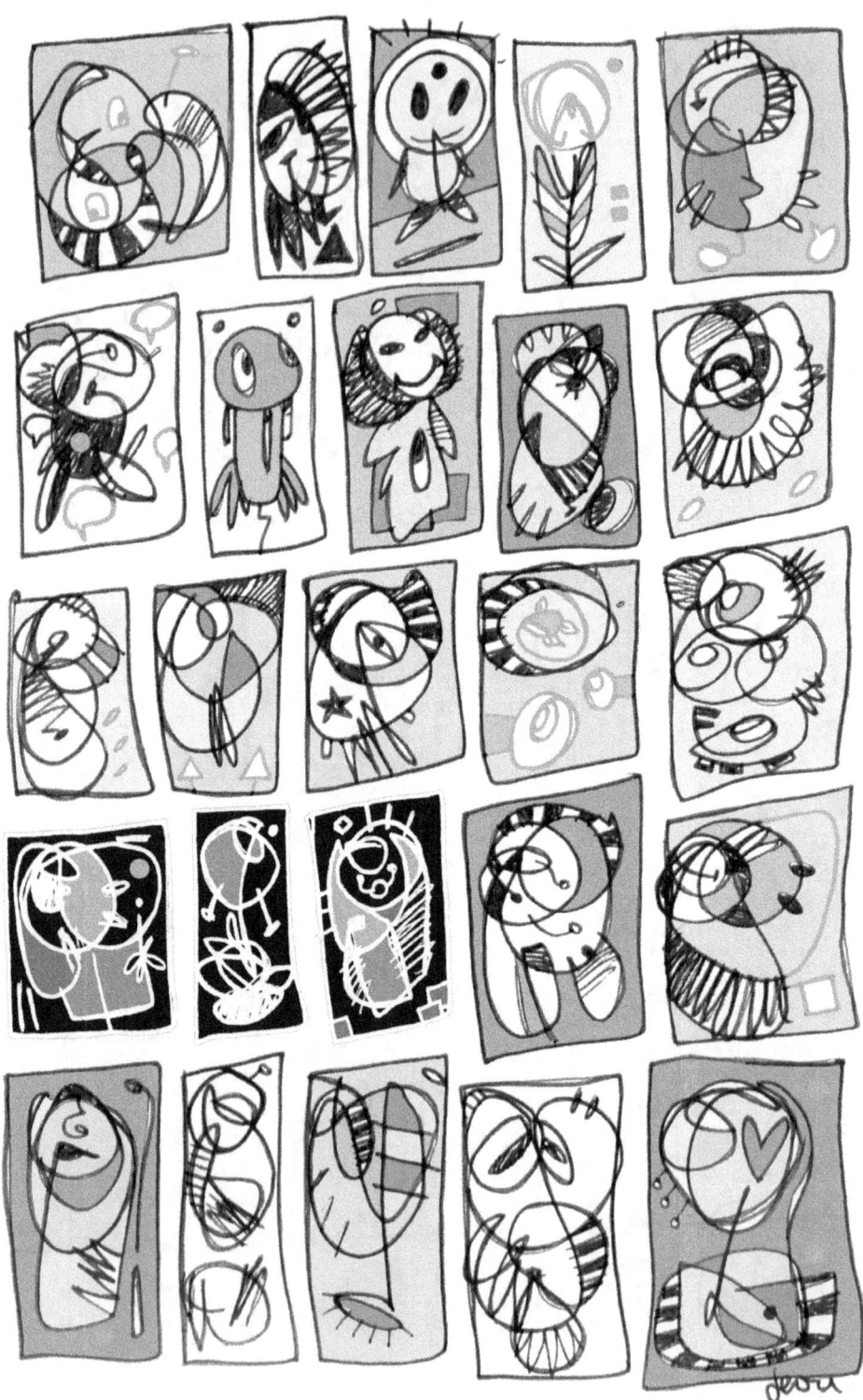

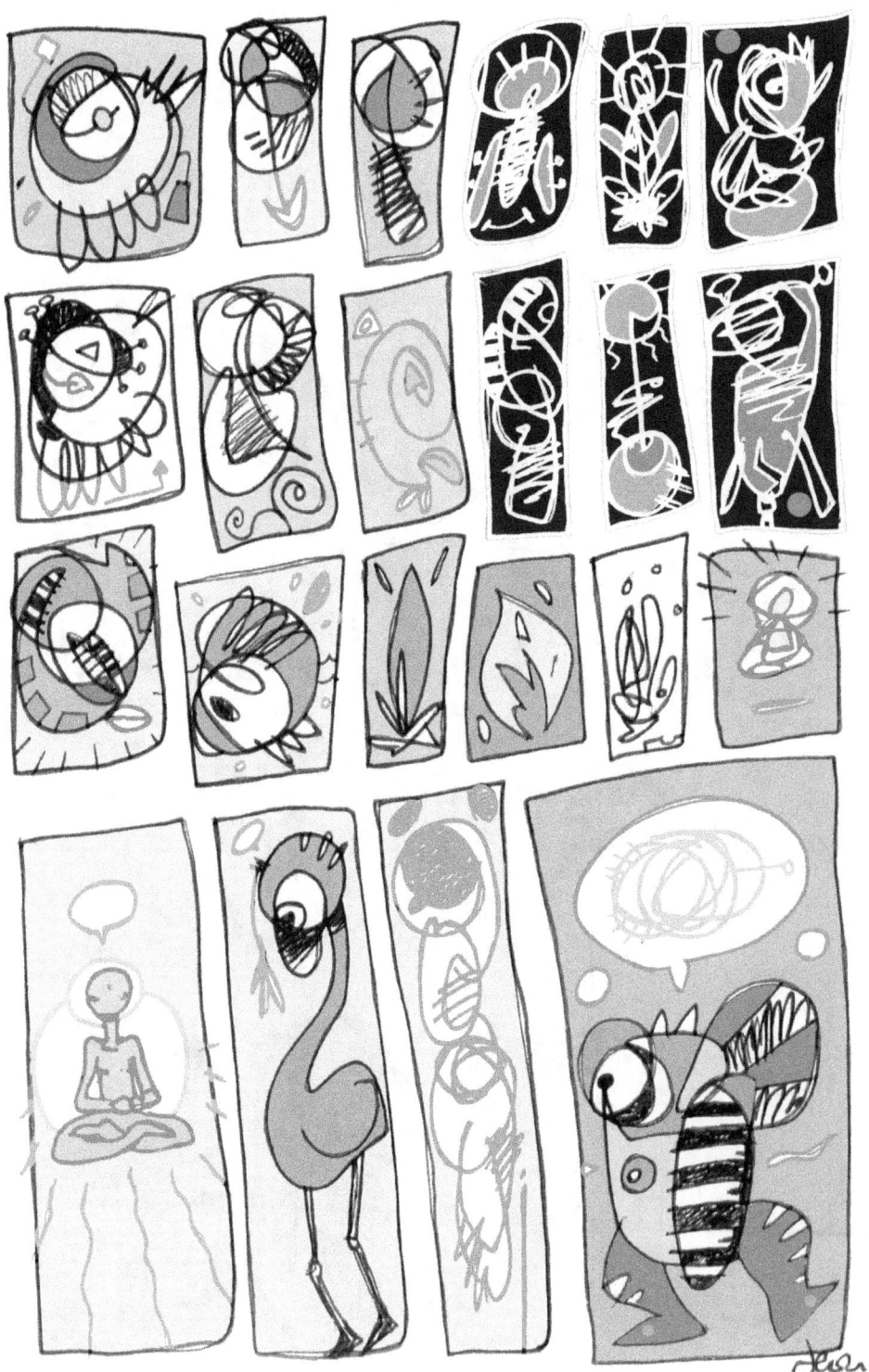

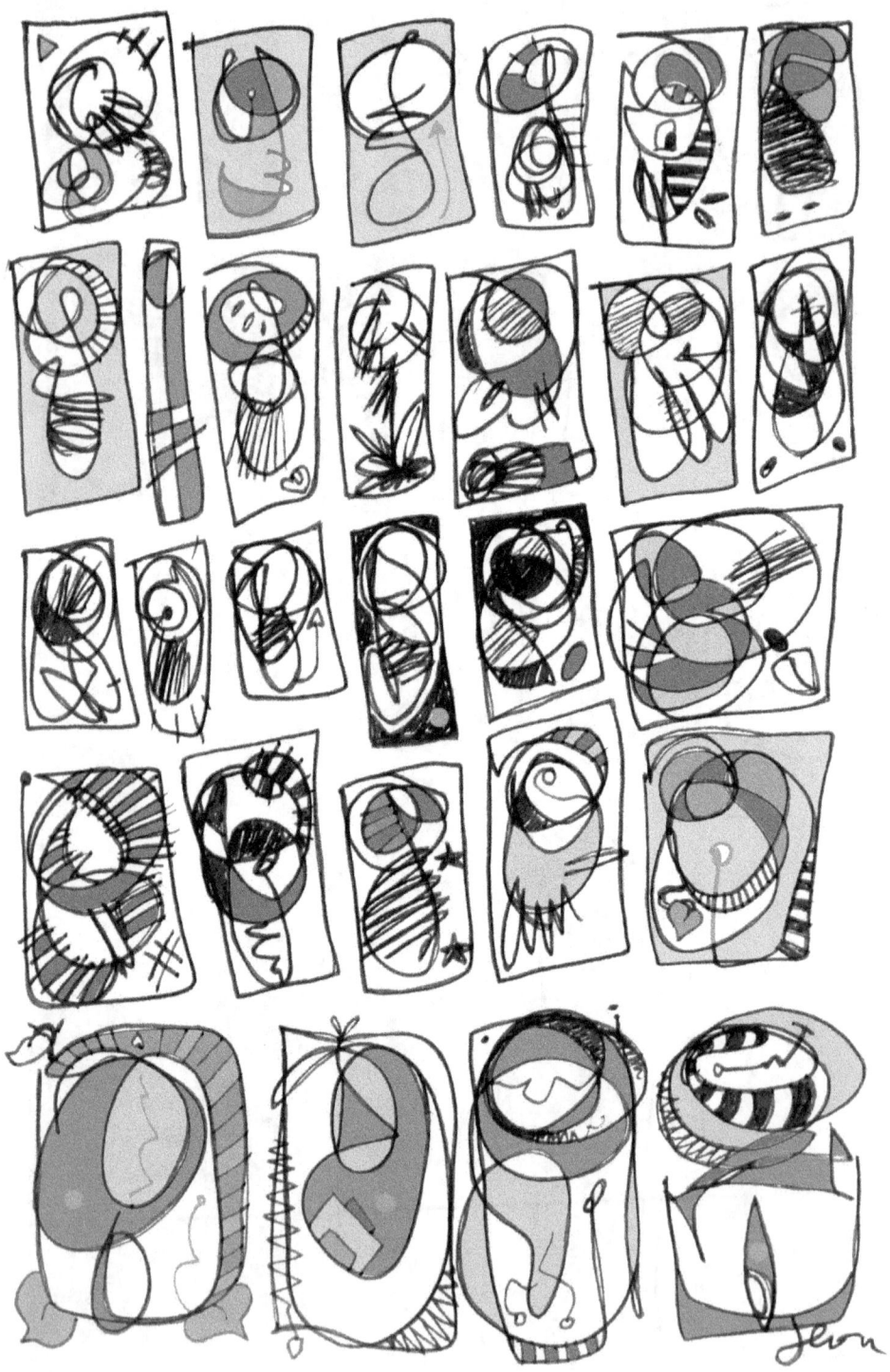

178

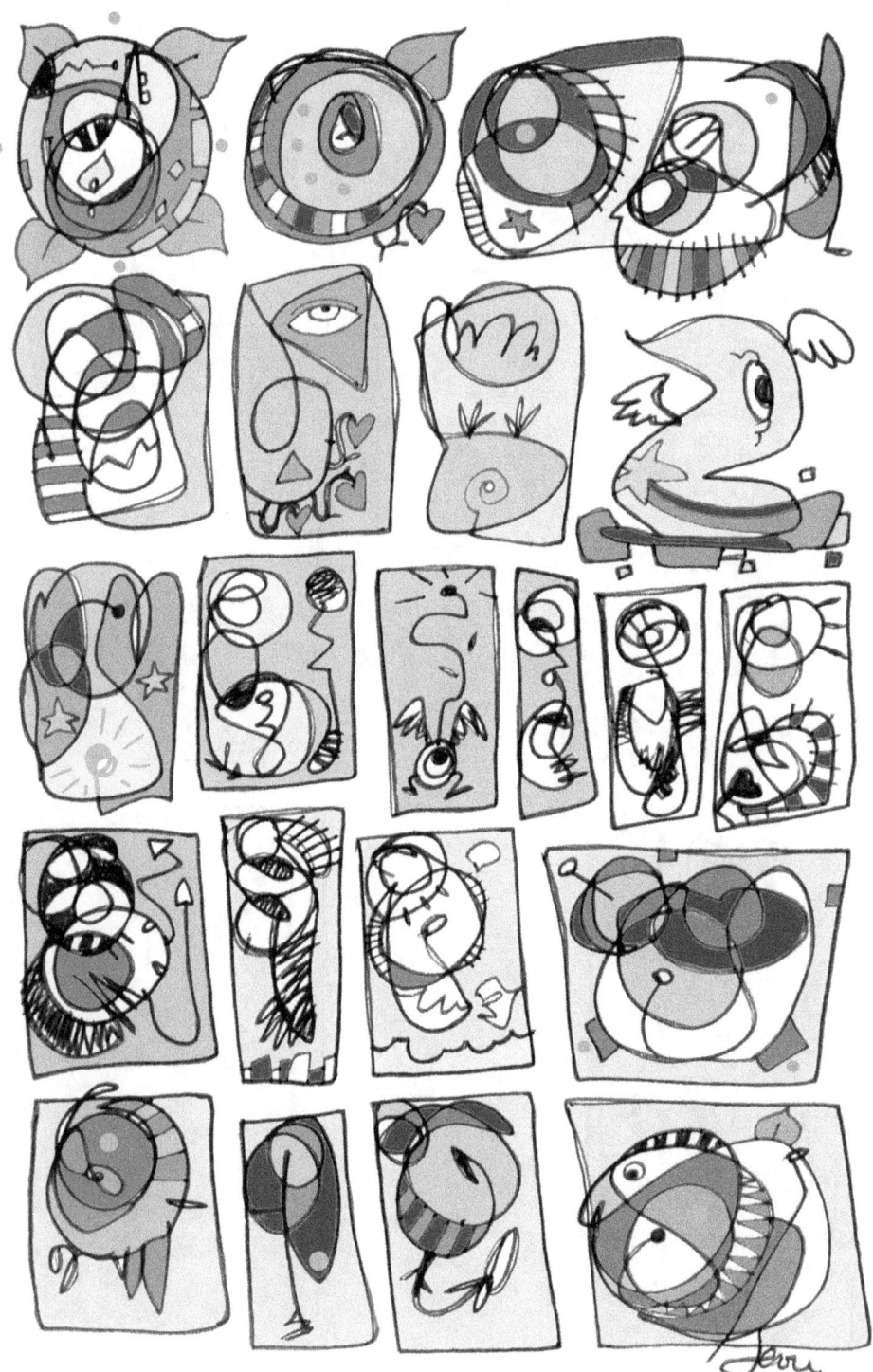

179

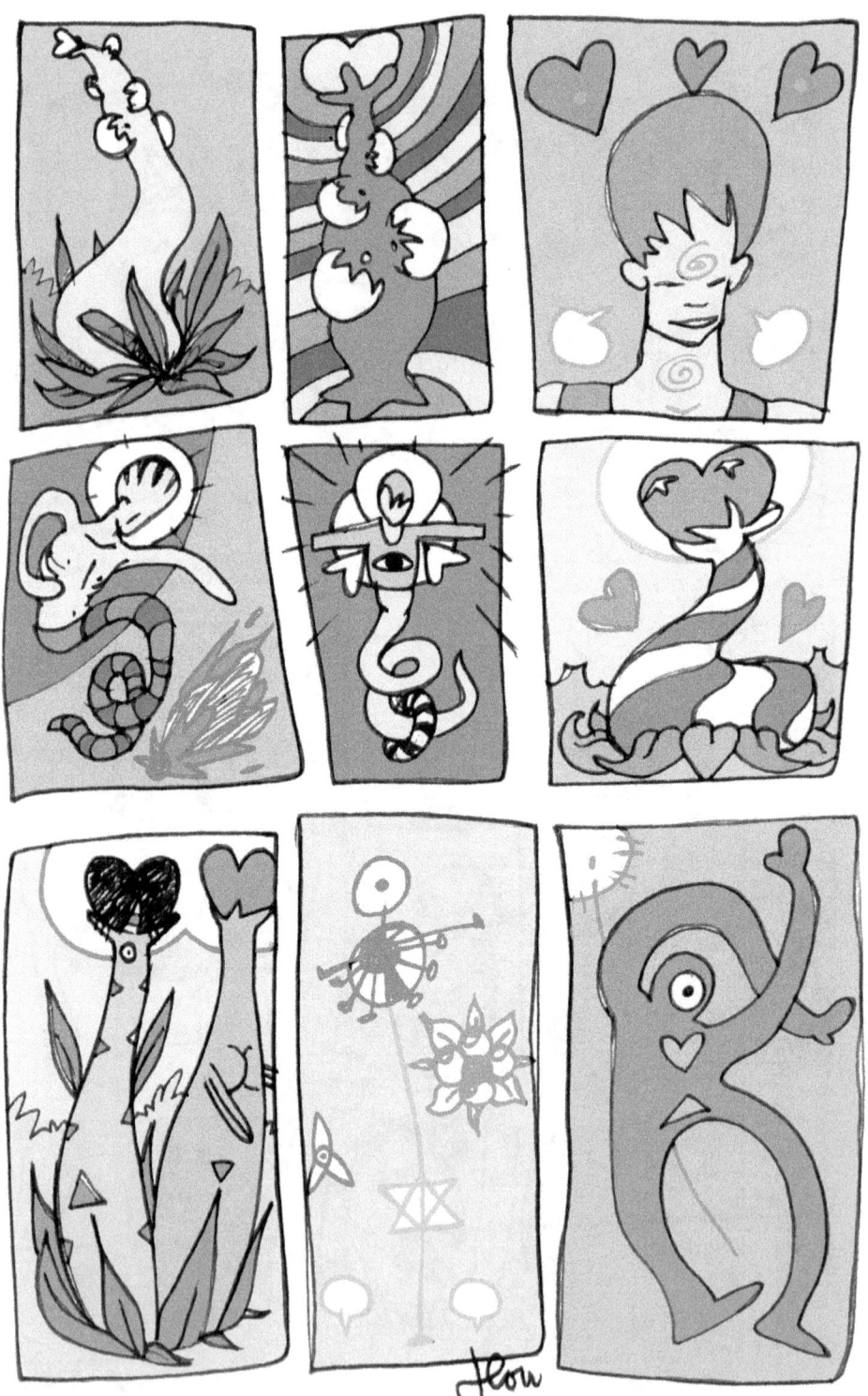

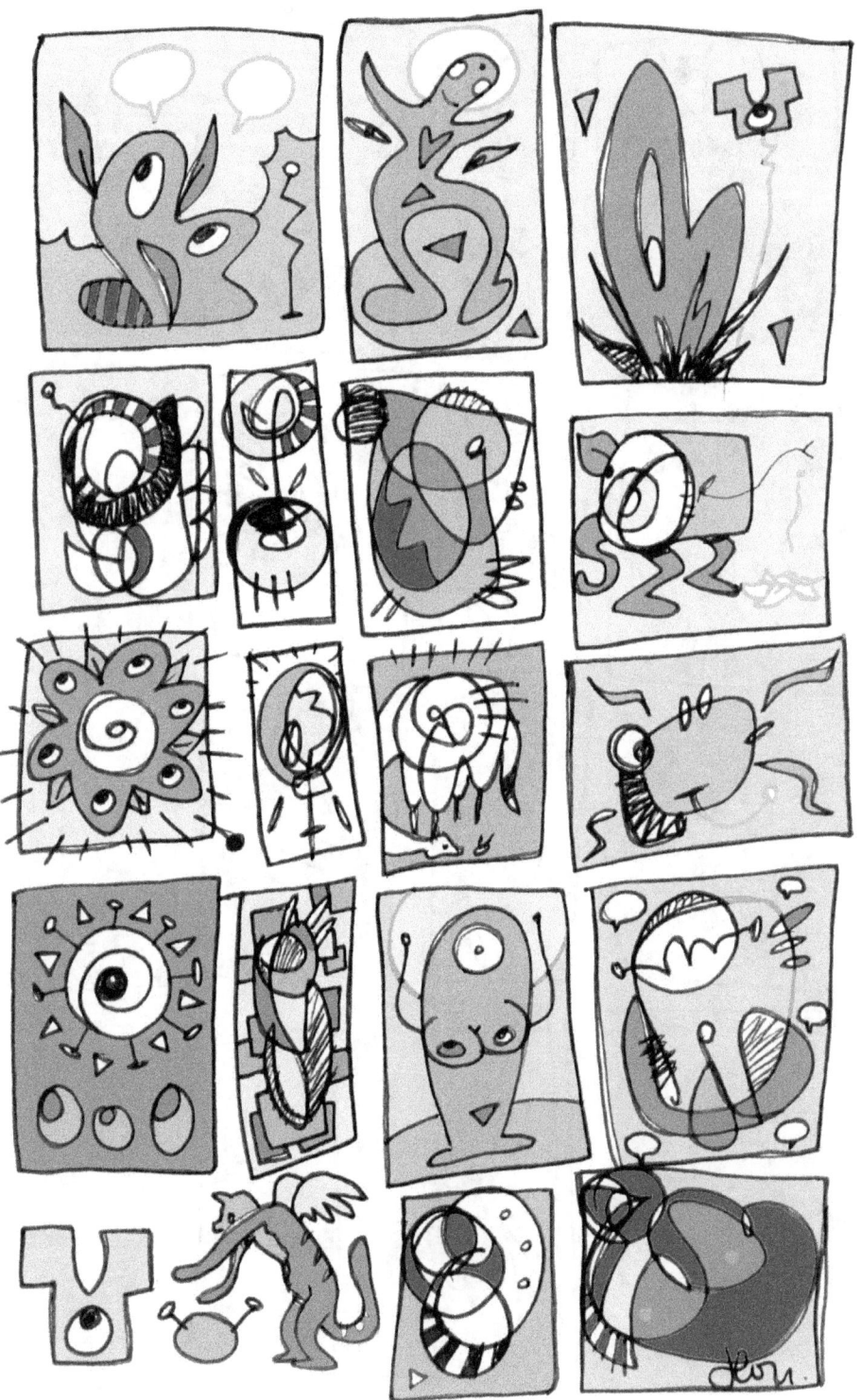

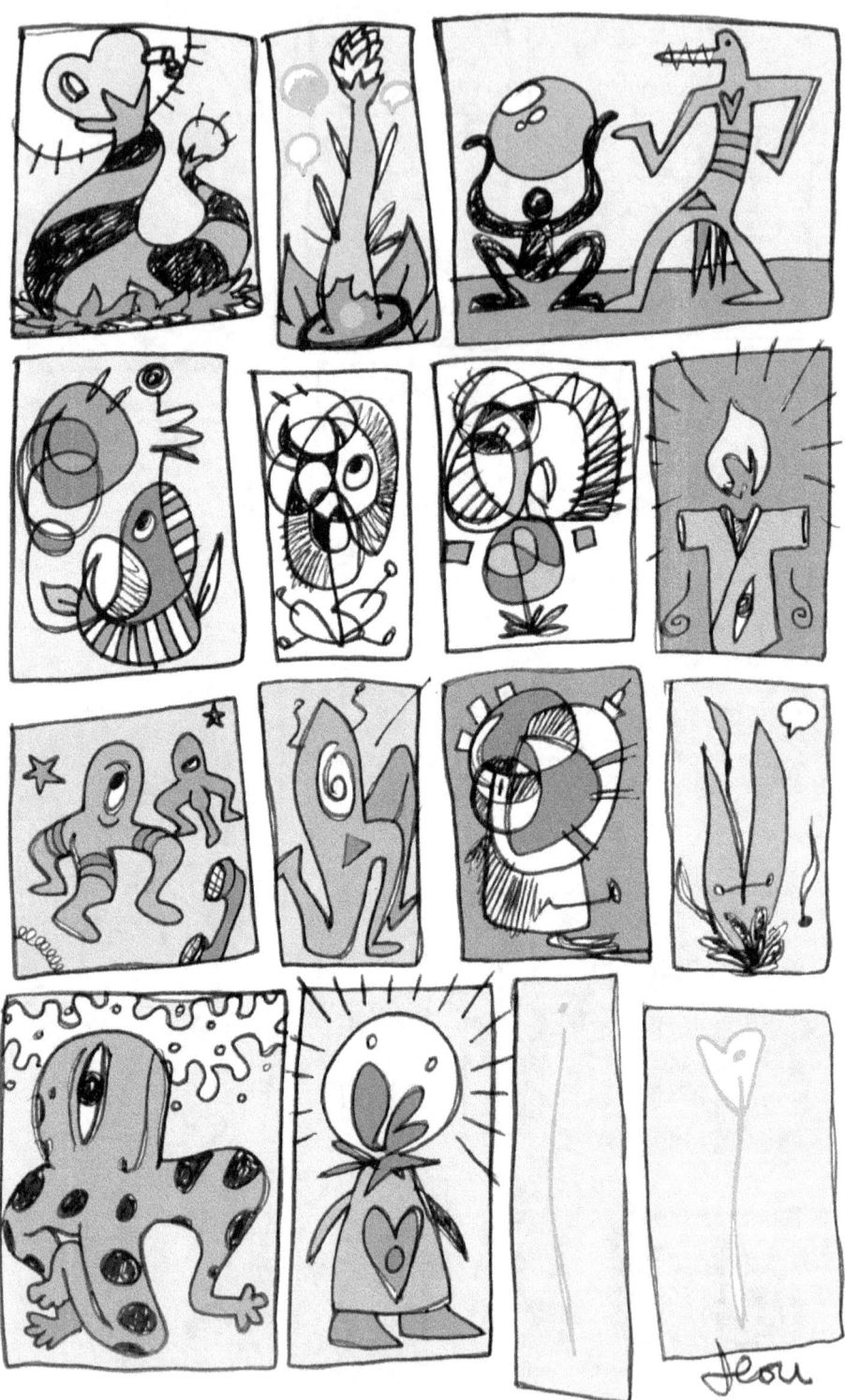

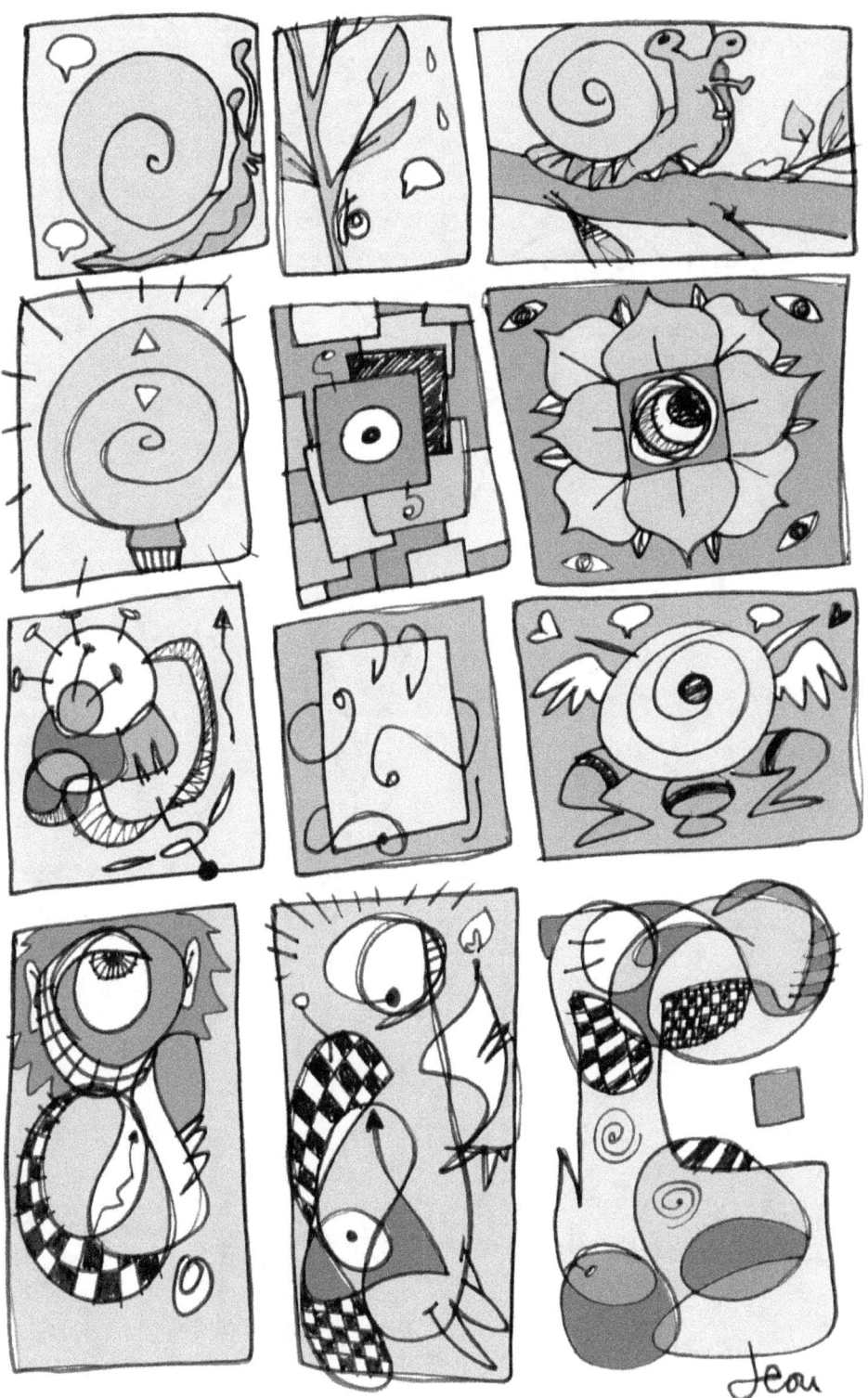

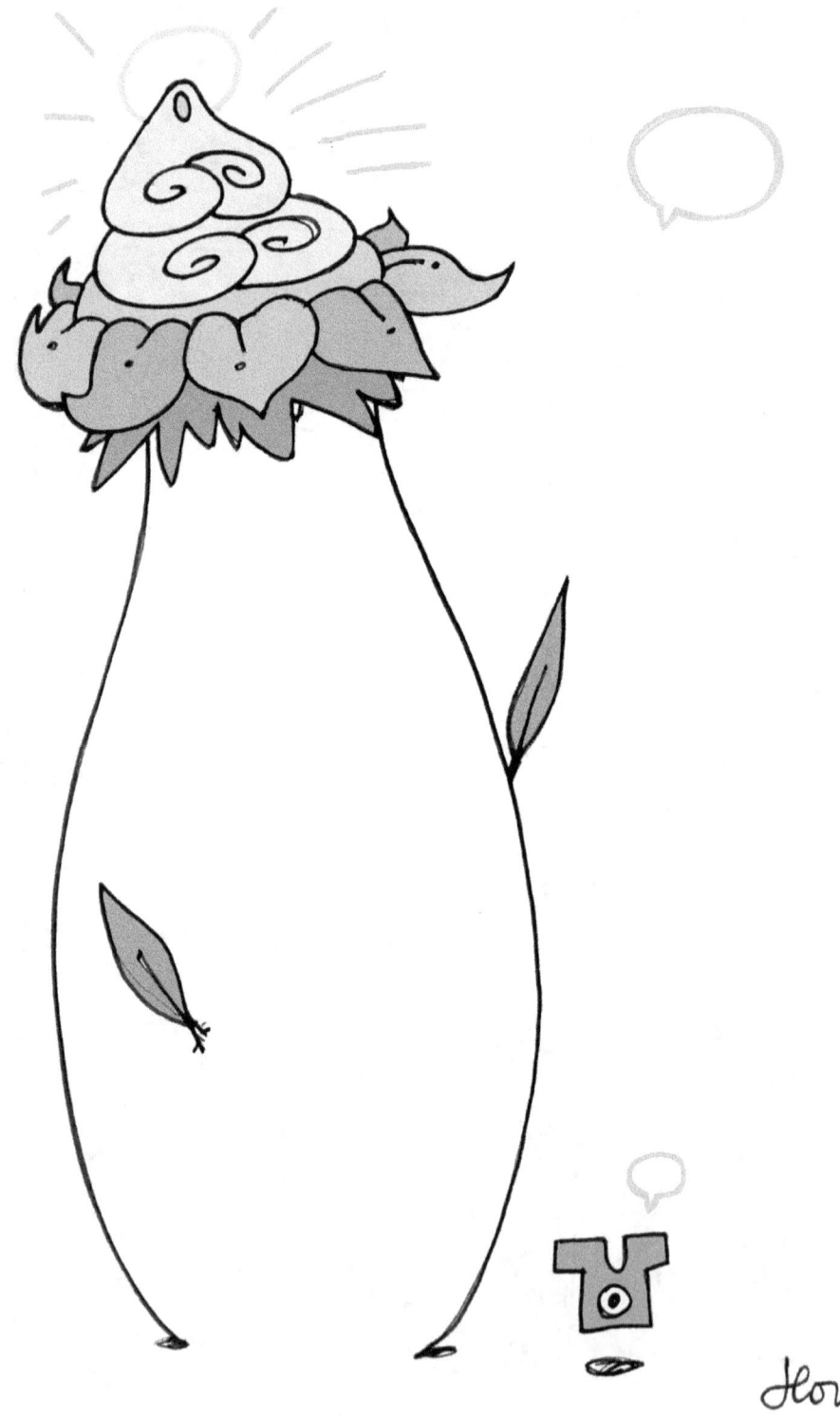

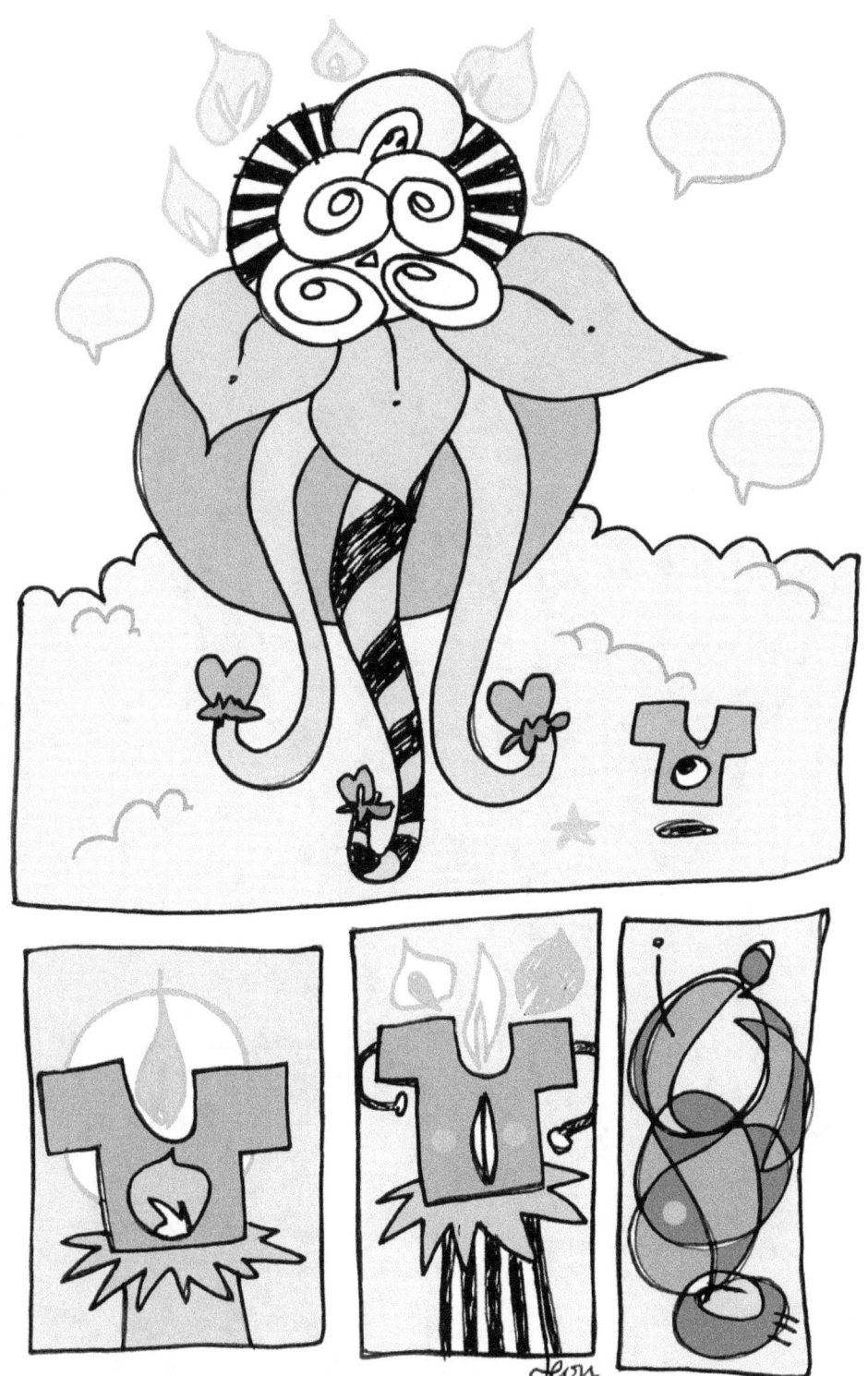

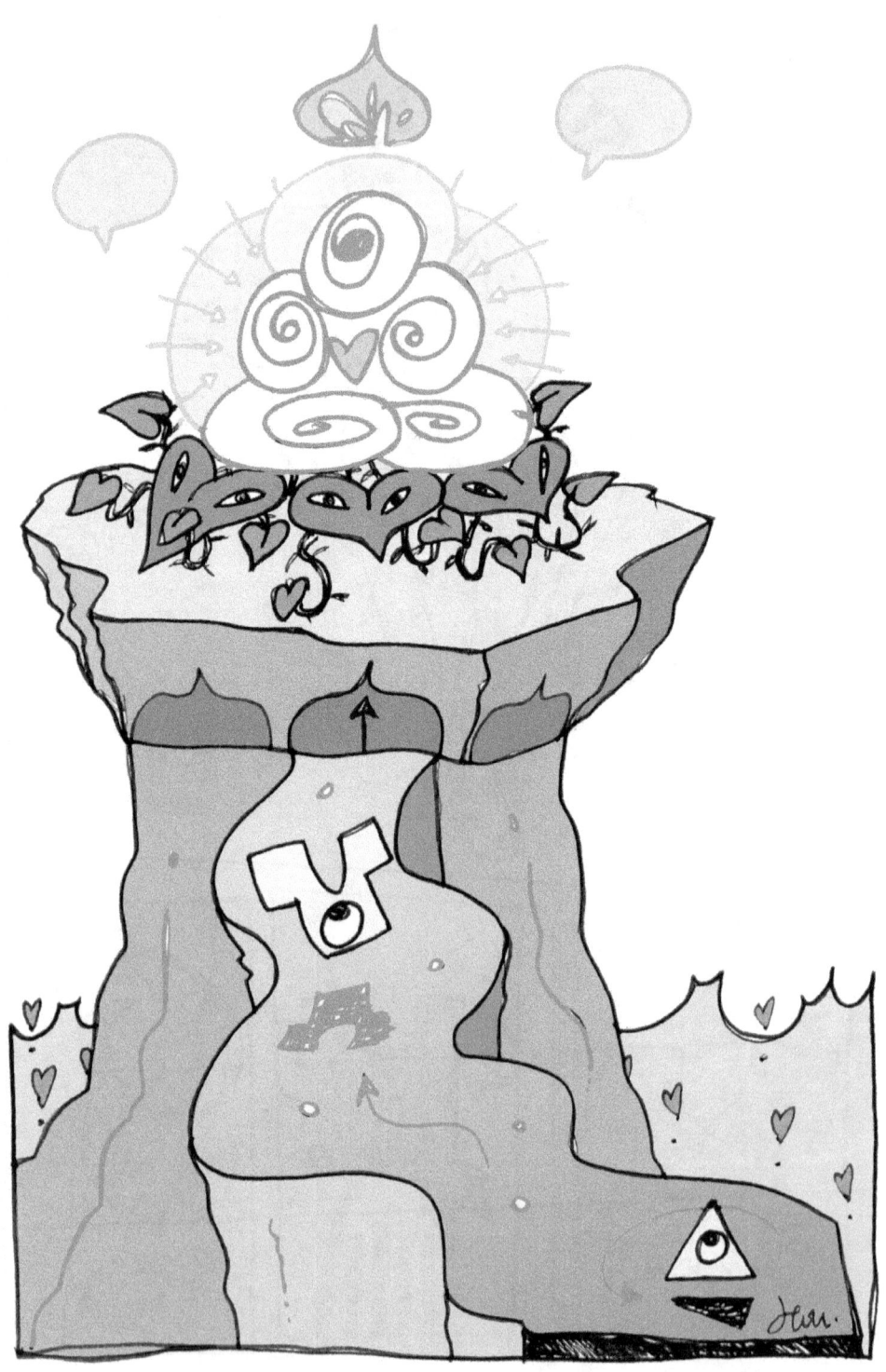

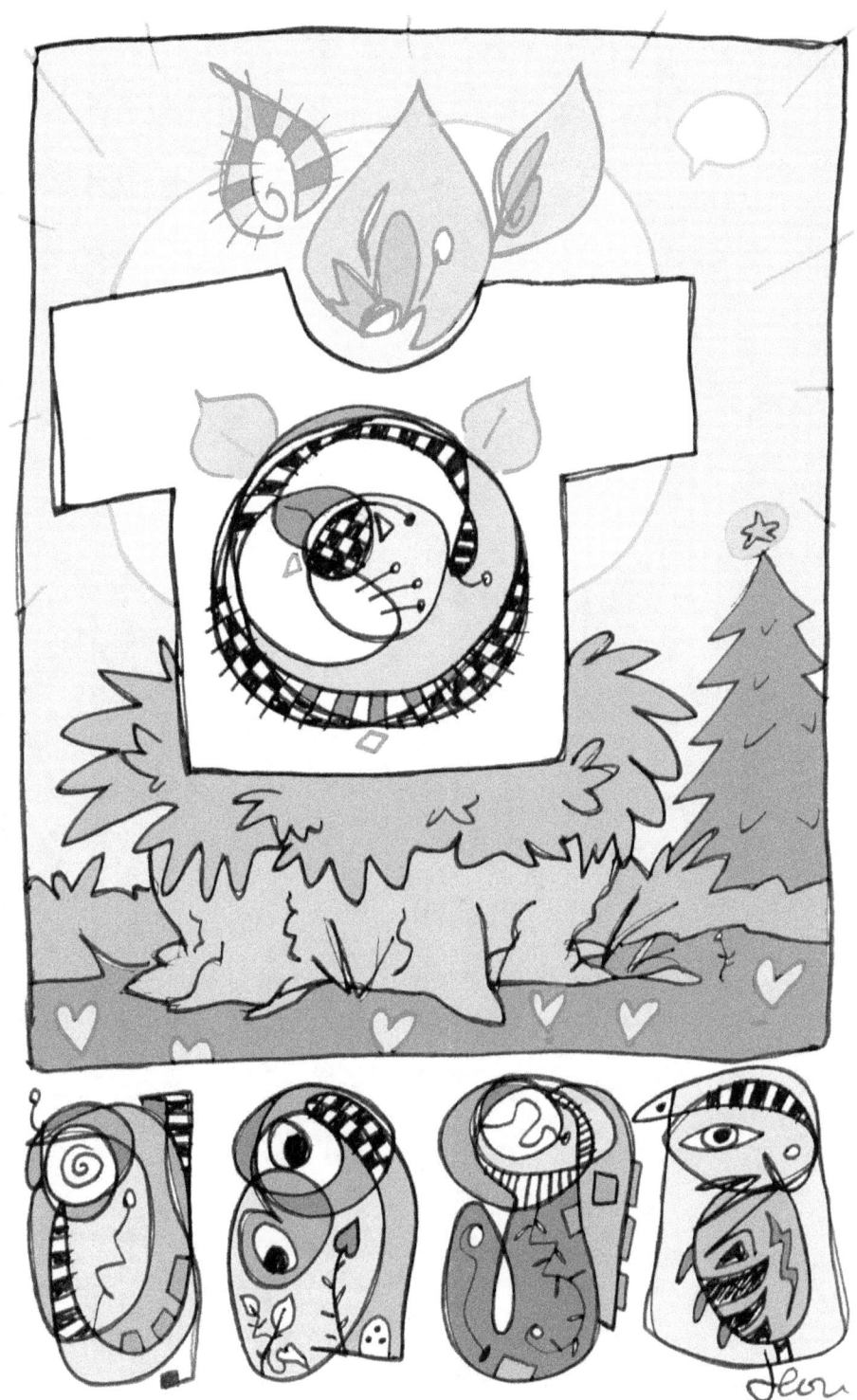

www.ingramcontent.com/pod-product-compliance
Lightning Source LLC
Chambersburg PA
CBHW072137170526
45158CB00004BA/1407